The Greatest Game of All

of All

MY LIFE IN GOLF

BY

JACK NICKLAUS

WITH

Herbert Warren Wind

FOREWORD BY ROBERT TYRE JONES, JR.

HODDER AND STOUGHTON

PRINTED IN GREAT BRITAIN FOR HODDER AND STOUGHTON LIMITED,
ST. PAUL'S HOUSE, WARWICK LANE, LONDON, E.C.4
BY COMPTON PRINTING LTD, LONDON AND AYLESBURY

ACKNOWLEDGMENTS

A good many people assisted us in the preparation of
this book. Four in particular were especially helpful:
Ray Cave; Janet Seagle, of the U.S.G.A.; Bill Foley, of
Columbus, who supplied a large number of the photographs; and Frank Hannigan, who kindly served as the
manuscript reader. We should also like to acknowledge
the courtesy of *Sports Illustrated* in making available
photographs from their fine collection.

J.W.N.
H.W.W.

For my father Charles
and
my wife Barbara.

CONTENTS

CONTENTS

FOREWORD

WHEN JACK NICKLAUS, at the age of fifteen, first appeared in our Amateur Championship, it was not difficult to see that a new talent of the first magnitude had arrived. Even though his presence in this championship was of brief duration, I am sure that most of us who saw him realized that he would become one of the greats of the game.

For my part, I made a special effort to see Jack and to meet him and his father. Since I enjoy nothing more than watching a graceful, powerful golfer, I have never missed any reasonable opportunity to watch Jack play. In the course of all this, I have come to know Jack and his father quite well and to have a considerable liking and respect for both.

Comparisons and superlatives have been liberally used on our sports pages. I do not like to compare players of one era with those of another, nor do I feel the necessity for proclaiming that anyone is the greatest, even in his own time. Insofar as contemporaries are concerned, the record book speaks for itself; comparisons from era to era involve too much of the unmeasurable effect of differences in golf courses and equipment. On the other hand, I do think it is completely safe to say that there has not yet been a more effective golfer than Jack Nicklaus.

Jack has a sound swing, constructed along classic lines, and majestic in its power; yet he is capable of a deftness in the strokes around the green that is astonishing in such a strong player. Occasionally he, like anyone else, has days when the putts will not drop. But he is essentially a very good putter, being most consistent in his ability to strike his putts solidly. There is no weakness in any department of his game.

There are times when I am tempted to think that Jack's enormous power can be something of a handicap to him. I think I have

9

noted one or two instances when he has hit a bad tee-shot at a crucial time because he was obviously going out for extra length. Why he should ever need to do this is beyond me, and I think it may be one of the things he will avoid in the future. I cannot say that I blame him, however, because if I had ever had the ability to do so, I can think of nothing I should have enjoyed more than ripping into a tee-shot with all of Jack's power. Oddly enough, this power seems to help him most in his iron play, possibly because he is able to play the same distances as other golfers with clubs that are more lofted than theirs, and so more readily controllable.

Nicklaus now holds the scoring record for the Masters Tournament and shares the Open record with Lee Trevino. With this and all the championships and tournaments he has won, it may seem strange to say so, but I think Jack will undoubtedly become better and better each year for a good many years, providing only that he retains his keenness for competition and his desire to win. It is in these subjective attitudes that the competitive golfer deteriorates long before his physical competence begins to wane.

Jack Nicklaus has a ready wit and very much enjoys the lighter side of a conversation; nevertheless, he is a very serious-minded young man when it comes to golf. Although he has an extraordinary natural ability in the game, he long ago realized that in order to play consistently well, he had to have a good understanding of the fundamentals of the golf swing. Applying his good native intelligence to this subject, he has, as one would expect, come up with a very good notion of what makes Jack Nicklaus play golf.

Herbert Warren Wind, who is collaborating with Jack on this book, writes about golf with a perception and charm excelled by no one. Herb plays the game well, understands it thoroughly, and has certainly not lost any of his keenness for championship golf reporting.

Jack and Herb make a good team; I am sure you will enjoy their book.

ROBERT TYRE JONES, JR.

10

Part One

I

Bob Jones,
Idol and Friend

MY FIRST GOLF HERO was Bob Jones, and this, of course, was a very fortunate thing. I became aware of Jones in 1950 when I started golf at the age of ten, for my father was a member of the Scioto Country Club in Columbus, Ohio, our hometown, and it was there that Jones had won the 1926 United States Open. It was a wonderful victory in many ways. First, Bobby—he was in his mid-twenties then, and he was known to everyone as Bobby—made a fine driving finish over the last nine holes to pick up five shots on the leader, Joe Turnesa, and edge him out by one. On top of this, earlier that season Jones had won the British Open at Lytham & St. Anne's, and with his victory at Scioto he made golf history by becoming the first man to carry off the two big national championships in the same year.

In any event, Scioto never forgot Bobby Jones. When I became a member of the club, a full twenty-four years had elapsed since Jones' victory, but a photograph of him still hung in a prominent position in the locker room, and another in the pro shop. The latter showed him at the finish of his follow-through on a drive. (I think it must be the photo General Eisenhower used as a model for his famous painting of Jones that is on display in Golf House, the United States Golf Association's headquarters in New York City.) In addition to this, many of the older members of Scioto, who had been deeply impressed by both Jones' golf and his personal charm, were always talking about him. The most devoted of these Jones-men was Stanley Crooks, a very capable golfer, by the way, who won the club championship several times. He was a good friend of Jones' and corresponded with him, and, if anything, the passing years had sharpened his memory of Bobby's performance back in 1926. He knew every one of the 293 shots Jones had hit.

When I first showed some promise in golf, Mr. Crooks began to tell me more and more about Jones—where he liked to place his drive on this hole and how he tried to play that hole; how he had missed his par on each of the four rounds on the relatively easy 145-yard ninth; how Bobby thought one of the best holes on the course was the eighth, a long par 5, where a virtual wheat field bordered the right side of the fairway off the tee and where, in second-shot range, a stream crossed the fairway and then curled to the left around the back of the green; and above all, how Bobby, needing a birdie to win on the last hole, a 480-yard par 5 that Turnesa had birdied just previously, laced out a drive that was fully 300 yards long, followed it with a 4-iron 15 feet past the pin, and got down in two safe putts. In 1950, I should bring out, Scioto had changed very little from the course Jones had tackled, and knowing how he had played it was a spur to me. It is a definite advantage for a young golfer, I believe, to grow up on a championship course, and there is something of additional value to be gained from knowing how a champion played the different holes. It gives you something concrete to measure your progress against.

Along with Stanley Crooks there were two men at Scioto who never stopped talking about Jones. One was Jack Grout, a tall, scholarly-looking Oklahoman who became the pro at Scioto the same year I took up the game. Jack was a tireless student of the golf swing. While he kept very much abreast of the times and was fascinated by the mechanics of Nelson's swing and Snead's and Hogan's, there were several respects in which he felt Jones' technique had never been improved on, and he made this very clear to his pupils. The other notorious Jones enthusiast was my father. The year the Open was held at Scioto, he was a boy of thirteen. He had played a little golf on the public courses, and for him, as for so many other Americans, there was no one like Bobby Jones. Through the kindness of the pharmacist he worked for after school hours, Dad got tickets for the Open, and he stayed on Jones' heels all four rounds. Watching his hero in action was the greatest experience of his young life, and it remained evergreen in his mind. I imagine his identification with Jones became all the stronger because of an offbeat incident that took place at Scioto when the Ryder Cup Match was played there in 1931. Jones, who had come up from Atlanta for the event, was twenty-nine at the time. There couldn't have been too much resemblance, really, between him and my dad, then just eighteen. However, my dad had the same chunky build as Jones, he parted his hair down the middle like Jones, and on this particular day he happened to be wearing knickers like Jones—and darned if the attendant at the front door of the clubhouse didn't sing out, "Yessir, Mister Jones," when my dad approached and fling the door open for him with a flourish. Dad's ticket didn't include clubhouse privileges, and he had just been edging up to take a squint inside. With the entrance suddenly opened, he tossed the attendant a friendly smile, the way he thought Jones would have, and sauntered around the clubhouse for an hour taking it all in.

For all these reasons, when I started playing golf I knew more about Robert T. Jones, Jr., than I did about any of the current champions. Later that year I learned a good deal about Ben Hogan, of course. This was the season, 1950, that Ben returned to golf after his near-fatal accident sixteen months earlier and then proceeded to astound the sports world by winning the U.S. Open at Merion. I also knew a little about Jimmy Demaret—very little; I knew he wore bright clothes and might stride onto the first tee any day wearing one blue shoe and one green shoe. Beyond this, the other "name golfers" were just a blur to me. That summer, however, I got a firsthand look at many of them, for Scioto was host to another championship, the 1950 P.G.A. (That was the year Chandler Harper beat Henry Williams, Jr., in the final.) By this time my dad was a member of the club, so there was no problem about the front door, but the locker room was off limits except for the players. However, Skip Alexander, one of the top touring pros, saw me with my autograph book at the door and put his arm around my shoulder and led me into the locker room. With Skip's help, I got the autographs of nearly all the players. Outside of how pleasant and considerate Skip was, little else sticks in my mind. I remember watching Lloyd Mangrum playing cards, a tall drink in one hand and a cigarette dangling from his lips beneath his moustache. It was a picture that would make an impression on any ten-year-old boy—there he was, the complete riverboat gambler come to life. I also remember catching a glimpse of Sam Snead. Sam couldn't have had too good a day. He was scowling and silent, and he was in and out of the locker room in thirty seconds.

Soon after that P.G.A. Championship, my friend Skip Alexander almost lost his life in an airplane crash. Although he made a phenomenal recovery from his injuries, he never regained full use of his hands and fingers, and his career as a tournament golfer was over. Skip stayed in the game, though. Today he is the pro at the Lakewood Country Club in St. Petersburg, Florida, and I get to see him when he comes over to the Palm Beach area for a tournament or a pro-am. Skip usually stays with my neighbor at Lost Tree Village, Cary Middlecoff.

I did not meet Bob Jones until five years later, in 1955, when I qualified for the United States Amateur Championship for the first time. It took place that year at the James River course of the Country Club of Virginia, in Richmond. Since 1955 marked the twenty-fifth anniversary of Jones' last appearance in that championship—his victory in the 1930 Amateur, at Merion, was the fourth and final trick in his incredible Grand Slam—the U.S.G.A. had asked him to come up from Atlanta and speak at the Players' Dinner. He undoubtedly would have honored this request anyway, but I have a feeling that the fact that this was one of the rare occasions when a national championship was being held in the South contributed to Jones' decision to attend. The day before the start of the tournament, when the field was getting in its final warm-up rounds, Jones parked his golf cart behind the last green to take in some of the play on that hole, a 460-yard par 4 over breaking, hilly ground. It so happened that I hit the eighteenth green that afternoon with two good woods and, furthermore, that during the time that Jones was watching, no other player had got home in two. He asked a newspaperman with him who I was, and on learning that I was only fifteen years old, he said he would like to talk with me. My father and I went over together. This session with Jones was a tremendous thrill for me, but I am sure it meant twice as much to my dad. Our chat lasted about twenty minutes—a good deal of it was about Scioto, naturally—and then Jones turned to me and said, "Young man, I've heard that you're a very fine golfer. I'm coming out and watch you play a few holes tomorrow."

My first-round opponent was Bob Gardner, a Californian who had moved to the New York area, a well-grounded golfer who was subsequently a teammate of mine in the 1960 Eisenhower Trophy and the 1961 Walker Cup matches. We had quite a battle that day in Richmond. At the end of the first nine we were even, and then

An early meeting with Bob Jones.

I went 1 up by birdying the tenth. As we walked to the eleventh, there was Bob Jones sitting in his golf cart on the edge of the tee. I wanted to play my very best in front of him, and I thought I might, for I'd been hitting the ball straight and crisp that morning.

Well, it didn't work out quite that way. I missed my par on the eleventh, a 412-yard par 4, when I took three from just off the green. I lost that hole to Gardner's par. On the twelfth, a par 4 423 yards long, uphill most of the way, I was even more brilliant —I took a double bogey: a drive pushed into the trees on the right, a choppy recovery, an underclubbed approach, and three more to get down from the apron. I lost that hole, too. The thirteenth is a short par 4 that doglegs sharply to the right as it falls down a hillside to a ticklish little green. I was weak with my second, and when I stubbed my chip, I had lost three holes in a row and had gone from 1 up to 2 down. Jones left at this point. As he later told my father, he felt that his presence might have led me to try too hard. After treating him to that splendid run of bogey, double bogey, bogey, I managed to settle down and won two of the next four holes to square the match. Then I lost it on the eighteenth when I hit my tee-shot into heavy rough and couldn't get home with my second. Gardner played it perfectly, an excellent drive and an excellent fairway wood onto the green, and that was that.

My next meeting with Bob Jones took place some two years later when he spoke at the banquet held in connection with the 1957 International Jaycees Junior Championship, which was played on the Ohio State University course. (We had our picture taken together, and it hangs today in my game room.) Then, another two years later, I qualified for the Masters for the first time, so I was able to get together with Jones that spring—and in the springs that followed until 1962—at the Amateurs' Dinner on the Wednesday night before the start of the Masters. Sometimes we just talked. I remember, for example, his reminiscing about the 1926 Open one evening and recalling that the wheat field of rough on the eighth hole was so high that on one round, after his caddie had laid down his bag in the rough so that they could better help Bob's playing partner find his ball, they had an awful time finding the bag. Other times we talked a bit more seriously. However, the most helpful piece of advice I received from Bob came to me secondhand, through my father. "I think I was a fairly good young golfer," Jones told him one evening, "but I never became what I would call a really good golfer until I had been competing for quite a number of seasons. You see, when I first started to play in the big tournaments, whenever anything went wrong, I'd run home to Stewart Maiden, our pro at East Lake. Finally, I matured to the point where I understood my game well enough to make my own corrections during the course of a tournament, and *that's* when I'd say I became a *good* golfer."

When my dad relayed this conversation to me, it made a particularly strong impression because, whenever something had gone wrong in a tournament, I had run home to Jack Grout. From the time Jack started to give me lessons, he wanted me to understand the mechanics of the swing, and, for my part, I wanted to learn all about them—why you made this movement in the swing, or what effect that movement produced. I wanted to be able to take care of myself out on the course. Somehow, though, I was still always running back to Jack Grout to fix me up. This is why Jones' statement hit me so right. It made me much more determined to learn everything I could about my swing so that, to some extent, I could diagnose my own errors and put myself back on my game. I cannot tell you what a big factor this is in tournament play.

18

A very happy moment with Bob Jones: at the conclusion of the presentation ceremony after the 1966 Masters.

It may be the biggest factor of all in shaping success or failure in the crucible of competition.

Bob Jones—I never call him anything but Mr. Jones—possesses the gift of intimacy and is always doing little things that make you feel that you are an old friend with whom he can be humorous, or frank, or spontaneous, as the case may be. One small illustration that comes to mind involved Bob only indirectly. In the 1959 Amateur, at Broadmoor, through the accident of the draw I came up against his son, Robert T. Jones, III, in the first round. Young Bob is a very good player who has qualified for the Amateur quite a few times, and on his day he can give any golfer all that he can handle. That morning at Broadmoor when young Bob and I met on the first tee, he greeted me with a big, warm smile. "You might be interested in knowing, Jack," he said, "that my father was thinking of coming out for this tournament. Then when he found out who I had drawn as my first opponent, he changed his mind. He decided it wasn't worth a trip to Colorado just to watch me play one round."

More to the point was a letter I received from Bob Jones shortly after I had broken through in the 1962 U.S. Open. If my victory hinged on any one single stroke, it was the four-foot putt I had to hole on the 71st green to save my par, stay even with Arnold Palmer, and set up a playoff. It was an extremely tough putt: it broke a little left and then, near the hole, it broke back to the right off a little rise. The more I studied the putt, the more convinced I became that, especially under the pressure, I probably wouldn't be able to handle that double roll with the exceptional delicacy it re-

19

quired. My best chance would be to rap the ball so firmly that neither the left or right break could really take effect. I hit the ball hard, for the back of the cup, and it fell—and if it hadn't, it would have gone miles past, it was moving that fast. As I say, I thought this was the pivotal stroke of the tournament for me, so it pleased me enormously when Bob Jones gave it primary emphasis in a letter of congratulation he sent me shortly afterward. Watching on TV, he had recognized exactly what my problem was and the risk I took in trying to solve it the way I did. "When I saw the ball dive into the hole," he wrote, "I almost jumped right out of my chair." I can't recall a letter that made me feel as good as that one did.

Apart from whatever other talks we may have at the Masters each year, I generally get to see Bob out on the course. When you come to the most dangerous stretch, the passage from the eleventh through the thirteenth, Bob is usually out there in his golf cart, studying you closely. Quite often, he'll pick you up on the fifteenth and sixteenth, too. I have managed to play some acceptable golf in front of him, but I know he was also watching when I hit one of the rottenest shots of my life—an 8-iron on the short twelfth in the 1964 Masters that I shanked so beautifully I still had a pretty full pitch left over Rae's Creek to the green. (I got my 4, one of the best bogeys I've ever made.) Because of my admiration for Bob Jones, the Masters—the tournament he created, played on the course he helped design—has always been something unbelievably special for me. When I have been fortunate enough to win it, I have treasured not only the victory itself but the generous things he has said about my play at the presentation ceremony. When Bob says something about your golf, you know there is substance and sincerity in it. Above and beyond this, you always feel that he understands what you are all about as a man as well as a golfer. This gives everything a deeper meaning, and it sticks to your bones.

Looking back on my friendship with Bob Jones, I am increasingly aware what a lucky thing it was for me that he happened to win one of his Opens at Scioto so that from the beginning, despite the differences in our ages, there was always a bond between us. I have learned an awful lot from him. We all have. More than any other person in our time, he has served to give us a sense of continuity with the game's earlier eras and its earlier players, to make us feel a part of an immensely worthwhile tradition. In a word, he has embodied the spirit of golf.

20

II

Partnered in the Open with Ben Hogan

THE GOLF SWING, for me, is a source of never-ending fascination. On one hand, the swings of all the outstanding golfers are decidedly individual, but, on the other, the champions all execute approximately the same moves at the critical stages of the swing. Through slow-motion movies, high-speed stop-action cameras, and other new devices, we have been able to isolate and examine those major moves and to understand more and more clearly how they influence the shot that ensues. However, there is still a lot about the swing we don't know and probably never will, since hitting correct golf shots can never be a purely scientific proposition.

In any event, scarcely a day goes by when I do not find myself thinking about the golf swing—what I must do to make my own method of hitting the ball sounder and more dependable; what are the strong points and not-so-strong points of other people's methods; what makes each of us go wrong when we go wrong; and so on. It is an inexhaustible subject, the golf swing. You can explore it endlessly and, like few things in the world, it never bores you, it enchants you. I do know one thing for certain, though. During the time I have played golf, the best technician, by far, has been Ben Hogan. No other modern player, as I see it, has approached his control of the swing, and I wonder if any player in any era has approached his control of the golf ball. Ben has probably hit more good shots and fewer poor shots than any man in history. He is the best shotmaker I've ever seen.

As I began to become a better player, I looked forward to the time when I would be paired with Ben with the same avidness that earlier, as a boy, I had looked forward to meeting Jones. That day finally arrived: June 18, 1960. We were playing partners on the third and final day of the U.S. Open at Cherry Hills, in Denver. Most golf historians remember that day in terms of Arnold Palmer, and understandably; that afternoon Arnold uncorked perhaps his most dramatic charge and won the championship with a marvelous finishing 65. In a slightly different way, it was also a significant day in my life. For the first time, I was a factor in a national open championship, and this transpired while I was playing with Hogan, who was making a tremendous bid for the title himself—his last serious bid. I think I may have come of age as a golfer that day.

In June, 1960, I was twenty—and when I look back on it now, a very young twenty. I hadn't played particularly well that spring, but in the weeks preceding the championship I suddenly began to hit my shots solidly. One morning, just before I flew out to Denver, my coach at Ohio State, Bob Kepler, said to me, "Jack, I think you'll do very well in the Open."

And what did I answer? "Bob," I told him, "I think I might win it this year." Terrif! The year before, at Winged Foot, I hadn't even made the 36-hole cut in the Open, but there I was honestly convinced I could lead the field at Cherry Hills. It's wonderful what a few good rounds can do for your confidence, especially when you're twenty.

I got off in fine style at Cherry Hills, matching par with a pair of 71s. That week I fell into a way of playing which I've never been able to recapture, though, goodness knows, I've tried to a hundred times. The main thing was the feeling I had at address: I felt that my right knee was directly under me, setting up my pivot nicely, setting it up easily. The sensation I had was that I was getting into the proper position on my backswing with a very restrained turn, and that, when I came down into the ball, I was in a great hitting position—there was no way I could go left; if I didn't hit the ball dead straight, I'd block it out a shade to the right. I was hitting my shots a little like Hogan, in fact. I was strong through the ball, and my irons were flying on a high trajectory with a touch of cut on them. And then, curiously, I drew Hogan himself as my playing partner for the double round on the last day. He had the same 36-hole total as I did, 142, offsetting a poor opening round of 75 with a 67. We trailed the leader, Mike Souchak, by seven shots, but I think both of us believed we still had a pretty fair chance. Cherry Hills wasn't an especially severe test, as Open courses go, and the short first nine could really be taken apart if you got your putter working. After all, if Souchak's 135 (68-67) was a new record low score for the first 36 in the Open, that only went to show that a player who got rolling on the final day might conceivably break par by that many or more strokes on the last 36.

Several golfers I knew had previously told me that Hogan was hard to play with. He was cold, they said, and he concentrated so explicitly on his own game that he was hardly aware that anyone else was on the course. This, I discovered early in the day, was absolutely wrong. Ben couldn't have been pleasanter to play with. He didn't talk a great deal, but whenever I produced a better than average stroke, he'd say, "Good shot," and in a way that you knew he meant it. In a word, he treated me like a fellow competitor, and I liked that. I don't go for the effusive types who are always passing out compliments as if they're going out of style. Ben is also extremely courteous in observing all the little things that add up to golf etiquette, such as standing well outside the rim of your peripheral vision on the tee and the green when it's your shot. The gallery doesn't notice these subtleties, but a golfer certainly does. Not only did I find him friendly and considerate but, more than this, I have never been partnered in a championship with a man who was in a contending position, as Ben was at Cherry Hills, who was so enjoyable to play with.

The weather on Saturday, the day of the double round, was perfect for golf. The sky was blue, the thin mountain air was clear, and there was a light breeze to make things interesting. In the morning, Ben and I were both around in 69, and this brought us to within three shots of Souchak, who had taken a 73. Ben, by the way, had been on every green in the regulation stroke in his morning round. In the afternoon I moved ahead of him with an eagle 3 on the long fifth and made the turn in 32, three under par. I started back with a bogey and a par, and this brought us to the twelfth, 212 yards long, a very good short hole on which the green is protected in front by a creek. This day the pin was set front-left—a rather tight position. In the morning, with a breeze blowing across the hole from the left and coming slightly against us, I had taken a 3-iron. Now, with the breeze up a bit, I shifted to a 2-iron and hit a nice useful shot about 20 feet past the flag. Then I watched Hogan. He had gone with a 4-wood in the morning and had played the most beautiful high, soft draw you ever saw. Now he took a

3-wood and hit an almost exact duplicate of that shot—ten feet from the flag. I holed my putt and then Ben holed his shorter one. Those two birdies did a lot for us. Ben's brought him back to three under par for the tournament and placed him in the middle of the fight. He now had a definite chance to win the record-breaking fifth Open he had been seeking since 1953. My birdie put me five under.

That afternoon more players than in any postwar Open were in a position to win. No less than ten of us were packed closely together: Hogan, myself, Souchak, Palmer, Julius Boros, Jack Fleck, Dow Finsterwald, Don Cherry, Dutch Harrison, and Ted Kroll. However, I learned from the small field scoreboard on the thirteenth that I was the only player who stood five under. I had moved into the lead a stroke ahead of Boros, Palmer, and Fleck. The prospect of possibly winning the Open didn't awe me at all. All I had to do, I said to myself, was to continue hitting my shots well and let the rest take care of itself. I was glad I was paired with Hogan. It gives you a firm sense of reality when you look across the fairway and see his familiar figure walking to his ball as you walk to yours.

The thirteenth at Cherry Hills is a straightaway 385-yard par 4. You don't want to be too far out on your drive. Some seventy yards before the green, the fairway is intersected by a creek, and it's important to be well short of the point where the terrain begins to dip down to the hazard. I drove with a 3-wood and put the ball where I wanted to—on the flat part of the fairway. From a fine level lie, I lofted a 9-iron approach up close, 12 feet below the pin. Then I became just a shade excited. If I got that putt, it would place me two strokes in front, and a two-stroke lead might stand up regardless of what anyone else managed to do. I hit a pretty fair putt that just slid by the cup and went about 18 inches past. And then I saw something that bothered me: directly on my line there was a small indentation, the remains of a ball mark which someone hadn't repaired properly. I remember well my thoughts at that moment. "I'm playing good golf and I'm twenty years old," I said to myself, "and I'm scared to ask the officials if I can refix the ball mark, though I know I shouldn't be." The fact of the matter, of course, is that a player has the right to repair a ball mark of this type on the green. I should have been aware of this but I wasn't, and it was costly. My putt hit the ball mark, the ball mark threw it a fraction left, and it caught the left side of the cup and spun out. So that was a 5 instead of a possible 3. Back to four under par. Tied for the lead with Boros, one pair behind, with Palmer, two pairs behind, and with Fleck, four pairs behind.

The fourteenth is probably the most rigorous par 4 at Cherry Hills —a 470-yard dogleg to the left, with the green, boldly contoured, sitting a little above the fairway. Hogan, who had made a routine par on the thirteenth, was on in two and down in two for his par. I missed mine again. My approach shot, a 4-iron that finished 40 feet from the hole, left me with a difficult putt over a hogback. I didn't play it quite right. My ball broke left off the hogback, leaving me with a seven-footer which I didn't get down. Two three-putt greens in a row. Two bogeys in a row. Only three under par for the distance now. Out of the lead.

On to the fifteenth, a par 3, 196 yards long. Hogan, as calm and methodical as he had been seven hours earlier, floated an iron 20 feet from the pin and holed his birdie putt. Aside from that ten-footer on the twelfth, this was the first putt of any length he had made all day. He had just kept moving along, hitting one fairway and one green after another—thirty-two consecutive greens, at this point—and, finally, a putt had fallen for him. It was something to take note of and admire, for all my concern with my own fortunes. Ben was four under par now and tied for the lead with Palmer and Fleck. (Boros had run into bunker trouble on the fourteenth.) I made my par on the fifteenth and trailed the leaders by a stroke.

Down the stretch now. We both had great chances for birdies on the sixteenth, a 402-yard par 4, but Ben missed from 12 feet and I missed from 5. I thought I had read the right-to-left break correctly, but evidently I hadn't, for my putt caught only the corner of the cup, and on fast Open greens you've got to put the ball right in the middle. You can't afford to miss those short ones. You don't get those opportunities very often.

I erased that putt from my mind as best I could and went to work to see if I could pick up the birdie I needed on the seventeenth. It wouldn't be easy. The green on the seventeenth, a par 5 that measures 548 yards, is set on a small island in a sizable lake that dominates the eighteenth hole. Some twenty feet of water separate the front of the green from the end of the fairway. Only when you have a strong wind behind you can you consider trying to get home on your second, and even then it's a big risk—it takes a near perfect shot to hit and hold such a tiny target. On Open Saturday, the question was academic. The wind wasn't helping enough, and con-

25

servative tactics were the only course. All you could do was to lay up short of the water on your second and hope to stick your pitch up close enough to have a reasonably short putt for a birdie. That wouldn't be easy either, not with the pin positioned on the front-right section of the green, only 15 feet or so beyond the far edge of the hazard; all of us had learned on our earlier rounds that you simply couldn't stop a pitch on that green no matter how fine you cut the shot or how much spin you put on the ball. I laid up with a 4-iron on my second, lobbed a little wedge that rolled 12 feet past the hole, and missed the putt. Still three under par for the tournament.

For Hogan the seventeenth proved fatal. He lay two, about 25 yards short of the water, in the center of the fairway. He took more time than usual before playing that crucial third shot. He had a difficult decision to make: Should he play a safe pitch and make sure of his 5? Or should he risk everything on getting his birdie? That would mean dropping the ball only a precarious yard or two beyond the far bank of the hazard. He chose to take the gamble. Laying the face of his wedge back almost flat with the ground, he hit the ball with a very decisive action and cut up a low-flying shot that was obviously loaded with backspin. I thought it was going to be perfect, that the ball would just clear the water . . . and then I saw it slap against the bank and topple back into the hazard. Ben tried to play it out, and played it out well, but it took him two more shots to get down, and that was a 6. As it transpired, that was also the tournament.

Had Hogan made the right decision, this man who throughout his career had just about always refused to gamble in a delicate situation, preferring to play the percentage shot and to let his rivals make the mistakes that cost them championships? It was debated into the wee small hours that night, and it has been debated ever since. For what my opinion is worth, I feel that under the circumstances Ben made the right move. As I remember it, the latest information we had at that time via walkie-talkie was that several players behind us were tied with Hogan at four under par. (That wasn't correct: only Palmer was.) In any event, I think that Ben probably felt that in this situation, with so many still in the fight, he had to go for the birdie. A birdie there might possibly win for him—even Palmer wouldn't be able to reach the seventeenth green in two. I am, of course, just guessing at Ben's thoughts, but I have

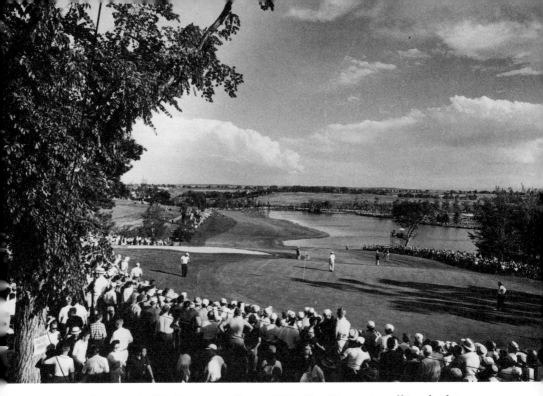

Anticlimax—the 72nd green at Cherry Hills. Ben Hogan is walking back to his ball after studying the area around the pin. I am off to the left in the rough, thinking out how to play my third.

an idea that he did not look forward to a playoff, not at forty-eight years of age, not right on the heels of 36 grueling holes. Since the same thing applies to nearly every sport, I don't much care for the cliché that golf is a "game of inches," but in this case 12 inches spelled the difference between success and failure for Ben's challenge. After Ben had gambled and lost, then to go into the lead Palmer had only to par the seventeenth, and this he did with no trouble.

By that time, though, the whole complexion of the tournament had changed. After Hogan's pitch had found the water on the seventeenth, he just went flat. He was completely drained—of drive, energy, concentration. It was all he could do to finish the round. He took a 7 on the eighteenth, hooking his tee-shot into the lake and ultimately three-putting the green. I remember our slow walk together up the hill to the last green. I was nowhere near as exhausted physically as Ben was, but my concentration was gone, too. I had no clear idea of how I stood in relation to the leader. I simply assumed I was out of the tournament. My approach on the last

27

hole had finished in the rough off to the right of the green, and when I saw Joe Dey, the executive director of the U.S.G.A., picking up some paper cups and cigarette butts near my ball, I thought Joe was just indulging his well-known passion for neatness. What he was doing was removing the trash so that I wouldn't have to do that myself and could fix all my attention on the 35-foot chip I was faced with. This was all lost on me, as I say. I hit a nice chip six feet from the hole but missed the putt. That gave me a 71 and a total of 282. It wasn't until some ten or fifteen minutes later, when I was in the clubhouse watching Arnold finish on television, that it dawned on me that I still had had an arithmetical chance when I was playing the eighteenth. Hearing the announcer say that Arnold, lying two off the edge of the green, needed a 4 for a total of 280, it suddenly hit me that if I had gotten that last six-footer and if Arnold were to take three to get down from the apron, why, we would have been tied.

I hasten to add several relevant facts. First, Arnold played a first-class chip to four feet and stroked his putt into the center of the cup to climax one of the most brilliant finishing rounds in Open history. When the chips were down, he had played the best golf of anyone in the field, and that is the man victory belongs to. Second, as I was old enough to realize at the time, all those *ifs* that golfers indulge in —*if* I had holed my approach and *if* he had whiffed his chip shot, and so on and so forth—are absolutely ridiculous. In golf, as in everything else, what didn't take place didn't take place, and that's the end of it. Third and last, at the conclusion of the 1960 Open, I was sitting on cloud nine. I had played with Hogan and had played well, I had finished second, and, as Joe Dey informed me in the locker room, my 282 was a new record total for an amateur in the Open. On top of this, over the three days at Cherry Hills I had received a priceless education in tournament golf.

I have had the pleasure of playing quite a number of rounds with Ben Hogan since that day in Denver. At the Masters, for example, we always play at least one practice round together. He names a day and we go out and play. I always learn something from watching Hogan. Of all the golfers I know, he's the best positioned throughout his swing, and he's so strong at the ball. The tempo of his swing is superb, all the time. We usually play a five-dollar Nassau, and as I don't have to tell you, there are easier ways of making money.

III

Arnold Palmer and the Contemporary Era

T HE GOLF WORLD TODAY is a far different place from the one Bob Jones inhabited in the 1920s and Ben Hogan in the late 1930s, the 1940s, and the early 1950s. In Jones' era, American professionals were just beginning to gain a spot in the sun. In that decade, they caught up with and passed the British pros, who had been the game's traditional leaders, and in the process they also demonstrated themselves to be better golfers than the Scottish and English pros who had come to this country and who had set the pace here in the tournaments. Most of the American pros who made their mark at this time—Walter Hagen, Gene Sarazen, Leo Diegel, Johnny Farrell, and so on—struggled up the hard way, from the caddie ranks. By and large, most of the talented young golfers who came from well-to-do families—Jones, for example; his father was a lawyer—chose to compete as amateurs throughout their careers. Since Jones could beat the pros, it followed that the amateur championships in those days had their own luster and considerable significance.

By the late 1930s when Hogan first came to prominence, the scene had changed a good deal. An amateur, Johnny Goodman, had won the Open in 1933—the last time an amateur was to achieve this wonderful feat—but, with the professional tour much more firmly established, it became the thing for the most successful amateurs, like Lawson Little, to graduate into the pro ranks. Most of the top pros of this period, however, had, like their predecessors in the 1920s, fought their way up the ladder the hard way. While there was more money in golf than before, the tour was nothing like the bonanza it is today. The hopeful young man who lived on oranges

29

and slept in a jalopy while he tried to make it on the tour was anything but a fictional character. There was another sizable change. In the earlier days our best pros had, for the most part, been the product of the eastern seaboard and the areas around the major cities. In the 1930s they began to sprout all over the country. Sam Snead came out of the hills of western Virginia, for example, Paul Runyan from Arkansas, Johnny Revolta from the upper peninsula of Michigan, Olin Dutra from California, and Ben Hogan, Byron Nelson, Ralph Guldahl, Jimmy Demaret, and Lloyd Mangrum all came from the new Scotland, Texas.

Today, in the 1960s, the world of golf, professional golf especially, has changed radically from what it used to be—as what hasn't. Since the close of the Second World War, the United States has enjoyed a period of unprecedented economic prosperity, and golf has not only shared in these good times but also enjoyed a special and remarkable boom of its own. To give you an illustration (not that figures tell everything): where the total prize money on the professional circuit came to about $600,000 in 1947, today it is in excess of $5,000,000 and it is climbing annually. There is such a fine living to be made in golf today that more and more young men, understandably, are thinking of making the game their career.

Most of them enter the professional ranks differently now—directly upon graduation from college. In the past dozen or so years, a growing number of our institutions of higher learning have come to pride themselves on their golf teams, with the result that golf scholarships are readily available for promising young players. Collegiate competition is now a formidable proving ground, and a high percentage of college stars who decided to turn professional have done very well indeed. In the period just before the present one, the pro field was sprinkled with young men with a college background —Cary Middlecoff, Art Wall, Bob Rosburg, and Frank Stranahan, to name a few who come quickly to mind—but nowadays the pro who has gone to college is the rule and not the exception. Let's see —there's Palmer (Wake Forest); Ken Venturi and Ron Cerrudo (San Jose State); Gay Brewer (Kentucky); Paul Harney (Holy Cross); Bobby Nichols and Billy Martindale (Texas A. & M.); Phil Rodgers, Rex Baxter, Homero Blancas, Kermit Zarley, and Marty Fleckman (all from Houston); Bob Goalby (Illinois); Joe Campbell (Purdue); Dow Finsterwald (Ohio University); Tom Nieporte, Tom Weiskopf, and myself (all from Ohio State); Bert Yancey

(West Point); Frank Beard, Dave Ragan, Tommy Aaron, Doug Sanders, Bob Murphy, and Dan Sikes (all from the University of Florida); Al Geiberger (Southern California); Dick Sikes (Arkansas); Labron Harris, Jr. and Bob Dickson (Oklahoma State); Don January and Jacky Cupit (North Texas State); Don Massengale (Texas Tech); and Dudley Wysong (North Texas State and Southern Methodist). And this, to be sure, is only a partial list.

The other major change has been the advent of televised golf. By introducing the game to such an immense audience, television has undoubtedly been the principal force behind golf's fantastic rise in general popularity. Gene Sarazen once remarked that the television audience for just one of the shows in the Shell series far exceeds the total number of people who have watched him in person during his long career. This will give you some idea of television's reach and its influence.

The commanding figure in the present era is, of course, Arnold Palmer. It is a classic case of the right man being in the right place at the right time. Arnold has many gifts, but first and foremost, I would think, is his magnificent flair for competition. In 1960 and 1962 particularly, just about every time a golf tournament was televised, there was Arnold pulling off just the sensational shot he needed at the critical juncture. In 1962, for example, there was one period in which, over the course of six weeks, he won four of the five tournaments he entered—and won them just about the way Frank Merriwell probably would have had he turned his attention to golf. In the Masters, in the first week in April, he gained a tie with Player and Finsterwald by holing a 50-foot wedge chip for a birdie on the 70th hole and then dropping a 15-foot birdie putt on the 71st green. In the playoff, after falling behind Player, he caught and passed him by rushing down the last nine in 32, four under par. The following week he finished only fifth in the Greater Greensboro Open, took a week off, and then came back to win the Texas Open at Oak Hills, in San Antonio, by birdying three of the last four holes. The next week, in the Tournament of Champions at the Desert Inn layout, in Las Vegas, he overhauled Billy Casper down the stretch with birdies on the 67th and 69th holes and bagged the winning birdie by holing a breaking 25-foot putt from off the fringe on the 72nd. He made it three in a row in the Colonial Open, in Fort Worth. Here he was unable to unleash the now famous Palmer charge on the final round and went into a playoff with Johnny Pott. He won it by four shots when he burned up the second nine with a 32. Then Arnold decided to rest up for a bit and let someone else win a tournament.

For the new-to-golf fan, who saw most of this series of finishes on television, Palmer's heroics made golf seem like the most exciting sport in the world. In addition, Arnold's personality struck a very responsive chord. He is an unusually appealing fellow: a handsome, clean-cut athlete, confident in his abilities but modest about them, natural in manner, very well-spoken, and, with all this, endowed with a rare brand of magnetism. He created the perfect image for the modern professional golfer. He was a type all Americans knew —the fellow they had gone to high school with, the boy next door —and here he was doing all these astonishing things under the most intense pressure. He also evoked the ideal atmosphere for modern professional golf: it was a game for gentlemen, played in beautiful surroundings, but a wearing, demanding game that might erupt at any moment into high drama. I don't think there is any question whatsoever that all of us who have flourished in golf in recent years owe Arnold Palmer a very great deal, to say the least.

Over the last half dozen years or so, I have spent a lot of time with Arnold both on and off the golf course. Each of us would like to be looked on as the outstanding golfer of this era—you must have this drive and ambition to succeed in a ruggedly competitive sport —and I think it is correct to say that there's no one I would rather beat than Arnold, and no one he'd rather beat than me. At the same time I would like to emphasize that, for all the seriousness of our rivalry, we are extremely good friends. In fact, of all the fellows on the tour, there are few people whose company I enjoy as much as I do Arnold's. We generally arrange to play a good many of our practice rounds together at the tournaments. For one thing, it puts both of us on our mettle. (I think that, technically, Arnold is a decidedly better golfer today than he was four or five years ago.) For another, the needling we both like to indulge in is a source of mutual relaxation. All you have to do to get Palmer started is to tell him that he has holed more good putts than any golfer in history. He

Arnold and I work on a putt during the 1966 P.G.A. Team Championship, which we won. We have had an excellent record playing together and have captured the World Cup four times.

probably has. He is far and away the finest clutch putter I've ever seen.

When we have teamed up together, we have fused extremely well. We took the 1966 P.G.A. Team Championship, and we have won the team championship in the World Cup (formerly the Canada Cup) match the four times we have been selected as the United States entry—in 1963 at Saint-Nôm-La Bretèche (near Paris), the following year at Royal Kaanapali (in Hawaii), in 1966 at the new Yomiuri course (in Japan), and in 1967 at the Club de Golf in Mexico City. Our record in the World Cup (where each player's score for each hole counts) stems, I believe, from the fact that we concentrate primarily on playing as a team and we forget about the concurrent individual competition—at least until we have the team championship wrapped up.

In the match in Japan, matters worked out somewhat different than we planned. With nine holes to go, after we had built up a safe lead in the team championship, Arnold gave me a little smile and said, "Okay, Jack, we're on our own now." Both of us were in the thick of the fight for the individual prize, along with Hideyo Sugimoto, of Japan, and George Knudson, of Canada, and from that point on it was understood that Palmer would shoot the works to win for Palmer, and Nicklaus would shoot the works to win for Nicklaus. So what happened? We both blew it. Knudson, who had played first-rate golf throughout his four rounds, eventually won out after a sudden-death playoff with Sugimoto.

In sports, the ideal attitude, as I see it, is to go all out to win, expending every last ounce of knowledge and skill and concentration and stamina, yet at the same time to regard your rivals with respect and even with genuine friendliness. The fact that Arnold and I have been able to do this is a source of considerable pride and pleasure to me. I would be less than candid, however, if I did not also say that there have been moments when I wished I had come up when golf had a less glamorous idol. When an athlete has captured the public imagination as completely as Palmer has, it is natural that at most tournaments he carries with him the largest and most keyed-up gallery. Arnie's Army isn't out merely to watch him play golf, it is there to see him win. This is all well and good, except that the extreme wing of the army has tended to look upon the men who stand between Palmer and victory not as golfers with careers of their own but as interlopers and upstarts. It is not an enviable position to be thrust into. One wants to be judged on one's own merits, of course, and it wasn't easy, I confess, to sense that on some occasions when I happened to play well enough to defeat Arnold, the result, shall we say, didn't exactly set people dancing in the streets in some quarters.

Everyone likes to think of himself as a basically appealing fellow —I know I do—so it puzzled me when I discovered, as I inevitably did, the reasons why I wasn't somewhat more popular with the Palmer-oriented sports public. I had come up too fast, some people felt. I had had things too easy. I had made too much money too quickly. In addition, I evidently came across all wrong, particularly on television: I seemed cold and grim and Teutonic and too darn sure of myself. Well, that just had to be faced up to. It is not easy to assess oneself objectively, but being as honest as I can, I think of myself as a fundamentally companionable fellow, a shade more sensitive than I appear to be, a bit too direct on occasions, a bit too stubborn on others, but, I trust, a good deal less cold and grim and Teutonic and cocksure than some people read me as being. I think I know my limitations. I am aware that I am not precisely the matinee-idol type. Rooms don't light up when I enter, and golf courses don't either. The best thing about my golf is my golf. While I enjoy the company of almost all the fellows on the tour when we're partnered together, when I am on a course in a formal competition, trying to play the best golf I can requires all my concentration. I was that way as an amateur. I took my golf seriously, and I liked to take it seriously. I am simply not one of those fortunate individuals who can operate on three different levels at the same time. However, to say things another way, whenever my golf has deserved it, I have found the galleries to be warm and supporting, and this I appreciate immensely. I also like to think that I have built up over the years a faithful following of fans who enjoy watching my golf and who gain a personal lift whenever I have a successful day or a successful tournament. That means a lot to me.

While I have tried to be myself, in the past few years I have made an effort to do things differently in one particular direction. I have tried to smile a little more and frown a little less on the golf course because I want my true attitude to be understood, and it is this: tournament golf is work, but my, what pleasant work! Some days projecting your feelings comes easier than on others. For example, on the opening day of the 1965 Masters, I was, for some reason that

35

quite escaped me, in such an uncharacteristically lighthearted mood that I was smiling at everyone in sight. As it turned out, I played nice golf that day without having to sweat at it, so without really being conscious of what I was doing, I practically smiled my way around the course. The next three days I continued to play good solid golf, with no absorbing crises, and I guess the pleasure I took in how things were going continued to be reflected in my manner. Anyway, when the tournament was over, I was rather astonished when the golf writers began to ask me to explain "the sunny new Nicklaus." This brought on a pretty funny scene in the press tent —funny because I was quite serious about it—in which I carefully explained that I really liked to smile but that, apparently, it was harder for me to adjust my facial muscles than it was for other people.

It was only a matter of months, though, before at least one of my close friends, Kaye Kessler, the golf writer for the Columbus *Citizen-Journal,* had already grown tired of "the sunny new Nicklaus." During the third round of the P.G.A. Championship that year—I was playing raggedly but was still in contention—Kaye was standing with my dad when I came beaming up a fairway even though I had just parked an easy approach in a bunker. "Great, Jack, great!" he groaned, heavy on the irony. "Just go ahead and smile yourself out of the tournament." All of which only goes to show how difficult it is, unless you're a born showman, to spend a part of your life in public in this era when "the image" is so important. You adjust as best you can, you try to keep on learning—and that's about it.

My story, as I see it, is somewhat different from the stories of most of my contemporaries in golf, and somewhat different also from the stories of the leading figures of the earlier periods. To a degree, my background is not unlike Jones', inasmuch as we were both lucky enough to come from well-fixed families and so had every opportunity to develop our games, but there the similarity ends. To a degree, my fascination with the mechanics of the golf swing is not unlike Hogan's, but, again, only to a degree. Ben has leveled many, many more practice tees than I have, or ever will, in his tireless, restless pursuit of technical perfection and the knowledge that leads to it. In temperament, for all of our differences, there is a resemblance between Palmer and myself, for we both thrive on competition and, somehow or other, the wheels within us turn best when we are in the ruck and must summon an extra effort to get back in the running. But, on closer inspection, Arnold and I are quite different essentially, and we look at golf in different ways. The son of a professional, Arnold grew up on the course at Latrobe, Pennsylvania, which his father operated. He learned to drive a tractor at about the same age that most kids are mastering the bicycle. The very fact that he is on a golf course has a reassuring comfortableness for him. He is at home, and everything from the smell of a new-mown fairway to the feel of a sticky new grip appeals deeply to him.

My approach to golf is a little different. While just being around golf has always been a source of genuine pleasure for me, golf really excites me only when I am playing a course with definite character and true interest, a course that tests your ability to play a variety of correct, intelligent, subtle golf shots. To try to meet the demands of such a course under tournament pressure, when you are up against the world's best golfers, is a challenge I respond to. In a word, I enjoy competing—competing against both fine holes and fine players. This makes me feel very much alive, somewhat in the same way that Sir Francis Chichester, the English sailor, explained his love of those perilous solo voyages he has found he cannot resist: life is intensified, and the efforts you make under those circumstances come to have a significance of their own.

My fondness for competition, I am sure, derives from the fact that I grew up, as so many American boys do, loving sports more than anything else in the world. I played them all in their season: baseball (I was a catcher), football (I was a quarterback), basketball (I was a forward), tennis, and track (you wouldn't believe it, but I was a sprinter). Like every kid, I wanted to be as good as I could at all the sports I played—good enough, at least, to win a place on the teams. All of America is sports-minded, and the area in which Columbus lies—that belt that sweeps down from Michigan through Indiana and across Ohio to Pennsylvania—makes as much of sports as any region in the country, and this rubbed off on me. It was bound to when you had a father like mine who lived, talked, and slept sports and who started taking me to Ohio State football games when I was six. (I didn't miss an Ohio State home game for thirteen years, not until 1960 when the dates of the Eisenhower Trophy match clashed with the big game against Southern California.) I gradually gravitated to golf because I liked it the best of all the sports I played and because I felt I had a reasonable chance of achieving something worthwhile in it. I had no other youthful ambitions.

The story you will be reading, you see, is about a young man with all the advantages who was able to do what he wanted most to do: play golf. While I have found life full of interest and complications, my story doesn't exactly crackle with drama. I don't think it would ever make a motion picture. If Hollywood ever attempted it, it would probably end up, according to a friend of mine who works in pictures, like "Night and Day." That was the movie about Cole Porter, the songwriter. Porter was a young man from a wealthy Indiana family who wanted to be a musical comedy composer. After being educated at the best schools, he tried to crack Broadway, and did so without too much trouble. The biggest headache he had for quite a while was that he married a beautiful woman who had even more money than he did. That's hardly Hollywood's idea of a conflict, so they invented some better stuff, such as having Porter join the French Foreign Legion where he was inspired by the chantings of the African troops to sit down on the Sahara and write "Begin the Beguine," which has a Caribbean rhythm. They'd probably have me winning the British Open at Muirfield by holing out a fantastic recovery shot from a bargeful of sheep that happened to be plowing up the Firth of Forth, just off the course, at the fateful moment. It wasn't that easy at all.

My story is simply about my career in golf. I will try to bring you the feel of the championships, to tell you something about my fellow competitors and the flavor of life on the tour, to set down my thoughts on technique and golf course architecture, and to say something about my family and friends. If the title hadn't already been used, I would have liked to have called this book *The Education of a Golfer*. That's what it is when it's all boiled down.

Part Two

IV

Dad and the Other Nicklauses

THE NICKLAUSES come from Alsace-Lorraine. We have never attempted to trace the family all the way back, but the "modern" patriarch is one Peter Nicklaus, who lived in the Alsace-Lorraine region in the early nineteenth century. The first Nicklauses to come to America were old Peter's grandchildren, who spread out and settled in Cincinnati, Columbus, and Wichita. The Wichita and Cincinnati branches pronounced the name *Nick-loss* (as in Santa Claus). The Columbus branch, which my great-grandfather started, pronounced it *Nick-lus,* and our branch has done so ever since. It is a name that gives people trouble. I remember that after my victory in the Open in 1962, my dad received a personal letter from General David Sarnoff, the head of R.C.A., asking for the correct pronunciation. I can only guess that the general was a little tired of hearing the sports announcers on N.B.C., an R.C.A. affiliate, pronouncing it three or four different ways and decided he would go straight to the horse's mouth. *Nick-lus,* accent on the first syllable.

Charles Louis Nicklaus, my great-grandfather, set up the Nicklaus Boiler Works in Columbus. The plant was situated on property adjacent to and behind his house lot. He and his wife had twelve children, ten of whom lived—three girls and seven boys. All the boys, my grandfather Louis included, became boilermakers. Louis Nicklaus was not as large in size as some later members of the family, for he stood only five-nine and weighed 175 pounds. He was a very strong man, though, and one of the few boilermakers who could swing those big overhead punches into position all by himself. In those days Columbus was an important railroad center, and my grandfather and four of his brothers worked for the Pennsyl-

41

vania Railroad. In time he moved up to the post of Foreman and
Yard Inspector and also became the secretary of the local chapter
of the railroad men's union. He must have been a person of unusual
principle and stubbornness, for in 1923, after the lengthy nationwide Pennsylvania Railroad strike broke out, he was one of the
very few men in the local union who refused to return to the Pennsylvania. The strike dragged on for years without a settlement. This
placed him under a severe financial strain. He had been getting
$1.75 an hour, good money in those days, and this was much more
than he could make at anything else. However, he would not give
in as long as the railroad would not meet the union's original demands. For five years he kept his family afloat by repairing school
and church boilers, and by working as a millwright, paperhanger,
and vacuum-cleaner salesman. When he finally went back to railroad work in 1929, it was for the Hocking Valley Railroad. He
was a strong man in more ways than one.

My grandfather and his wife Arkie Belle had five children, three
boys and two girls. My uncle Frank was the oldest, followed by my
father, Louis Charles, Jr., two years younger, and then by Jessie
(who died at age six) and by Dorothy and Bob who were eight and
fifteen years younger, respectively, than my father. They were a
closely knit family, and everything went into the family wallet; there
was no other way to make ends meet, particularly during the years
my grandfather was waging his private war against the Pennsy. For
all of the physically exhausting nature of his work, my grandfather
found the time to play some baseball. He was a catcher in the Columbus industrial league. It was his job to take care of the equipment between games, and I mention this because of the impression
it made on my father. The sight of all those gloves, bats, and balls
piled inside the house provided the most blissful spectacle of his
boyhood, a notch above even the pleasures of fishing with his dad
—"poor man's fishing" for bass, crappies, and bluegills in the
nearby streams.

My father has been called Charlie since he was a boy. It is a
name that suits him well, for he is a friendly, outgoing man. There
is also a good deal of substance to him. I am not talking about his
physical make-up, though that would be applicable, too: he has a
big, broad build, like mine, except that his legs are nowhere near as
heavy. (As Gary Player never lets me forget, his waist measures
31 inches and my thighs 27 inches.) What I am referring to, of

course, is the solidness of Dad's character, his sense of values, and his abilities. When I look back and think about how hard he worked as a boy and a young man, I am filled with admiration and, truly, with not a little awe—my life has been so much easier. The great thing about him is that he is one of those men who has never allowed himself to be consumed by business. He has always played as hard as he has worked, and he has had time and a half for his family and his friends. I don't mean to be corny, but he has always been my best friend.

If you were setting down in outline form the main facts about my father, they would be: Born in Columbus, 1913. Graduated South High, 1931. Graduated Ohio State University, College of Pharmacy, 1935. Married Helen Schoener, of Columbus, 1937. Children: Jack William, born January 21, 1940, and Marilyn, born February 8, 1943. Opened his first pharmacy in 1942. Hobbies: Ohio State football, golf, fishing, and watching his son play golf. It is, I suppose, a typical, unsplashy American success story, but I think there is more color to it than most and I want to tell you a little about it.

When Dad and his older brother Frank were boys in grammar school, three mornings a week their day started at four o'clock when they loaded the vegetable wagon for a man in the neighborhood who was a house-to-house vendor. This gave them time to get through their paper route—they delivered the Ohio State *Journal*, now the Columbus *Citizen-Journal*—before going to school. After school they delivered the Columbus *Dispatch*, and in the evenings they clerked in a drugstore, Mebs' Pharmacy, operated by Fred J. Mebs, or Doc Mebs, as he was called. (A lot of the kids in Dad's generation worked this hard, he tells me.) The day that Doc Mebs opened his place, Dad, then eleven, was perched at the soda fountain early in the morning. Doc asked him if he knew of an older boy who would like to earn some money helping out, and Dad convinced him that he could handle the job himself. In a way, I think, it was the turning point in his life. He stayed on at Mebs' Pharmacy until he finished college, and Doc Mebs became sort of a second father to him. I knew Doc pretty well. He was a bald-headed little man, about five-six, with a wide dimpled smile, very German. He was a clown at heart. He used to keep a big curly wig under the counter, and when he saw a familiar face entering the front door, he'd duck down, pop on the wig, and, changing his voice, say, "May I help you?" If the disguise worked and the regular customer asked, "Is Doc Mebs here today?" the old Doc's day was made. He was always cutting up like that. His customers were his friends, and he wanted them to leave with a smile.

Doc Mebs was the man who introduced my father to golf. Doc and a few of his cronies played at the nine-hole course at the local army depot, and Dad caddied for him whenever he could arrange it. It was another way to make a buck. When Dad was in high school, he began to play some golf with Mebs' group, filling in whenever a player was needed to round out the foursome. It was typical of Mebs that he gave Dad the tickets he had purchased for the 1926 Open at Scioto. Doc was simply too busy to go himself, he explained, but Dad knew that this was just a pretense and that Doc had meant to give him the tickets all along. It was like Doc Mebs, too, that in 1932 he sold Dad his set of Bobby Jones woods and irons for fifteen dollars, slightly below their market value. He wanted Charlie to have them, and went through the leisurely formality of deducting one or two dollars a month from his paycheck until the transaction was completed. Dad loved those clubs, first, because Jones was his idol and, second, because they suited the long Jones-like swing he had developed. Considering he never got onto a course more often than once a week, he was a darn good golfer. He played number-one on the South High golf team, scoring between 73 and 79. A little later he set a course record at the Bridgeview public course, a nine-hole layout; the record lasted for two years.

Even after Jones went into retirement, he remained Dad's hero, but he was fascinated also by Hagen after watching him in the 1931 Ryder Cup match at Scioto. On the morning of the second day of the match, when the eight singles were played, Hagen put on one of those unforgettable shows of his before teeing off with his opponent, Charles Whitcombe. As he stood on the tee with a coat thrown majestically over his shoulders, a waiter appeared from the clubhouse carrying a tray on which was poised a martini in a shining stem glass. Walter took a sip or two of the martini and nonchalantly swung his driver a couple of times with his free hand, his left. He took another sip or two, shifted the martini, and took a couple of swings with his right hand. When his name was announced, he drained the martini with a flourish, and after taking a few practice swings with both hands on the club, hit a beautiful drive right down the middle of the fairway. He went on to beat Whitcombe 4 and 3. No one on the tour today would be permitted to get away with a performance like that. Some of the fellows, like Doug Sanders, drink deeply at the fountain of life, but when they are on the course, compared to Hagen, they are about as free-wheeling as Doris Day.

Dad was a very fine all-round athlete. He played fullback on the high school football team, guard on the basketball team, and left field (his regular position), third base, and catcher on the baseball team. Baseball was probably his best sport. I don't know how he ever found the time in the spring, but he was also a member of the high school golf and tennis teams, both of which scheduled a half-dozen or so matches. At the request of Coach Rodney Ross, a young member of the faculty, Dad helped start the golf team. That same spring they started a tennis team. Dad rounded up five or six students he knew who played some tennis, and Rodney took over the coaching duties. Dad continued to play tennis for recreation throughout his college days, and in 1935, the year he graduated, he won the Columbus Public Courts Championship.

Because of his athletic record and his good marks, Dad was offered an attractive scholarship deal by the Hun School, which specialized in preparing boys for Princeton. He turned it down because Princeton had no course in pharmacy. Idolizing Doc Mebs as he did, Dad had made up his mind that he wanted to follow in that profession himself. He entered Ohio State, which had an outstanding college of pharmacy.

During his freshman year, typically, he tried to do everything. He attended classes from eight to five most days during the week, and from eight to eleven on Saturdays; he was of half a mind in those days to become a doctor, and for a while he tried to carry the full pre-med curriculum. He sandwiched in freshman football, basketball, and baseball, and he continued to work at night at Mebs' Pharmacy. At midnight he was generally still up studying, along with his brother Frank, who was attending Ohio State's College of Dentistry. They would turn the radio on to the "Moon River" program, the popular music show from station WLW, Cincinnati, that began at twelve, and keep pounding away at the books.

Early in his sophomore year, Dad was confronted with a crisis of sorts. He had gone out for the varsity football team and had been shifted to end, since his forte was defense and Ohio State then went in for big, heavy, turn-them-in ends, like Sid Gilman, the present coach of the San Diego Chargers. On the eve of the opening game against Cincinnati, his appendix acted up and the team physician sent him to the hospital. The idea was that, with good luck, he would be back after the operation in time to play the last half of the season. "While I was lying in that hospital bed," Dad has told me, "I began to ask myself, 'What the deuce am I doing here? The only reason, apparently, why I need an operation is so I can play college football. But if I have that operation, I'll fall behind in my subjects. That doesn't make sense. I'm supposed to be here to get an education, not to play football.' " So he got up and left the hospital and never had the operation. Instead of playing for Ohio State, he played for the Portsmouth Spartans of the National Football League, on Sundays, under assumed names. He spelled "Father" Lumpkin, the All-America back from Georgia Tech, whenever Lumpkin needed a breather, backing up the line when the other team had the ball. He played some jayvee basketball his sophomore year, but then gave that up when he found it took too much time from his studies. His last two years he concentrated on just two things: his college courses and his job at Mebs' Pharmacy.

When my father received his degree in pharmacy in 1935, he went to work as a regional salesman for the Johnson & Johnson Company. After several years of this, he was offered the position of divisional manager, to be based in Chicago. He spent a week there making up his mind and decided against the promotion; he felt the new job would entail too much traveling. In 1942, what had been a Walgreen drugstore on the corner of High and Chittenden Streets, directly across from the Ohio State campus, came up for sale. With the help of loans from a drug wholesaler, an ice cream company, and his brother Frank, my dad bought it. He prospered. By 1960 he owned four pharmacies in and around Columbus. He later sold two of them to employees of his. Today he owns and operates two pharmacies, one in Arlington and one in Worthington. My uncle Bob, who also graduated from the Ohio State college of pharmacy, is a partner with Dad in the Worthington store. As for Uncle Frank, he's a dentist in Bath, New York, a town seventy miles southeast of Rochester. He has been the town mayor many times—all in all, for something like eighteen or twenty years. Until recently it was no trouble at all to recognize Uncle Frank at a golf tournament. All you had to do was scan the horizon for a gigantic fellow, about six-three, dressed in such gaudy sports clothes that it looked as if he was wearing his warm-up suit for a basketball game. He has gradually quieted down the past few years, and some days now his outfits are so muted he looks positively British.

It is easy, too, to recognize my dad at a golf tournament. He is always in my gallery—a man in his mid-fifties who looks a good deal like me. He is a very unobtrusive rooter. He makes it a practice to slide his name card out of his tournament badge, and he plods along outside the fairway ropes like everyone else. The 1965 P.G.A. Championship at Laurel Valley was the one and only time I've ever seen him exercise any privilege at a tournament. On the last day at Laurel Valley, the marshaling broke down almost completely, and when Dad found he could not watch me play half my shots, near the end of the round he slapped on a press badge he was carry-

Father and son—a pointer from the Old Maestro.

ing in case of emergency and joined the reporters inside the ropes. I spotted him bustling along just after I'd driven off the sixteenth, and I called over to him, "Hey, big boy, who you covering for?" He hesitated a moment and then responded, *"Evening News."* When I saw him that night, he was very amusing about that incident. *"Evening News!"* he said, shaking his head. "Can you imagine a duller answer? There I was with the opportunity of a lifetime to say something bright and witty, and I blew it. The *Evening News* indeed!"

My father knows golf, and his observations are generally very much worth listening to. As is only natural, though, there are occasions when we see things differently. Sometimes when, in my estimation, I've hit the ball well, he'll be critical of my play, and the other way round. I remember one evening when I dropped in for dinner at the house he rents in Augusta during the Masters just as he was describing for a golf-writer friend of ours, Gwil Brown, how it was I hadn't birdied the long eighth that day. "Jack played every shot faultlessly," I heard him say. "A big drive just left of center. Then a perfect second to the right of the entrance to the green, exactly where he wanted to be. Then a great little wedge pitch to about four feet. How he missed that putt, Gwil, I'll never know. It rolled right for the middle of the cup but somehow it twisted out. He really deserved a birdie." For a while I didn't know what hole Dad was describing, for as I remembered the eighth, I'd almost duckhooked my drive, I'd come way off my second and lost it far out to the right, I'd hit my wedge heavy and was lucky some unintentional overspin carried it up close, and finally I'd jerked that four-footer so badly the ball was traveling much too fast and never had a chance of falling when it caught the corner of the cup. I was lucky to make 5.

Most of the time, however, I hasten to add, my dad's views on what comprises good golf, both the tactics of play and the execution of the shots, are much the same as my own. As "stage fathers" go in sports, I don't think there's a better one. He always has my interest at heart, never his. When I seek his advice—he never offers it otherwise—he presents his opinions clearly and honestly, but he never pressures me to accept them. He has always held that I must be responsible for my own decisions. He has watched with quiet patience and understanding while I played disappointing rounds; and when I have played well, for all his natural exuberance he has

From the family album. Age five.

always been modest in talking about his son—just the way his son has wanted him to be. I hope he is as proud of me as I am of him.

There was a wonderfully heart-warming finish to the exceptional relationship between Doc Mebs and Charlie Nicklaus. When Dad opened his first pharmacy at High and Chittenden, Doc came to work for him. He was sixty-four then. He continued to work with Dad, at the Arlington store, until 1961 when he died at the age of eighty-three. I never remember his being in anything but good humor. Right to the end he loved the pharmacist's life because it brought him into contact with so many people, and as Doc hoped would happen, few of them ever left the store without a smile.

V

Getting Started with Jack Grout

ARLY IN MY CAREER as a professional, newspaper and magazine writers, in search of anecdotes about my formative years,
regularly approached my father for background material. He was
very cooperative, for he enjoyed reminiscing, but after a while,
when he had covered the same ground on fifty different occasions,
he was amazed that there still remained any readers, let alone
reporters, who hadn't heard about "The Famous Ankle Injury,"
as he came to call it—the injury to his right ankle that got me
started in golf.

Briefly, in 1944 my dad had hurt that ankle while playing volley-
ball. It was diagnosed as simply a severe strain, since no disloca-
tion showed up in the x-rays. His foot had not mended well, however, and over the next five years it gave him quite a lot of trouble.
In 1949, when it flared up badly, he finally discovered why. A small
bone, the calcaneus, had been chipped. Over the years it had been
covered with an outgrowth of bone, and arthritis had set in. In
the autumn of 1949, Dr. Jud Wilson, an orthopedic surgeon, operated to fuse the ankle. Dad wore a cast for three months, and when
it was removed, Dr. Wilson instructed him carefully, "Give your
foot as much movement as you can—the sort of movement you
get when you walk on soft ground." To Dad this suggested one
thing: golf. In 1935, when he had graduated from college, he had
given the game up, but thirteen years later he had joined Scioto
and had started to play again. In the spring of 1950, after the
operation, he quickly discovered that he could play only a hole
or two before he had to sit down and rest the ankle. Since this
ruled out his usual games with his friends at the club—golf carts

50

were not in use yet—the thought occurred to him to have his ten-year-old son come along as his golfing companion. He got me a set of cut-down Hillerich & Bradsbys, and we started hacking around together. We would play a hole or two, and then while he took a breather, I'd practice chipping or putting or hitting sand shots.

Before that season, I had never thought about golf. I was crazy about baseball, and that had occupied me fully in the spring and summer. Then in the fall, like most other Midwestern boys, I had been swept up in the football mania. In fact, at the age of five, I had almost cost my mother the best maid she ever had. Her name was Annie, and one afternoon after I had been watching some older boys playing football in a nearby lot, I went home and promptly leveled Annie with a flying tackle. She phoned for a taxi and left the Nicklauses, presumably forever. My mother later was able to persuade her to return, and Annie was with us for many years—untackled.

The spring that I took up golf, a new pro, Jack Grout, came to Scioto. One of the things he instituted was a weekly two-hour class for juniors on Friday mornings during the summer. About fifty boys and girls between the ages of ten and seventeen took advantage of this. That June my father turned me over to Grout. I took a private lesson from him every two or three weeks, and I joined the Friday morning class. We met at the practice area, an unusually large one, perhaps 150 yards wide and extending some 400 yards in length, down to the edge of the club's nursery. The one thing wrong with this practice area is that the wind generally blows from left to right. That is not a good wind to practice in—it breeds hooking—so nowadays when I tune up at Scioto, I often go down to the far end of the field and hit back toward the clubhouse. In 1950, of course, I wasn't that finicky.

During those Friday morning sessions, Grout would line his pupils up in one long row across the practice area. He would discuss some point he wanted us to absorb, and he would demonstrate it himself or use one of us to do so. Then, when we started to hit out practice balls and work on that point, he would walk down the line and look us over individually. Funny thing about that first year. The first time I played nine holes I had a 51. My second time out I had a 61. Then, for weeks, I got worse and worse, though I played every day and was beginning to develop the rudiments of a golf swing. (I probably told my buddies, "I'm hitting the ball great but I'm just not scoring.") Finally it began to come, and before the summer was over, I had a 95 for eighteen holes.

I was a member of Grout's Friday morning class the next two years, the summers of 1951 and 1952 when I was eleven and twelve. By my second summer, I had become his prize demonstrator. Let's say he was working on getting us not to scoop the ball on the upswing, one of his basic tenets. "Jackie," he would say, "come out here and show us what it means to hit down on the ball." I'd trot out and hit a few shots emphatically on the downswing and, after some complimentary remark by Grout, trot back to my place. I came on very quickly that second summer—I shot an 81 before it was over—thanks to that Friday morning class and my private lessons with Grout. One of his strongest qualities was that he regarded his pupils not as products to be stamped out in the same mold but as individuals, each with his special problems and aptitudes. That second summer, I remember in this connection, he wanted to change my grip. My father had started me with the interlocking grip, which was popular in the 1920s—Sarazen and Ouimet used it, for example. Grout thought I might do better with the overlapping grip, the so-called Vardon grip which has become almost standard. I didn't like the overlap. No matter how much I practiced with it, I still felt that my right hand would slip off my left either on the backswing or the downswing. Grout watched me closely and at length suggested that perhaps, after all, the interlocking might be better for me. He never tried to change my grip again, and I have stayed with it ever since.

Jack Grout, as you can see, was more than just a run-of-the-mill golf pro. He was both a fine player and a thorough student of the game. An Oklahoman by birth, he had started his real education in golf in 1930, at the age of twenty, when he became an assistant to his older brother Dick, the pro at the Glen Garden Club in Fort Worth. He stayed at Glen Garden for seven years. During that time he learned a great deal about golf from Dick, a popular and talented teacher, and from his rounds with two local boys, just under twenty, who had earlier caddied at Glen Garden and now came out frequently to play the course—Byron Nelson and Ben Hogan. He learned much from his own competitive experiences— he won the Oklahoma State Open during this period—and from observing and talking with the professionals he met when he took a crack at the P.G.A. tournament circuit.

52

The touring pro Jack was closest to was Henry Picard, one of the leading golfers of that day, and when Grout left Glen Garden in 1937, it was to go with Picard as his assistant at the Hershey Country Club in Pennsylvania. (Because of his connection with Hershey, Picard was referred to by the press as "The Chocolate Soldier," naturally.) Grout remained with Picard until 1940, then took a series of jobs in Pennsylvania and one in Chicago, and in 1950 came to Scioto. He was forty then, a tall, slim fellow whose tanned complexion, black patent-leather hair, and glasses gave him somewhat the look of a Peruvian lawyer. He was a lovely golfer to watch—a hands player, essentially, with a long graceful arc to his swing and a beautiful, consistent tempo.

I don't think Jack had come close to fulfilling his potential, or his aspirations, as a tournament golfer. He had scored only two notable victories. In 1939 he and Picard had teamed to win the Mid-South Four-Ball Championship at Pinehurst, and in 1947 he had outdistanced the whole pro pack in the Spring Lake Invitational, nosing out Craig Wood. Most of the time, though, he had been forced to be content with coming close. In the 1941 P.G.A. Championship, for instance, when Vic Ghezzi beat Nelson in the final, Grout and Ghezzi had had a tremendous battle in the fourth round, which Ghezzi won on the 36th green. However, unlike most golfers of tournament class whose achievements had fallen below their hopes, there was nothing sour or backward-looking about Grout. His ambition was now to be as fine a teacher as he could, and he went at it with thoughtfulness, vigor, and a contagious enthusiasm for anything and everything that had to do with understanding the golf swing. I happened to be at the right club at the right time.

Grout's assessment of the true fundamentals of the golf swing were, you might say, triple-distilled: he had arrived at his conclusions after his studies with Picard, and Picard had previously studied with Alex Morrison, the most advanced and controversial theorist of the 1920s and 1930s. Some of Morrison's ideas seem extreme even today, but many of his thoughts on technique which were once considered revolutionary—his thoughts on the work of the feet, for example—are now as accepted and as orthodox as the straight left arm. In any event, Jack Grout, a man with an active analytical mind, had by 1950 formulated an approach to the golf swing that rested on a mere handful of fundamentals. I will take

53

my time in presenting them, for I want to be sure and get them across lucidly. I ask you to bear in mind that Grout was teaching these fundamentals back in 1950 when the golf swing was not understood anywhere near as well as it is today. He was far ahead of his time.

The first fundamental that Grout impressed on us was the necessity for keeping the head still. This was not a new idea. Harry Vardon had stated decades before that the player who does not maintain his head in a still position cannot expect to play good golf —nothing was more important. Down through the years, however, it became more and more customary to instruct a golfer not to keep his head still but to keep his eye on the ball. This new phrase was meant to be just another way of saying the same thing, but it did change the emphasis in a golfer's mind, and, in a way, the value of the still head had to be discovered all over again.

The head is the balance center of the swing. If it moves, it changes your balance as well as your arc, your movements, your timing. It has to. At address the head should be set just behind the ball. It must remain there, *still but not rigid,* during the backswing and the downswing. It takes practice to master this. It didn't come easy for me, I know. When I was eleven or so, Grout, a very gentle man, had to resort to a rather rough teaching device. His assistant, Larry Glosser, would position himself directly in front of me, as I stood at address, and grab hold of my hair with his hand. If I moved my head while hitting a shot—oh, did it hurt! It was as if someone was tugging at the roots with all his strength. Many times the pain this caused sent tears running down my face. To repeat, Grout wasn't the sort of fellow who went in for Tower of London stuff, but this was the only way he could get me to stop bobbing my head, and in time I learned to hold it still no matter how hard I swung at the ball.

The second fundamental also had to do with balance: proper foot action. The great players, almost without exception, have had superb foot action. Otherwise, they would never have become great players. Unless a golfer possesses excellent balance, he cannot move freely and swiftly through the ball on the downswing. The feet are the key. Everything else follows. For a long time the essentials of correct foot action were taught by only a few professionals. It was conventional in those days to tell a pupil that on the backswing he should move up onto his left toe as his weight shifted onto his right foot, and that on the downswing this was reversed. The trouble here is that in the course of this left-toe, right-toe procedure, many golfers will bend their left knee the wrong way and turn their hips the wrong way on the backswing and continue to make wrong moves throughout an off-balance swing. *Good foot action is based on rolling the ankles.* To put it simply, the left ankle rolls in laterally, toward the right foot, on the backswing; the right ankle braces against this motion. On the downswing, as the left ankle rolls back to the left and into a firm bracing position, the right ankle rolls in toward the left. This enables a golfer to turn properly going back and to move forward properly into the ball—and to avoid a hundred and one faulty movements. Wasn't it Bob Jones who remarked, "Good golf is played on the inside of the feet"?

Even though it can be said that when you roll your ankle you have to roll your heel along with it, for myself I always think of footwork as being a combined rolling of the ankle and heel. This undoubtedly goes back to those early days with Grout. He had the members of his class keep their heels on the ground at all times during the swing. This not only makes you roll the entire foot but also promotes several other beneficial habits: it deepens your sense of balance; it helps you to develop a good arm swing, and, in the process, it increases the suppleness you need to make a full shoulder turn. I must have been playing golf for three or four years before Grout permitted me to raise my heels at all during the swing. Even then, he would remind me to practice occasionally keeping both heels on the ground. Hogan, he told me, used to practice that way, sliding his right foot into the shot as he hit it. There's a lot in this. When your swing is getting out of kilter, practicing with your feet hugging the ground is a wonderful way to rediscover the essentials of a good, compact swing. I recommend it unreservedly for all golfers.

A third fundamental that Grout stressed for young golfers was to *develop as full an arc as possible;* the best shoulder turn was the fullest shoulder turn. His thinking was that by extending, extending, extending, a young golfer stretched his muscles, and he could not do this later when the muscles had become so much less flexible. And right from the start he encouraged us to hit the ball as hard as we could and as far as we could. This went directly counter to

55

the traditional approach. Most young golfers, then and now, are counseled to strive first for accuracy, not distance; distance will come naturally as you grow bigger and stronger. Grout's reasoning went like this: There is no getting away from the fact that the man who can hit the ball farthest has an advantage. Accordingly, a player should develop a power swing when he is young and his muscles are limber. That will stay with him. Control can come later.

There is no question in my mind but that Grout is right about this. Length has helped me immeasurably in tournament golf. If I hit the ball farther than most people, it isn't because I am stronger physically than they are but because it became second nature for me at a young age to be fully extended muscularly as I performed the golf swing and hit through the ball.

There were other fundamentals that Grout gave tireless attention to, such as the grip, the stance (we were all taught the square stance in the Friday class), and, as I touched on earlier, the necessity of hitting the ball on the downswing, not on the upswing. Each of these is important, but my own feeling is that discussing them here might weaken the spotlight I want to put on the three fundamentals I have described at some length. I consider them the ABC of Grout's method:

A. The head must be still throughout the backswing and down-swing.

B. The key to balance is footwork—the correct rolling of the ankles.

C. The young golfer should develop the fullest possible arc.

The summer I was eleven, as I noted earlier, I got down to 81. I did this qualifying for the Columbus District Junior Championship. In the first round, however, I was knocked out on the 19th hole by Larry Snyder, a tottering veteran of thirteen. That year, by the way, I got my first set of full-length clubs—a set of Bobby Jones woods and irons, with tan-coated shafts, which my dad had stored in the cellar. I used the woods for two years, the irons for one; I replaced the irons with a set of Spalding Top-Flites I bought at the pro shop. As my father periodically pointed out, I was developing not only a pretty good golf game but a pretty good signature on those Scioto charge slips. It was nothing for me to go through ten or eleven buckets of balls on the Fridays I went to Grout's class. When the bills came, my father would say to me, half-frowning, half-pleased, "From what I gather, Jack, most of the kids in the class hit out one or two buckets of balls. You, ten buckets, a dozen buckets. How does anyone hit out that many balls?" The answer, I told him, was that I stayed after class and practiced and that I always practiced before I went out to play on the other days. He would close his eyes and rub his head, and that would be it.

This steady practicing led to some real progress. The summer I was twelve, I broke 80 for the first time. It was odd how it happened. I shot eight straight 80s, and just when I was wondering what I had to do to break that barrier, I shot a 74. The following summer, when I was thirteen, I reached the next goal I had set for myself: I broke 70 for the first time. I remember that afternoon as clearly as if it were yesterday. I was working at the drugstore that summer, and my dad and I went out to the club around four, as we often did. Par at Scioto was 36-36–72. I was out in 34. I don't know what my father could have been thinking of, but at the end of the nine he said to me, "That was wonderful golf, Jack. Well, now, home for a good dinner."

"Dad, we can't do that," I told him. "I've got a chance to break 70."

He thought for a moment. "I'll tell you what we'll do, Jack. We'll eat and come back."

"No, we won't have time," I protested. "It'll get dark. It won't hurt Ma to hold dinner."

He shook his head. "We'll do it my way," he said. We drove home and I raced through dinner. Dad wasn't bad. He got through his faster than I'd ever seen him do before, and we tore back to the club. We couldn't have cut it much finer. When we got to the eighteenth, the twilight was fading so fast you could hardly see where the ball was going, and it was getting darker every second. At that stage, I was one over par on the second nine, so in order to get the 35 I needed to break 70, I would have to eagle the eighteenth, a par 5 about 500 yards long. I hit a good drive and a good 2-iron. I couldn't see the flag in the darkness but I could see the water-sprinkler on the green, and I had played for that. I was on, all right, 35 feet from the cup—35 very wet feet. I remember

57

pulling the sprinkler back and somehow, through all the water, I holed that putt. 34-35–69! The promised land!

The two accompanying photographs will give you an idea of what my swing looked like during this period. If I seem to be a little thinner than you might have expected, there is an explanation. That summer of 1953 I had a mild case of polio. Before we knew what was wrong, I had felt rotten for two weeks; my back ached and I had a slight temperature some days and other days I had headaches. However, even though there was a bad polio epidemic that summer, it didn't seem that what was bothering me was anything that serious. Then one afternoon my dad came over to the club and took me off the golf course. My sister Marilyn had come down with polio. I obviously had it and she'd gotten it from me.

Hers was a **much** more severe case. It took her two years to regain full use of one of her legs, but with therapy it became as good as new in time. (Marilyn grew up to be very good-looking—an auburn-haired girl with green eyes.) As I say, I was luckier that summer, my case of polio being nonparalytic. The only visible after-effect was how thin I was—I went from 165 pounds down to 145. That is why I look more like Tab Hunter than Jack Nicklaus in these shots.

There is one other comment I should like to make about the two photographs above. If you compare my thirteen-year-old swing with my present swing, you will observe, I think, that there's very little difference between them. To put it another way, Jack Grout

Jack Grout (at left), the man who taught me golf.

started me so well that although I made minor adjustments in my swing in later years, there was never any need to change its basic pattern. I have never gone to any other teacher except Jack. Of course, when I have been in the middle of a sour streak and he hasn't been around, I have experimented with tips and suggestions that my fellow players and other friends have kindly offered, but down through the years Jack is the one person I've worked with. I need hardly underline how fortunate I was to meet up with him when I was so young, for countless promising golfers I know have become hopelessly confused by switching from one teacher to another and attempting to play twelve different ways at the same time. I was spared all that. I still go back to Jack regularly to get checked out. He's now at La Gorce Country Club, in Miami Beach, and, if anything, he's keener about golf and the golf swing than he ever was. He is still turning out fine young golfers because, in addition to his technical virtuosity, he is still teaching his pupils, as he taught us at Scioto, not to be afraid to experiment and to think for themselves. This, I would say, is the hallmark of a great teacher.

VI

High School and College

O NCE I BEGAN to play golf, it became a large part of my life. At the same time, it wasn't till I was seventeen—graduating from high school and heading for college—that I started to realize that, to some extent anyway, my future might be seriously bound up in the game. Up to then, I had looked on golf almost as just another seasonal sport. The ideal in those days was to be an all-round athlete, not a specialist, and I threw myself just as hard into football, basketball, baseball, track, or whatever I was playing. It meant as much to me to be considered a good basketball player, say, as a good golfer. Growing up, I wasn't a bad student, but, really, with the exception of girls, I never thought of anything but sports.

In football I started as a lineman, which was logical because I always was big for my age—by thirteen I was five-ten and weighed 165. Also, I was pretty slow. In junior high, where we had an organized league and a six-game schedule, we played an advanced brand of football, for kids. Since everything revolved around the quarterback, I got it into my head, midway through the seventh grade, that this was the position for me. My father didn't think that I was either fast enough or agile enough to play in the backfield, which was all the spur I needed. I went out for track that spring to improve my speed. It helped a lot. I won the quarterback spot the next fall, and in our last game, which we won 54-0, I had a big day, scoring three touchdowns and kicking six points after touchdown. I was a fairly good place-kicker because I liked kicking, and next to our house there was a pie-shaped lot with two crab apple trees that made perfect practice goalposts. I would stay out there for hours place-kicking by myself, making believe I was Lou Groza of the Cleveland Browns.

Columbus is now a city of almost a million. In my day there were twenty or so high schools. Ours, Upper Arlington High, was about average size. There were then about twenty thousand people in Upper Arlington, a comparatively new suburb and one of the nicest sections of town. Now there are over forty thousand. My freshman year in high school I gave up football. By then I realized it had to be either golf or football. The schedules conflicted: the Jaycee Juniors, the U.S. Juniors, and the U.S. Amateur usually took place in late August and September, so if you wanted to play in these championships, you had to miss pre-season football practice. When I decided not to go out for the high school football team, it broke my dad's heart a little, for he had been looking forward for years to watching me play for the team.

In junior high we had only an informal baseball team that played three or four games. I did the catching and was a good hitter. My dad had turned me into a switch-hitter when I was eight or nine, and that is always an advantage. At that time, track was the or-

The colorful star of Upper Arlington High goes up for two.

ganized spring sport in our area. I first went out for track, as I mentioned, to improve my speed for football, but my second year out, when I was in the eighth grade, I was a sprinter on the school team. I ran the 100 (in 11 seconds flat), I ran the 220, and I was anchor man on the 880-yard relay team. I also high-jumped but there was never any question, I am happy to report, about choosing between the decathlon and golf. My freshman year at Upper Arlington High, I also gave up both baseball and track and played on the golf team.

In high school, golf was not my favorite sport. Basketball was. I was one of those kids who had a hoop in his back yard. In the winter, whenever I had a free moment, I'd be out there popping away. I was plain crazy about the game. In junior high I played center on the team, being the tallest guy in the class, but in my freshman year in high school I was shifted to forward. We had a really outstanding freshman team. The next winter, four of us who had been regulars on it became starters on the varsity, and the other freshman regular became the sixth man. In our junior and senior years—same four starters and same sixth man. We were a taller than average team—our five regulars were 5'11", 5'11¾" (me), 6'2", 6'4", and 6'7"—and by our senior year we had developed into a solid, smooth-working group, even by Midwestern standards, which are high. Our record that last season was something like 17 wins and 4 defeats, and we went to the fourth round in our district in the Ohio High School Championship before losing a squeaker 56-55. By my junior year I weighed 185 or 190. Though I played forward, I helped bring the ball down the court. I was a good outside shot, I'd say, a good driver, and a fairly good rebounder.

I don't want to bore you with all the "glamorous" details, but I remember everything about high school basketball. I was the team's second high scorer my last two years. As a sophomore, I averaged only 8 points a game, as a junior 17.5, and as a senior 18. My percentage from the foul line those three years was almost 90 percent. My last year I had a streak in which I sank 26 in a row, which my coach told me surpassed the Big Ten record held then by Miller of Wisconsin. All the team could shoot fouls. As a junior and senior I made all-league forward in the Central Buckeye League, and my last year I received honorable mention in the All-Ohio selections.

63

I certainly thought I'd be going out for college basketball, but when I reached Ohio State, I settled for inter-fraternity ball. I really don't know whether I had enough ability to have made the squad. Probably not. In 1950, Ohio State had won the Big Ten and made an unexpectedly strong showing in national competition, and after that exploit, basketball became very big and the college attracted terrific talent. Larry Siegfried, who is now with the Boston Celtics in the National Basketball Association, was in my class; John Havlicek, who's also with the Celtics, and Jerry Lucas, the Cincinnati Royals' star, were in the class behind me. We had great teams. In 1960, we won the N.C.A.A. Championship. That year and the following two, we were the Big Ten champions. Lucas, Siegfried, and Havlicek all made All-America, but Havlicek was my particular favorite. He always took the other team's top star and concentrated on defense, and his hustling, unselfish teamwork made the difference in many tough games.

And then there was golf. At thirteen, I remember well, I got my first complete set of new clubs—Tommy Armour woods and irons, the irons with the Silver Scot blade. (I stayed with Tommy Armour clubs until I began to design my own for MacGregor. In truth, the first irons to bear my name were basically the same club as the Silver Scot.) From my last year in junior high on, I played quite a bit of tournament golf. Jack Grout thought there was nothing like a touch of competition to impress on a young golfer what he had to measure up to, and my father was very much in accord with this. Oddly, whereas I can remember all the details of my high school basketball career, my youthful triumphs and defeats in golf are sort of a blur in my mind. My father, however, kept a scrapbook, very assiduously, and looking back now over those old clippings and jottings, I see that the following occurred:

1953 (age thirteen). Won Ohio State Juniors (for boys between thirteen and fifteen) by one shot over Bill Muldoon, at Sylvania in Toledo. My score for the 36 holes of stroke play was 161. . . . Won Columbus Junior Match-Play Championship at Groveport C.C., beating Bill Muldoon 1 up in the 36-hole final. (Bill, my chief rival when we were kids, later played on the Ohio State team. He's a dentist now and lives in Fort Walton, Florida.) . . . Played in my first national tournament, the U.S.G.A. Juniors (seventeen and under), at Southern Hills. Won my first three matches but lost to Bobby Ruffin 5 and 4. (Rex Baxter won.)

. . . Entered the Columbus Amateur Championship and was put out in the quarterfinals.

1954 (age fourteen). Made my first hole-in-one, on the 145-yard seventeenth at Scioto, in the final of the club junior championship. (I've made seven holes-in-one in all, six of them in competition.) Won that final on the 38th green from Bill Cowman. (My hole-in-one came on the morning round after Bill had put his tee-shot a yard from the cup. In the afternoon Bill tied the match with a 2 on the seventeenth after again firing his tee-shot a yard from the pin. I remember his father saying to him, "I told you that if you kept making twos on this hole, you'd win it.") . . . Won the Columbus Juniors, both the stroke-play and match-play tournaments. However, in the U.S.G.A. Juniors, at the Los Angeles C.C., Hugh Royer beat me 4 and 3 in the second round. (I've never played well in L.A.!) At that tournament, incidentally, Byron Nelson put on the best clinic I've ever attended. The caddie never moved sideways, just back, as Nelson went through the whole bag. . . . Played on the Upper Arlington High School team. In the Tri-State Championship (Ohio, Indiana, and Kentucky), I was low scorer, with a 64 on one round. . . . Lost in the final of the Columbus Amateur, at Scioto, to Bob Rankin, a fine golfer in his middle twenties. He and Tom Nieporte had alternated at number-one on the 1950 and 1951 Ohio State teams. . . . Entered the Ohio State Amateur, at Sylvania, and was eliminated, 1 down, by Dale Bittner. (The winner was a fellow named Arnold Palmer who was working in Cleveland that year.)

1955 (age fifteen). Repeated in the Columbus Junior match-play and stroke-play tournaments. In the latter, Dave Daniels and I finished in a tie, we remained tied after an eighteen-hole playoff, and we were still tied after a second eighteen-hole playoff. Sudden death was ordained, and I won on the second extra hole with a par 3. (I shot one 63 in the tournament proper and another in the playoffs, two of the five 63s I had that summer. All of them came on the Gray Course at Ohio State, which is only some 6400 yards long and far easier than the Scarlet Course. I didn't have another 63 until the 1965 Australian Open at Kooyong, in Adelaide. That was the tournament that Gary Player won with an unbelievable score: 62-71-62-69–264.) . . . Won the Ohio Jaycees. Tied for the medal in the National Jaycees (eighteen and under), at the Columbus C.C., in Georgia. (Phil Rodgers won the title. Boy, was Phil ever a cocky kid!) . . . In the U.S.G.A. Juniors, held at Purdue, Billy Dunn, the eventual winner, defeated me 4 and 2 in the quarterfinals. . . . Won the Columbus Amateur. Won the medal in the Ohio State Amateur but was knocked out in the first round. . . . Qualified for the U.S. Amateur for the first time but lost to Bob Gardner, 1 down, in the first round at the C.C. of Virginia. (Met Jones there.)

1956 (age sixteen). Won the Ohio State Juniors. . . . Low scorer in the Tri-State High School Championship. . . . In the National Jaycees, tied for first and lost in a playoff to Jack Rule. He pitched and putted beautifully. . . . Lost to Rule again, 1 down, in the semifinal round of the U.S.G.A. Juniors, at the Taconic Club, in Williamstown, Massachusetts. . . . Lost in the quarterfinals of the Ohio State Amateur to Frank Gacek, a veteran from Cleveland. . . . Won the Ohio State Open at the Marietta C.C., beating a good field that included Frank Stranahan, Gordon Jones, and Leo Biagetti. . . . Played in the Sunnehanna Invitational, for amateurs, and finished fifth. Bill Campbell couldn't make the tournament and kindly suggested that I be invited as his replacement. (Gene Dahlbender won.) . . . Qualified again for the U.S. Amateur, held at Knollwood, near Chicago. Eliminated in the third round, 3 and 2, by Ronnie Wenzler. . . . Tried for the first time to qualify for the U.S. Open. Didn't make it. Was second alternate.

1957 (age seventeen). Won the individual prize in the Ohio State High School Championship. . . . Won the Ohio Jaycees. Won the National Jaycees in my last crack at it. It was played over the Scarlet Course at Ohio State. (John Konsek, the runner-up, was tied with me until he double-bogeyed the last hole.) . . . In the U.S.G.A. Juniors, at the Manor C.C. outside Washington, Larry Beck gave me a good licking in the third round, 4 and 3. . . . Didn't defend in the Ohio State Open, but succeeded in qualifying for the U.S. Open for the first time. Played badly at Inverness, a pair of wild 80s. Missed the cut by ten full shots. . . . Lost to Dick Yost, 3 and 2, in the fourth round of the U.S. Amateur, at The Country Club, in Brookline. A little unlucky. I was out in 32, but Dick was so hot I was still 1 down. (It seemed that as soon as anyone came up against me in the Amateur, he'd promptly play one of his career rounds.)

The high point during these five years, of course, was winning the Ohio State Open at sixteen. It was a 72-hole stroke-play event, with two rounds on the third and final day. That year it was held at the Marietta Country Club, a hilly course with very lush fairways. After starting with a 76 and a 70, I broke the tournament open with a 64 on Saturday morning and added a 72 in the afternoon. One of the reasons why my golf may have been so sharp that last day was that the previous afternoon I played an exhibition with Sam Snead at the Urbana (Ohio) Country Club. Bob Kepler, who was later to be my golf coach at Ohio State, was running the State Open that year, and when I told Kep I would like to play this exhibition set for Friday afternoon, he arranged for me to get an early starting time that morning. After completing my round, I was flown to Urbana in a Beechcraft D-18—the man behind the exhibition, Warren Grimes, was in the aviation instrument manufacturing business—and flown back to Marietta early in the evening. I had a 72 against Sam. My recollection is that I hit all the fairways and greens in the regulation stroke and took two putts on every green. Sam, in excellent form, had a 68. We hit the ball about the same distance off the tee, but his irons were far superior. I enjoyed playing with Sam but I would have enjoyed it even more if he hadn't kept calling me "Junior." The important thing, however, was that some of his wonderful rhythm must have rubbed off on me. The next day, in the last two rounds of the State Open, I hit the ball with ease and tempo and timing all day long. Throughout the afternoon there was never any doubt in my mind—or in my dad's, either— that I would be able to hold onto the lead I had built up with that 64 in the morning. I simply had a tremendous day.

Dad attended most of these tournaments with me. He handled things very well, I can appreciate now. He made tournament golf seem like a natural extension of my life. Jack Grout was extremely

My mother and dad check a session in our cellar practice range.

helpful, too. Like my dad, he seemed to know exactly when I needed to have my confidence built up or when I was getting too big for my britches. Along with Stanley Crooks and other Scioto members, Dad and Jack knew Bob Jones' boyhood record by heart, and on some of those occasions when they thought I was a bit too complacent about my golf, they would reel off the things Jones had done: at nine, he had won the junior championship at East Lake; at thirteen, he had won the invitational tournament at Roebuck Springs, in Birmingham, plus the club championships at East Lake and Druid Hills, in Atlanta; at fourteen, along with the invitational tournaments at East Lake, the Birmingham Country Club, and the Cherokee Club in Knoxville, he had taken the Georgia State Amateur and gone to the third round of the U.S. Amateur, at Merion, before losing a darn good match to the defending champion, Bob Gardner; at fifteen, he had become the Southern Amateur champion; at seventeen, he had been runner-up in the Canadian Open, runner-up to Jim Barnes in the Southern Open, and runner-up to Davy Herron in the U.S. Amateur; at eighteen, in his first U.S. Open, at Inverness (where, incidentally I played my first Open), he had tied for fourth, four strokes behind the winner, Ted Ray. As I say, Jack or Dad would run through a few of Jones' early accomplishments for my benefit, sighing in admiration, and that usually did the trick.

On the other hand, whenever I stumbled badly—like shooting those two 80s in the 1957 Open—Dad and Jack were always there to buoy me up with understanding and encouragement. Sometimes Jack would relay a meaningful compliment through my father. For instance, my father might say to me, "Jack Grout tells me he never saw any young golfer more determined than you are to be a really first-class player." Or maybe he'd say, "Jack Grout was telling me today that when Hogan and Nelson were your age, they couldn't touch you. And you know Jack Grout—he wouldn't say it if he didn't believe it." At other times Jack would approach me directly. "I am honestly awed by the shots you can already play at your age," he might say. "You'd make any teacher look good. You've not only got natural ability and golf intelligence but a flair for competition as well." I could have listened to him all day.

During my years in high school, Grout set out to implant in my game certain basic characteristics of play which he thought would serve me well in the years ahead, and which surely did. We worked on two main points. First, he wanted me to hit the ball high. Bob Jones had, he emphasized. In fact, all the great Open players had. It was self-explanatory: when the pin is tucked in a difficult position on a hard-surfaced green, in order to hit and hold the green with a long iron a golfer must flight the ball in a high trajectory. Hitting the ball high came easily for me. It was always natural for me to hold my head a shade further behind the ball than most people, and when you do that, it helps you to stay behind the ball at impact, and you will hit it high. The ball will come fluttering down softly, almost vertically, and there will be relatively little run even on a 2-iron or a 3-iron. As a matter of fact, one of my main troubles for years was my inability to keep the ball as low as I wanted to in windy conditions. I wouldn't class myself as a good wind player now, but I have made some improvement over the past four years.

Grout's second major concern was improving my control by getting me to hit the ball in a left-to-right trajectory. Jack could be eloquent when hammering home why a fade (a ball that moves from left to right) is far preferable to a draw (a ball that moves from right to left). Under pressure a draw frequently turns into an outright hook, and a hook is the worst shot in the world to hit. It snaps quickly and fast to the left, with heavy sidespin; it can finish so far off the fairway and so deep in trouble that it takes an absolutely brilliant recovery shot for a golfer to retrieve his par. In contrast, a ball that moves from left to right carries a less pronounced sidespin. As a result, when a fade degenerates into a slice, the ball doesn't break half as viciously or sharply as a hook—you can duck-hook but you can't duck-slice. All in all, because the degree of error is so much less severe, left-to-right is by far the safer method of play. That is why Ben Hogan went over to it in midcareer, and it was only after he did that Ben began to win in a big way. (When the article on "Hogan's Secret" came out in *Life* magazine, all of us at Scioto, as you would expect, discussed it at great length.)

Grout felt the complete golfer had to be able to draw or fade the ball when the situation demanded. If a man couldn't move the ball from left to right, he seriously reduced his chances of winning the Open. For example, Harry Cooper, Grout believed, had lost the Open in 1927 because he hadn't been able to fade his approaches into certain greens at Oakmont. "You can count on one thing," he used to say. "Mr. U.S.G.A. always sets a good number of pins on the right-hand side of the greens. Mr. U.S.G.A. is no fool. He always tries to provide a test that will produce a champion who can play all the shots."

The first step in learning to hit the ball from left to right is to adopt a slightly open stance. Grout, who started all his pupils with a square stance, had shifted me to a modified open stance when I was just a youngster. His feeling was that a heavy-set fellow could pivot through the ball much easier from an open stance. I was fourteen when we really began to work on left-to-right in earnest. It is a fairly complicated technique, and I think it best if we wait until the instruction chapters before discussing it. Suffice to say here that with Jack Grout's help I caught onto it rather quickly and stayed with it.

In the spring of my senior year at high school, when I was seventeen, it suddenly became clear to me that, much as I loved basketball and the other sports, first and foremost I wanted to become a golfer. I didn't sit down and consciously arrive at this decision. It just happened, the compound of many things. I was influenced certainly when I received golf scholarship offers from a number of colleges. I accepted none of them because I knew where I was going to college. I had known since I was six. I was going to Ohio State. As far as I was concerned, there was no other college. I did not receive a golf scholarship from Ohio State, but the $1000 scholarship that went with winning the National Jaycee Championship in 1957 took care of the cost of my tuition and books for three years.

By that time it had also crystallized in my mind that I liked golf more than any other game, that it was the greatest game of all. One reason why I felt this way was that golf was the only game I could play by myself. I could practice shooting baskets or place-kicking by myself, but if I wanted to play basketball or football, that necessitated rounding up enough other fellows. Golf—all I had to do was walk through a couple of backyards and there I was on the fourth tee at Scioto, ready to go at it, needing no one else. I had done this all my life, particularly during the long days of summer when I could still get in a round after playing some other sport in the afternoon. Another aspect of golf that appealed to me was the tremendous variation implicit in the game. In basketball the hoop never changes; it's always ten feet high. In football the goalposts never change; the crossbar is always the same height. But in golf you are never confronted with an identical shot. You play from different lies off different kinds of grass in different weather conditions on different holes where the target is continually being changed and different demands set up. You can pour yourself as deeply into golf as you want to. There are fourteen different clubs to be mastered, an endless diversity of shots, and, beneath it all, the most refined technique of any game, I honestly think. Then, if you contemplate competitive golf, you must school yourself to develop a kind of live composure that is far harder to come by than the simpler poise required in team sports where the pressure doesn't build during three or four days and is over in an afternoon or evening. The all-encompassing demands that golf makes on you are, of course, the source of its fascination. When I was seventeen, I didn't begin to appreciate that you never really master golf, that more often than not the game masters you, but I had set my sights on becoming the best golfer I could, and I loved the prospect and the challenge.

VII

The 1959 Walker
Cup Match

Ohio State is a very large university with a total enrollment of about thirty-five thousand students, including those in the graduate schools. At O.S.U., the fraternities dominate undergraduate life, as they do at most Big Ten colleges. In my time there were something like seventy fraternities and forty sororities. The general atmosphere, I gather from the late late movies on television, was not unlike what prevailed in those old Hollywood musical comedies about coed colleges where the boys wore shaker-knit letter-sweaters as they carried Mary Carlisle's books home from class or tried to inveigle Toby Wing into a stroll down the Old Ox Road. It was a happy place. If he wanted to, a fellow could play sports, do well in his studies, and still enjoy a full social life—and quite a few people I knew did. Tom Matte, the backfield star for the Baltimore Colts, was one.

Tom comes to mind because he was a classmate and fraternity brother of mine, and I was fairly close to him. Like many exceptionally good athletes, he had his own ideas about things, and, as a result, he had his differences with Woody Hayes, the excellent O.S.U. coach. Woody used him at right halfback most of his sophomore year, a position Tom didn't think he ran well from. Woody used him at half and quarter his junior year and entirely at quarter his senior year, and that last season Tom really came into his own. Great competitor, Matte! Nobody who knew him was at all surprised when, after both Unitas and Cuozzo were injured during the 1965 N.F.L. season and Matte was hastily pressed into service to run the Colts' offense, he proceeded to turn in one solid performance after another, although he had never been used at quarterback during his pro career.

At O.S.U., fraternity rushing starts even before classes begin. During pre-induction week, the freshmen are invited to breakfast, lunch, and dinner rush parties where they get looked over and do a little looking over themselves. I joined Phi Gamma Delta because I liked the kind of fellows they had. Phi Gams, according to the campus thumbnail rating system, were big guys and good athletes. Our chief rivals in everything were the Betas and Sigma Chis. It was crucial to make a fraternity, for the undergraduate who didn't had no social life at all.

All in all, counting the five-year men and the transfers from other colleges, there were around a hundred fellows in our Phi Gamma Delta chapter, twenty or so being pledged from each new class. Fifty of us lived in the fraternity house. (I did during my sophomore and junior years. My freshman year I lived at home. My senior year, having been talked into marriage the summer before by a classmate, Barbara Bash, I lived off-campus in our small house in Upper Arlington.) A few years ago, the Phi Gams built a new house, a crisp, symmetrical structure. I guess we needed it. Phi Gamma Delta was the first fraternity on campus, going back to around 1878, and in my time we occupied the oldest fraternity house, a beige stucco building with green shutters that dated from the turn of the century and was called "The Grain Elevator" because it was so blocky and unstylish. It had three floors, with the dormitory section broken up into single, double, and triple rooms. We ate all our meals at the house. Between times we played cards, lots of cards—bridge, gin rummy, poker, euchre (we were a very classy bunch), and hearts. On Monday nights we had our fraternity meeting, and every Saturday night we had a party. Of course, during the football season everyone had lunch at the house with his date before going on to the game—that was making the scene.

Our biggest social event was the annual Fiji Island Party held in the spring quarter. A couple of days before the weekend, the boys and their girls would go out to whatever farm outside Columbus we had lined up for the party, and they would build grass huts that looked Polynesian and get the place generally decorated. Things got moving on Saturday when we all drove out for lunch. The girls wore sarongs and brown makeup. The boys wore South Seas material pinned at the waist, and maybe a grass skirt. There were loads of fried chicken and fresh pineapple, and we washed them down with such famous "native" vodka drinks as Purple Passions and

73

Barbara and I and two other Fiji Islanders.

Screwdrivers. In the evening we had a dance that lasted long into the morning. Corny? Too much like Hollywood? Maybe. I loved it.

In my day the standard outfit for the fellows was sweater, slacks, and dirty white bucks or dirty saddle shoes. It was very embarrassing when you were breaking in a new pair of whites that had that telltale spotlessness. I used to have the guys step on them. As for the girls at O.S.U., they wore sweaters and skirts and clean saddle shoes. They shaped up a little different, depending on their sorority. It was agreed (by us) that Kappa Alpha Theta, our sister sorority, was the best group on campus. They weren't the dazzling girls, they were the real nice girls.

Barbara, as if that lead-in didn't make it obvious, was a Theta. Very pretty, too—a tall, slender blonde with blue eyes. I met Barbara my first week in college, before I really had a chance to try my wings. I was dating a girl I'd gone with in high school, and she introduced me to Barbara, who was also a freshman, in front of Mendenhall Lab. A couple of weeks later, after I had had a falling-out with this girl, I called Barb and asked her to fix me up with someone attractive in her sorority. She fixed me up with a girl who drank too much and got sick. I called Barb back (1) to tell her off and (2) to ask for a date. Playing it cool, I named a night three weeks away. She thought this was ridiculous, but she went out with me. We got along okay, so I asked her for a date the next night, which she agreed to, and then we began dating regularly.

Barb wasn't too wild about me, however. She had gone to North

Big Woman on Campus and escort.

High School in Columbus, and she held it against me that the winter before, in an inter–high school fraternity carnival, I'd been elected the Snow Ball King. She told me point-blank that her group figured that my group must have known the judges—it was the only possible explanation of my election. Two months after we had started going together, we broke up. It was sort of complicated: on New Year's Eve I went back to the girl I'd previously been dating, and Barb began dating the fellow who'd been dating *that* girl. We got back together on Barb's birthday, February 28, and after that we stayed together. I had no chance for escape after what her father did for me that spring on the eve of my final exam in Math 401, an algebra-trigonometry course. My professor was a German with a terrible accent, and going into the final, I still didn't know what he was talking about. Anyway, the night before the final, I went to see Barb's father, Stanley Bash, a mathematics teacher at South High School, and he showed me a different way to do every type of problem. I got a 100 in the exam and an A in the course.

It took Barbara almost two years in all to get me pinned, though. Actually, the boy pins the girl, but any man of the world knows that who pins whom is just a technicality. For the record, I pinned her in June, 1959, the day I got back to the States after the Walker Cup match. I was tired, obviously, after the grueling flight from London and definitely not myself.

Barbara was a very bright girl. Her major was elementary education. She did some teaching—the second grade—and graduated in March, 1961, a quarter early. She was also extremely popular, I have to admit. Freshman year she was Pledge Princess of the campus, junior year she was on Homecoming Court, and senior year she was Rushing Chairman, not to mention her being Fiji Island Queen at our 1960 party—a real B.W.O.C. and a fitting consort for the old Snow Ball King.

My first three years I was in the College of Arts and Sciences where I completed the pre-pharmacy course. The next year I transferred to the College of Commerce, where I majored in insurance. In July, 1960, the summer before our senior year, Barb and I had got married, and in the months before we took this step, I naturally had to do some serious thinking about how I would make a living, immediately and in the future. I decided against the pharmacist's life, and since I had begun to sell insurance, the wise move seemed to be to enter the College of Commerce where I could study all the ramifications of insurance and get a firm business background. There were some moments, to be sure, when the idea of making golf my profession occurred to me, but deep down I felt that it would probably be for the best if I remained an amateur and made my living outside the game. My dad, with whom I talked these things over, was very much of this opinion.

My golf record at Ohio State was respectable, but I could never really get enthusiastic about college golf, since my general golf horizon was expanding so fast. As a matter of fact, I didn't play on the O.S.U. team until my junior year. My first year, when I was ineligible for the varsity, I was on the informal freshman team; as a sophomore, I left college during the spring quarter so that I could play in the Walker Cup match, at Muirfield in Scotland, in mid-May. However, the two years I did participate in college golf, I enjoyed it very much, largely because our coach, Bob Kepler, was such a first-rate fellow to be with and play for. Kep, who had played on the O.S.U. team in 1929–30–31, was the college's first official golf coach. A big, broad-shouldered man, then in his late forties and beginning to gray a bit and develop the first ripples of a paunch, he was a very easygoing guy. Once a week, typically, he would take a few of us out to the Zanesfield Rod and Gun Club, an hour west of Columbus, and teach us the fine points of fly casting. That is when I first learned to fish, which has long been my favorite change-of-pace sport, my surest relaxation. When Kep left O.S.U. in 1965, after twenty-seven years as the golf coach, his chief reason was that he had a chance to become the pro at the Hound Ears Club in the North Carolina highlands, a resort where he could indulge his passion for fishing to the full.

Kep knew his golf. He would suggest changes in some of the boys' swings occasionally, but if a member of the team was more comfortable left alone, Kep let him work things out for himself. The comments he made on my golf I found helpful. My swing was a lot like his—an upright arc with the hands high—and he understood what I was after. In his unpressuring way, he brought his boys along well. He developed four N.C.A.A. individual champions: John Lorms in 1943, Tom Nieporte in 1951, Rick Jones in 1956, and myself in 1961. He won his share of Big Ten titles—five in all, I believe. In the late 1950s and early 1960s, the only Big Ten rival we ever had any trouble with was Purdue. They were the big power then. Sam Voinoff, the Purdue coach, was a gifted recruiter, and it required top-notch golf to defeat teams composed of the likes of John Konsek, Joe Campbell, and Don Albert.

We played our college matches on Saturdays. One weekend we might play Ohio University in a dual match; the next, an alumni team; the weekend after that, perhaps a match with Purdue, Michigan, and Indiana at Ohio State, with another quadrangular match against the same teams the following Saturday at Purdue; then maybe it would be Michigan, Michigan State, and Illinois at Ann Arbor; and so on. In these quadrangular matches, each man on the six-man teams played his opposite number over thirty-six holes, usually at Nassau stroke play with six points at stake: one for the first nine, one for the second nine, and one for the first eighteen, and the same thing in the afternoon round. As goes without saying, whatever teams you out-totaled, you beat.

Then, in the latter part of May, just before exams, came the Big Ten Championship. The machinery worked like this: each team was made up of six men, and the team total for each day was arrived at by adding together the lowest five scores; it was a four-day, 72-hole event, with each team's grand total the sum of its daily totals. In 1960, when the championship was held at Michigan State, Purdue was the winner. We finished fourth, I think. Konsek won the individual title with a total of 282 to my 284—his third straight individual victory in the championship. (Very nice golfer,

77

very nice fellow, John Konsek. He graduated from Purdue that spring at twenty, entered medical school, and is a doctor now.) The next year when the Big Ten Championship was held at Indiana's course, Kep took me aside and asked me to try as hard as I could—if I could finish well ahead of the field, we'd have a good chance to win the team championship. I tried very hard, won the individual by 22 shots, and we took the team title by 5. This was by far my most meaningful performance in college golf.

Our other important annual competition was the N.C.A.A. Championships. Here the team championship is contested over 36 holes. Each team is made up of five men, with the four players who bring in the lowest grand total for the two rounds being the winners. The 64 lowest scorers simultaneously qualify for the individual championship, at match play. My junior year, in my first start in the N.C.A.A., at Broadmoor in Colorado Springs, I won my first match against Bert Yancey, who was then at West Point, but was knocked out in the next round by Steve Smith of Stanford. (Dick Crawford of Houston was the winner.) I did better the next year, at Purdue, defeating a teammate, Mike Podalski, in the final.

I will leave college golf at this. While it means a very great deal to the players to gain a spot on their team and come through creditably in their matches, college golf, I'm afraid, has little meaning for most outsiders. Today the spotlight tends to shine so brightly on professional golf that the general sports public doesn't care much about what is happening in any phase of amateur golf. It's too bad, but at the moment it is a fact. I remember when I first began to do well in the Open and the Masters, well enough so that a few reporters would come over and ask me about myself. Well, the moment I'd refer to some round I'd played in the N.C.A.A., the Big Ten, the Trans-Mississippi, the North and South, or even the U.S. Amateur, the reporters' eyes would glaze over; some of them would begin to yawn, others would edge away and light up a cigarette, and I felt like the biggest bore in the world. Amateur golf deserves far more attention and respect than it gets. I think of the case of Deane Beman. Here is a wonderful little golfer who as an amateur had taken the U.S. Amateur twice and the British Amateur once, and who several times distinguished himself in our Open, and if you asked most people then if they knew who Deane Beman was, they'd shake their heads. The name rang a few bells for some people. "Sure," they'd say. "He's our Secretary of State."

The ambition of every American amateur is to make our Walker Cup team and play in the match against the British team which takes place every two years, alternately at home and abroad. In a way, this is completely understandable: there is nothing quite like representing your country in an international competition. In another way, the lure the Walker Cup holds is hard to explain, for with the exception of the America's Cup yachting races, no other international sports series has been so one-sided. Since the Walker Cup was inaugurated in 1922, twenty-one matches have been played, and only once, back in 1938, have the British been victorious. You would think that the series would have long ago been abandoned. Not at all. No matter how crushing their most recent defeat, the British always snap back with a resilience and a vigor I doubt we could muster were we put in their position. By the time the next match rolls round, having discovered one or two up-and-coming young players (and been cheered a little by the news that a few of our amateur stars have turned pro), the British are all stoked up for another try. Some years they are genuinely hopeful of victory, but they never concede anything even in those years when on paper they would seem to have only the remotest chance. In 1965, for example, when they had only an ordinary team and, furthermore, were supposed to be at a definite disadvantage since the match was being held on an American course—Five Farms, outside of Baltimore—the British really caught fire, tied us 11–11, and were unlucky not to have scored an outright triumph. You have to admire them. It is their refusal to regard the Walker Cup as a lost cause that has given the series its remarkable spirit and significance—and made it the continuing goal of every American amateur to be chosen for our team.

It is an attainable goal, too. What I mean is that there are nine or ten places on the team, so you don't have to be a superstar to make it. A good overall record plus a strong showing in a few of our top tournaments will warrant you serious consideration. With the 1959 Walker Cup match scheduled for Muirfield in May, throughout the 1958 season the hope of winning a place on that team was always at the back of my mind, an almost tangible extra incentive in every tournament I entered. When the team was announced in January, 1959, at the annual meeting of the U.S.G.A. and I learned I was on it, I felt I had finally accomplished some-

The Columbus airport. Off to Scotland in style for the Walker Cup match.

thing. Every young golfer feels that way. Before, you were just one of the mass of capable American amateurs—and what a mass there is! Now, you're one of the top ten. You must be—otherwise they wouldn't have picked you. The next day there's a little more swagger in your walk, and you expect to be stopped everywhere for autographs.

Looking back, after our 1959 Cup team was named, it seemed to me that my selection had rested chiefly on my performances in four tournaments:

1. The U.S. Open. My four rounds at Southern Hills, in Tulsa, were nothing spectacular (79-75-73-77–304). However, I made the cut in the Open for the first time and finished in a tie for 41st. Tommy Bolt, the winner, had a total of 283; to my mind, this represented some of the finest golf ever played in the championship, for the greens were hard and burned, and if you missed a fairway you couldn't get out of the Bermuda grass rough with anything except a wedge.

2. The Trans-Mississippi. This is one of the top amateur tournaments, ranking alongside the Western and the North and South, on the next rung below the U.S. Amateur. It was played at Prairie Dunes (in

Hutchinson, Kansas), which is called "The Pine Valley of the West," justifiably. The grass in the rough is literally a yard high; you're lucky if you can hack the ball back onto the fairway in one blow. The course plays pretty long, and there are dunes all right! Very much like a British seaside links, all in all, except it's drier. It rains about one minute a year in Hutchinson. Anyhow, I don't think anyone broke par. I got to the final with some fair golf, and there defeated Richie Norville. After this, for the first time, I thought I had a chance of making the Walker Cup team. A lot would depend, I knew, on how I made out against Harvie Ward in the Amateur at Olympic. When the pairings were published, I saw that we were set to bump into each other in the second round.

3. The U.S. Amateur. I lost to Harvie on the eighteenth green. I must say it was a tough match to lose. In 1955 and 1956 when Harvie had won the Amateur, he had been in a class by himself—the best American amateur since the Second World War, a golfer truly comparable to the top pros. Then he had an awfully bad break. The U.S.G.A. suspended him for a year for accepting some tournament expenses—it really wasn't his fault—and afterward he was never the same player again, the suspension had hurt him that much inside. When we met at Olympic, in San Francisco, Harvie's tee-to-green game had lost its edge. He could still putt, though. And how! He had no fewer than 13 one-putt greens against me, and only one of those putts was under six feet. For good measure, he also chipped in once. Going to the seventeenth he was dormie: 2 up and 2 holes to play. After he had chipped up tight for his par 4, I holed a 30-foot wedge chip from the greenside rough for a birdie and kept the match alive. I blew a great chance on the eighteenth, a drive-and-pitch par 4 to a tiny plateau green that is heavily bunkered. Harvie put his approach over the green, but going for the pin, set at the front of the green, I caught the top of the protecting bunker with an 8-iron. (I felt Harvie would get his 4 and that I had to play for a 3.) Well, Harvie left his chip 20 feet short, and then I tossed away a second chance by taking three to get down from the bunker, missing from 12 feet. We were around in 70 and 71.

4. The Rubber City Open. This was my first P.G.A. tournament. It was at Akron, not far from home, on the old Firestone course. Partnered with Jerry Magee and Charley Sifford the first two rounds, I had a 67 and a 66 which placed me only one shot behind the leader, Art Wall. On the third round I was partnered with Art and Tommy Bolt. The galleries were the largest I'd ever played in front of, and I was nervous as could be. On the first nine I missed half a dozen putts of under three feet. You know how it is—if you miss one, it's hard to re-establish your confidence. Wall tried to settle me down with some quiet words, and Bolt kept telling me, "Just relax and enjoy yourself." Tommy was then in one of those periods when he was acting up a storm. I don't think there's been anything like it in golf before or since. On the twelfth, for illustration, he hit a gorgeous sand shot from a buried lie 12 feet

from the flag, whereupon he brandished his wedge overhead at arm's length, like Douglas Fairbanks, Sr., and plunged it blade-first into the bunker. He left it quivering there and strutted out. He just missed the putt, and then, lunging forward like Fairbanks, drove the blade of his putter against the flagstick and sent it vibrating. Returning to the duller side of life, I was out in 41 and back in 35 for a 76. The next day I was paired with Julius Boros. You know how you imitate other golfers when you're young? Suddenly I had a new swing. I was swinging with Boros' tempo. It didn't hurt. I had a 68 and finished twelfth. (Wall won the tournament after a playoff with Dow Finsterwald.) Twelfth was not bad for an amateur, and I think this showing helped my Walker Cup chances considerably.

The American Walker Cup team flew to Edinburgh, via London, about a week before the match, scheduled for May 15 and 16. There were nine of us on the team. Five were veterans, in their thirties or forties, with previous experience in the Walker Cup and in Britain: Charley Coe (the playing captain), Billy Joe Patton, Bill Hyndman, Bud Taylor, and Harvie Ward. The other four were kids: Ward Wettlaufer, twenty-three, from Hamilton College, a quarter-finalist in the 1958 Amateur, a big, congenial, chubby fellow with a powerful hitting-action and an excellent golf temperament; Tommy Aaron, twenty-two, from the University of Florida, the tall, bespectacled son of a Georgia professional, a finalist (against Coe) in the 1958 Amateur, the possessor of a long, lazy swing that may have been a trifle loose at the top but which was most impressive nevertheless; Deane Beman, twenty-one, a student at the University of Maryland, a little fellow about five-seven-and-a-half with one of the least impressive swings you ever saw—among other things, the arc was too flat, the upper part of his trunk tipped the wrong way on his backswing, and his knees shot out all over the place—but, for all this, a natural golfer who had first qualified for the Open at seventeen and who had won a slew of sectional titles; and Jack William Nicklaus, nineteen, the holder of the Trans-Mississippi and the North and South titles. (All the members of the team had received invitations to play in the Masters earlier that spring, and, following the tournament, I had gone to Pinehurst for the North and South and won a hard-fought 36-hole final 1 up over Gene Andrews.) I don't think any of us, old or young, got more than two hours sleep on the night flight to London. Late the next afternoon when we arrived at Graywalls, the inn where we were staying—it's right off the tenth tee at Muirfield—we were all having trouble keeping our eyes open. However, it was such a glorious evening, the sun spilling over the links, that we forgot our tiredness, changed into our golf gear, and charged out to play nine holes with the British ball before dinner.

From the beginning I liked Muirfield, very much. I think we all did. While it has the intrinsic qualities of a British seaside links—fairways that tumble every which way, magnificent low-cropped turf, deep bunkers, and hard, unwatered greens—it is a frank and open course, unlike such links as the Old Course at St. Andrews with its hidden fairway bunkers or Royal St. George's in Sandwich with its blind carries off the tee. There are something like 190 bunkers at Muirfield, but they are all visible. They were, incidentally, the most fastidiously built bunkers I had ever seen, the high front walls faced with bricks of turf fitted together so precisely you would have thought a master mason had been called in. The credit belonged to Colonel Evans-Lombe, the secretary of the Honourable Company of Edinburgh Golfers, the world's oldest golf club, which has made its home at Muirfield since the 1890s. The Colonel, we heard, was so fanatic about course maintenance that he was not above dressing down golfers whom he caught carelessly replacing a divot so that the grain ran against the grain of the fairway.

Muirfield measured 6806 yards but it played fairly short, not only because the smaller British ball can be hit appreciably farther than our ball but also because we had struck the course when the east coast of Scotland was undergoing a most untypical drought. We didn't have a drop of rain during our week of preparation or during the match, so the fairways had a lot of run to them and the greens putted very fast. We all adapted to the British ball quickly enough, but what we had to work on during practice was gauging the approach shot. You couldn't fire the ball right at the flag as you can on our soft, watered greens—it would bound way over. You had to drop it on the fairway before the green, figuring out how much to allow so that the bounce and roll would take it onto the green close to the flag.

From the outset, Charley Coe had us practice as foursome pairs, the pairs he planned to use. (In foursomes the two partners play alternate strokes and drive from alternate tees. In the Walker Cup in those days, there were four foursomes on the first day, followed by eight singles on the second.) Coe and Patton formed one pair.

83

They were good friends, and congeniality is a factor that seems to help in foursome play. Ward was partnered with Taylor. These two California golfers also knew each other well and liked each other very much, and I would think this had a good deal to do with Coe's decision to put them together. Hyndman was partnered with Aaron. In teaming a veteran with a young man, Coe was taking a chance that Hyndman's experience would keep them on an even keel. And last, Wettlaufer and I were paired. We got along very well as in- dividuals and at Muirfield we were both hitting the ball solidly. I suppose Charley was taking a gamble in putting two young kids together, but there was no question in Ward Wettlaufer's mind or mine about our ability to handle the pressure. Each day we read in the papers that the match would undoubtedly hinge on how successfully the untested American "Whiz Kids" stood up under fire, but being very young, we thought the writers had got things mixed up a little. *We'd* be all right. It was the veterans we were worried about. You know, they were all over thirty, and thirty-six holes is a lot for old people.

At the same time, we had formed an exceedingly high opinion of the senior members of the team during the practice sessions. In- deed, we should have. They were five of the finest amateurs this country had produced over a score of years. Charley Coe, thirty- five, an oil broker from Oklahoma, was a very disciplined golfer. When he had first won our Amateur in 1949, he had a long and involved swing, but after undergoing some lean years, he had re- vised it so that it was shorter, simpler, and more dependable. It had taken him to a second Amateur title the summer before and to sixth place in the 1959 Masters, only four shots behind the winner. Off the tee Charley was "sneaky long"—much longer than he appeared to be—and the rest of his game was very sound. He was excep- tionally quiet in manner, like an Oklahoma cowboy, and he walked down a fairway as if it were the showdown street in some frontier town.

Billy Joe Patton was the exact reverse in temperament. He was always "up." If he wasn't talking, you knew he was ill. However, when he talked he was invariably interesting or witty, or both, a very alive fellow who gave you a lot of himself and sensed a lot about you. Billy Joe was thirty-seven then, a lumber broker from North Carolina, and he had the fastest swing in golf. You couldn't

The 1959 U.S. Walker Cup team. Seated, left to right: Harvie Ward, Deane Beman, Charley Coe (captain), Billy Joe Patton, Bud Taylor. Standing, left to right: Tommy Aaron, myself, Ward Wettlaufer, Bill Hyndman.

even *see* the backswing. He hit the ball pretty far, he had a wonderful touch with the wedge and the putter, and he thrived on competition. I used to love to play bridge against him in the evenings.

Bud Taylor, forty-one, was a dentist from Pomona, California, who had twice won the state amateur and, when he later found the time to travel to tournaments in other parts of the country, had shown himself to be one of the best technicians in the game. He had been a finalist in the 1957 Amateur and had played very well in the Walker Cup that year. He was a relatively short hitter but marvelously accurate, for his swing had a fine groove and his tempo never varied. His nature was like that, too. He had a very even disposition and a nice companionable sense of humor.

Bill Hyndman was forty-three, an insurance man from Philadelphia. From his schoolboy days on, he had been a leading local player but he had been late in gaining a national reputation. He made his first big splash when he was thirty-nine by going to the final of the Amateur. When he was in top form, he could do brilliant things. The autumn before, for instance, in the first Eisenhower Trophy Match at St. Andrews, he had been the American hero when he made a great finish (including a 3 on the 71st, the Road Hole) to pull our team into a tie with Australia, but we lost in the playoff. Tall, angular, and fidgety, Bill was a real kid about his golf, terribly enthusiastic, fretful about his errors in an amusing way, but underneath he was a sturdy, courageous match player.

And finally there was Harvie Ward, then thirty-three. Before the match we were all more concerned about Harvie than anyone else. He wasn't hitting the ball at all well for him. His timing was off, and he couldn't seem to get it back, hard as he worked at it. He was picking the club up on the backswing and hurrying his moves and missing a lot of fairways and greens. He was hardly recognizable as the Harvie Ward the Scots and English had admired so much on his previous trips. No one was more aware of this than Harvie, and it worried him conspicuously all during the week of practice. Despite this burden, he was, as usual, the life of the party, full of merriment and quips from morning to night. About two days before the match, he concocted a set of nicknames for the team. They were so good they stuck. Coe was "Wyatt Earp." Patton was "White Lightning." Taylor was "Bulldog Drummond." Hyndman was "The Praying Mantis." Aaron was "Cotton Mouth." Beman was "B-B Eyes." Wettlaufer was "Baby Fat." I was "Snow White." And E. Harvie Ward was "E. Mickey Mouse."

We expected a tough match. We were facing a team that was not only the best that the British had assembled in years but, according to many observers, the strongest team the British have ever assembled. A quick review of the personnel will bring this out, I think. To begin with, as always, there was Joe Carr from Dublin, a Walker Cup perennial. Joe at this time had won two British Amateurs and was to win another in 1960. Along with Joe, there were four other veterans of the 1957 Cup match at Minikahda where the British had given us a much harder fight than the final score, 8–3, would indicate; midway through the second day, they had actually been in the lead. These four were Guy Wolstenholme (who had won both his singles and foursome at Minikahda), Reid Jack (British Amateur champion in 1957 and a fine-looking shotmaker), Douglas Sewell (an artisan golfer who, like Wolstenholme, later turned professional), and Alec Shepperson (a young law student with an excellent competitive temperament). The British were also counting heavily on two young men new to Walker Cup play, Michael Bonallack and Michael Lunt, both of whom were to make good on their promise in later years by winning the British Amateur. The team was filled out by Arthur Perowne, who had been a member of the 1949 and 1953 teams, and by Dick Smith, an experienced Scot with a strong tournament record.

In the days before the match, we got to know the British players a bit, since although they were staying down the road at the Marine Hotel in North Berwick, they ate their meals in a small private dining room at Graywalls and we ate in an adjoining private dining room. In their quiet way, they struck us as being quite confident. They had reason to be. First, they had that encouraging showing at Minikahda behind them. Second, the previous summer a team of ten British amateurs had thoroughly whipped a team of British pros at Turnberry—the same British pros who had beaten our Ryder Cup team in 1957. Then, in the fall of 1958, in the first Eisenhower Trophy match, the British team (Carr, Perowne, Jack, and Bonallack) had finished only a shot behind Australia and the United States. Gerald Micklem, the nonplaying captain, and Raymond Oppenheimer, the chairman of the selection committee, had for four years devoted practically their whole lives to putting this team together and bringing it along. They genuinely believed it was at least as good as the American team, maybe better; and more to the point, they had succeeded in instilling this conviction in their players.

In the Walker Cup, as in the Ryder and Curtis Cups, the two captains do not announce beforehand the players they intend to use or how they intend to position them. They hand in their lineups at a formal ceremony the afternoon before the match, when they are read out. Only then do the two teams, the press, and the fans learn who will be facing whom. When four foursomes make up the format for a day's play, it is the customary strategy for a captain to lead off with his strongest pair, to play his next best pair either second or fourth, and to stick his least solid pair in the third slot. Oftentimes a captain will fare best by following this order to the letter. At other times, anticipating that the rival captain will be playing things this orthodox way, he may choose to switch his order around. For example, he may stick one of his strong pairs in the third spot and lead off with a somewhat less formidable pair, gambling that in the end his team will pick up more points that way. At Muirfield, Coe decided to gamble. To set up one almost sure point, he placed his strongest pair, Coe and Patton, in the third spot. They were drawn against Bonallack and Perowne, the weakest British pair. In the top spot he placed Taylor and Ward. It was a calculated risk; if the two Californians got hot, they could very well steal a point from the top British pair—Jack and Sewell, as it turned out. Hyndman and Aaron, in the second spot, drew Carr and Wolstenholme, a big assignment. In their final warm-up, this British pair had beaten Henry Cotton and Dai Rees, two of the best British pros. In the last foursome, Wettlaufer and I drew Shepperson and Lunt, the youngest British pair.

Ten thousand fans turned out on Friday, the first day of the match, a warmish day with only a slight breeze out of the east, blowing off the Firth of Forth. The galleries were subdued, even by British standards. Somewhat tense, too. They knew this was a good British side, but they had attended too many Walker Cups in which their teams had failed to play up to expectations, so they didn't want to get their hopes up too high. The day started fairly well for the British. At lunch, after the morning round, only their third pair, Bonallack and Perowne, were in bad shape—4 down to Coe and Patton who had been really charged up. However, this was not too surprising. Sewell and Jack were holding their own and a little more against Taylor and Ward in the first match. Ward was still playing erratically, so the percentages favored the British here. In the second match, however, the favored British pair, Carr and Wolstenholme, were 2 down to Hyndman and Aaron. It wasn't that they had played badly. Hyndman and Aaron were simply fusing together wonderfully. They had come back in 33, two under par. Still anybody's match, though. In the fourth match Wettlaufer and I were 1 down at lunch. At one point we had been 4 down but we had swept the sixteenth, seventeenth, and eighteenth. Again, still anybody's match. At the start we had been jittery, and it had taken us a while to collect ourselves. At lunch I was still feeling keyed up. I hadn't bargained for the Walker Cup being as exciting and as draining as I was discovering it was.

That Friday afternoon the eighteenth Walker Cup match was

decided. Wettlaufer and I had our hands filled all afternoon long—we squared our foursome at the 20th but couldn't move away from Shepperson and Lunt—and so we had only a vague idea of how things were going in the three front matches. Briefly, this is what took place. In the third foursome, Coe and Patton, never letting up the pressure, kept widening their lead and closed out Perowne and Bonallack on the 28th green. One point for us. . . . Up ahead, in the first foursome, Ward and Taylor, trailing Jack and Sewell down the stretch, were hanging on only because of some incredible putting by Ward. On the 26th, he had holed from 30 feet, on the 31st from 25 feet, and on the 33rd from 40 feet. Coming to the last hole, a tight 427-yard par 4, the match was all square. Here the British were just over the green in two, the Americans on about 25 feet from the pin after a first-rate approach by Taylor. The British chipped up close for a sure 4, and then Harvie Ward lined up that 25-footer and barreled it into the middle of the cup. That was a little too much. It must have broken every British heart. . . . In the second foursome, Hyndman and Aaron, holding their poise in the face of a British counterattack, were all even coming to the 35th, 513 yards to a punch-bowl type of green. The Americans never looked like birdying this hole, but Carr and Wolstenholme, trying too hard for their 4, ended up by taking four shots from not too far off the front edge. They lost the hole and, with it, the match, for they could do no better than a half on the 36th. This was another crusher. The British had been counting heavily on a point from Carr and Wolstenholme. . . . Wettlaufer and I completed the whitewash by closing out Shepperson and Lunt on the 35th green, 2 and 1. The shot that really won the match was a great iron that Ward stuck four feet from the pin on the 13th, or 31st, a difficult short hole to a high, slippery plateau green nearly surrounded by bunkers. Our birdie there had finally put us in front, and we had held it. What a black day this was for the British! Losing all four points was bad enough, but what really hurt was that three of the four matches had been so close. In each of them, as had happened so often in the past, the British had let their opportunities slip away. The Americans hadn't.

With a 4–0 lead, all that our team had to do to insure victory was to win three of the eight singles. We actually won five. Only a few comments seem necessary. Ward Wettlaufer, continuing his splendid play, did the best scoring; he had a 69 in the morning and was five under even fours for the duration of his match. Deane Beman did a big job for us. Replacing Bud Taylor in the singles— Bud had thoughtfully offered to step down—Deane was 3 down at lunch to a 69 by Michael Bonallack. Typically, he kept plugging away, caught Bonallack at the 27th, and took the 35th and 36th to win 2 up. Harvie Ward again had it when it counted. Standing 2 up at lunch against Wolstenholme, he ripped through the front nine in 33, and that was that. In the eighth and last match, I played Dick Smith, a bald-headed fellow of forty-one with a little moustache, an affable, courteous man and a darn good fighter. At one time it looked like I would win by a huge margin. I was 5 up after a 70 in the morning and then won the first three holes in the afternoon. Smith then began to play the pants off Muirfield. He threw four birdies at me and was still coming on strong when the match ran itself out on the 32nd. The most humorous note of the day came in the top singles, Coe versus Carr. On the 29th, when Carr was holding a narrow lead after losing a large one mainly because of his poor putting, a spectator crossing before the green accidentally stepped on his putter and broke it. Forced to use his 3-iron on the greens, Carr immediately began to putt much better than he had all day, and it won him the match.

As we all appreciated at the time, the significant thing about the American victory was that it had been a true team victory: every player had contributed at least one point to our winning total. Of course, the junior members of the team were ecstatic. We had, as we knew, been the question marks, but we had more than held up our end, and we were proud of that. I suppose, though, that if there was an individual hero, it was, fittingly enough, Harvie Ward. Relying on experience and heart and that old wooden-shafter putter of his, old E. Mickey Mouse had pulled out the crucial foursome for us, and the next day he had set the pace for us in the singles. He made his farewell to the Walker Cup a memorable one.

Here is how the eighteenth Walker Cup match looks in the record books:

GREAT BRITAIN		UNITED STATES	
		Foursomes	
R. Reid Jack and Douglas N. Sewell	0	E. Harvie Ward, Jr., and Dr. Frank M. Taylor, Jr. (1 up)	1
Joseph B. Carr and Guy B. Wolstenholme	0	William Hyndman, III, and Thomas D. Aaron (1 up)	1
Michael F. Bonallack and Arthur H. Perowne	0	William J. Patton and Charles R. Coe (9 and 8)	1
Michael S. R. Lunt and Alec E. Shepperson	0	H. Ward Wettlaufer and Jack W. Nicklaus (2 and 1)	1
Total	0		4

		Singles	
Joseph B. Carr (2 and 1)	1	Charles R. Coe	0
Guy B. Wolstenholme	0	E. Harvie Ward, Jr. (9 and 8)	1
R. Reid Jack (5 and 3)	1	William J. Patton	0
Douglas N. Sewell	0	William Hyndman, III (4 and 3)	1
Alec E. Shepperson (2 and 1)	1	Thomas D. Aaron	0
Michael F. Bonallack	0	Deane R. Beman (2 up)	1
Michael S. R. Lunt	0	H. Ward Wettlaufer (6 and 5)	1
W. Dickson Smith	0	Jack W. Nicklaus (5 and 4)	1
Total	3		5
Grand Total Great Britain	3	United States	9

One brief footnote: At the ceremony at the conclusion of the match, the British captain, Gerald Micklem, stepped forward and, after congratulating us, said in a ringing voice, "We intend to go on learning and trying, and we will be after you again in 1961." The British had to wait a little longer than that, but in 1964 their day at length came: they won the Eisenhower Trophy for the World Amateur Team Championship at Olgiata, near Rome. The next year they tied us in the Walker Cup at Five Farms. Boy, you have to hand it to that British amateur group! I wish I could have been at Olgiata when all those years of perseverance and hard work finally paid off.

The second hero of our British trip was Deane Beman. When he was left out of the foursome structure at Muirfield, it was rough on him, as it would have been for anyone. A fellow of less determination might have been harried by all manner of doubts and worries. Deane just kept working on his game until he got it going better, and when he was called on in the singles, he was ready. Nevertheless, when the scene shifted from Muirfield to Royal St. George's, in Sandwich, for the British Amateur, I don't think that too many people looked for Deane to be a factor in the championship, let alone win it.

The British Amateur was preceded by a historic 36-hole medal event that is held annually, the Royal St. George's Challenge Vase. It seemed the perfect occasion for trying out a new putter I'd gotten while at Muirfield; Wettlaufer and I had gone into Ben Sayers' shop in North Berwick and had him make us each a hickory-shafted blade putter. On the first green I used my new acquisition four times before I got the ball into the cup. Then I couldn't miss with it. I had nineteen putts on the next seventeen holes, and won the Challenge Vase by a comfortable margin, with Deane second. My prize was the last of the fifty sterling silver cups, replicas of the big trophy, which had been made back in 1909. They're beautiful little cups, about sixteen inches high, and I gather they're worth in the neighborhood of fifteen hundred dollars. At Sandwich my father and I stayed with Hugh and Penelope Wilson, two wonderful people. Brigadier Brickman, the secretary of the Royal and Ancient Golf Club of St. Andrews, the British counterpart of our U.S.G.A., had arranged this. I also remember that week because it was the first time I tried to drive a British car. I never really got the hang of it, though all I was doing was driving down a country road. In a mile and a half I passed only two cars—and I almost hit them both. I had someone drive me to the club after that.

Royal St. George's is a rather old-fashioned kind of course with many blind tee-shots and fairways that pitch like the Atlantic in a storm. For the championship, the fairways averaged about 35 yards in width. The rough adjoining them was so high you were lucky if you could find your ball in it, so control was the ticket. In my quarter-final match against Bill Hyndman, I started spraying my drives, and that was the end for me, 4 and 3. Bill drove handsomely and did everything else well. He made his way to the final where he met Deane, who had beaten Wolstenholme in the semis, and Deane won an excellent match 3 and 2. It was one of those times when you wanted both men to win, but Deane was certainly the better player that day. He kept splitting those narrow fairways, and around the greens he was, as he always is, just terrific.

I have known Deane since 1953 when we met at the U.S.G.A.

Juniors in Tulsa. Deane was the national qualifying medalist that year. He was a cocksure little fellow, and I was delighted when Bill Muldoon beat him. Down through the years Deane and I have spent a good deal of time together and have become close friends. I have immense respect for his golf. He probably gets more out of his game (while looking like he's getting less) than anybody I know. People keep wondering how he hits the ball so straight, and reasonably long, with such an ungainly-looking swing. Well, as he enters the hitting zone his clubhead is square on the line and he keeps it on the line for a long while. Besides, even if he sways back, he always sways forward square. As I remarked earlier, in the green area—except for his bunker play, which is only good—Deane is fantastic. He can improvise any kind of pitch or chip, and he has the best putting stroke I've ever seen. Palmer's is the only one that comes close to it. Deane's secret here is his phenomenal nerve control and rhythm. His stroke is almost a slow-motion stroke, the hit is so perfectly timed. He's been smart enough to stay with the simplified putting method he grew up with; the one thing he concerns himself with is keeping his hands ahead of the putter head. He turned professional a year or so ago, and I look for him to be a very successful one.

VIII

Broadmoor and Merion

I T IS GENERALLY AGREED that playing in a Walker Cup match
serves as a sort of finishing school—or better yet, a postgraduate
course—for amateur golfers. You come out of the match—particularly if it is your first Cup match, and more particularly if it was
played in Britain—a discernibly better golfer than you were before.
It is hard to put your finger on the exact area where you have improved. It is chiefly a matter of having gained experience, and
experience is an elusive quality to define. After Muirfield, though,
I know I had a deeper confidence in my ability to produce a good
golf shot when I had to. It seems you are always facing "big"
shots in match play, and certainly in foursomes. I had more confidence, too, about my capacity to function under pressure. Until
he has actually been through an international team match, a young
golfer cannot begin to understand how much heavier is the sense
of responsibility one feels when he is playing not merely for himself but for his team, his country. Late that summer, for example,
when I successfully defended my Trans-Mississippi title at Wood-
hill in Minnesota—I met Deane Beman in the final—compared
to Muirfield it all seemed like a friendly walk in the country.

I started to grow up in another way. In the Walker Cup, I realized, I had been lucky. I had been in excellent form on those two
critical days. But what if I hadn't been? What if I had been struggling with my game? Would I have had the golf savvy and the re-
sourcefulness to have still managed to play with reasonable effectiveness? I began to ponder these questions almost daily after the
1959 U.S. Open at Winged Foot. It wasn't that I was overly bothered when I missed the cut after two 77s; I was still tired from all

94

that golf in Britain and knew beforehand that I wouldn't be able to get my game together at Winged Foot. But what struck me in the Open was how well Doug Ford and Gene Littler, my playing partners, were able to score despite the fact that neither of them played well from tee to green. On those first two rounds Littler was bunkered thirteen times in the green area, and twelve of those times he got down in two. As for Ford, he was bunkered eleven times, and all eleven times *he* got down in two. Ford salvaged a 72 and a 69, Littler a 69 and a 74. Boy, that impressed me! I decided right there and then I had better start learning how to get my figures on those days when I wasn't playing well. While I was about it, I had also better start learning how to adapt quickly to new conditions, as the touring pros do who play a different layout each week, sometimes with only one practice round. I couldn't count on always having a week of preparation in which to get to know a course.

That summer, accordingly, I entered three P.G.A. circuit events: the Gleneagles tournament at St. Andrews near Chicago, the Motor City Open, and the Buick Open. I did acceptably in them—I finished around twelfth in the Buick, my best showing—but what I was concentrating on was golf management: learning how to get my bunker shots into one-putt range; learning how to chip so that the ball finished on the side of the cup that left me with the most makeable putt; learning how to gear my putting, lagging a longish putt if the situation dictated prudence or charging it when the percentages were favorable; learning better when to let out on the tee and when to give first priority to placement; and, above all, learning how to play the intelligent approach shot when my lie or the position of the pin presented a problem.

In those days my method on approaches was to play the ball for the center of the green, drawing it in if the pin was on the left, fading it in if the pin was on the right. I was happy with this method. Indeed, looking back now, I must admit that in some respects I used to play much more carefully in my amateur days, and this does not please me at all. However, the orthodox approach shot was not what concerned me. What did were those odd approaches I couldn't handle when, after a poor drive, I ended up at an awkward angle to the pin or was playing from rough and couldn't put spin on the ball or otherwise control it. This is where I had always lost strokes. I would try to play "wonder shots," and when they didn't come off, I would be in serious trouble. What I learned that summer

95

was how to work the ball on those approaches so that if I missed the green, I would miss it on the proper side—the side that left me with a simple chip or a routine sand shot.

In 1959 the Amateur was held in September at the Broadmoor Golf Club, in Colorado Springs. In my four previous shots at the championship I had never gotten beyond the fifth round. I felt sure I would this time. I considered myself a much sounder golfer after digesting Muirfield and those P.G.A. tournaments. Even if someone threw a hot round at me, as always seemed to happen in the Amateur, I believed I might be able to cope with it. However, chances were that no one was going to tear Broadmoor apart. While it played shorter than its yardage—7010 yards—since it was situated 6400 feet above sea level and the ball traveled far in the thin air, it was still a fairly lengthy course. Most of the greens were plateaued, and their surface was so hard and fast that the ball had to be dropped softly onto them to hold. The man who hit these greens in regulation figures would have a distinct advantage over the scrambler, for holing putts of any size would be troublesome, as it always is on a mountain course. It is one thing to know that every putt will break away from the mountains; it is another thing to know how much break to allow for. Moreover, on mountain greens a putt, which looks absolutely level, appears to be only because of the contours of the adjoining terrain. It might turn out to be slightly uphill or slightly downhill. Which reminds me that I had one thing going for me at Broadmoor that I was quite unaware of at the time. We've all heard the remark, "He's too young to understand how difficult putting really is." That applied perfectly to me. I was just nineteen then, and I had no fear of anything on the greens. Like any kid, I relied primarily on instinct. I just aimed at the hole and then rapped the ball. I expected to make my share of putts, and as a result I did, even at Broadmoor. Not that I am exactly a graybeard now, but it seems years and years ago that this blissful ignorance of youth left me and I began to worry about everything that could go wrong with a six-footer. How dumb you get the more you know!

Playing what I would describe as steady but not spectacularly good golf, I reached the final where I met my old Walker Cup captain, Charley Coe, the defending champion. Charley, who knew Broadmoor well, had been hitting his shots so accurately all week

Broadmoor. As is true of all mountain courses, its greens took lots of reading.

that he had had only one tight match. In the quarterfinals he was 5 up on Bill Hyndman with 7 to play when Bill, moving into one of those purple passages of his, won four of the next five holes, three of them with brilliant birdies, and carried Charley to the home green before surrendering.

I had had two close calls. The first came in the fifth round against big Dave Smith, a buddy of Patton's from North Carolina. The morning of our match, Broadmoor was shrouded in the heaviest fog I have ever seen on a golf course. It was so thick that all you could make out were the markers on the tees. I can remember Dave's saying as we stood on the first tee, "I wouldn't send my mother-in-law out to plow in weather like this!" Not only did we have to use forecaddies, but forecaddies for the forecaddies. On each tee we would instruct them, "When you boys get out there, yell back so we can get an idea where the fairway is." When either Dave or I would drive, we would holler out the general direction of the shot. "Left, left," we'd yell, and then you'd hear the cry echoing up the fairway from caddie to caddie, "Left . . . left . . . left." I won that match in the mist 1 up, but it could just as easily have gone to Dave.

After getting by Dick Yost, who had beaten me at The Coun-

97

try Club two years before, in the quarter-finals, I had another
squeaker against Gene Andrews. Gene was in his forties, a heavy-
set, talkative fellow from Pacific Palisades, California, who first
came to national attention by winning the U.S. Public Links Championship in 1954. He had developed into quite a character. He
wore a big, wide-brimmed banana planter's hat, he played up his
folksiness, and at Broadmoor he had his own oxygen tank to help
him cope with the rarefied air. A purposeful competitor beneath
his easygoing exterior, Gene always carried along a notebook in
which he had charted hole by hole the distances to the center of
the green from certain points on each fairway, the better to help
him select the right club for his approach. Gene not only charted
the holes, he charted the greens, drawing outline maps of each in
which he used arrows to delineate the direction in which the terrain broke. He was the sort of golfer who made few mistakes, as I
knew from our battle that spring in the North and South final.
If you didn't play good forcing golf, he'd walk right in and beat you.

After our morning round, I was 3 up after a 70, but knowing
Gene, I took pains not to let up when we resumed the match in
the afternoon. Even so, when I hit an erratic patch, he won four
holes in a run of six (between the third and the eighth) to erase my
lead and go out in front. I got back to even with a conceded 3 on
the long ninth. Gene was not yielding for a moment. He took the
tenth with a birdie, the eleventh with a par. Then the match swung
my way again. I squared it with a birdie on the thirteenth and went
1 up with another birdie on the fourteenth. We halved the next
two holes. On the seventeenth, a 613-yard par 5, Gene had his 5
all the way. I hooked my drive badly and, after a succession of
poor shots, lay 4 on the upper tier of the two-level green about
25 feet beyond the pin. I had left myself a lovely putt: for the first
18 feet or so it was relatively flat, but then it broke down to
the lower level at about a 15-degree angle. The cup was at the foot
of the slope. I had to drop that putt to halve Gene's par, and somehow I did, mainly because that particular green was a little heavier
and slower than most. When we halved the 18th, or 36th, I had
again scraped past Gene by the skin of my teeth and was in the final.

John English, then the Assistant Executive Director of the
U.S.G.A., called the final at Broadmoor a "classic drama" in his
account in the *U.S.G.A. Journal*. Most of the other reports also
used the word *classic* in referring to the match. It merited that

term, I think, and I believe I would feel that way had I lost and not won it. It certainly was both the most exhilarating and exhausting duel I have ever been engaged in—the personification of that special kind of suspense that comes only in match play. Everything was right for the final. The weather was great, the sun bouncing off the salmon-colored walls of the mountains. Charley Coe was at the peak of his game. I was at the peak of mine.

I got off like a bolt of lightning, barely missing my birdie on the first and then birdying the second and the third. Thanks to that terrific start, I stood only 1 down. Charley had started birdie, birdie, birdie. He slowed down a notch after that but not much. He was around in 69 in the morning and I was 2 down after matching par with a 71. I was pleased with my golf. I was hitting the ball far and accurately, allowing for about 20 yards of drift on my tee-shots and getting it. Charley was right out with me, though. His typical tee-shot is rifled on a fairly low trajectory with right-to-left draw that gives the ball quite a bit of run. As I mentioned earlier, he's deceptively long, the way some baseball pitchers are deceptively fast. You watch him hit a drive and you say to yourself, "That'll be fifteen yards behind me. I really powdered mine." Then you watch his ball finish out with yours, and sometimes a few yards past it. You don't have to be a physical powerhouse to hit a long ball. A good swing and timing will do it for you.

When our afternoon round began, Charley hooked his opening tee-shot—his first poor shot of the day—and I won that hole. A birdie on the long 21st squared the match for me. I was starting to wonder if Charley wasn't possibly beginning to show the effects of six straight days of match play, when he flew his approach five feet from the flag on the 24th and won it with a birdie. We halved the next five holes, the par-5 27th with 4s, and then Charley made a costly slip: he three-putted the 30th from 25 feet. All square again. I went 1 up on the 32nd when Charley missed the green with his approach. On the long 35th I gave it back, snapping my tee-shot even deeper into the rough than I had against Andrews and then hitting a metal gallery-control stake with my attempted recovery. After seven hours of golf we came to the 36th all square.

The home hole at Broadmoor was a par 4, 430 yards long, that ran straight out and a shade uphill for some 275 yards, then broke acutely to the right. (Now it is the sixteenth.) The tee-shot should be aimed down the left side, for the right edge of the fairway falls off quickly and the ambitious tee-shot meant to cut the corner nearly always kicks down into the clumpy rough. About halfway between the green and the high left side of the fairway, the land slopes down to a small but menacing pond, then swings up to the green—a large, hard-surfaced green that sits at about the same level as the fairway area from which the golfer will be playing his approach after a well-placed drive. It's a good hole.

Charley, with the honor, took a 3-wood and hit a fine shot to Position A. He was still wearing, as he had all week, the red baseball-type cap, with a white O, that is standard equipment for the football coaches at Oklahoma. Bud Wilkinson, a close friend, had given it to him, and it certainly wasn't doing Charley any harm. I took a 3-wood, too. I must have been in a wonderful playing mood that day, for on the tee I never once thought about my duck-hook off the seventeenth, just concentrated on the shot at hand. My ball finished about three yards past Charley's—three very important yards, as it turned out, since he would be playing his approach first, and the shot to the home green was difficult to judge. With the pin at the back, about 20 feet from the fringe at the rear of the upsloping green, Charley went with an 8-iron. (That was the club I would have picked.) As usual, he made crisp contact with the ball and had it right on line. However, it carried a little farther than Charley probably intended. It landed about hole-high on the green, got a very fast first bounce, and, rolling on through the back fringe, trickled down a three-foot bank into a little hollow of rough. I decided I had better go with a 9-iron. I hit quite a good shot. It came down in the front-middle section of the green, bounced up toward the pin, and expired eight feet below it. That shot did not end the match. After finding his stance in the hollow, Charley took a little tug at the bill of his red cap and got the feel of his sand wedge in his fingers. Then he lobbed the ball delicately over the bank—a great touch shot. The ball came rolling slowly, slowly down the incline dead on line for the cup. One more half-turn and it would have gone in. Charley and I sort of smiled at each other. After Charley had checked to make sure his ball had no chance of toppling in or being blown in, I began to line up the eight-footer on which our match now rode. I read it to break ever so slightly from left to right. I hit a firm putt and the ball went into the center of the cup. It was a good thing that it did. I didn't relish the thought of extra holes with Charley Coe.

100

It took me a little while to realize that I was the new Amateur champion—the youngest, the press informed me, since Bob Gardner, the winner in 1910. Most of my thoughts and emotions were still focused on the long day's battle with Charley. The best way, I think, to bring out what a marvelous match it was is to set down its progress hole by hole:

HOLE	DISTANCE	PAR	COE	NICKLAUS	STANDING OF MATCH
1	391	4	3	4	Coe 1 up
2	350	4	3	3	"
3	573	5	4	4	"
4	165	3	3	3	"
5	415	4	4	4	"
6	400	4	4	5	Coe 2 up
7	460	4	4	5	Coe 3 up
8	170	3	3	3	"
9	531	5	5	4	Coe 2 up
	3455	36	33	35	
10	400	4	3	4	Coe 3 up
11	430	4	4	4	"
12	220	3	3	3	"
13	413	4	5	4	Coe 2 up
14	404	4	4	4	"
15	465	4	5	4	Coe 1 up
16	180	3	3	4	Coe 2 up
17	613	5	5	5	"
18	430	4	4	4	"
	3555	35	36	36	
	7010	71	69	71	
19	391	4	6	4	Coe 1 up
20	350	4	4	4	"
21	573	5	5	4	Even
22	165	3	3	3	"
23	415	4	4	4	"
24	400	4	3	4	Coe 1 up
25	460	4	4	4	"
26	170	3	3	3	"
27	531	5	4	4	"
		36	36	34	

HOLE	DISTANCE	PAR	COE	NICKLAUS	STANDING OF MATCH
28	400	4	4	4	"
29	430	4	4	4	"
30	220	3	4	3	Even
31	413	4	4	4	"
32	404	4	5	4	Nicklaus 1 up
33	465	4	4	4	"
34	180	3	3	3	"
35	613	5	5	6	Even
36	430	4	4	3	Nicklaus 1 up
		35	37	35	
		71	73	69	

When I looked back at that long, intense final, what I was most impressed by was Charley's sportsmanship. True sportsmanship is more than abiding by the rules and displaying outwardly good manners. It is being genuinely considerate and maybe a touch on the friendly side toward one's opponents. A golfer can tell the difference. I really liked playing with Charley, and the funny thing was that I hadn't thought I would. At Muirfield he had seemed overly reserved to me, possibly because he was the team captain and felt that it was necessary to keep a discreet distance between himself and the players. Well, he wasn't that way at all in our final at Broadmoor. I don't go for pseudo-sportsmen who put on an act, but I love to play with golfers who are confident enough of their ability to be honestly pleasant as we both go about the business of seeing who can muster the winning shots that day. That is golf.

The following year, 1960, my golf was much more of an up-and-down proposition. Some weeks I played better than I knew how, and then abruptly I'd be all over the lot. My first tournament was an amateur get-together in Florida called the International Four-Ball. Deane Beman and I used it as a tune-up for the Masters, and we won it. In the driving contest Deane outdrove me with a skillful "drop-kick" tee-shot, a specialty of his: the clubhead bounces off the turf before contacting the ball and, consequently, imparts tremendous overspin to it. That tee-shot of Deane's must have rolled a hundred yards on the baked-out fairway. Deane never lets me forget about that driving contest.

In the Masters I made the 36-hole cut for the first time and finished in a tie for thirteenth, splitting the low-amateur loot with

Billy Joe. Palmer won at Augusta for the second time that year, nipping Venturi by birdying the last two holes. In the Big Ten Championship in May, I lost the individual title to John Konsek by two strokes. A month later, paired with Hogan on the last two rounds, I finished second to Palmer in the U.S. Open at Cherry Hills, after holding the lead with six holes to go. Then the week after that I got knocked off in the second round of the N.C.A.A.

I continued to be erratic. In August, when we played an Americas Cup match at the Ottawa Hunt Club against Mexico and Canada, I took my singles matches but Deane and I were shut out both days in the foursomes. The first day we had an excuse. On the fifth hole, when we stood 2 up and 3 up on the opposing pairs, Deane reached into his bag for a pitching club and didn't know which sand wedge to play, his or Charley Coe's. Extra club penalty: loss of the first five holes. The second day we had no excuse. We were outplayed. All down the line the Canadian and Mexican boys were beginning to make the matches close, as witness the final team totals: United States, 21½; Canada, 20; Mexico, 12½.

In the Amateur, at the St. Louis Country Club, I made a weak defense of my title. Charley Lewis eliminated me, 5 and 3, in the fourth round. Phil Rodgers was partially to blame. Phil and I are good friends, and you must understand this when I write about him, but, man, can he bug me on occasions! He sure did at St. Louis. The way the draw was set up, we would meet in the third round providing we won our earlier matches. Well, from Monday on, that chesty little bantamcock was strutting around telling everyone, "Baby, if I ever get a crack at that Nicklaus, I'll bury him." After that, I just couldn't wait to play him. Phil was one under par for the thirteen holes of our match—and out of the tournament. I was seven under. I had never played such fantastic golf. The only trouble was that in the afternoon, against Charley Lewis, I had nothing left. I three-putted six times, once from three feet. Lewis played nice golf and putted well, and I could never mount a rally. Two weeks after that comeuppance, I redeemed the whole year in the second World Amateur Team Championship, at Merion, by playing what may still be the four finest consecutive rounds I've ever put together.

As I see it, the reason why my golf was so inconsistent in 1960 was that I got married that July—July 23rd, to be precise. (That was the weekend of the P.G.A. Championship for which, being an

103

amateur, I was ineligible. As I explained to Barbara, it was a logical date for our wedding.) In truth, in the months before and after our marriage, my thoughts were centered on that big step, and golf became just a sport, a recreation, for me. The morning before our wedding, I remember well, I played a round at Scioto with three friends who were ushers—Ward Wettlaufer, Bob Hoag, and Bob Barton, the last two from Columbus. When we got to the eighteenth, a short par 5, I announced grandly, "Gentlemen, this is my last tee-shot as a single man. Step back. I'm really going to crush it." I came hurtling into that shot like a wild bull, barely ticked the top of the ball, and watched it trickle down into the creek twenty yards away. One of the great farewells of our time!

The wedding went better. I'm not so sure of the honeymoon. What I mean is, there were a few rough corners in the itinerary that perhaps could have stood a little polishing. New York was our destination. Barbara had never been there and burned to see it. That was fine with me, so after spending Saturday night, our wedding night, in Columbus, we headed for the big city. As we were driving along that Sunday afternoon, it suddenly occurred to me that our route through Pennsylvania would take us very close to the Hershey Country Club, where Jack Grout had worked with Picard. Jack had talked a good deal about the course, but I had never had a chance to play it. Here it was, right in my lap. We spent Sunday night near Hershey, and the next morning I teed it up on Grout's old course and brought it around in 71. Barb, I should mention, didn't play golf in those days. One year at Ohio State, she had taken the game up during the last quarter of her Phys Ed course and had done pretty well with it. Once she played the first five holes of the Gray Course in two over ladies' par. But golf didn't grab her, and when that Phys Ed course was over, she had no further interest in playing. She walked around Hershey that day—she was always very obliging whenever I asked her to come out and follow me—and then we hit the road for New York.

We stayed at the Astor. The next day, Tuesday, we just walked around the city. We were thinking in terms of a two-week honeymoon, so there was no need to hurry. I turned the day over to Barbara. The first item on her agenda was to buy some new shoes. This surprised me since she had brought along more shoes than she could have worn out in a lifetime. Nevertheless, she wanted some shoes, so I bought her two new pairs. I told her firmly that they would have to last her five years, little knowing at the time that I was married to a woman who never stops buying shoes. Compared to her, Doug Sanders is a barefoot boy. Anyway, that evening we saw "Music Man" and went to the Copacabana afterward, and the next morning I got up and called Claude Harmon, the pro at Winged Foot—we were so close to Winged Foot it would have been criminal to have passed up this chance to play it. Claude arranged everything. When we arrived at the course, however, it was pouring down rain, and it never stopped or eased up all day. I managed to play eighteen very wet holes. Barbara walked the whole way with me, and I was glad she did: Winged Foot is a course no one should miss. Back in New York, we got into some dry clothes, had dinner at Sardi's, and went to a musical revue called "La Plume de Ma Tante."

The next morning Barbara said that she had had enough of New York. Except for that thing of hers about shoes, she's an extremely thrifty girl, and the amount of money we were running through in New York bothered her. It bothered me, too. Here I was, a part-time insurance salesman with an income of $6000, blowing over a hundred bucks a day. I hadn't appreciated how expensive New York was. We talked a little about that, and then, as we were packing our bags, I said to Barb, "Hey, I just thought of something. Wouldn't it be terrific if on our way home I stopped off and played Pine Valley?" A heavy silence followed.

Pine Valley is situated near Camden, not too far off the New Jersey Turnpike. It's hard to get on the course without an intro-duction, but at the club I met a member, a youngish middle-aged insurance man from New York named Dave Newbold, and he ar-ranged for me to play as his guest. There was one slight hang-up: Pine Valley is strictly a man's club. Except for one day a week when women are allowed to play, they're not permitted even to step onto the course. We fixed that up. Dave drove Barb around on the club's private roads so she could see the course, one of the greatest in all the world. She got to watch me hit some shots, too; there are several spots where the roads run close by a tee or a green. I had a 74, but, as I told Barb, I didn't think it was a fair test having to play Pine Valley under those conditions. I wasn't just talking. The next year Dave Newbold took me down to Pine Valley again, and without Barbara to worry about, I hit all eighteen greens in regula-tion and had a 66.

Barb and I stopped over at Atlantic City that night. We were terribly disappointed with it. The next morning, after we had taken a short stroll up the boardwalk, we were ready to leave. Before we did, I made a purchase. There's nothing I like better than steamed clams, so I bought twelve dozen clams to take back to Columbus with us—heady old Jack! Granted, this created a few small complications, such as having to drive miles out of our way every three hours to pick up ice to keep the clams fresh. At twelve-thirty that night, I recall, we were wandering around Zanesville, Ohio, looking for ice—but the big thing is that we found it. We got to my folks' house, where we were staying, at two in the morning. The first thing I had to do was steam those clams. Everything was coming along beautifully until my mother got up and came into the kitchen to see what was going on. She examined the clams and then said brusquely, "You're not eating these, not unless you want to get sick. These aren't the sort of clams you steam." She gave me one of those when-will-you-ever-learn-to-take-care-of-yourself looks, picked up the pot and the rest of the clams, and threw them all in the garbage can.

Since we had originally planned a two-week honeymoon and had cut it to a week, Barb, I suppose, had a right to complain a little. She didn't. I guess she realized how lucky she was—after all, how many new brides get to see three such famous courses as Hershey, Winged Foot, and Pine Valley? In the middle of August, anyhow, we had that second honeymoon week. I took Barb with me to the Americas Cup match, and she got to see another fine golf course, the Ottawa Hunt Club.

The last week in September that year, the top amateur golfers from all over the globe gathered at Merion, on the edge of Philadelphia, for the second World Amateur Team Championship for the Eisenhower Trophy. Two autumns earlier, when the event was launched, the most celebrated course in the world was selected, the Old Course at St. Andrews in Scotland. The format of this championship called for it to be held every two years, the next time in the American zone, after that in the Asia-Australia zone, after that in the Europe-Africa zone again, and so on. In 1960, when it was our turn to stage the event, the U.S.G.A. was anxious that we put our best foot forward. They chose Merion. They couldn't have done better. Although it is difficult to compare golf courses since they

106

differ so much in character, in my book Merion is one of the few truly great courses in our country.

Merion's setting is nowhere near as picturesque as the Augusta National, the most beautiful meadowland course I know, or as majestic as Pebble Beach, with its awesome cliffs and ocean headlands. It is a park-type course, set in the suburbs. It occupies pleasant rolling terrain, but it is what its designer, Hugh Wilson, did with that terrain that makes Merion exceptional. Each of the eighteen holes has its own personality. Each is interesting to play. Each requires that you use your head to get your par. As courses go today, Merion isn't a long course. For the 1950 Open, which Ben Hogan won, it measured only 6694 yards, but Ben's four-round total was 287, seven over par, and this will give you some idea of Merion's quality. Its strength is its subtlety. Raw power off the tee may be a big asset on a lot of our fake new "championship courses," but at Merion it will do you more harm than good unless it is combined with accuracy. The majority of the par 4s are doglegs or modified doglegs, and so placement of the tee-shot is everything. If you try to cut off too much of the corner and don't carry the ball far enough, you wind up in the rough, short of the swinging fairway, with no opening to the green. On the other hand, if you're too conservative, you end up just as badly off; your ball will run through the fairway and into the rough on the far side—and in some instances, like on the fifteenth hole, out of bounds. Even if you have positioned your tee-shot accurately and have opened the entrance to the green, you have your work cut out for you to put your approach within birdie range of the pin. The greens are medium in size and tightly bunkered. All in all, there are something like 117 bunkers on the course.

Each green at Merion is different from the others. One will slope sideways from right to left, and another will fall off to the right; one will be abruptly plateaued, and another will sit well below you; one will come off the shoulder of a rugged ridge, and another will be a gentle extension of a flattish fairway; one will tip toward you, and another will slide away; one will give you a lot of secondary green area to shoot at, and another will present a frighteningly tiny target. The size of the openings to these greens varies judiciously in proportion to the difficulty of the shot required, but there is not, in my estimation, anything like a routine approach at Merion. Once

Just before Merion. Bruce Devlin (Australia) and Walter Grindrod (South Africa) join Ward Wettlaufer and me for a round at Scioto.

you're on the greens, you can't relax either. They're fast and tricky, very tricky. The break breaks. Every four-foot putt is a real "character builder." I could go on at much greater length about Merion, but I will leave it at this: acre for acre it may be the best test of golf in the world.

Because the team totals run into the hundreds, the system of scoring in the World Amateur Team Championship seems much more complicated than it actually is. Each team has four players, and on each of the four days of the tournament a team's score is the sum of the three lowest rounds turned in by its four players. A team's grand total is the sum of its four daily totals. Thirty-two countries sent teams to Merion. The ones we were most worried about were Australia (the defending champion), Great Britain and Ireland, Canada, New Zealand, and South Africa—the traditional golfing countries. The "we" were our nonplaying captain, Tot Heffelfinger, Deane Beman (who had just won the Amateur), Bob Gardner (the runner-up in the Amateur), Bill Hyndman, and myself. While we were all business about winning, we were also out to enjoy the occasion.

What sets this championship apart from the others and gives it meaning is that you get to meet golfers from all over the world.

108

The first day, for example, my playing partners were Mauri Vikstrom of Finland and Hans Schweizer of Switzerland; the second day, Duarte Espiritu Santo Silva of Portugal and Johannes Le Roux of South Africa; the third, Reg Taylor of South Africa and Carlos Raffo of Peru; and the fourth, Guy Wolstenholme of Great Britain and Eric Routly of Australia. While most of the amateurs assembled at Merion were only average golfers, nearly all of them struck me as being miles above average as individuals. (Of course, many of them were relatively new to golf. Schweizer, the Swiss boy, confided to Barbara at the start of our round, "I hope I don't upset Jack's game. No one has ever watched me play but cows.") I got to meet and talk with a lot of fellows besides the ones I played with. I had met a few of them earlier at the U.S. Amateur, in St. Louis. That is where my friendship with Bruce Devlin started, for example. After the tournament Bruce and Walter Grindrod of South Africa came out to Columbus for a few days and we played Scioto.

In the first round our American team jumped off to an unexpectedly large lead. We had a nine-stroke margin over New Zealand,

Merion. The greens range in size from quite large to very small. They're fast and they're filled with difficult rolls. Championship greens.

Last round of the Eisenhower Trophy match—the 16th, the famous Quarry hole. I played one of my best shots here, an intentional hook with an 8-iron around the trees and over the quarry and onto the green.

the closest team. (Bob Charles, incidentally, was on that team.) I had a 66, a new amateur record for Merion, and Hyndman, Gardner, and Beman all had 71s. I hadn't anticipated playing that kind of golf. On the first nine holes of my last practice round I had been just terrible, and though I had started to hit the ball better on the second nine, I wasn't any too confident that I'd be able to maintain that groove. I certainly didn't start off auspiciously in the championship. I put my opening drive in a bunker, and then put my recovery into a bunker off the green. However, I laid my explosion shot dead and got my par, and after that everything just went right. I turned two under par, birdied the tenth and the eleventh (the renowned Baffling Brook hole), and went on to birdie the seventeenth, a rough 230-yard par 3, when I drilled a 3-iron seven feet from

110

the flag. On the eighteenth, a good 458-yard-long par 4, I had a 20-footer for another birdie and a 64. I three-putted it.

On the second day our team pulled even farther away—20 shots in front of the second-place team, Great Britain and Ireland. The three scores that counted for us were a 71 by Gardner and 67s by Beman and me. After the third round we led by an incredible 38 strokes. All of us broke par, 70. Hyndman had a 67, and Gardner and I 68s. Beman had a 69 and we couldn't use it. "Sorry about that, Deane," I told him. "Guess you'll just have to play a little better." We ended up by winning by 42 strokes. On that last round Hyndman and Beman had 75s and I had another 68. I don't think any team in any similar competition will ever come close to winning by such a vast margin. It was just one of those things: all four members of our team were at their very best, and Merion was simply too much even for the experienced golfers from Britain and the Commonwealth countries.

My four rounds—66, 67, 68, 68—created enormous attention, much more than my victory in the Amateur had the year before or my second-place finish in the Open that June. It wasn't so much that I had beaten the runner-up, Beman, by a full 13 strokes. Rather, it was the fact that my total of 269 was 18 strokes lower than Hogan's total at Merion in the 1950 Open. This calls for a few words of explanation. To start with, the course we played was somewhat shorter than the Open course. It was also set up easier. The fairways were wider, the rough a bit lower, and the pin positions less difficult. Additionally, there was a lot of mist and some rain the first three days, and in the clammy weather the greens were holding much better than they had during the Open. Deane, for example, hit a good number of them with fairway woods, and his shots sat down as if they were medium irons. Then, too, except for the fourth day, when they got fast, the greens were only medium fast and comparatively easy to putt.

At the same time, I must confess, I was gratified at the hubbub my scoring had stirred up. Favorable conditions or not, I had never dreamed that I could get it going and keep it going like that over 72 holes on a course like Merion. Everything had just come together for me. Every time I stepped up to the ball I knew I was going to hit a good golf shot. I played the ball straight for my target that week, one of the few times in my life I have. Usually at address I feel as if my clubhead is a shade open and that the left wrist is breaking and sliding under. At Merion I felt absolutely straight-wristed, the back of my left hand an unbroken continuation of the line of my wrist. I was so comfortable before the ball I never gave a thought to the mechanics of my swing; all my attention was riveted on producing the shot I had decided to play. To top it off, my concentration was astonishing. On the fourth round, for illustration, I was crouching over the four-footer I needed for my par on the eighteenth when a gust of wind blew my cap off. I hardly noticed it. I kept working on the putt and holed it. I'd like to have a little of that concentration today!

When I think back to Merion, it brings to mind a conversation I had with Gene Littler at the Vancouver Open a couple of years back. There was a tie-up at a short hole, and we were killing the time by chatting. At one point Gene astounded me by saying, "It's a long time since I've played real good golf. It must be at least five or six years." I don't recall that I said anything much in reply, I was just struck by Gene's extreme candor. However, there are many moments these days, even when arithmetically it looks as if I'm playing pretty good golf, when I think of what Gene said and how it applies to me. At those times I wonder if I have ever hit the ball as squarely or sustained my shotmaking at as high a level as I reached at twenty at Merion.

The victorious American team at Merion: Tot Heffelfinger, our non-playing captain, with Bob Gardner, Bill Hyndman, Deane Beman, and me.

IX

My Last Season as an Amateur

ACCORDING TO BILLY JOE PATTON, a good man to listen to, it is an incalculable help in our modern world to have an identity—or "ahdintitee," as Patton pronounces it. What Billy Joe means is that today, with so many people coming into contact with so many other people and with everyone in such a hurry, a fellow can get lost in the shuffle unless he is lucky enough to have done a little something, just enough so that people know who he is and can find the time for him. After my performance in the 1960 Open and the Eisenhower Trophy match, I had the most enviable identity a young man could hope for. Whether or not I deserved that status, I was called by the press "the greatest amateur since Bobby Jones" and "the only amateur since Jones who could give the pros a run for their money." I wouldn't have blamed Lawson Little if he took exception to these generalizations which swept so glibly past his accomplishments and, for that matter, past those of Johnny Goodman (who won the 1933 Open), Bud Ward (who almost won the 1939 Open), Frank Stranahan (who had come awfully close in both the Masters and the British Open in 1947), and certainly Harvie Ward.

In any event, as "the amateur the pros feared" not only was I now a golf celebrity but, as I say, I occupied the most wonderful position imaginable. An amateur hopeful—a young amateur hopeful especially—is always a strong sentimental favorite. People root for you, not because they dislike the pros, but because it is human nature to want the little guy to beat the big guy. They invest you with every romantic notion they have stored up. You are David against Goliath, Horatius at the bridge, Sir Galahad wherever he was, Washington at Valley Forge, Teddy Roosevelt at San Juan Hill, and Moishe Dayan in the Sinai Desert, not to mention Tom Brown at Rugby, Centre College versus Harvard, and the Mets versus the old Yankees.

The facts of the matter are somewhat different, as I need hardly explain. The difference between an amateur and a professional boils down to this: a pro makes his living from golf and plays it continuously; an amateur depends on some other job or profession for his livelihood, plays less golf, and doesn't get paid for it. It doesn't follow from this—though there are some people who consider every amateur the emblem of purity and every pro an over-dressed caddie—that for most pros golf is only a means to an end. I know of no golfer who loves the game itself more than Palmer does. I also know of few amateurs who embody the "amateur spirit" as completely as Roberto de Vicenzo or Kel Nagle, to name two pros who come quickly to my mind. The pro inhabits a different world than the amateur, but while this necessarily changes his outlook in some basic ways, where the actual playing of golf is concerned both are essentially the same people. It all shakes down finally, as everything does, to the individual.

Be that as it may, in 1961, it was thought in some quarters that I had a solid chance to become the first amateur ever to win the Masters and the first since Goodman to win the Open. It was an angle that appealed to the sports public, and it received a good bit of play in the press. (I was hoping I would be asked if I rated myself 18 shots better than Hogan off our totals at Merion. I had my answer all set: "Not 18. Maybe only 11 or 12.") I did play sound golf in the two big tournaments. At Augusta I finished in a tie for seventh, seven shots off Gary Player's winning total of 280. However, after a 75 in the second round I trailed the leaders, Player and Palmer, by eight shots and was never really a serious challenger. In the Open, at Oakland Hills in Detroit, I tied for fourth, three shots behind the winner, Gene Littler. There I was definitely in the fight on the last day, and I did have a good chance to win.

I had headed for Oakland Hills immediately after my last exam and began my preparation there a full week before the start of the championship. Ben Hogan, as is his habit, was an early arrival, and I got to play a couple of practice rounds with him. (You don't play stroke play or match play when you practice with Ben. You play a little game Ben made up years ago in which the winner is the man who hits the most fairways and greens. It's kind of like talking on the telephone with Alexander Graham Bell.) That week I got in 36 holes each day, for I was overweight and needed to take off ten pounds. After my morning round I'd have a piece of melon and a glass of iced tea for lunch, and then go out again.

I scored well in practice, but my opening round was a disappointing 75. A 69 and a 70 placed me in contention at the 54-hole mark, four strokes behind the pacemaker, Doug Sanders, three behind Mike Souchak and Bob Goalby, two behind Dow Finsterwald, and one behind Littler. On the last round I was the first of the leaders to go out. On the first hole I aimed my tee-shot for the trap on the left side of the fairway and put it into the trap on the right side—I didn't want quite that much fade—but I settled down quickly. When I walked onto the twelfth tee, I was only one shot behind Littler, who was then playing the eighth. Sanders was still in the lead but Littler was narrowing the gap between them. Eventually he overtook and passed Sanders with a birdie on the eleventh. He then went on to birdie the thirteenth and finished strong.

Now back to live action. Standing on the twelfth tee, after having birdied the eleventh, I realized that, all things considered, I would have to make one or two birdies on the last seven holes to stand a chance. The twelfth, a par 5 that measured 566 yards, offered me by far the best birdie opportunity. I could reach the green with two big shots—it was a mildly plateaued green heavily trapped in front. I would try to hit my second onto the right side of the green, the larger side. If my shot ended up in the trap at the right front of the green, that was okay. It was a shallow trap, and since there was plenty of room between the trap and the pin in which to stop my ball—the pin was on the left side—there was a good probability I could get down in two.

I cranked up on that drive and hit a long one just where I wanted it, down the left-center of the fairway. I had a perfect 3-wood lie. On this second shot, the line I wanted to take ran a few yards to the left of a bushy tree that hung out over the right side of the fairway some 140 yards away. What follows, I appreciate, is a perfect example of those Munchausen fables that every loser inflicts on the victims he corners in the locker room, but so help me, just as I hit that 3-wood, a little twister ripped across the course. It blew hats into the air, it swept sand out of the traps, and it bent that big bushy tree five yards to the left—into the line of flight of my ball. My ball crashed into a limb and dropped straight down. I was on with my third about 30 feet from the cup, but with my mind fixed on getting that birdie, I went much too boldly for my putt and took two more to get down. That was a 6. I had two good cracks at birdies after that but got neither putt, and when I missed my par on the seventeenth, I was out of it. I should add that, like everyone else, I was delighted by Gene Littler's victory. There isn't anyone on the tour who doesn't respect Gene as a golfer and as a fellow. When he's going bad, he never grouses. When he's burning up a course, he's still the same quiet, modest, unegotistical guy. We can all learn something from Gene.

I carried a rather full golf schedule in 1961, considering that I was also attending college and trying to keep up in my studies, selling insurance and trying to increase my income, and, with Barbara, settling into the pattern of married life and trying to adjust to its responsibilities. I realized at the time that I was attempting to do too much, but I wanted to get in all the golf I could. That year, as my tune-up for the Masters, I played in, and won, the Western Amateur, held in New Orleans in late March. In May I played in the Colonial Classic, in Fort Worth. After the Open, I played in the N.C.A.A. Championships, the Buick Open, the American Golf Classic, the Colonial Invitational, the Walker Cup match, the Amateur, and the Americas Cup match. That was stretching things for a guy with an income of less than $10,000. (In addition to my insurance job, I was now doing public relations work for a slacks company.) My father would have been only too happy to have helped out, but the day I got married was the last day I took a penny from him. I knew he was there if I needed him, but it was time I tried to stand on my own feet.

At certain periods I was bothered by muscle spasms in the lower part of my back, which slowed me up, but by and large I hit the ball well that season. My only defeat in match play came in the Colonial Invitational, in Memphis, where Bobby Greenwood, after winning the eighteenth with a great eagle, beat me on the first extra hole with a birdie. In the Walker Cup, in Seattle, Deane and I won our foursome handily, and I won my singles from Joe Carr in a match in which we both scored well. However, this Cup victory filled none of us with the elation we had felt at Muirfield. With Guy Wolstenholme and Douglas Sewell in the pro ranks and with

Alec Shepperson and Reid Jack retired from competition, the British fielded a thin team. The only question was the size of the score we would win by—11 to 1, as it turned out.

Two vignettes from that Cup match stick in my mind. The first is of Michael Bonallack coming into the locker room after we had virtually clinched the match by sweeping the foursomes, 4–0, and asking Deane and me—with the sadness and puzzlement of a man who has looked forward for two years to a certain day and then seen everything crumble at his feet—the reasons, as we saw it, why American golfers played so well and British golfers so disappointingly under the pressure of a big occasion. The other is a much lighter scene. At the concluding ceremonies, after the U.S.G.A. had thanked the Seattle Golf Club for hosting the match and had officially turned the course back to the members, the club president, Lloyd Nordstrom, swung around to face the course and, at his signal, two gang-mowers, which had stood poised, began to mow down the high rough along the narrowed fairways and restore them to their normal width. The whole membership stood up and applauded like mad. I guess no one had hit a fairway for weeks.

From Seattle we went down to the Monterey Peninsula, below San Francisco, for the Amateur at Pebble Beach. This was the first of the many pleasant visits I've made to Pebble, the key course in the annual Bing Crosby tournament. Golf is such an ornery game you can never be sure what sort of form you'll be in on any given day, but, as a rule, if you like a course it seems to increase your chances of playing good golf. Pebble Beach always stimulates me. I love the strategic concept of its holes, not just the famous ones perched above and along Carmel Bay—the 4th, 6th, 7th, 8th, 9th, 10th, 17th, and 18th—but many of the interior holes.

For example, I think that the second, which most people regard as a weak hole, is anything but. It's a straightaway par 5 only 497 yards long over rather humdrum terrain. The major hazard, presumably, is a small ravine, filled with sand at the bottom, that cuts across the fairway about 70 yards before the green, but no touring pro worth his alpaca sweater is going to have any trouble carrying it with his second if he has hit a good drive. On the face of it, the second is a logical birdie hole, except that there's a lot more to the hole than first meets the eye. To begin with, your tee-shot should be down the right side of the fairway. I aim for the trap on the right— the far bank is 222 yards out—and hit the ball as hard as I can.

If my tee-shot finishes not on the right but the left side of the fairway—well, now we have a horse of a different color: I must play the hole cautiously, since I will have to hook my second out and around the trees that overhang the entrance to the green on the left. Get into those trees and your ball may ricochet out of bounds, to the left; even if you avoid that drastic penalty, you can end up in bad trouble. If I put my tee-shot down the right side of the fairway, however, I will go for the green without hesitation, but I never try to fly it all the way home. The two small greenside traps, one on the left and the other on the right, don't worry me. Two things do: (1) knowing that my ball might kick off that small, hard green and run over the back of it into rough and bushes; (2) knowing that a shot calculated to carry onto the green can all too easily get tangled up in those dangerous branches at the left of the entrance if it's a shade off-line. I play a defensive second shot. I take a 2-iron or a 3-iron and try to hit the ball with a little draw, a little overspin. If the shot comes off as planned, the ball will land about 20 yards short of the green, and the run on it may take it onto the green. At worst, I'll have a crack at getting down in two for my 4 from off the edge. Generally, I don't think highly of holes that are penal in character, but I like the second at Pebble very much, perhaps because it looks like such a pushover but can destroy you unless you handle it with care. A good many of the other plain-looking inland holes, such as the thirteenth, have this same exacting nature.

My hat is off to the two men who designed Pebble Beach back around 1919—Jack Neville and Douglas Grant, two well-known California amateur golfers who had never before attempted anything important in golf architecture. They did everything right. They couldn't have made better use of that breathtaking cliff-lined shore, and, as I mentioned, they put a great deal of thought as well into the less glamorous inland holes. After all these years, and with no major revisions, Pebble Beach still stands up, a superb championship test.

I had a bye in the first round of the 1961 Amateur. From my second-round match on, I tried to bear down every moment, to think out and execute each shot just as deliberately when I had a comfortable lead as when I didn't. That week, for some reason or other, my concentration was practically invulnerable, and I believe that my golf was every bit as good as it was at Merion—that is,

On the 13th green at Pebble Beach, semi-final round of the 1961 Amateur.

slightly over my head. All in all, I was 20 strokes under par for the 112 holes I played, and in each of my seven matches I was under par at the point where the match terminated. As it turned out, it was a fortunate thing that I was in the midst of a torrid streak. In the fourth round against Dave Smith, whom I had just slid by at Broadmoor two years before, I must have been four or five under par, but Dave played such terrific golf that I barely got by him again, 2 and 1. Same thing in the next round. Despite my subpar pace, Johnny Humm, a veteran from Long Island, led me at the turn and carried the match to the seventeenth green. I breathed much more easily once I had reached the semi-finals which, like the final, were played over 36 holes. I won my semi from Marion Methvin 9 and 8 and then defeated Dudley Wysong (who had put out Joe Carr) 8 and 6.

I have never since handled Pebble Beach this capably, never hit as many accurate, full-blooded long irons to those small greens, never made so few erratic shots. In January, when the Crosby takes place, the weather conditions are usually fierce, but we have also had a few nice calm days. Still and all, if I matched just those good-weather cards against the ones from the 1961 Amateur, I would lose a bundle.

A week after my return home from the West Coast, our first child, Jack William, II, was born, on September 23. It made me feel very happy and, suddenly, very old. In Columbus I resumed my college studies and at home finished work on converting the cellar into a game room complete with paneled veneer walls, acoustical ceiling, and vinyl flooring—the whole modern bit. I also had a talk with Mark McCormack, the young Cleveland lawyer who managed Arnold Palmer and Gary Player. I had first contacted Mark at the American Golf Classic in Akron in August, a couple of weeks before the Amateur. I wasn't seriously thinking of turning professional at that time. I was thinking more along the lines of what I would have to do to double or triple the $6000 I was making by selling insurance. However, I wanted to find out the facts of life about professional golf. When Mark, at my request, came to Columbus to see me after the Amateur, he went over, item by item, a breakdown he had prepared on the various contracts he believed would be available to me if I decided to turn pro. They came to about $100,000, exclusive of the tournament prize money I might win. I told Mark that my plans were to remain an amateur but that I would like to think matters over more fully at my leisure, and we left it at that.

The venue of the Americas Cup that year was the Club Campestre Monterrey in Monterrey City, Mexico, and the dates were October 21 and 22. Shortly before the match, I was informed that the UPI wire service had come out with a story that I was turning pro. One of their sportswriters, who had got wind of my conference in Columbus with Mark McCormack, had rushed to that conclusion. Will Grimsley of the rival wire service, the AP, happened to be at Monterrey, and he naturally wanted to know if there was any foundation to the story. I told Will that at the present time I had no intention of turning pro. Then I sought out Joe Dey, the Executive Director of the U.S.G.A. With these stories breaking just when I was set to represent the United States in an international amateur match, I was in a most embarrassing position, to say the least; under the U.S.G.A. code it is an infringement of the rules of amateur status for a golfer to play in amateur events if he has definite plans of becoming a pro. I had known Mr. Dey since I was a little kid trying my luck in the Junior Championship, and I told him the whole story, just as it had taken place. I guess my agitation was apparent. "You've done everything correctly," he assured me after listening me out. "If you were my son and you had this golf ability, I would certainly have advised you to look into the matter of turning pro. Rest easy. You've broken no rules."

When I was back in Columbus after the Americas Cup match, my last golf of the year, I began to weigh the problem all over again. Would it be better for me and my family if I remained an amateur golfer or if I became a professional golfer? There were many ramifications to think about. I talked them over at length with Barbara and also with my father. He was, as always, just right with me. It was clear from our discussions that he inclined toward my continuing as an amateur, but he presented his opinions without pressuring me and, at the close of each talk, reminded me that I had to be responsible for my own decisions.

A good many of my friends in golf also got in touch with me around this time. One was Bill Campbell, the fine amateur from West Virginia, who was the American Walker Cup team captain in 1955. Knowing Bill to be the epitome of the true amateur, I was somewhat taken back when he counseled me to give full consideration to the benefits of a professional career. "As an insurance man myself," Bill said in part, "it strikes me that, if you remain an amateur, a very large amount of your time will be spent playing golf with prospective customers, both at home and when you travel to tournaments. I don't think you'll enjoy that kind of golf. It's not so much that you'll be playing with average golfers but that you'll be playing dull courses. If a young man like you is going to spend a considerable portion of his time playing golf, I think he'd be much wiser to play professional golf. First, you'd enjoy it more and get more satisfaction out of it. Second, professional golf today presents a talented young golfer with an opportunity to make a marvelous income—far more than you'd ever make in insurance. In short, if you really expect to devote a good part of your time to golf, you should think over the advantages of going the whole way and becoming a professional."

I thought over what Bill and my other friends said, but on November 6 I was firmly committed in my own mind to staying amateur. I liked being "the greatest amateur since Bobby Jones." I still thought of Jones as the greatest golfer who ever lived. My ambition, as it had been since I had first broken 80, was to see how close I could come to duplicating Jones' superlative record. If I turned pro, that would all be finished.

121

The next day, just like that, I decided to turn professional, definitely, once and for all. I felt I owed it to my family—the financial benefits couldn't be disregarded. I felt I also owed it to myself—if I continued to play as an amateur, I wasn't at all sure I would be able to realize my full potential as a golfer. That same day I wrote a letter to Joe Dey informing him of my intentions. It wasn't the easiest letter to write: I felt I had an obligation to amateur golf— it had been wonderful to me. Later that day when I found that I had difficulty mailing the letter, I decided to telephone Mr. Dey and reached him in Washington. I wanted him to know what I was doing before I made any formal announcement. It was the least I could do. (I should add that we have remained close friends and that this is a tremendous source of pleasure for me.)

Two days later at a press conference in Columbus I announced that I was turning pro, that Mark McCormack would be managing my business affairs. That same night I received a call from a Mr. Joel Gordon of the Revere Knitting Mills, in Boston. He had heard the news on the radio, he explained, and wondered if I would be interested in endorsing a line of sports shirts and sweaters. I told him to get in touch with Mark, and later that month we all met in New York and worked out the contract. (The line was eventually called the Golden Bear, a name for me that the Australian press dreamed up.) I mention this affiliation with Revere, my first commercial plum, not only because it proved to be a long and happy one but also because of its importance to me at that time. Now that I had taken the plunge, in order to compete on the tour I would have to get an Approved Tournament Player card from the P.G.A., and one of the requirements was that the applicant be able to show that he had $12,000 in the bank or was backed by a sponsor who did. By taking to my banker the written commitments from the Revere people and from a deal that Mark had quickly arranged with a publishing house (actually for this book), I got the letter I needed.

There's no particular reason to go too deeply into the details involved in getting an Approved Tournament Player card. In brief, the golfer first makes application to the national headquarters of the P.G.A., which in turn routes the application to the golfer's local P.G.A. sectional organization for its approval. My section, the Southern Ohio P.G.A., speeded things up as fast as it could, knowing that I wanted everything cleared up by the first of the year so that I could play in the opening tournament on the tour, the Los Angeles Open. The secretary polled the members of the committee by telephone, and since they all had known me since I was a high-school boy, they agreed to dispense with (a) a personal audience and (b) a trial round to establish my qualifications as a golfer. The local section then sent my approved application back to P.G.A. headquarters, and I sweated out the national body's final approval. It arrived on December 30.

While I was waiting for my credentials, I did some practicing at Scioto. Since 1951, when he had arrived at our club, Jack Grout had spent most of each winter up north. To facilitate practice on cold or snowy days, he had devised an ingenious setup. This was half a quonset hut—the open side, naturally, faced the range—with the corrugated steel sides lined with polyethylene. There was a stove at the back of the hut, and since the flow of the warm air followed the curve of the roof, it was nice and warm for the practicers—

Winter at Scioto. With Bob Obetz and Jack Grout in the quonset hut.

fifty-five to sixty degrees. I had put in a lot of hours there every winter. First, I'd hit out my own practice balls. If there was snow on the ground, there were always a few the caddie couldn't locate, so after I'd exhausted my own shag bag, I'd hit out my dad's practice balls and, after those went, I'd move on to Grout's. That December I was at the hut almost daily, but it wasn't quite the same that year. Jack wasn't around. He had left Scioto to take a new job at La Gorce, in Miami Beach, and was already south. There was another difference. That year, for the first time, I said good-bye to the other winter practicers just before New Year's Day and headed for the West Coast and a whole new life.

Part Three

X

The Longest Year: 1962

THE TIME IT TAKES a year to go by, I gather, grows shorter and shorter the older you get. My mother, for example, tells me that when she sits down now to address her Christmas cards, it seems like only five months have elapsed since she sat down to do her cards the year before. While I am still too young to experience the sensation that the years are contracting, I do know that the longest year of my life by far was 1962. That was my first year as a professional, and during it I traveled so much more continuously than ever before, met so many new people, grappled with so many new thoughts, and faced so many new situations that it seemed like twenty-four months were packed into it.

Before turning pro, except for the Walker Cup expedition in 1959, I had never been away from home for an extended period, and I had never been on my own. My dad missed few tournaments I played in, but if he wasn't on hand, someone else was. I had really led a comparatively sheltered life. The only place I knew was Columbus. I had lived there all my life, I had gone to college there. At twenty-two, however, I was still so young that, all in all, breaking from my old Columbus groove wasn't a hard thing. In fact, I relished the challenge of trying to make good as a professional and the chance this would give me to widen my orbit. Nonetheless, as I sensed it would be beforehand, the itinerant life on the pro tour *was* hard in certain ways. From time to time Barbara came out and joined me on the circuit—later in the year when Jackie was old enough to travel, she brought him along—but there were long stretches when I was away from my wife and son, and I missed them deeply. My father also came out and watched the tournaments for a couple of weeks at a time, and I enjoyed his visits a lot. It wasn't that I was exactly lonely on the tour. I had known a good many of the pros before, and I found them hospitable and helpful. Mark

McCormack, my lawyer and business manager, came out frequently to talk things over with the members of his growing stable. Then, too, at many of the stops, a representative of the MacGregor Company (with whom I had signed in January) was on hand to replenish my supply of golf balls, check with me on how I liked my clubs, and assist me with any small problems.

Transportation was no problem. Mark had worked out an arrangement whereby I had a Buick at my disposal whenever I needed a car. The Buick people, for instance, supplied me with one of their new models when I arrived in Los Angeles in early January, and I drove it to the tournaments in San Diego, Pebble Beach, San Francisco, and Palm Springs. I dropped it there and flew to Phoenix where another new Buick was waiting for me at the airport. The world of professional golf, I was discovering, was populated with companies and individuals who were only too happy to oblige a "name player." My chief regret was that I hadn't signed up with a good Chinese laundry and a nationwide we-pick-it-up-anywhere dry cleaning service. It seemed I was always either taking my soiled stuff out or else collecting it, and besides, the prices were steep.

One thing for sure—I had certainly chosen the right time to turn professional. Thanks primarily to television but also to Arnold Palmer's impact on the sports public, to the golf salesmanship of Ben Hogan and General Eisenhower before him, and to our steady national prosperity, tournament golf was entering a prodigious boom period. In 1962 the purses at most tournaments ran between $20,000 and $35,000, but the Lucky International, the Doral Open, the Indianapolis 500 Festival Open, the Buick Open, the Houston Classic, the Western Open, and the American Golf Classic were now offering $50,000 or more in prize money. As for the major tournaments, in 1962 the purse in the Masters came to $109,100, in the U.S. Open to $68,800, and in the P.G.A. Championship to $72,000. Most significantly, in 1962 we had the first $100,000 tour tournament, the new Thunderbird Classic. Considering the millions that are spent annually on advertising and promotion by large companies such as the auto manufacturers, $100,000 was like a grain of sand in a bunker for them. But it was a lot of money for the pros to be shooting at, especially if you remembered that twenty-five years before no golfer had earned as much as $20,000 in prize money over a full season. Here we were now with a crack at $25,000 for winning a single tournament. The Thunderbird was the breakthrough. Five years later the $100,000 tour tournament had become almost ho-hum, a new record purse of $250,000 was established by the Westchester Classic, and the total prize money on the tour had climbed to $4,500,000. Along with this, when you take into account that a top pro earns at least the equivalent of his prize money from his subsidiary activities (golf club royalties, product endorsements, exhibitions, instructional articles, and so on), it was El Dorado. If a young man was going to turn professional, the 1960s were the time to do it.

In 1961, my last season as an amateur, the leading money-winner on the tour had been Gary Player. Gary's winnings, official and unofficial prize money combined, had come to around $68,000, some $3000 more than Arnold Palmer's. When I joined the tour in 1962, however, there was no question whatsoever who was king—Palmer. He had been since 1960 when he had captured the Masters, the U.S. Open, and the excited admiration of the whole sports world. Arnold had solidified his position in 1961 by winning the British Open. In 1962 he was destined to have a remarkable season: apart from being the leading money-winner, he was to win eight tournaments in all, including his second British Open and his third Masters, and to win most of them with the dramatic closing charges that had become his trademark. I had known Arnold since 1954, when I'd met him at the Ohio State Amateur. Now that he had grown so much in stature, I didn't know quite what he would be like. I found he had time for everyone, including the rookie pros. He was always extremely nice to me—friendly and informal and enjoyable.

As a matter of fact, I found the touring pros as a group to be a great bunch of fellows. So many of them went out of their way to make me feel at home, it would be hard to list them all. Walter Burkemo, Stan Leonard, Bob Rosburg, Art Wall, Fred Hawkins, Doug Ford, Ed Furgol, Jack Fleck—they were all darn nice to me. So were Dow Finsterwald, Jay and Lionel Hebert, Billy Casper, Gary Player, Mike Souchak, Gene Littler, Jack Burke, Gardner Dickinson, Johnny Pott, Wes Ellis, and Mason Rudolph. Bo Wininger was super. So was Dave Ragan. Really, it's difficult to think of anyone who wasn't cordial and pleasant. The veterans like Cary Middlecoff, Byron Nelson, Pete Cooper, Ted Kroll and Ben Hogan were, and so was old Tommy Bolt. So were the new pros—fellows like Dan Sikes and Bobby Nichols and my old sparring partner,

Phil Rodgers. Tony Lema was most considerate. What pleased me as much, and surprised me more, was that I also found a very high level of what you might call "competitorship" on the tour. Each man regarded the men he was paired with as his equals. We were all out to make a living, and if you happened to be playing better that week than the next guy was—well, good luck to you. There was a minimum of pettiness and, I thought, a strong basic sense of fairness and sportsmanship. I don't think this has changed.

That winter I had the blinkers on. What I mean is that I thought only of two things: trying to make a successful start as a pro, and trying to do the right things as I learned the ropes in the new world. For all my precautions, I did have some trouble, minor trouble, with the press on the West Coast. Ninety percent of the sportswriters are first-class fellows, I have found, but there are always a few guys who have to attract attention to themselves and like nothing better than being controversial. For example, one California writer took as his premise that the pros "resent the intrusion of this highly publicized newcomer," and went on from there. I also made the mistake of saying in an interview, when I was asked how much money I expected to win, that I hoped my year's take would come to $30,000. After that appeared, I had to explain that I didn't think I was going to drive the established pros off the circuit and to make clear, past any misunderstanding, that I didn't have any particular money goal: I'd be happy to take whatever I won. Actually, I didn't think that aiming for $30,000 was having ideas above my station—I did win something more than that amount— but I learned quickly from this experience that you cannot be as honest or as spontaneous as you would like to be. You must always consider the circumstances.

Speaking not just in relation to my freshman year on the tour but in general, I admire plain speaking in personal relations, and I am inclined to forget that public relations are different. As an amateur, I know, I was so forthright that if someone asked me how I was playing, it never occurred to me not to say, "Just great," if I was really playing that well. Sometimes this was interpreted as cockiness and brashness when all it was, in truth, was delight. You must have a certain style, I think, in order to get away with confident statements. I have in mind Gary Player's famous declaration to the press a few years back: "How am I playing? Actually I'm playing so well that I am positively embarrassed." Gary can be very amusing, and this being Gary at his Gariest, everyone took it that way. While diplomacy has never been my long suit, I believe I have learned to recognize its virtues. Today, if any young athlete were to ask my advice, I would counsel him not to be too slick, to be himself, and to try and temper honesty with tactfulness. . . . Now, if I can only follow this myself.

The opening tournament of the 1962 tour, the Los Angeles Open, was played, as it customarily was in those days, on the Rancho Municipal Golf Course. I had a 74 on my first round and added spotty rounds of 70, 72, and 73. My total of 289 was good for a tie for fiftieth, the last money place, which was worth $33.33. The winner, with a closing 62, was Mr. Philamon Rodgers, then in his second year as a pro.

At the next stop, the San Diego Open, held at the Stardust Country Club, I played a little better. A final 67, following a 72, a 69, and a 74, lifted me into a six-way tie for fifteenth. My check came to $550. (Tommy Jacobs was the winner, defeating Johnny Pott in a sudden-death playoff.) Next, the Crosby. There I ended up in a five-way tie for twenty-third and earned $450. (Doug Ford won out over Joe Campbell in a sudden-death playoff.) I was pleased with myself for finishing in the money in these three tournaments, but I was anything but happy with the brand of golf I was playing. I was driving the ball badly, and on the greens I had no touch at all. During our next stop, the Lucky International at the Harding Park Course in San Francisco, I went over to the Olympic Club to see if I could straighten out my driving. I found a good practice spot behind the seventeenth tee of the Ocean Course and hit out hundreds of balls. I decided there to change drivers. Beginning at L.A., I had been using a driver with an X (or extra stiff) shaft—I thought that now that I was a pro, I should be using a less-flexible-shafted driver than I had before. After fiddling around at Olympic, I went back to a driver with an S (or moderately stiff) shaft, the type of shaft I was accustomed to. I started using that driver in the next tournament, the Palm Springs Classic. I stayed with that driver, incidentally, the next four years.

The best that I had been able to do in the Lucky—71-73-73-73—290—was 16 strokes above Gene Littler's winning score and good enough only for a tie for forty-seventh and last money, $62.86. Once again, as in my first three tournaments, my putting had been atrocious. All in all, over those first 16 rounds, I managed only once to take less than 35 putts, which is about four more than a winning professional averages. At Palm Springs I got some help. Jackie Burke, who knows as much about putting as anyone, played a practice round with me and studied my stroke closely. Jackie's diagnosis was that, instead of stroking through the ball with the palm of my right hand, I was dragging the club into the ball with the fingers of my right hand. He suggested I modify my right-hand grip. I had been setting that hand on top of the shaft, and Jack had me move it back a shade to the right so that the palm would be squarely behind the putter. I began stroking the ball better right off the reel and actually holed a few. One round at Indian Wells I got down to 33 putts, a real triumph. Once again, however, I finished way off the pace in the last money spot; this was worth $164.45 despite the fact that no less than nine of us were tied for that last place, thirty-second. After viewing me in action in this swing around California, very few established pros had packed their bags in panic and headed for home.

On to Phoenix. I made another change there. One day before the tournament when I was practicing at the Phoenix Country Club, I ran into George Low. George, a former professional, is a big, beefy, expansive fellow who for years has been one of the ripest characters who follow the tour. For a long while, the story had it, he had supported himself on the practice green: he was always ready to wager that he could outputt any pro, and it was rare when he didn't. In 1959 George had "gone straight." A company was formed to manufacture George Low putters, and they sold very well. Be that as it may, I explained to George that I was having a lot of trouble adapting myself to the greens we played on the tour; composed of many different types of grass, the greens varied considerably in speed from one course to another. After watching me stroke a few balls, George told me that part of my trouble, quite obviously, was that the Ben Sayers model putter I was using was too light for the circuit greens. He went into the pro shop and returned with one of his Bristol models. This was a blade-type putter backed up by a pronounced flange—a sort of combination, you might say, of a mallethead and a blade. I liked its feel and decided to try it out in the Phoenix Open.

I proceeded to play my first good tournament as a pro. I drove well with my new driver, and thanks to Jack Burke's adjustment and the new putter, I had the ball rolling for the cup at a uniform speed all four rounds—69, 73, 68, 71. My 281 put me in a four-way tie for second with Bill Casper, Bob McCallister, and Don Fairfield, and it brought me my first sizable check, $2300. I had never been in contention for first place, though, and, for that matter, neither had Casper, McCallister, Fairfield, or anybody else. Palmer, who had won at Palm Springs the previous week, was in absolutely brilliant form at Phoenix. He had led off with a 64, which put him 5 shots ahead of the field, and, piling it on, he eventually finished 12 full shots in front. How often do you see a tournament won by half that margin!

After Phoenix I went home for a week's rest, skipping the Tucson Open. After that second-place haul, I felt I could afford to do this. My game still wasn't right, but I thought that it was beginning to fuse somewhat better. During those first six weeks I had received quite an education, but one point stood out above the rest: Everyone on the tour shoots good rounds; the trick is to weed out your bad ones. That's easier said than done, of course. When I rejoined the tour for the New Orleans Open, I failed to weed out an 80 on my second round, so although my other three rounds were respectable (two 71s and a 70), I finished a good ways down the list, sharing seventeenth with Mike Souchak and winning $650. The following week in the Baton Rouge Open, I tied for ninth. This was worth only $753.33, since Baton Rouge was a small $20,000 affair. The week after that, at Pensacola, I thought that my modest streak of having finished in the money in every tournament was over. Scores always run low at the Pensacola Country Club. Each day there are fifteen or twenty rounds in the 60s, so after a pair of 71s and a 74, I was miles back. Then on the last day—it was about time—I finally came up with a hot round, a 64. It shot me all the way up into a tie for eleventh, and I won $450. This was helpful, but what really mattered was knowing I had been able to come through with a good low round when I needed one.

The winter wore on. I passed up the next tournament, the St. Pete Open, and visited that week with my folks who were vacationing that year at Port St. Lucie. The rest of the time I spent with Jack Grout at his new club, La Gorce. I hadn't been satisfied with my short irons, so we worked mainly on them. Jack thought that the pattern of my swing in general looked okay, and he wasn't

THE GREATEST GAME OF ALL

at all worried about the position of my right elbow. That was a big relief. After Phoenix, whenever I picked up a newspaper, it seemed that some authority or other was expounding that my less-than-sensational debut on the tour was due to the fact that I had developed a fatal flaw in my swing: my right elbow was not folding in toward my body on the backswing but breaking away from it. This "flying elbow," they said, was putting me into a position where I had to come into the ball all wrong. There was no question but that my elbow was not in the old-time classic position. Somewhere along the way, I had gotten into the habit of letting it break out, perhaps in my preoccupation with keeping the arc of my backswing as full as possible. (To go into the details a bit further, a golfer who has a conventional right-hand grip, in which the V points to the right shoulder, is less likely to move his elbow away from his side than a golfer like myself whose right-hand grip at that time was more on top of the shaft, with the V pointing at the chin.) Anyhow, after Jack had studied my swing, he told me not to worry about my elbow. "Your position on the backswing is perfectly all right," he told me. "You don't have a real flying elbow. That's a different thing entirely—at the top of the backswing the golfer's right elbow is pointing up, and the outward thrust of the elbow pushes the shaft of the club out so that it points far to the right of the target. At the top of your backswing, Jack, your elbow still points toward the ground—as it should. Your club's in perfect position—pointing right at your target. Now let's forget all that nonsense and play some real golf."

A session with Jack Grout always does wonders for me. I went out the next week in the Doral Open—the first Doral Open held—and finished third, two shots behind Billy Casper and one behind Paul Bondeson, who really should have won the tournament. My four rounds—69, 74, 69, 73—at Doral, a long and trouble-filled layout designed by Dick Wilson, added up to my best golf of the year. Aside from the transfusion from Grout, I was helped by the fact that Doral was in excellent condition—the first course on the tour that was. (A possible exception was Stardust in San Diego, where the turf was pretty good.) The other courses we played generally had wet, marshy fairways with high grass, or, if they were in the desert, bone-hard fairways with high grass.

Very simply, it was too early in the year for the average tour course to have had a sufficient growth of grass. On the other hand, despite the frequent winter rains, the greens had very little receptivity to them. When you are playing from tall wet fairways to hard bouncy greens, you have the toughest parlay in golf. On your approach shots, you must manufacture some half-punch compromise version of your usual swing, or otherwise all you'll hit is "fliers" —shots that sail well beyond your target area and keep on running when they land, since they have no backspin on them. (If your ball has a mild back rotation, that doesn't mean it has true backspin.) On those winter tour courses, you also get a high percentage of plain bad lies on the fairways. You have to gouge the ball out of them, and before you know it you're gouging everything out whether you have a bad lie or not. These were some of the items, anyhow, I found myself explaining when, passing up the Azalea Open, I went on to Augusta for the Masters and became involved in intricate discussions with Billy Joe Patton, Bill Hyndman, Charley Coe, Deane Beman, Ward Wettlaufer, and my other old amateur pals. After some practice rounds together, some of them thought I was hitting the ball sharper than I had before, but at least as many intimated politely that my swing wasn't as smooth as it had been—so there was a lot to talk about.

Probably because of my third-place finish at Doral, but also because the Augusta National is a course on which a big hitter has quite an advantage (as long as he is hitting the ball in the right direction), I was made a co-favorite with Palmer in the Masters. This seemed sort of ridiculous to me. I hadn't won a pro tournament nor had I been in a position to, except at Doral—I might have broken through there had I mustered a better fourth round than my 73. In this connection, I had a talk right after Doral with Jim Gaquin, then the director of the P.G.A. tournament bureau, which had bucked me up a good deal. I had received a good-sized check at Doral, but Jim sensed my disappointment with my finishing round and my general frustration at failing to win on the tour. "One of these days," he said, "you'll go into the final round of a tournament and shoot a 34 instead of a 39 on the back nine, and you'll win one. Then it will be easier. Some of the fellows out here are content just to finish in the money and collect a nice check each week. Then there are fellows like you who are used to winning and who must play winning golf to be happy with themselves. Not all of them become winners, but, in my experience, most of them do."

However, I didn't think I was ready to win the Masters—I wasn't hitting the ball that well—but since this was the first major tournament of the year, I wanted terribly to play four strong rounds and show my friends (and my critics) that my game hadn't slipped and had, in fact, matured in some ways. Well, I didn't show them much. In my three previous starts in the Masters I had come up with at least one 75 that had killed my chances then and there. I did once again. It came on the second round after an opening 74, and I was darned lucky to make the 36-hole cut. Since I started the third round 13 shots back of the leader, Palmer, no one was especially impressed when I finished with two fairly good rounds, a 70 and a 72. I couldn't blame them. I ended up tied for eleventh, which looks all right in the record book, but I was never a force in the tournament.

Palmer, by the way, won that Masters, his third, defeating Player and Finsterwald in a playoff. The day before, Arnold had tossed away a commanding lead, but being Arnold, he had bailed himself out at the eleventh hour with a birdie on the 70th (where he holed a wedge chip) and another on the 71st. Then he nailed down the playoff with a 32, four under par, on the in-nine. There was a man who knew how to win. Three weeks later, as some of you may recall, he went off on the most fabulous streak of his career. He won the Texas Open with a birdie on the 72nd. Then he won the Tournament of Champions by holing a 25-footer for a birdie on the 72nd. The following week he won the Colonial, at Fort Worth, beating Johnny Pott in a playoff with a subpar burst on the second nine. Most of these heroics were visible on television, and after this, Arnold, who had been a hero only to golfers, was a hero to everyone.

My own fortunes improved in the weeks following the Masters. After tying for seventh at Greensboro, I finished in a three-way tie for first with Bobby Nichols and Dan Sikes in the Houston Classic. The evening before the final round, when Dan and I were having dinner together, he said, "Jack, I've just got a feeling that one of the two of us is going to win this tournament." We came close, anyhow. In the playoff, Dan and Bobby had 71s—I had a glittering 76—and Bobby then defeated Dan on the first hole of the sudden-death overtime.

I skipped the next event, the Texas Open, but the week after that, when the fellows who had won tournaments were in Las Vegas for the Tournament of Champions, I joined the also-rans at the Waco Turner Open in Burneyville, Oklahoma. I tied for third there, and the following week was fourth in the Colonial. Then, in mid-May, I did a rather foolish thing. Earlier in the year, when I had been collecting all those flyweight checks, Mark McCormack had sounded me out as to whether I'd like to go to England in the spring and play in the 72-hole Piccadilly tournament that the Carreras tobacco people were putting on. (This was the forerunner, in a way, of the Piccadilly World Match-Play Championship, established in 1964, which is held annually in October.) When Mark had broached the idea of playing in a British tournament, I was all for it: I figured I could use a couple of hundred bucks.

At any rate, I flew over two days before the tournament, which was set up so that the first two rounds were split between Southport & Ainsdale and Hillside and the last two were held on Hillside. These are two of the many links clustered along the Irish Sea just north of Liverpool. (Birkdale, which is right next to them, was used for parking cars.) It was a dismal expedition. The weather was bitter cold and damp. I never adjusted to the time change—London is five hours ahead of New York—and was yawning during the daytime and wide awake at midnight. Forget about that. I simply played rotten golf: 79, 71, 70, 78. I learned a couple of things the hard way. First, a golfer can't pop over to Britain just before a tournament, switch to the small ball, and expect to produce anything like his best game. (Tony Lema managed this successfully in winning the 1964 British Open, but I think of Tony's victory as the exception that proves the rule.) Second, the field of British pros, augmented by pros from Ireland, continental Europe, South Africa, and Australia, was much more formidable than I had imagined it would be. I realized that spring how narrow the gulf between the American pros and the foreign pros had become.

I returned home in a discouraged mood. The Open, at Oakmont, was only three weeks off, and unless I got my game straightened out, I probably wouldn't finish even in the first thirty. I decided not to play in the Memphis Open and devote a week solely to practice. It went well. I decided also to familiarize myself with Oakmont. In the middle of that week I flew to Pittsburgh and played Oakmont twice. On those rounds I stepped off every fairway on the par 4s and 5s, measuring the distance from the tee to each fairway trap, then the distance from those traps (or some other permanent feature) to the front and back edges of the greens. On the par 3s I took some permanent feature near the tee, such as a tree or simply the front bank of the tee, and measured the distances to the front and back edges of the green. In the 1961 Amateur at Pebble Beach, to help me in my club selection, I had started this practice of charting the yardages and marking them down on a scorecard I carried throughout the tournament. Deane Beman, who had been doing this for a number of years, had suggested I try it. I found it to be an invaluable aid, so after that, knowing its worth, the chore of pacing off a course was never tedious for me. During my reconnaissance of Oakmont, two things stood out. First, good driving would be imperative, since the rough was thick and several new fairway-flanking traps had been added to the course's record number—something in the vicinity of 250. Second, a very high standard of putting would be required on the large, weaving greens.

My mind, I think, was still half on Oakmont and the Open when I started my first round the next week in the Thunderbird Classic at the Upper Montclair Club, in New Jersey, even though a record purse of $100,000 was at stake. I was out to get a good slice of the cake, of course, but a corner of my concentration was devoted to checking my putting to make sure that my ball had the proper rotation, and to checking my driving to make sure the ball was moving properly from left to right. From time to time, sometimes because injuries made it difficult for me to play left-to-right, I have had periods when I have played the ball for a draw instead of for a fade. When I draw the ball, I am a very ordinary player. Moreover, it is beyond my abilities, evidently, to play right-to-left for as short a period as three weeks before the draw becomes an outright hook.

At Upper Montclair, a good course with a number of exacting holes, I started with a 69 and a 73, and was close to the leaders. On the third round, I three-putted the first three greens, and on the fourth hole I pulled my drive under a shrub. After hacking it out left-handed, I hit the green with my approach and got down a fair-sized putt for my par. This gave me such a lift that I couldn't do anything wrong the rest of the round. I birdied ten of the last fourteen holes for a 65 and a share of the lead with Dow Finsterwald. On the last round I was paired with Gene Littler, who was a shot behind us. All Gene did was birdie the 1st, 2nd, 3rd, 5th, 7th,

9th, and 11th. (A pity about that birdie on the 2nd—it ruined the pattern.) Gene made a few mistakes coming in, so when we arrived at the last hole, a 600-yard par 5, his lead was down to three strokes. I reached the home green in two with two well-hit 3-woods. Gene, bunkered off the tee, was bunkered again on his third, before the green. He played a fairly good explosion and lay four, 12 feet from the flag. I still had a chance, though a small one. If I could hole the 20-footer I had for my eagle 3 and if Gene missed his putt, I'd pick up three shots and we'd be tied. I made a good run at that 20-footer but when it slid by, that was that. Gene then finished his superb pressure round in style by holing for his par. His prize money was $25,000 and mine was $10,000.

This was by far my largest haul—it boosted me to seventh place, I think, among the money-winners—but I meant every word I said when I told some friends that night that I would rather have won the Thunderbird and received only $500. I had now played sixteen pro tournaments and still hadn't won a single one. I was beginning to wonder if I ever would.

The 1962 Open marked the fourth time that Oakmont had been the venue of the national championship. (I had picked up *venue* on my trip to England—about the only thing I did pick up.) Situated about twenty miles from downtown Pittsburgh, Oakmont is routed over strong, hilly countryside—the foothills of the Alleghenies. Today the Pennsylvania Turnpike cuts through the course. Eleven holes are on the clubhouse side, and a footbridge over the turnpike takes you to the other seven holes, the second through the eighth.

Oakmont has always been respected as one of the most fearsome of the regular Open courses. Along with its rugged terrain and its ample length, it is pocked, as I mentioned earlier, with over 200 bunkers. As if this weren't enough, the bunkers are given a special treatment: they are furrowed with a deep-toothed wooden rake. For the 1962 Open the furrows in the bunkers were not very deep but even the light furrowing worried the field. If your ball came to rest between two ridges of sand, a conventional recovery was out of the question; all you could do was splash the ball out as best you could. Furrowing the bunkers had begun years before at Oakmont. Since the course has a clayey soil, it wasn't feasible to dig deep bunkers, for this would have presented a drainage problem.

139

William Fownes, Jr., who for many years was the club's one-man green committee, thereupon decreed that the bunkers be furrowed to compensate for their comparative shallowness.

Oakmont's greens are also celebrated. They can be fast as lightning. At the start of the 1962 Open, they had a nice pace to them, but one knew that by Saturday's double round they were bound to be pretty slick, which indeed they were. It should be stated, that the greens were hardly as severe as they had been for earlier championships. During the 1935 Open, they had been like glass —a main reason why Sam Parks, the unexpected winner, had been the only man in the field to break 300 for his four rounds. Eight years before that, when Oakmont had held its first Open—the one in which Tommy Armour beat Harry Cooper in a playoff—*no one* had broken 300. Finally, in the 1953 Open, Oakmont had been tamed: Ben Hogan's winning total was 283. Oakmont, however, had still dominated the rest of the field. Sam Snead, the runner-up, was six shots back of Hogan at 289, and Lloyd Mangrum, the third man, another three shots back at 292. As a matter of fact, on the final two rounds that year, the par of 72 was broken only six times, and there wasn't a single round below 70. For the 1962 Open, par was 71; the first hole, previously a short par 5 down a hillside, had been converted into a long par 4. There were some other minor changes, but none of them affected the course's fundamental character. In Oakmont we were up against a real test that called for superior driving to hit and hold the sweeping fairways, for first-class iron play to the well-protected greens, and for excellent approach putting across fast, dipping contours. If you weren't right at the top of your game—forget it.

I was paired with Arnold the first two rounds. We drew enormous galleries. Latrobe, Arnold's hometown, is only thirty-five miles outside Pittsburgh, and his local admirers were out in full force—and full throat—to root him on to victory, which seemed like a reasonable probability. From tee to green Arnold's game was sharp. If his putting on those first two rounds had been up to his usual standard, he could have been out in front at the half-way mark by two or three strokes. As it was, his 139 (71-68) placed him in a tie for the lead at that point with Bob Rosburg. Billy Maxwell was at 141, with Nichols, Player, and me at 142. Littler was at 143, and Rodgers at 144 despite an 8 on the first round on the seventeenth, a short uphill par 4, where his drive had lodged itself in a small evergreen.

I hadn't played quite as well as Arnold those first two rounds but I hadn't played badly. From the moment I had gotten back to Oakmont after the Thunderbird, I had been in an almost ideal frame of mind, burning with energy and low-register assurance. On my tune-up round on the Monday, I had a 71 and then had practiced till nine. Tuesday I played with Burke, Finsterwald, and Dickinson. We all played pretty well, one or two over. Following that round, I practiced driving for an hour, and after chipping and putting for another hour, I went out to play the handy three-hole loop—the twelfth, thirteenth, and fourteenth. I was hitting my shots so well I went on and played the last four holes, finishing four under par. I don't know what possessed me that day, but I still wasn't ready to quit. A little before nine, I was out practicing my putting, oblivious of the darkness and a light drizzle, when a member strolled onto the practice green and offered me his flashlight.

At the start of my opening round on Thursday, I was in this same go-at-'em mood. I birdied the first three holes, the first and the second with relatively short putts, and the third by sinking a 50-foot wedge chip. You can't ride roughshod over Oakmont like that, and by the ninth (where I took two to get out of a fairway bunker and also visited a drainage ditch) I had given those three strokes back to par and one more to boot. Then I settled down and played the in-nine in par. On Friday, I was one under going out, and again came back in par. I was doing the two most important things right: I was staying out of the rough off the tee, and I was handling the greens well. A half-dozen times I had misread the speed of a green on a lengthy approach putt and left myself a five- or six-footer, but I'd made them all. In fact, I hadn't three-putted a green. If I continued to play like that, maybe I could still win the Open.

On Saturday, a warm and cloudless day, I was paired for the final 36 with Billy Maxwell, always a congenial partner. Arnold, paired with Bob Rosburg, was playing just behind us. A 72 in the morning enabled me to gain a stroke on Arnold and move within two shots of him. After 54 holes, Arnold was tied for the lead with Nichols at 212, Rodgers was at 213, and I was at 214. Arnold, I gathered, had played better than his score, a 73. His putting was

141

still letting him down. He had taken 38 putts and had missed three 2-footers. One had come on the home green after Arnold had eagled the 292-yard seventeenth by driving the green and dropping a 12-footer. Otherwise he would have been the undisputed leader with a round to go.

With ten holes to go, Palmer *was* the undisputed leader, well on his way to winning his second Open. In retrospect, the pivotal hole was the ninth. A par 5 only 480 yards long, it is uphill all the way from tee to green. There's a sizable bunker directly in front of the green, so getting home in two requires two big blows. Coming to the ninth, Arnold, one under par for the round, led me by three strokes. Though I am not absolutely sure of my arithmetic, I believe he led the other two remaining contenders, Rodgers and Nichols, by either two or three strokes. Rodgers was on about the fourteenth, Nichols on about the twelfth, and I was coming off the tenth when Arnold was driving on the ninth. He hit a long tee-shot and then a strong second that cleared the trap in front. It was pushed a little, though, and the ball finished not on the green but in the tangle of rough along the right edge. Still, Arnold was only 50 feet from the flag, so there was a good chance he would be able to get down in two for a birdie 4 and widen his lead. He fluffed his wedge chip, however, advancing the ball only a few yards and leaving it in the rough. His fourth was a wedge chip about seven feet from the cup, but when he failed to hole the putt, that was a 6. Instead of bolstering his lead by a shot, he had lost a shot. Now he led me by only two. A moment later, when I got down an eight-footer for a birdie on the eleventh, he led me by only one. Now I had a darn good chance. I matched par on the next three holes. Arnold did the same, but when he bogeyed the short thirteenth (his tee-shot found the bunker to the right of the green), he had lost the last shot of his lead. Up ahead Phil Rodgers had fallen off the pace with bogeys on the fifteenth and sixteenth, and Bobby Nichols' bid was over when he missed his par on the fifteenth and later on the eighteenth. Down the stretch it was to be a two-man fight.

Playing as carefully as I could, I completed my round with an unbroken string of pars. So did Arnold. Accordingly, we finished tied at 283—72, 70, 72, 69 for me, 71, 68, 73, 71 for Arnold— and a playoff was necessary.

My pars on the closing holes had not come as easily as Arnold's.

Going down the 72nd at Oakmont. (That's me in front of the woman scorer, Billy Maxwell to her right.) Arnold and I both missed birdie chances on this same hole—a 462-yard par 4—and finished deadlocked at 283.

On the sixteenth I had to hole a hard three-footer up a slope, and on the next green I had as worrisome a four-footer as I have ever faced. I had tried to drive the green on that mongrel par 4—292 yards up the side of a hill to a green closed in by bunkers, save for a narrow gap on the left. I had aimed for the opening, naturally, but I pushed the shot and put it into the right side of the large front bunker, a deep one. Considering that the ball was wedged in the groove between two ridges of sand, I came within inches of playing a super recovery. Had my explosion shot carried a foot farther, it would have landed on the trimmed fringe of the green, and since it had little or no backspin on it because of the lie I had played from, it might possibly have rolled within birdie distance of the pin, positioned at the right center of the green. As it was, my ball died just where it landed in the rough, and from there I ran my chip four feet past. (Thanks to a lesson from Art Wall on the eve of the tournament on how to chip from the rough bordering the greens, I chipped well throughout the Open.)

I get goose pimples just thinking of that short putt. Overall, there was a faint break to the left to take into account, but the cup itself was sitting on a little left-to-right slope. I didn't dare play a touch putt off the double roll at that stage of the championship—I couldn't count on having the nerve or the delicacy. The wisest course, I decided, was to aim for the left-center of the cup and hit the ball firmly so that neither break would really affect its line. I blasted it into the middle of the cup. (This was the putt of which Bob Jones, who had watched it on television, wrote me, "I almost jumped right out of my chair.") Arnold, on the other hand, had a crack at a 12-footer for a birdie on the seventeenth. I had been very lucky, for that was exactly the kind of clutch putt he had been making in tournament after tournament that spring. On the last green, where I had missed a birdie putt of approximately 15 feet, Arnold had another crack at a birdie putt, a 12-footer slightly uphill, that would have won for him. This was a much more difficult putt to make, for the cup was cut at the top of a tiny knob. As I watched Arnold from the scorers' tent, I was a trifle less relaxed than Don Knotts, but having had just about the same putt myself, I thought there was a fair chance that Arnold might be fooled by the line, as I had been. I had played my putt straight for the cup, and as it crept up the knob, it had veered off to the right. Arnold must have played his the same way. It veered off just the way mine had.

On Saturday I had worn what I thought was a very snazzy outfit, a white T-shirt and a pair of iridescent olive pants. Few of my friends shared my enthusiasm for those trousers. Barbara hated them—my "army refugee pants," she called them. Nevertheless, I wore them again for the playoff. Like many athletes, I am superstitious when it comes to that sort of stuff. If things are going right, I don't want to disturb them. I'll wear the same outfit, order the same breakfast, collect a Coke at the same stand on the course, eat at the same restaurant at night. When I'm playing a tournament, anyway, I love to set up a routine. When I'm home, just the opposite.

It was an exciting playoff. To begin with, the gallery—a Palmer gallery, of course—was really up for it. Some years later, Tom Fitzgerald of the Boston *Globe* told me that he couldn't recall a rougher gang of spectators at a golf tournament. "At one green, when you were lining up your putt," Tom said, "I was standing in front of a couple of bruisers and I couldn't believe my ears. 'Walk around, Arnie baby,' one of them was yelling. 'That'll shake him up.' Things like that. I thought I was at a wrestling match." But I didn't find Arnie's Army disconcerting that day. I don't think any golfer does if he's playing well, and I was fortunate enough to be at my best. I was never behind during the playoff.

On the first, which I parred, Arnold went one over when he missed his second. (The afternoon before, at the start of the fourth round, I had three-putted the first—my first three-putt green of the tournament and, as it turned out, my only one.) After six holes I was out in front by four shots. I'd birdied the fourth, and on the short sixth, which I birdied, Arnold had three-putted for a bogey. A four-stroke margin is no margin, though, when you're up against a competitor like Palmer who believes in his star. I kept telling myself not to let up, and I don't think I did, but one by one those four strokes started to slip away. I lost one on the ninth, the par 5 up the hill. Arnold birdied it after chipping to four feet. I lost another when he birdied the eleventh by punching a great pitch a yard from the pin. I lost one more on the twelfth, a par 5 598 yards long, on which Arnold made his 4 after almost reaching the green with two big woods. Even with my lead whittled down to a single stroke, I still felt quite composed, since I had continued to play my shots well. Yet with Arnold off on one of his charges, I wondered if my best would be good enough.

I didn't stop Arnold's charge. He stopped it himself on the thirteenth, a rather undistinguished par 3 that is 161 yards long. Arnold, as you know, allows for right-to-left draw on most of his shots. On the thirteenth, going with a 6-iron, I think, his timing was a shade fast. The draw didn't take and the ball hung out on the right. It looked for a moment as if it would catch the bunker to the right of the green, but it came down inches to the left of it, and bouncing off the outside bank of the hazard, kicked sharply to the left, well onto the green. This was a terrific break for Arnold. Most uncharacteristically, he failed to exploit it. He three-putted. My lead was back to two again.

A two-stroke lead is an entirely different thing than a one-shot lead with five holes to go. Except for the seventeenth, none of those five holes was what you would call a birdie hole. I felt that if I could match par in, hole by hole, I would not be tied. I played four good pars in a row, and when we came to the eighteenth my two-stroke lead was still intact. I was almost home.

On the tee of the eighteenth, a swaybacked 462-yard par 4, I made an error. In my anxiety, I let my right hand get into my drive too quickly, and I pull-hooked it into the edge of the heavy rough. The ball ended up in a really ugly lie, lodged tight on hard ground and half-covered by coarse, bunchy grass. Arnold's drive was down the fairway. He was away, and I watched carefully as he played his second. After much deliberation, he hit what looked to me like a 3-iron. He must have caught the ball a little fat. Halfway in its flight it began to slide off to the right. It came down short of the green and rolled into rough fringing the green on the right. With a two-stroke lead and Arnold off the green, I could afford to play a cautious, conservative recovery from the rough—I felt sure a 5 would win. There was no sense trying to carry the bunker in the middle of the fairway 130 yards away and about 80 yards from the green. If I put it in the bunker, it could be disastrous. Accordingly, I played a pitching wedge from the rough and laid up safely short of the bunker. I had only a 9-iron left, and hit a good pitch 12 feet to the left of the pin. Arnold needed a miracle shot now. He took a wedge. The ball jumped out of the rough fast, bounded for the hole, nearly hit the pin, and ran past it on the right—well past. It was all over. Arnold missed his tap-in when we putted out, but this had no bearing on anything except our final scores, a 71 and a 74.

I walked off the green in a slight daze. I knew that I had won the Open Championship, but when you have thought about something for years and it finally happens, your emotion blurs the whole scene and makes it unreal. Gradually I settled down and merely walked on air.

A good many things happened after that. I made the cover of *Time*. I was in great demand for exhibition appearances. Back in Columbus a Jack Nicklaus Day was organized by my friend Bob Barton. There was a parade to the State House with confetti, ticker tape, and all the rest. I rode in one car with Barbara, my folks rode in another, Jack Grout and a delegation of local professionals in a third, and so on. That was the best thing about it—all my old friends were in the act, including Stanley Crooks, the first man who

The 18th at Oakmont, the day of the playoff. I have just played my third. Arnold watches prior to playing his third from the rough near the green.

had looked on me as a golfer who might develop into a champion and follow in the footsteps of Bobby Jones. Later that summer Arnold and I played an exhibition at Scioto, one of the several we played.

My own reaction after winning the championship was to try to perform like a true champion and play better golf than I had done before. I think I did, for the most part. Most of the problems that had cropped up during the winter when I was adjusting to the professional tour—my erratic driving, my troubles with my putting, my unorthodox elbow position, my inability to weed out bad rounds and to finish strongly, the difficulties of getting used to the playing conditions of tour courses, the constant travel, and all the rest—had resolved themselves, temporarily at least. With the exception of the British Open, at Troon, where my golf was as dismal as Arnold's was remarkable, I didn't play a bad tournament the rest of the year. In the Western, at Medinah, a tie for eighth; in the P.G.A., at Aronomink, a tie for third; in the Canadian Open, at Laval-sur-le-Lac, a tie for fifth; in the American Golf Classic, at Firestone in Akron, a tie for third. In early September I won the first World Series of Golf, a television event in which, as the U.S. Open champion, I met Arnold, the Masters and the British Open champion, and Gary, the P.G.A. champion. Later that month I won two tour tournaments, the Seattle World's Fair Open and the Portland Open. Financially, too, it had turned out to be a tremendous year for me. Palmer led the money-winners with $82,456.23, Littler was second with $67,969.01, and I came third with $62,933.59.

Inevitably, there were a few sour notes, and I should mention them. In the second round of the Portland Open, I was penalized two strokes for slow play by the P.G.A. tournament supervisor, Joe Black. No one was more aware than I that I had become a slow player—far slower than I wanted to be or meant to be. I don't know how it was I fell into the habit, but I suppose it came from trying to check too many things before each shot and from a conscious resolve not to hurry things. Joe's explanation for assessing the penalty was that I had failed to heed a warning at the ninth hole to speed up. That wasn't quite right. I had tried to speed up. Our threesome—Bill Casper and Bruce Crampton—played the back nine in 1 hour and 48 minutes and we completed our round in 3 hours and 50 minutes, ten minutes faster than we had the day before. Besides, I wasn't the only slow player on the tour by a long shot, and I felt I was being singled out unfairly.

The slow-play habit, let me say, is like the cigarette habit—it is so hard to break that a man is wisest not to begin it. Some weeks now I play at a good quick pace but, all in all, I haven't entirely licked my tendency to play too slow.

Having mentioned cigarettes, I am reminded that I gave up smoking on the golf course that summer. One of the scenes in the movie the U.S.G.A. made of the Open showed me on the thirteenth green during the playoff picking up my cigarette after my approach putt and then putting out with the cigarette hanging from my mouth. I had never realized before how disgusting a golfer looks when he does that. Then and there I decided to smoke only socially, away from the tournaments.

The other sour note was struck by the dean of the College of Commerce at Ohio State. Following the Portland Open, I had returned to Ohio State for the fall quarter—I needed to make up three quarters I'd missed in order to graduate. When it came to the dean's attention that I planned to leave college for two weeks that autumn to play in two tournaments in Australia—this was a part of my contract with the Slazenger company—he asked me to withdraw from college. I thought that I could meet my golf commitments and still keep up academically—I was doing all right—but the dean was adamant and I had to withdraw.

Everything considered, though, 1962, the longest year of my life, was a very happy one. The complicated transition to professional golf had gone all right, finally. The first tournament I had won turned out to be the Open, which had been way beyond my dreams. Six months later, I was still getting used to it.

XI

Major Championships:
The Ones That Count

S CIOTO WAS SUCH a Jones-conscious club that practically from the time I took up the game I knew one golf statistic cold: Bob Jones had won thirteen major championships over an eight-year span. I could also break those championships down into four neat piles: one victory in the British Amateur (1930); three victories in the British Open (1926, 1927, 1930); four victories in the U.S. Open (1923, 1926, 1929, 1930); and five victories in the U.S. Amateur (1924, 1925, 1927, 1928, 1930). It was made clear to me early by my dad, Jack Grout, and others at the club (including those two well-known senior golfers, John Roberts and Allen Rankin) exactly why this was such a prodigious achievement. To win one of the traditional major championships a man has to be a really wonderful golfer, since they are held on much more testing courses than the general run of tournaments. Along with this, he has to be an equally outstanding competitor. With the whole field keyed up for the big events, the tension is fierce and the pressure on the leaders becomes so nerve-wracking that in countless championships it has proved too much for seasoned golfers with reasonably good temperaments. The essence of Jones' greatness was that he could play great golf on the great occasions.

When all is said and done, this is how the champions of every sport must be measured. Harry Vardon and Ben Hogan, who rank alongside Jones as the greatest golfers of all times, both built monumental records in the major championships. Over a nineteen-year period, 1896 through 1914, Vardon won the British Open (then the most important event in golf) no less than six times. No one has matched this. Vardon also won our Open in 1900

150

and came very close on his two other tries: in 1913 he and Ted Ray were defeated in that historic playoff at The Country Club by Francis Ouimet, and in 1920 at Inverness, when Vardon was in his fifties, he was headed for victory with only a few holes to go when he was battered by a tremendous gale off Lake Erie and blown into a second-place tie (with Jackie Burke's father), a stroke behind the winner, Ted Ray. As for Ben, he has won a total of nine major championships: one British Open (in 1953, on his only attempt); two P.G.A. Championships (in 1946 and 1948, when it was still a match-play tournament); two Masters (1951 and 1953); and four U.S. Opens (1948, 1950, 1951, and 1953).

There is, as you have no doubt gathered, one unavoidable inconsistency in discussing major championships. For an amateur, like Jones, the British and U.S. Amateurs must be counted as major championships whether or not a victory in them demands the skill it takes to win an open tournament. For American professionals the counterpart of the U.S. Amateur is, of course, the P.G.A. Championship. Since the rise of the Masters after World War II as a tournament of great importance, it has become customary to look upon the Masters, our Open, the British Open, and the P.G.A. (naming them in the order they are played each year) as constituting the four major championships for professionals. Over the last few years, a few tournaments have sprung up which offer more prize money than any of the four major championships, but, so far, they have not eclipsed the status of the two national opens, the Masters, and the P.G.A. It would be wrong, and sad, if it were otherwise. Who knows how many seasons the rich new Continental Super-Classic at the fabulous new Vermilion Creek resort development will continue on the tour schedule? Who knows how long the even richer Papaya Open at lavish new Mango Manor will go on before its sponsors, the distributors of calorie-free Polynesian foods, decide they can get more for their advertising-and-promotion dollar by putting it into magazine ads, say, or into spot commercials on television? It may be a matter of only a few years before events like these are gone with the wind and forgotten, but the traditional championships will always be with us, and the men who have won them will be remembered as long as the game is played.

In 1964, my third year as a pro, I did not have what I would call a truly successful season, despite the fact that I was the leading money-winner. I was much more pleased with how things had gone in 1963, even though I earned a smaller amount of prize money that year and trailed Arnold in the standings. The big difference was that in 1963 I won two major championships, while in 1964 I won none. If I have any one goal in golf, it is to try and capture one major championship each year. I was brought up to think that they were the only victories that really mattered, and I later concluded on my own that this was absolutely correct. This was why 1964, at base, was a season of disappointment. At the tail end of that year I put a little polish on an otherwise lackluster campaign by winning the individual competition in the Canada Cup (in Hawaii) and the Australian Open. For a couple of weeks after returning from that trip to the South Pacific, in conversations with friends I referred to the Australian Open as a major championship, but they knew and I knew I was kidding myself. Being the national championship of a golf-minded country, the Australian Open was a most estimable tournament to have won, but it simply wasn't a major championship except in the eyes of the Australians. Of course, the men who have won it have prized it highly. Only three Americans have—Sarazen, Palmer, and myself.

The first of my two victories in major championships in 1963 came in the Masters. Previous to the Masters, I had gone through a winter I find difficult to characterize. Some things had gone well, others hadn't. One of my main disappointments, certainly, was my stumbling finish in the Crosby. To tell the story briefly, I came to the last hole—the famous 540-yarder that is bordered from tee to green along the left by the waters of Carmel Bay—needing a par 5 to tie Billy Casper and a birdie to win. It was calm and beautiful at Pebble that Sunday afternoon. Granting that the eighteenth is never easy to birdie, that afternoon I had a much better chance of pulling it off than in the wild, stormy weather that usually prevails during the Crosby. I began with a good drive, about 280 yards down the tight fairway. Since I couldn't carry the bunker before the green in two and didn't want to wind up buried in that bunker, my plan was to lay up short of the hazard with my second and gamble on sticking my third close enough to the pin to give me a makeable putt for a 4. I hit a pretty bad second. I pushed a 2-iron far out to the right near the trunk of a pine, about 75 yards from the green. Luckily, I had room to swing at the ball and played what was a rather good wedge under the circumstances—25 feet past

and to the right of the cup. I studied the line of the putt painstak-
ingly with my caddie, Dede Gonsalves, who had caddied for me
in the 1961 Amateur at Pebble and who always caddies for me in
the Crosby. We agreed that the putt, which was a touch downhill,
would break a shade to the right near the hole and that I should
play it for the left corner of the cup. When I hit that putt, I thought
I had it, but the ball didn't come down at all and just skimmed by
the corner. Either we had misread the line or I had misgauged the
speed of the green—probably the latter, for my ball had gone a
good three feet past. Dede and I put our heads together and decided that the line on the three-footer was the right-hand corner of
the cup—a tiny bit of break had to be allowed for. I thought I hit
that putt perfectly, too. I had it right on the corner. Again, it slid
straight over the rim. I had made the same mistake twice, and was
thoroughly disgusted with myself.

Two weeks later I almost succeeded in throwing away the Palm
Springs Desert Classic. This took some doing. With a round to go,
I held a five-shot lead on the nearest man, Gary Player. I proceeded
to lose all five shots to Gary—he had a 67 to my 72—and only a
birdie on the last hole, a short par 5, saved me from losing six. I
was so peeved with myself after that exhibition that I was in a help-
fully mean mood for the playoff, at Indian Wells, and took it by a
comfortable margin. Coming to the twelfth, a short par 4, I was
leading Gary by a couple of shots, and when he took a 7 there,
that was it. Gary is probably the most consistently straight tee-to-
green player in the game today, and I can't ever remember seeing
him get into as much trouble as he did on that hole. His tee-shot
ended up at the base of a palm on the right side of the fairway;
his second, from a bunched-up stance, was hooked across the fairway and finished next to the trunk of another palm; his third, a
7-iron played left-handed, struck the trunk and rebounded 30 yards
back toward the tee; on his fourth he was bunkered before the green,
and, after a good out, he blew the putt. Nice straightaway golfers
like Gary are not at their best dealing with exotic situations. A
veteran tree surgeon like Patton would probably have scraped out a
par on the hole.

I had not expected to play nearly as well as I had in the Palm
Springs Desert Classic. The week before, I had run into an ex-
tremely serious problem during the Lucky International Open in
San Francisco. I am not referring to the fact that my first two

153

This scenic hole at Indian Wells moves right into the mountains. Indian Wells is one of the courses in the Palm Springs-Palm Desert area used in the annual tournament now called the Bob Hope Classic.

rounds, a 79 and 73, were a stroke too high to make the 36-hole cut. (This was the first time in twenty-eight pro tournaments that I had missed the cut, and also the first time I was shut out of the prize money.) What upset me was the sudden flare-up of bursitis in my left hip on the eve of the tournament which had brought on this bad golf. Before the second round, I took some shots to relieve the pain, and afterward the doctor I consulted advised me to pass up the next tournament and give my hip some rest. Barbara (who had joined me on the coast) and I went to Las Vegas for a few days. My hip began to feel a good deal better, so I went to Palm Springs and played in the Desert Classic and won it. I never did stop worrying about that bursitis, however. Every athlete lives in dread of sustaining an injury that will affect his career and possibly terminate it. I certainly did that winter.

After I had played satisfactorily and with very little pain the next week at Phoenix, my hip acted up again at Tucson. I started that tournament off by hitting three tee-shots out-of-bounds on the first hole. I finished out the first two rounds—I missed the cut—and then did something I obviously should have done much sooner: I went home to Columbus to see Dr. Jud Wilson, a wonderful orthopedic surgeon. Dr. Wilson gave me an injection of Hydeltra and Xylocaine, and some ten days later, following his instructions, I got another shot in Coral Gables. In the interim, Barbara and I had enjoyed a short holiday with Gary and Vivienne Player on Paradise Island, near Nassau, a plush new winter colony which Huntington Hartford was developing. (Gary was affiliated with the golf course as the pro, and Pancho Gonzales was the tennis pro.)

The rest and the injections did me a world of good, and at the beginning of April, after having been away from golf for two weeks, I picked the tour up in New Orleans. There I had a terrific piece of luck. On the third round, I had to get an iron shot up quickly to clear a tree that was directly on my line to the sixteenth green. When I was hitting through the ball, something in my left hip popped. Dr. Wilson and the other doctors had previously asked me if I had heard a popping noise at about the time the hip had begun to hurt. I hadn't. After the tournament, when I went home to Columbus and saw Dr. Wilson, he told me that what had probably happened in California was that a tendon had slipped over the hip bone the wrong way and caused the bursitis; at New Orleans it had popped back into place. He gave me a series of injections,

155

about fifteen. I stayed at home, missing Pensacola and St. Pete. Starting back gradually, I tied for ninth at Doral, and after skipping the Azalea, went up to Augusta to get in some good serious practice before the Masters.

There was a lot of work to be done. To keep from hurting myself once the bursitis had set in, and afterward when it had abated somewhat, I had altered my swing a little—or to put it more accurately, my swing had altered itself, since I couldn't get my left side out of the way with my usual speed. I was just sliding my left hip forward and easing through the ball, generally favoring the hip. As a result, I had gotten away from hitting the ball from left to right. To do that, you must get your left hip out of the way very fast —faster than I could. I went to Augusta as a right-to-left player and tried to sell myself on the advantages of this changeover. I sold myself extremely well. The more I thought about the Augusta National, the more I was convinced that the course favored a right-to-left player. I started the tournament in a very positive frame of mind.

Weather conditions during the 1963 Masters were the roughest in years. On Thursday, the day of the opening round, a heavy wind gusted over the course, and it wasn't surprising that only two players, Souchak and Wininger, broke 70. I was back in the crowd with a 74, but there was no question in my mind that I had hit my shots much better than my score indicated. On Friday the wind was down considerably—it was to be the one good day we had during the tournament—and since the greens had been watered to make them hold better, the course played much easier. I went out and shot by far the best round I'd ever had in the Masters, a 66 on which I hit every green except the first in regulation. This put me a shot behind Souchak at the halfway mark. On Saturday we had a deluge. For a time it looked as if some of the lower greens might become completely covered with water and that play would have to be stopped and the whole round played over again. The field just did get around before sections of the course became unplayable. In that downpour Souchak had a 79, and my 74 put me in the lead.

There was a funny little moment when I came up the eighteenth fairway that afternoon and studied the big leader-board. As you know, the Masters pioneered the superb scoring system whereby each of the ten leaders' rounds is posted hole by hole, showing only the number of strokes he is over or under par for the tournament at that particular point. Red numbers are used to denote that he is under par, green numbers that he is over par, and a green 0 if he is even par. This system enables the players and the spectators to take in at a glance the relative positions of the leaders. I have trouble with the boards, however, because I'm partially red-green colorblind: when I'm over a hundred yards from an object, I can't distinguish between the two colors. That afternoon as I gazed at the big leader-board, all I could make out was a mess of 1s for the other players along with the 2 beside my own name. (I knew my 2 had to be red.) "Willie," I said to my caddie, Willie Peterson, "are we leading this tournament by three strokes or by one?"

"Them others is all green numbers," Willie answered. "You're leading by three."

I was until Ed Furgol birdied fifteen and sixteen to move one under for the tournament. With a round to go, I led him by one, Boros by two, Snead and Lema by three.

With eight holes to go on Sunday, I stood one under for the tournament and held a one-shot lead on the closest man, Snead, playing three holes ahead of me, and a two-shot lead on Boros, with whom I was paired. When I was looking over my approach putt on the eleventh green, a salvo of excited whoops and yells went up from the huge gallery packed along the nearby slope. I turned my head to study the large leader-board beyond the eleventh green and saw a red "1" being posted beside Snead's name. Sam had birdied the fourteenth—he had caught me. I putted out for my par and then walked slowly up the slope to the twelfth tee.

I reminded myself I would have to be especially vigilant on the twelfth and thirteenth. All the great sports events seem to develop their own set of patterns, and in the Masters the man who is in the lead (or sharing it, as I was) as often as not comes to grief on these two holes on the fourth round. Ralph Guldahl did in 1937, for example. Four shots ahead of Byron Nelson, Guldahl took a 5 on the par-3 twelfth and a 6 on the par-5 thirteenth, and when Nelson came along and played them in a birdie and an eagle, he not only caught Guldahl but moved two strokes in front—his ultimate margin of victory. Two years later it was Guldahl who overhauled and passed the leader, Snead, by eagling the thirteenth. Only 475 yards long, the thirteenth, a dogleg to the left, with the green protected by an arm of Rae's Creek, can be reached with two first-class

157

shots. Guldahl gambled on carrying the creek with his second, a 3-wood, and hit a beautiful shot four feet from the stick. There are numerous other instances of the make-or-break role the twelfth and thirteenth have played on the fourth round, but I will give you only two more. In 1958, Arnold Palmer, then just another promising young pro, was out in front when he came to this perilous corner of the course. After a scrambling par on the twelfth, he eagled the thirteenth, and right there and then, he won his first major championship. The very next year, leading by three shots when he came to the short twelfth on the last round, Palmer pushed his 6-iron just a fraction, the ball plummeted into Rae's Creek before the green, Palmer took a 6—and, just like that, it was anybody's tournament again. Art Wall, who had been nowhere in sight, won it by birdying five of the last six holes.

As I stood on the twelfth tee thinking these thoughts, a few of the rabid Snead partisans in the immense gallery—there must have been twelve thousand people packed at the corner—let me know explicitly just where their sympathies lay. This unnerved me, I confess. Every tournament golfer is aware, of course, that some of the spectators have to be pulling for the other players, but, ordinarily, when you come by they are polite and quiet; they don't root openly against you. Anyhow, I wanted to get that shot to the twelfth over with just as soon as I could and get on with things. It's always a dangerous shot. The hole measures 155 yards, with the green set at a diagonal tangent to the tee, like the hour hand of a watch at two o'clock. Rae's Creek, which is seven or eight yards wide, swings in front of the green, almost to the edge of it. It is an exceedingly narrow green, and along the far side a bank of rough rises steeply. To compound the terrors, a treacherous wind is almost always swirling over the creek and the green. On this Sunday, happily, the pin was not in one of the more difficult positions. It was toward the front of the green—left-middle, as I recall, about 25 feet to the left of the single bunker that is cut into the bank between the creek and the putting surface. Boros, with the honor, hit a pinsplitter 12 feet past the stick. I didn't hit a very good shot. It just got over the creek by a matter of feet and plopped into the right-hand corner of the bunker. The course's superlative drainage system had digested nearly all of the water that had fallen on Saturday, but there were inevitably some boggy places, and if your ball ended up in casual water or in an area deemed unplayable, you could lift and drop without penalty. It was ruled that my ball lay in casual water in the bunker. I walked two paces to the right and dropped it over my shoulder onto the moist sand. Not a bad lie. Not too much lip to the trap. Okay. Down to work.

The second after I'd hit that bunker shot, I thought I'd played a beauty, for the ball came out fast and struck the green about 15 feet before the pin—just where I'd hoped it would. The trouble was it had come out too fast. Because of the wetness of the sand in the bunker, it had a lot of overspin on it and really took off. It kept rolling and rolling and finally slid off the putting surface and into the rough, 25 feet beyond the pin. The rough in that area, stiff rye grass, was rather scrubby. It was close by the bridge to the green and had been trodden on a good deal. Chipping from it would be risky; there was too much of a chance of stubbing the blade in the wet soil. I decided I would putt the ball instead. All I wanted was to get out of the hole with a 4, and I felt sure I could lag the ball up close to the cup with my putter.

I ran that putt nine feet past. I had played a really bad shot, misjudging how much the rough would slow up the ball and the speed of the green as well. Now I was staring at a very possible 5. While I was fretting about that, Julius stepped up to his birdie putt and, with his typical aplomb, rolled it into the cup.

Man, how fast the situation had changed! Boros had already picked up two strokes on me on the twelfth. We were tied now, and if I missed my nine-footer . . . I read it to break about a half inch to the left just before the cup, so I played it a hair inside the right corner. It took the break at the very last moment, but it took it and dropped. I walked to the thirteenth tee thankful I had escaped with a 4.

I made a conscious effort to pull myself together then. Okay, I was tied now with Boros and, undoubtedly, a shot behind Snead— Sam wouldn't miss his par on a par-5 hole like the fifteenth. If he birdied it, which he might, I'd be two shots back. Only minutes later, I learned that he had birdied it. At that moment, I had also fallen back into a tie with Lema, playing the fourteenth, and I trailed Gary Player, who had mounted a four-birdie rally through the fifteenth, by a shot. I wasn't aware of what Lema and Player were up to, though. My thoughts were on the leader, Snead. Okay, the job was to forget about other people's golf and to focus all my attention on my own. Things could have been far worse, I told myself. I still had six holes in front of me including two par 5s, the thirteenth (475 yards) and the fifteenth (520 yards)—two possible birdie holes. By the time I had driven off the thirteenth, and driven well, I had gotten a firm grip on myself.

I made my birdie 4 on the thirteenth. I was on in two. I think I used a 2-iron for my second. I forget. On the fourteenth, I got my par 4. I know I put my approach about 15 feet behind the pin, but I can't recall how I missed the putt. However, I remember just about everything about the fifteenth; it was the sort of hole you don't forget.

My tee-shot on the fifteenth was well hit, straight and fairly long, but it ended up in a shallow fairway divot. Since I wouldn't be able to get under the ball on my second, my main concern was to take enough club to carry the water hazard before the green—a small pond that runs the width of the green, which sits slightly above it. I took a 3-wood. I made good contact with the ball, but because of the lie, the shot had a lot of hook spin on it, and as the ball flew over the pond it started to break sharply to the left. It came down on the mounded bank at the left of the green and kicked in the direction of the pond in front of the sixteenth tee. It was moving fast when it suddenly struck a mass of red mud, a section of the spectators' pathway between the two holes that had been churned up into mud during Saturday's downpour. When the ball struck the mud, it stopped instantly—a colossal break for me. Under normal conditions it would have surely bounded on into the sixteenth's pond.

Under a local rule instituted for the fourth round, I could lift my imbedded ball from the mud and drop it without penalty. Standing on the far side of the unplayable area, I dropped the ball over my shoulder, and it imbedded itself in the mud again. I was under the impression that the rules permitted me to lift and drop again, but a member of the Rules Committee told me no. I asked him if he was sure, and spotting Joe Dey of the U.S.G.A., who was also serving on the Rules Committee and who was only a few paces away, I suggested we get his opinion. According to Mr. Dey, the rules were explicit on this point: a player whose drop had reimbedded itself was entitled to lift and drop again. My second drop wasn't much of an improvement, finishing in a patch of flat, wet mud. From there—about 50 feet from the near edge of the green and another 30 feet from the pin—I played one of the best touch

160

shots of my life, a little low pitch into the bank with my 7-iron. Just as I intended, the ball hopped up onto the putting surface on its first slowed-down bounce and crawled to within four feet of the cup. I blew the putt. And yet, I couldn't be unhappy about that; I had made 5 and it so easily could have been a 6 or a 7 or more. I suppose the accompanying circumstances made it even easier to be philosophical: my birdie on the thirteenth had put me a shot ahead of Boros and only one behind Snead, and on the fifteenth I had been informed that Sam had bogeyed the sixteenth, taking three from the front edge. With three holes to go, I was back in a tie for the lead.

The sixteenth is a stiff one-shotter of 190 yards over a fairway of water. The flag was positioned to the right and to the back, on a little deck above the dip in the middle of the green. My 6-iron landed on the deck and stopped about four yards short of the hole. The putt had a clearly readable break to the left of about a foot, and I holed it. Now I was a shot ahead of Snead. As I was walking off the green the word came down from the hill that Sam had failed to get his par on the eighteenth. That gave me a two-stroke margin. I could bogey one of the last two holes and still win.

I hit a good straight drive on the seventeenth and was strolling up the fairway when a loud roar came from the eighteenth green. News travels like lightning on a golf course, and before I played my second, I knew the whole story: Tony Lema had sunk a long curving putt to finish with a birdie and a total of 287. I hadn't thought of Tony all day. I hadn't even realized he was in contention. Now to edge him out I would have to get my pars on the seventeenth and eighteenth. I managed to do this despite one of those patented Nicklaus drives on the eighteenth, a pull into the rough on the left. I must not think that hole is hard enough.

When I had climbed the slope onto the home green after hitting the green with my second, Ralph Hutchinson, who served as the announcer there, said to me, "If you win, Jack, save the ball so that you can give it to Bob Jones at the presentation ceremony." Consequently, after I had holed the winning putt, I had to restrain myself. I'd always liked throwing the ball to the crowd—it relieved my tensions. As a kid I'd loved watching other golfers do it, and it was one of the things I'd looked forward to doing myself when I grew up. After that long, hectic, tiring afternoon, I had to throw something, so I whipped off the baseball-type cap I was wearing

161

and threw that. At the presentation ceremony, I handed my ball to Bob Jones, and I shall never forget the look in his eyes: he was so delighted for me.

The 1963 Open was a different story, a shorter one. As the 1962 champion, I hoped to make a strong defense of my title at The Country Club, in Brookline. I didn't even survive the 36-hole cut. I played loose golf, a 76 and a 77 during which I spent a good portion of my time digging the ball out of the thick *poa annua* rough. There were some complicating factors. I mention them not to provide myself with an alibi—I felt fine during the Open and had no alibi—but to introduce a typical problem that every professional on the tour is confronted with from time to time and must learn to handle.

The week before the Open, during the second round of the Thunderbird, I suffered a muscle spasm in the left side of my neck and in my left shoulder. It was a strange morning, cool but humid—too warm for a sweater but quite cold when the wind blew. I must have caught a chill in my neck and shoulder. I had never withdrawn from a tournament, so I wanted to finish the Thunderbird, and I did. My neck had continued to bother me, but it seemed to be getting better. The injury, however, confused my plans. I had intended to go back to my old left-to-right flight for the Open and had meant to work on this during the Thunderbird. I had to postpone that because of my neck trouble, and when I began my three days of practice at The Country Club I was in a dither. With so little time left now, I didn't know whether to try and switch back to left-to-right or to stick with right-to-left. I ended up by doing both and neither. When I played right-to-left, my shots hung out on the right. When I played left-to-right, they hung out on the left. Either way, I was missing the fairways. By the time the championship started, my neck, as I say, felt fine, but I hadn't put in enough work of the right kind on my game. Had I been a little calmer and more mature, I would have been able to have thought things out more clearly and arrived at a sensible program.

In early July, when I went across for the British Open, the next major championship, I was back on my game again, back to left-to-right.

The scene of the British Open that summer was Royal Lytham

& St. Anne's, off the Irish Sea, a few miles from Blackpool, the English version of Coney Island combined with Atlantic City. Lytham has been on the R. & A.'s championship rotation since the 1920s—Jones won the Open there in 1926, and later Lawson Little and Joe Conrad won the Amateur there—but it is not nearly as well-known to Americans as some of the other regular championship courses, such as St. Andrews, Muirfield, and Carnoustie. I liked it very much at first look, much more than I had Troon the summer before. Troon had been brown and as hard as a rock; Lytham was green with a lovely growth of turf.

Admittedly, Lytham is merely a very good course and not a great one, and it surely doesn't present much visual beauty, what with the sea a mile away and the links bordered by unbroken rows of identical tomato red brick houses. However the better I got to know it, the better I liked it. Its terrain has a pleasant modified seaside character, and there are plenty of good holes, the last five especially. They are all par 4s. The fourteenth, 448 yards, has a tight fairway and the green area is contoured very subtlely. The fifteenth, 456 yards, presents a difficult approach to a green that slants down from

A pause in the day's occupation as I wait for one of the frequent trains to puff on past the 8th hole at Royal Lytham. The rail line runs parallel to the 1st, 2nd, 3rd, 8th, and 9th holes—one of the course's unlisted hazards.

the back. The sixteenth, only 354 yards, is a possible birdie hole, but in order to get the right angle into the green, you must place your drive ·down the left side, which is studded with pot bunkers. The seventeenth, 428 yards, is a strong 4, a dogleg to the left that sweeps to a low, flat, elusive green. The eighteenth is only 379 yards but it requires an almost perfect tee-shot: seven fairway traps, in sort of a U formation as you look at them from the tee, nose into the landing area.

For the Open, Lytham wore a very odd, ungolfy look. The British, who had started roping off the fairways for their championships years before we adopted this gallery-control measure in 1954, had gone a step farther for the 1963 Open. The perimeters of the individual holes were fenced with wood palings about four feet high. The year before, at the climax of the Open at Troon, the crowds had gotten out of hand and had swarmed over the course, and the R. & A., I presume, wanted to prevent any recurrence of this.

Sometimes it doesn't work out exactly that way, but every now and then a golfer will get a special feeling about a tournament. I did about the 1963 British Open. From the start, I felt I was going to win it. More than that, round by round everything fell neatly into place for me, almost as if the plot of the tournament had been scripted to my order. After a par 71 on the first day, I was four strokes behind the leaders, Phil Rodgers and Peter Thomson, the Australian veteran who was trying for his fifth British Open 'title. After a second round of 67, I moved to within three shots of Rodgers and Thomson, who were still in front. On the third round I gained another shot, closing to within two shots of the new leader, Bob Charles of New Zealand. Early in the fourth round, that afternoon, I picked up another shot on Charles, and on the seventh hole I jumped into the lead, watched by a large gallery (including Leopold of Belgium and his wife) which seemed to share my feeling that it had been clearly ordained by destiny that I win the 1963 British Open.

I couldn't have made my move more dramatically. The tee on the seventh, a par 5, 551 yards long, is elevated, so you can fly the ball a long way. If you do and keep it on the fairway, you can reach the green in two. That takes a well-played second, however, for you're hitting to a punch-bowl green, with a large mound rising just to the right of the small entrance. I hit a fantastic tee-shot there, if I do say so. (I must be frank and admit that I have never outgrown the thrill one gets from a big drive.) What particularly delighted me about that tee-shot was that it was as accurate as it was long. It had to be. The fairway, you see, swings out from the tee to the left of the direct line over the rough that a player trying for lots of distance must take. As a result, what you have to do is figure out just how much of the rough you think you can bite off, so that your ball, when it lands on the narrow fairway—it's only forty yards wide or so and tilts to the left—won't run on through and finish in the rough on the far side. There was no wind to worry about, only a light breeze coming off the right, and since I felt strong and confident and, moreover, was playing the small British ball, I took aim on a patch of fairway that must have been almost 300 yards away. At the time I had no idea of its distance in yards, I simply felt I could fly my ball to that point if I caught it flush. I managed to, and after carrying the long expanse of rough, it lit right on that patch. The shot had a wee bit of fade on it, and the bouncing ball swung with the fairway and stayed on it. When we left the tee, some of the golf writers who were with our pair (my partner was Tom Haliburton) paced off that drive. The consensus was that it was out approximately 350 yards, that it had carried about 300 yards and rolled another 50. That measurement must have been fairly accurate, because, as I say, the hole was 551 yards long and I got home with a 5-iron. As a matter of fact, my approach finished only four feet from the flag. I made the putt for an eagle 3, and when I did, I had taken the lead in the Open. I felt wonderfully easy and relaxed. A golfer does when he's swinging well, and my swing had felt great throughout the tournament.

In the British Open it's more difficult than it is in our championships to know how you stand in relation to your opposition. The scoreboards out on the course are few in number, too small to be readable from a distance, and well behind the action as a rule. You depend primarily on the reports that the officials with your group give you on request; they get their information from walkie-talkies. When I made the turn, I knew I still had a stroke on the closest men, Bob Charles and Phil Rodgers. On the eleventh I went one over par, but I got that back with a birdie 3 on the fourteenth, the first of those five tough finishing holes. At that stage I had opened a two-shot lead on both Charles and Rodgers, who were playing together, a hole behind Haliburton and me. I wasn't aware of it myself at the time, but a number of people later told me they had never seen me so talkative in an important event. Apparently, I was chatting away between shots the way I normally do only on a practice round. Some of my friends, knowing me, thought I was perhaps too relaxed. Possibly. All I can say is that I was continuing to hit the ball so well that it buoyed me up.

On the fifteenth I hit the best long iron I'd hit all year, a 2-iron that covered the flag. The ball, I remember, was hardly on its way when Bruce Devlin, who had come out to watch, sang out, "Perfect, Jack, perfect." It nearly was. The ball almost went into the cup on the fly. It sat down 15 feet past—a chance for another birdie. I took some time over the putt. It was a little downhill and the green looked fast to me. It wasn't. I left the ball two feet short. Then I missed that two-footer. A 5, not a 3. That shook me up a little.

I needed a birdie now to feel safe. On the sixteenth I got one, holing from 16 feet. I felt in command again. What I wanted now were two solid pars.

I drove with a 3-wood off the seventeenth, a dogleg to the left. The best line is down the right, and I wanted to be sure I didn't hit the ball too far and reach the rough. The ball ended up on the right side of the fairway, about ten yards short of where I'd driven in the morning. On that round I'd played a 3-iron on my second and had been about 25 feet short of the pin. There seemed to be about the same amount of breeze coming from the same direction— slightly against—so I selected a 2-iron. I hit a good-looking shot, but somewhere in my calculations something had gone wrong. The ball carried too far, past the middle of the green, and hopped on through the fringe and into the high, springy rough beyond it. Again, I was a little shaken: I'd hit the shot the way I wanted to and couldn't figure out where I'd made my mistake in estimating the distance.

From the rough I played a wedge, a poor one. I barely got the ball onto the green. The high grass had been much more giving than I had expected it to be, and my club had slid under the ball. My long putt was wide of the cup. A bogey 5.

I did some rapid arithmetic. Charles and Rodgers were now on the sixteenth green. By my count, I could still wrap things up tight with a par 4 and could even win with a 5—unless either Bob or Phil picked up a birdie on one of the last three holes. I took a little time before teeing up on the eighteenth. I wanted to know whether either Bob or Phil had birdied the sixteenth. That green was within hearing distance, and I would be able to pick up the applause if either made his 3 there. I heard nothing.

Applause or no applause, both Charles and Rodgers, as I was to learn later, had birdied the sixteenth. And as I also learned later, I had another thing wrong—my basic arithmetic. With my 5s on the fifteenth and seventeenth, I had dropped one more shot to Charles and Rodgers than I thought I had. In a word, if either or both matched par on the last two holes, I had to par the eighteenth to tie.

Then I made my final mistake, the one that cost me the championship. The last place I wanted to put my tee-shot was in the gorse bushes off to the right of the fairway. With the breeze blowing across the fairway from left to right, I took aim on the farthest bunker on the left edge of the fairway; I'd let my fade and the breeze bring the ball back into the middle of the fairway. My drive had no fade on it. In fact, it was hooked—not much, but hooked nevertheless. I hadn't hit a hook all week. Well, I had now. The ball headed straight for that last bunker, held its line into the breeze, and thumped into the sand at the foot of the high, heavy-lipped front wall of the bunker.

From that lie I had no option but to wedge the ball back to the fairway, almost laterally. My recovery actually rolled through the fairway into light rough on the right, about 90 yards from the pin. I needed a champion's shot now. I didn't have it in me. My pitch with my sand wedge rolled 20 feet beyond the pin and finished on the back fringe. My putt never had the line. This third 5 *was* fatal. Rodgers and Charles made no errors. They both made their pars on the seventeenth and eighteenth: 277 for them, 278 for me. I had thrown it away.

In a 36-hole playoff the next day, Charles prevailed and history was made: for the first time ever, a left-handed golfer had won a major championship. I didn't stay around for the playoff. The P.G.A. Championship was scheduled to begin the coming Thursday, at the Dallas Athletic Club course, and I had no time to spare. I hated that flight. Not to take anything away from Bob Charles or Phil Rodgers, but if anyone had ever blown a championship, I had at Lytham. I suppose I would have felt even worse if I hadn't previously won the Masters that spring, but it kept burning into me that I would have few such opportunities in the years ahead to win the British Open. I finally decided just not to think about Lytham any more.

I didn't think too much about the P.G.A. Championship either. It was too darn hot in Dallas to think about anything. During the three days I played practice rounds, the thermometer was never below 100 degrees. It was uncomfortable just to walk from your motel room to an air-conditioned car. Fortunately, the D.A.C. course weathered the intense heat remarkably. The greens were a trifle soft, since they had to be watered generously and there was not a ripple of a breeze to dry them, but they stood up splendidly during the tournament. They would hold a well-played shot but a mediocre shot would slide off. They putted fast. The rest of the course had been carefully prepared. The fairways were wide but not too wide. The rough was neither sparse nor clumpy. Under the brutal circumstances, a good honest test—7046 yards, par 71.

The afternoon before play began, I won the driving contest with a poke of 341 yards. I mention this because, while I have driven the ball farther, this is my longest measured and recorded drive. As this attested, I had made the switch from the small ball back to the large one successfully. The British ball, as you know, is 1.62 inches in diameter, our is 1.68 inches, and both weigh 1.62 ounces. You wouldn't think so, but you can actually spot one ball from the other with the naked eye. That six-hundredths of an inch, as you also know, makes for an astounding difference in the playability of the two balls. The small ball, because it is "heavier" and denser, will bore through winds that would flip the American ball back in your face. There are other differences. The small ball, for instance, doesn't accentuate your errors as much; a hook or a slice doesn't break as acutely. Furthermore, you have to strike the large ball better to get it out a good distance, whereas the small ball travels quite a ways even when it isn't struck properly. Taking all these factors into consideration, the large ball requires finer hand action and a superior overall technique, and, I would say without hesitation, it produces better golfers. As regards the side issue of switching from one ball to the other, when I first went over to Britain as a kid of nineteen, the scoop was that it was easier for Americans to go from the American ball to the British ball than the other way round. I found it worked out just the opposite. While the British ball takes less skill and builds up your confidence, returning to the large American ball is usually easier for me than adapting to the small ball because of my ingrained familiarity with the American ball.

When the championship started, Dallas, if anything, became even more scorching. I don't believe we had one afternoon when the temperature stayed below 110 degrees. Away from the course, I didn't leave my motel room except for meals. On the course I felt hotter and more sweat-drenched than I ever had in my life. I just wanted to get each round over with as soon as possible and escape from the furnace. Dick Hart, who had set the pace on the first two rounds, crumpled in the heat on Saturday, and Bruce Crampton became the 54-hole leader with a total of 208. Dow Finsterwald was at 210, I was at 211 (69-73-69), and Dave Ragan at 212.

On the final day Crampton and I played together in the last two-some, directly behind Finsterwald and Ragan. I remember more about the heat than the golf. Crampton, I believe, held the lead until the twelfth hole, when he got into trouble off the tee, and I think I took over the lead when I birdied the fifteenth at the same time Ragan was en route to a bogey on the seventeenth after spraying his drive. In any event, I came to the eighteenth, a 420-yard par 4, needing only a 5 to win. (This time, you can be sure, I had my arithmetic correct.) A creek crosses the eighteenth fairway about 290 yards from the tee, so to be on the safe side, I drove with a 3-iron. I eased up on it and pulled it into the rough. I chipped out conservatively, short of the creek, for I could reach the green from there with a pitching club. I played a 9-iron and played it un-heroically for the center of the green—a large green that sloped down from the back. My ball landed about 20 feet past the flag and spun back down the green 4 feet above the cup. I made the putt for a 68 and had won by two strokes.

The P.G.A. trophy had been toasting in the sun in front of the clubhouse the whole day. It was so hot that if you touched it you would have blistered your fingers. I left it alone during the presentation ceremonies. The moment they were over, I made a beeline for the clubhouse with the security officer assigned to me. A couple of steps from the door, the poor fellow collapsed from heat exhaustion.

I always link those two championships together in my mind—

the British Open and the P.G.A. of 1963. I lost the one I thought sure I was going to win, and I won the other before I had hardly realized it was within my grasp. Such are the fortunes of golf. There is nothing you can say about the game that the earliest tournament golfers didn't know. All you can do is repeat what others have said so often before: You can never be certain of winning until the last putt is in the cup, and on the occasions when you win you can usually look back and find a number of spots in which you were rather lucky. I would also agree with the first golfer who said—no doubt as he sewed the stitches in the cover of his feather-stuffed ball—that while some championships are won, most of them are lost.

XII

The Tour and the Touring

THE 1964 P.G.A. CHAMPIONSHIP was played in my hometown, Columbus, at the Columbus Country Club. Before, during, and after the championship I spent nine straight days at home, the longest uninterrupted stretch during the two and a half years I had been a professional. Over that period I had slowly adjusted to the gypsy life the modern golf pro leads: a new town and a new tournament every week, annual trips to two or three other continents for tournaments, and, in between times, one-day or two-day jaunts here, there, and everywhere for exhibitions, business conferences, television appearances—the whole bit. Through practice I had become a much neater packer of suitcases, an authority on steak houses from coast to coast, and a promising geographer. While I still couldn't make an after-dinner talk I was proud of, I had become more adept at somehow getting through a hard day after traveling most of the previous night. And through meeting so many people, my memory for names, I was relieved to find, was finally improving.

In July, 1964, the same month I was home for that record-breaking nine days, I took a decisive step. To make my life of constant travel easier, I purchased a plane, a twin-engine Aero Commander 680 FL. Called the Grand Commander, this model had a cruising speed of 220 miles an hour, a 1000-mile range, and seating accommodations for seven persons other than the pilot and co-pilot. Arnold Palmer had earlier bought himself a private plane, and it had greatly lightened the pressures of his heavy schedule. I found it worked the same for me. I got home much more regularly between tournaments and other engagements, and besides, I loved the hours in the air—stretching out and napping when I was really bushed or, at other times, taking over at the controls or observing

171

how my pilot, Stan Pierce, handled them. I enjoy flying very much and I've logged over a thousand hours, but I'm strictly a student pilot. I have never tried to get a license. My only incentive for getting one would be if I wanted to fly by myself, and I don't want to fly without Stan. Golf is my business, flying is his. I think I was very lucky getting Stan Pierce. A native of Glassboro, New Jersey, who is now starting into his fifties, Stan is a fine companion, pleasant, stable, and accommodating. Though he still needs a little more exposure to rival Bernard Darwin as a golf critic, he loves the game and the tournament scene, and he thinks I play all right.

Barbara, I thought, made an exceptional adjustment to the unorthodox pattern my professional life imposed on our family life. (On April 11, 1963, four days after the Masters, we had had our second child, Steven Charles.) To appreciate how tough this adjustment must have been for Barbara, you must know her—she's the most organized person you ever met. Her folks have always kidded her about this trait. Once, quite a few years back, when she and her mother were shopping in a supermarket, a customer asked a clerk where the baking soda was. The clerk didn't know but Barbara volunteered the information—two rows over, third shelf on the right. "Barbara," her mother said, aghast, "don't tell me you've got this supermarket organized, too!" Living with an unperfectionistic, easygoing guy like me did wonders for Barb. Now she is just organized enough, and she does everything so easily, so invisibly, that I am all admiration—and appreciation.

Today Barbara knows her golf, very well. It took her about two years after we were married to get the hang of things—to be able, say, to remember the individual holes on a new course after one or two rounds. She is very amusing when she talks about the transition period. "When I heard someone say, 'No Mulligans allowed,' " she told me once, "I thought that amounted to saying, 'If you're not good enough to play this course, go and play an easier one.' " She tells me that gallerying at tournaments with Vivienne Player, who's the daughter of a pro and an excellent golfer in her own right, helped her a great deal. Now, as I said, she's a knowledgeable observer and thoroughly enjoys coming to the tournaments. Barb is beginning to play golf again, and I would think that in a year or so she may overtake my mother, who's not a bad player at all, as the low-handicap female in the family. Her golf Bible up to now has been a copy of Cary Middlecoff's *Advanced Golf,* which the

172

author, our Florida neighbor, inscribed, "Happy birthday, Barbara. If *he* won't tell you the secrets, here they are."

By 1964 Barb had acquired a sufficient understanding of the vagaries of tournament golf to realize what a strange bitter-sweet season it was for me. From one point of view, it had been very successful: I won four tournaments here and two abroad. At the same time, I had shown a lack of a strong finishing punch on several occasions: I was second or tied for second in no less than six tournaments, and three other times I tied for third. On the other hand, looking at my record in a different light, I had never played as consistently well as a professional: after three poor tournaments in California, I had a run of seven straight starts in which I finished no worse than fourth. Then, after four mediocre performances, I went off on another streak in which, with the exception of one tie for eleventh, I finished 5th or better in ten consecutive tournaments. When the P.G.A. bookkeeping was all wrapped up for the year, because of this week-after-week steadiness I emerged as the leading money-winner, my total earnings of $113,284.50 in official events coming to $81.13 more than Palmer's.

A golfer's status, in my opinion, shouldn't depend primarily on his annual winnings, but the fact is that it does: the standings are publicized regularly and golf fans follow them closely. This brought about a real Broadway climax to the 1964 P.G.A. season —or perhaps I should say, a real off-Broadway climax, since the last tournament on the schedule, the Cajun Classic, is put on in the small town of Lafayette, Louisiana, deep in the Hebert brothers' country. The purse is, understandably, on the small side—only $25,000 in 1964—but that year both Arnold and I entered. Since each of us aspired to be the leading money-winner and I trailed Arnold by only $300 or so, how we finished in the Cajun could make all the difference. On the last day, Arnold, a few holes in front of me, had a 71 which gave him a total of 284. I duplicated that 71 for 282 which, as it turned out, put me five shots behind the winner, Miller Barber. Temporarily at least, it also put me in second place in the tournament, and to edge by Arnold in our personal fiscal contest, I would have to finish second or in a tie for second. Ultimately, everything swung on whether or not Gay Brewer, who was playing just behind me, made a par or a birdie on the 72nd, a dogleg par 4 that called for an 8-iron or a 9 to a slightly elevated green. Gay dropped his approach 20 feet behind the hole. If he missed the putt, he and I would tie for second, and I would nose Arnold out; if he made the putt, I would wind up third and Arnold would nose me out. Just before Gay lined up that 20-footer, he walked to the back of the green, where I was standing, and asked me with that cockeyed grin of his, "How much is this worth to you, Jack?" I handed him my wallet. We all quieted down then and Gay went to work on the putt. He pulled it a fraction and it trickled by the cup on the left.

My four domestic victories in 1964 came in the Phoenix Open, the Tournament of Champions, the Whitemarsh Open, and the Portland Open. My two foreign victories were in the Canada Cup individual competition and the Australian Open. You will notice that in this list the major championships are conspicuous by their absence. This took much of the glitter off the gold I won. Moreover, to add a wry little twist to things, in three of the four major championships I came in second. I won't inflict any blow-by-blow accounts on you. In each of the championships there was one repeated theme or one set scene that summed up the event—at least my part in it.

Taking the championships chronologically—first, the Masters. Palmer led all the way and won by six shots with rounds of 69, 68, 69, and 70 for 276. I would rate this his outstanding performance in an American championship and place it on a par with his 276 at Troon in the 1962 British Open, undoubtedly his top performance overseas. Never, before or after, has Arnold's swing, to my mind, possessed such perfect tempo as it did in 1964 at Augusta. Arnold is not the type of golfer you would call effortless, but those four days he hit the ball with an ease that *was* almost effortless. Ordinarily his longer approach shots will come steaming into the greens on a low hot trajectory, but that week at Augusta they were fluttering down as softly as leaves in autumn. There was one short period during that Masters when I might have been able to have given Arn something to think about. On Saturday, after having started with a 71 and a 73, I was making a run at him until I shanked my 8-iron on the short twelfth into deep right field. I didn't play especially well the rest of the way in, and Arnold had a real good back nine and moved away again. On the last day, Dave Marr tied me for second by holing a wicked, downhill, 30-foot putt for a birdie on the last hole.

The Open. There's not too much to say about it. It was at Congressional, near Washington, and this was the year of Ken Venturi's spectacular triumph. Just before the tournament I changed putters, switching from the George Low Bristol model I was still using to a Tommy Armour blade model with a compact flange. It belonged to a friend of mine, Curtis Person, Sr., the fine senior golfer from Memphis, and I thought it would suit the fast but grainy greens at Congressional. To make a long story short, I was headed for a 69 on the first day when I ruined the round by blowing putts on the last three greens, two of them under two feet. My second round was somewhat similar. I finished weakly again, bogeying three of the last four holes, as I recall. My 145 (72-73) was eight strokes off the pace. On Saturday morning I started off hitting the ball awfully well but I putted atrociously. On the first seven greens I missed eight putts of four feet or less. After those seven holes I was six over par. That was my tournament. The following week Arnold stole that Armour putter from me and I've never seen it since. After the way I had putted at Congressional, I didn't hound him too much about it.

The British Open was another story. There was one moment when I honestly thought I might win it. Most moments of that type come on the fourth round, but this one came on the third, on the morning of the final 36. We were at St. Andrews that year and Tony Lema held the lead after the first two days. I had started 76, 74 and was nine big strokes behind him. Tony's golf had really been something, but I must say he had been luckier than I had those first two rounds. On Wednesday he had an early starting time and I had a late one, on Thursday it was the other way around, and both days he missed the worst weather and I caught it. It had been particularly fierce on Wednesday afternoon—cold rain and a sixty-mile-an-hour wind that literally blew you over when you were putting. On Friday, the day of the final two rounds, playing conditions were excellent. I was out about an hour and fifteen minutes before Tony. A birdie 3 on the first got me rolling and I added birdies on the fourth, seventh, ninth, and twelfth to stand five under even 4s, as the British calculate their rounds, after twelve holes. As I walked down the thirteenth fairway, Tony was coming up the sixth. I looked at the scoreboard for Tony's twosome and saw that Tony had taken three 5s on the first five holes to go three over even 4s. He looked at the scoreboard for my twosome and saw that I was five under even 4s through the first twelve holes. I had made up eight strokes of my nine-stroke deficit! We looked at each other for a brief moment and then moved on. I finished the round with five pars and a birdie on the eighteenth for a 66 that equaled the course record. It didn't do me much good, though. The knowledge that his lead had been trimmed to a single stroke set Tony off on a great driving comeback. He proceeded to birdie the seventh, ninth, tenth, fourteenth, fifteenth, and eighteenth. This gave him a 68, and so all I had picked up was two strokes; I was still seven behind. In the afternoon I had another good round, a 68, but Tony, staying right with the Old Course, added a 70 and was the winner by five full strokes. A magnificent victory.

Last but not least, the P.G.A. Championship, at the Columbus Country Club. It was a course I knew well. I'd shot it in 66 when I was sixteen, and since we were playing substantially the same course save for narrower fairways, I was hopeful of giving my home-town friends something to cheer about. I must say I was very proud of the folks at the Columbus Country Club. I think they did as fine a job as has been done in recent years with the P.G.A. Championship, with a course that was a good course but not the severest test of golf. It was an exciting tournament. Arnold was in top-notch form. He had consecutive rounds of 68, 68, 69, 69, the only man ever to break 70 on all four rounds in a major championship and still not win it. I didn't win it either. After some sloppy golf in the middle rounds, I came up with a 64 on the last day to tie Arnold for second. Only one man was meant to win that tourna-ment—Bobby Nichols. There was no other way you could look at it. Round after round Bobby got in all kinds of trouble and always came out of it smelling like a peony garden. He grabbed the lead the first day with a 64, six under par. He did it on the greens, using only 13 putts on the last nine and holing three of about 20 feet. After a second round of 71, he led Arnold by a shot and continued to after a 69 on the third. Providence had to be watching over him. As Bobby was the first to admit, he could easily have been 80 that third round. Look at this: he was bunkered on the first but got down a 10-foot putt for his par; he was bunkered again on the sec-ond and got down a 20-footer for his par; he hit a tree on the eighth, had to play down an adjoining fairway, and made his par when he threw a wedge a foot or so from the hole; on the twelfth, after he had been in trees off the tee and in a bunker on his second, he holed a longish putt for his par; on the fifteenth he drove under a tree, hit another tree 50 yards down the rough with his second, played an intentional slice with a 6-iron 25 feet from the pin, and made the putt for his par; on the sixteenth, where he drove into a ground-under-repair area, he put a 6-iron 18 inches from the hole for a birdie; on the seventeenth, a par 3, he half-shanked a 2-iron into a cluster of trees and all but holed out his recovery— the ball struck the pin and stopped inches away. Did you ever hear of anything like that! His fourth round, a 67, was almost as fantastic. Down the stretch, with Arnold and me on his neck, Bobby birdied the 69th with an 18-foot putt, saved his par on the 70th with a 12-footer, and rolled in a 50-foot snake to birdie the 71st. He won by three strokes. Had Arnold and I dared come any closer, Bobby's guardian angel probably would have stuck an illegal extra club in our bags or had us penalized for slow play. He'd have fixed our wagons one way or another.

I don't know how future golf historians will rate the professional field of the 1960s, but I think of it as a strong one—some very skillful golfers at the top and, on the rung just below, twice as many really competent golfers as had ever before come along at the same time. After three years on the tour, I had gotten to know my colleagues fairly well and had reached some definite conclusions about their golf. Let me present a gallery of quick portraits of ten of the leading players of this period, as I saw them and see them.

Since I have already talked about Arnold Palmer at some length, I will add here only a few observations I haven't touched on. Arnold had a relatively lean year in 1968 when his main problem was concentration. At the same time, though, he's become much straighter off the tee in recent years. He no longer has that closed-clubhead position at the top of the backswing that sometimes produced a big hook in pressure situations. Now he has a square position at the top and doesn't have to block out his right hand from taking over as he hits through the ball. . . . Arnold doesn't think he's as good a putter as he used to be. Maybe so, but he's still excellent on the greens. He does miss an occasional four-footer, but any golfer like Arnold who charges the hole is bound to miss some putts coming back. I never did see Bobby Locke, and perhaps he was even better than Arnold, but Arnold's the best putter under pressure I've even seen. . . . The chief weakness in his game is much the same as my own: neither of us is much of a

They used to talk of the Big Three, and here we are at the Sands Point club with Perry Como, filming a segment for Mr. C's television show.

short wedge player. One other thing about Arn. He's the best bad-weather golfer I know. Every time it's raining or chilly or blowing hard, he has a definite advantage over the field. Part of this comes from his determination not to let things distract him, part of it comes from his confidence in his ability to function in any weather, and the rest comes from his extraordinary physical strength and stamina.

With the exception of Ben Hogan, who's in a class by himself, Gary Player is the most accomplished technician in the game today. I would certainly rate him as the most consistent striker of the ball: every shot looks like it's been struck with the same hitting action, and the flight of his shots is extremely uniform. To compensate for his lack of size and produce bigger and more powerful swings, Gary thrusts himself into many artificial positions, but he's such an exceptional athlete and has such great coordination that he can get away with it. I don't know any other golfer who could. Sometimes

178

Gary falls off the ball on his follow-through, but when he's playing well he doesn't. In the past, at times, he's tried to play his shots from right to left, and that's silly for Gary since he's such a fine straight player and since he's long enough to begin with. . . . Gary is solid in every department. He's as good as they come with the fairway woods, he's a top-class putter, and, as I see it, he's the best sand-player in golf. His bunker-play technique is different from that of most other golfers, who think in terms of getting the ball out with a smooth, flowing, soft stroke. Gary positions his weight forward, sets his hands well forward, takes a short backswing swing, and drives his wedge into the sand firm and hard. It takes nerve and a great eye to do this. In short, he's a complete golfer—which a man of his size (5 feet 7 and a half) must be to compete successfully in today's game of power golf. . . . Some people ask why Gary plays only fifteen tournaments a year now in America, since, at thirty-two, he's still a young man. People tend to forget that Gary started playing tournament golf around the world when he was nineteen, hardly more than a schoolboy. He has been knocking himself out for a dozen years. Aside from his appearances on the American tour, he has had to support the pro tour in South Africa (which wouldn't exist if Gary didn't play in the tournaments), and in addition he has had to fulfill obligations in Britain, Australia, and the Far East. He has traveled more miles and has been forced to spend more time away from home than any golfer who ever lived. This has required sacrifice and effort, but in the process Gary became a true champion and deserves everything that has come his way. He and his wife Vivienne have five children, and I can't blame him for wanting to spend a sizable portion of his time nowadays enjoying his family and his beautiful farm. . . . Gary is ideal to play with, a wonderful sportsman, a good winner and a good loser. He never takes his golf away from the course—a 66 or a 76, it stays there. He has unusual charm. So many people become fond of him that, as I keep telling him, he has got to be the world's greatest gift-getter. (Just to give you an idea, Dale Robertson, the cowboy actor, sent him a quarter horse.) With crowds around, Gary projects himself rather theatrically, but underneath he has worth and warmth and humor. "You wish a player good luck at a tournament," I remember his telling me not long ago. "On the first hole he slices his drive, it kicks off a tree back onto the fairway, and you say, 'Can you imagine the luck!' " (Our favorite exchange

179

Two of the steadiest—Bob Charles and Billy Casper.

lines are "All the best for Monday," and "Let's have a nice game.")
Gary is one of my closest friends and I think a lot of him. I hope
my boys grow up to be as fine an all-round person as he is.

Billy Casper looks phlegmatic but he has intense drive and fire.
He is a stupendous pressure golfer, one of the few men to whom it
honestly doesn't mean a darn what the other fellow is doing; he
still plays his own game. It's quite a game. To start with, he is one
of the best drivers of our time. He can play the tee-shot both ways,
left-to-right and right-to-left, but he is sounder, I'd say, left-to-right.
That would go for the rest of his game. Billy's iron play is dependable rather than brilliant, but he can get pretty hot on occasions
with his middle and short irons. Of course, he is simply amazing
on the greens and around the greens with the wedge. We all have
our weak points and one of Billy's is that the flight of his long irons
is too low for certain golf courses that have extra firm and resilient
greens on which the ball doesn't sit down quickly. . . . Billy is a
super competitor. He never plays a foolish shot. He has a sure
ability for recognizing an opening and seizing it. He is direct and
pleasant, aware of the other fellow in the right way. I always enjoy
my rounds with him.

Before his tragic death, Tony Lema had just started to realize
what a good player he had been for years. His career, really, was
packed into his last three seasons; somehow or other, he hadn't
been able to express his talent until 1963. It would have been his-
torically wrong if an accomplished golfer like Tony had not won a

180

major championship. His victory in the 1964 British Open assures him of being remembered for all time, and for his friends and admirers there is some solace in that. . . . Tony, I suppose, was just about the prettiest player of the 1960s. He had natural timing and rhythm, he used his legs very well, and he had a delicate feel for the clubhead at impact. Indeed, when he was playing his best, he had a greater sense of artistry than any of his contemporaries. He was a superior driver—that's for sure. He didn't lash at the ball. He worked under it with his body, and the club continued way out toward his target. He was a reliable iron player, a good putter, and he stood up well to the strain of tournament play. . . . There was a strong streak of the Route 66 swinger in Tony and an equally strong streak of the poet. A complicated person, he was intelligent and companionable. I liked talking things over with him very much. . . . Anything one says is bound to be inadequate, but we have all missed Tony Lema a great deal.

Julius Boros has won two Opens a dozen years apart, and last year at forty-eight he won the P.G.A. Only a golfer of the first rank could stay at the top as long as Julius has. His swing doesn't have

With Tony Lema, a genuinely talented golfer and man.

the best conceivable path—he takes the club back too much on the inside—but his lovely tempo makes up for that and other minor technical idiosyncrasies. (I think of tempo as the rate of speed throughout the golf swing, and I think of rhythm as the flow; the cadence, that knits the various elements of the swing.) . . . As Ben Hogan has pointed out, it is crucial for a golfer to be able to repeat the same swing under tournament stress, and Boros does this about as well as anyone. He is a perfect example of a professional athlete who found a method that worked for him and who stayed with it. He reduces shotmaking to its essentials. He gets into a comfortable stance before the ball in no time at all, and from that moment on he stays in motion until he has completed his shot. This is the foundation of his relaxed style. . . . Julius has a marvelous temperament for competitive golf—easygoing, confident, affected by no one and nothing. He is sure around the greens and expert at handling greenside rough. He is not supposed to be much of a holer, but he has always been a good streak putter. Correct that: he's a darn good putter—period. . . . Finally, the strongest feature of Julius' game is probably the soft flight he gets. Even his long irons come down as if the ball were attached to a parachute. Along with his straightness off the tee, this makes him especially effective on tough championship courses where a man must be able to hit the ball a fair distance and still control it.

Everyone talks about Doug Sanders having a bad golf swing. That isn't true at all. His club travels on the correct path more regularly than any other player's. Sure, it's a shorter path than the blueprint calls for, but, going back and coming down, it's the right path and Doug's on it all the time. He is not too long off the tee, but there are few men who play the fairway woods as well, and this makes up for it. . . . Another quality of Doug's golf that is often overlooked is his skill at manipulating the ball. He can hit it high or low, draw it or fade it, play a soft flight or a boring flight. On his approaches he has a flair for estimating the amount of run he'll get, and, like all winners, he has a good sense of distance on and around the greens. He reads break and grain well, and he is an excellent putter from all distances when the burden of a tournament is on him. . . . In recent years, when Doug has blossomed out as golf's answer to Twiggy, his consciousness of his gallery impact and his television appeal has tended to impair his concentration, but when he is in a serious mood, he can play.

In temperament Gene Littler is at the opposite pole from Sanders —quiet, placid, about as unshowboaty as a man can be. When I first watched Gene, I thought he had one of the prettiest, smoothest swings I had ever seen. In 1962, when he set out to hit the ball harder in search of more distance, his accuracy and his scoring fell off. He has come back, of course, to play many fine tournaments, but I don't think Gene has ever fulfilled his basic potential. For one reason or another, he appears to lack the drive, the inner stimulus, to reach the heights he should have attained. . . . This does not mean that Gene is not a good competitor. He is. He's surprisingly bold around the greens and on them. He can afford to be because, when he leaves himself a big putt for his par after attacking the hole, he generally gets it down. A wonderful recovery putter. He has one of the sweetest backswings in golf. You hear a lot about one-piece takeaways. Gene's is. . . . As I remarked earlier, there isn't a nicer man in sports than Gene. When I find I'm paired with him, I look forward to our round.

Sam Snead, I would imagine, has ripped out more long, straight drives and covered the pin with more approaches than any golfer in the game's long history. Technically, Sam's swing isn't quite as polished as it used to be, but for a man in his middle fifties he's a wonder. No one has a better position at the top of the backswing; the arms are fully extended, the hands fully cocked. He has great control of his legs during his swing, and he is still awfully strong. Though he plays all the shots well, I have always been particularly impressed by the accuracy of his 7-iron and 8-iron pitches and by the precision of his bunker play. . . . As has been appreciated for many years, Sam's long list of victories would have been even longer had he been a surer short putter. He has always been one of the best approach putters. . . . He is still capable of classic shotmaking today. His longevity, I'd guess, is due primarily to his rare physical endowment, but he can also be regarded as the perfect illustration of the old adage that a swinger will last long after a hands-player has had to pack it up.

I have known Gay Brewer for over ten years—we used to bump into one another in the Cincinnati area when I was an amateur— and his success in recent seasons has been a source of pleasure to me. Gay's rise has been a triumph of hard work. He has improved every phase of his game. For example, by changing from drawing the ball to fading it he made himself a much less in-and-out driver.

183

He has become more consistent with his short irons and around the greens. Gay has also worked diligently to become a smarter golfer, and today he manages all kinds of courses shrewdly. . . . Once he builds up confidence in his game, Gay sustains it over a long period. His main trouble is that when he hits a slump, it takes him a correspondingly long time to get out of it. He is an interesting player to watch not only because of his control of his unconventional loop swing but also because of his aggressive attitude when he's hitting the ball. He can show you some great shots.

Like Gene Littler, Ken Venturi, the last golfer in this brief gallery, is a player who has not fulfilled his tremendous potential. Of all the young professionals of the post-Hogan era, Ken without a doubt possessed the best talent. The only weak club in his bag was the putter. His stroke with it was too variable, and he was inclined to be jabby. However, when he was playing well, he was effective on the greens. . . . Ken has an extremely simple golf swing. He presets his hands very definitely—much as I try to do—takes the club back on a straight path from the ball, and then, with just a small movement of his hips, gets into a sturdy position to hit the ball. He has remarkably good hands, and this is why his iron play can at times be superlative, as it was at Congressional. . . . Had Ken not had the misfortune to run into those circulation problems with his hands, he might well have developed into a truly great golfer.

I feel impelled to comment on one other golfer, Chi Chi Rodriguez, perhaps because I am asked so many questions about Chi Chi. The most frequent question, of course, is whether or not that 118-pound elastic band from Puerto Rico can hit the ball as far as I can. The answer is that he certainly has on quite a few occasions. He must be the longest driver pound for pound there has ever been. The technique Chi Chi has devised gives him maximum leverage and a hard, boring flight, almost as if the ball carried topspin. He gets it way out there. At one stage in his career—I don't believe he really understood how out of place it was—Chi Chi overdid his Caribbean showmanship and annoyed the fellows he played with. When he was spoken to about it, though, he toned down his behavior immediately and since that time it has been exemplary. He's a very good fellow. When he began to win prize money, he gave it all to his family back in Puerto Rico until they all had suitable housing and comfortable lives. Only then did Chi Chi begin to think about himself.

On the eve of the 1965 Open. Left to right, Ken and Conni Venturi; Arnold and Winnie Palmer; Gus Benedict, president of the U.S.G.A.; Ralph Hutchinson, the golden voice of the home green; the Nicklauses; and Julius Boros.

In the 1960s, what with the purses on the American tour doubling and trebling, many professionals from foreign countries found they couldn't stay away. You couldn't blame them. Tenth place in many of our tournaments was worth more than first place in most of the tournaments in their own countries. Among the visiting players who have become familiar faces on our tour, I would say that Bruce Devlin, of Australia, has the most natural talent. Bruce has played some wonderful stretches of golf, but he hasn't accomplished as much as he should have. His temperament is good but his attitude toward professional golf isn't. He should travel more, play more tournaments, and work on his game harder. If he made these sacrifices, I feel he would stand alongside Gary Player as the best foreign golfer in the world. Bruce, who is tall and lanky, should be an upright swinger, and he is when he's playing his best. Often, though, he lets himself slide out of his natural style—which is to play the ball from left to right with an open stance—and starts drawing the ball. When he does, he gets flat and runs into alignment troubles.

Kel Nagle, a much older Australian, is one of the most admirable men in golf. He has a friendly, even disposition, and he has character. Kel is not long with his woods, and his iron play is more steady than sparkling, but few people can match his short game. What makes it so efficient is the rhythm with which Kel executes his strokes with his pitching and chipping clubs and with his putter. It's absolutely uniform—the same rhythm, basically, that he uses on his full shots.

Bruce Crampton, also from Australia, has played in more tournaments on the American tour than any other foreign golfer. Come to think of it, the last few years Bruce has probably played in more of our tournaments than any American golfer. Bruce, as a result, suffers at times from being over-golfed. Then he loses the tempo of his swing, and frequently he gets into the bad habit of taking the club back on the inside—so much on the inside, after a while, that he hits out and around on everything and hooks shot after shot. Then he'll stop, get back to fundamentals again, take the club back square, and play first-class golf for a series of tournaments. He has the stuff to be an outstanding scorer, for few players are better natural putters. What Bruce needs is to be more pacific and self-disciplined.

Bob Charles, from New Zealand, is another uncommonly gifted putter. When he has his touch, he probably holes more putts in a streak than any other touring golfer. Bob's biggest problem derives from the fact that he does everything right-handed except play golf. It is difficult for him to get helpful instruction when he hits a bad patch, for it isn't as easy as you would think for a right-handed instructor to check the fine points of a left-hander's action. A reserved, likable, gentlemanly man, Bob has become much more gregarious since his marriage to Verity Aldridge, a wonderful girl who was Vivienne Player's best friend when they were growing up in South Africa. Bob can still look terribly solemn on a golf course, however. For me, the funniest line in any golf film is the one that accompanies the scene in the movie of the 1966 British Open in which, after Bob has rolled in a mammoth putt, he walks across the green stone-faced and glum to retrieve the ball. As the walk begins, the narrator states in a brisk voice, "And Bob wants all of you to know how deliriously happy he is."

From time to time, since the pro golf tour, as I had come to know, amounts to a small set world of its own, I would arrange for a change of pace by inviting some of my old friends from Columbus to come out for a visit. For example, Bob Hoag, a fellow about ten years older than me who's in insurance, regularly made the Crosby and played as my partner in the pro-amateur competition. Hoag is an excellent all-round athlete. A banged-up knee cut short his football career, but he played on the Ohio State basketball team. I got to know him at Scioto where he was a 2 or 3 handicap. A big fellow who stands about six-two-and-a-half and weighs about 190, Bob not only has a cultivated, fluid golf swing but is really long; on occasions he has outdriven me not just on one hole but over a succession of holes. He always took the Crosby very seriously, but we never came close. One year, I think, we were nine shots back of the winning team, another year only eight. Hoag doesn't exactly suffer from an inferiority complex where his golf is concerned, though, and he was always telling people in Columbus, "If Nicklaus ever gets in shape for the Crosby, we'll kill them in the pro-am. I practically have to carry the team." So what happened? In 1967 I won the Crosby and the team of Nicklaus and Hoag missed the 54-hole cut. They'll never let him live it down in Columbus.

A little setback like that doesn't slow down a guy like Hoagy very much. Like every old athlete, he loves all kinds of competition and he is always bristling for action. He got a lot of it the week after we played the Crosby in 1965. That year Arnold and I both skipped the Lucky International the next week, and eight of us went to Erawan Gardens in Palm Desert for a holiday—Arnold and Winnie, Barbara and I, Hoag and his wife Louise, and Bob and Jean McCall, friends of the Palmers and ours from Gary, Indiana. Every day Palmer and McCall, a former All-American guard and a good golfer, took on Hoag and me at Indian Wells, and every day they flattened us. One round I had eleven pars and seven birdies for a 65, and Hoag and I lost eighteen $10 bets. The last of them went down the drain when Arnold eagled the last hole. He had a 66 with four penalty strokes. Then, every night Palmer and McCall took on Nicklaus and Hoag at the bridge table. Every night we lost the dinner rubber and had to pick up the tab for eight. Hoag's assessment of the week was that I had played rotten golf and worse bridge, and that he had been flawless. He had just gotten bad lies and bad cards.

The winter after that, at the conclusion of the Crosby, six of us took off for a holiday at a secluded spot in Baja California, Hacienda a Cabo San Lucas, which is renowned for its marlin fishing. Our party included Barbara and me, the flawless Hoag and his wife, and another old Columbus friend, Pandel Savic, and his wife Janice. Pandel—he's of Macedonian extraction, was born in Yugoslavia, and came to the States when he was nine—was an outstanding quarterback at Ohio State. He made the All-Big Ten team and led O.S.U. to a 17–14 victory over California in the 1950 Rose Bowl game. I've known Pandel since I was a boy, for he used to hang around my dad's drugstore, the one across the street from the college campus. (If I can believe Pandel, our first encounter came when I was nine. He was sitting at the soda fountain when he spotted this kid filling his pockets with candy, and called the clerk's attention to it. "Oh, don't bother about him," the clerk said. "That's Charlie's boy.") Pandel, as I keep telling him diplomatically, has a very artificial golf swing. He's strong as an ox, though, and he concentrates like a beaver on each shot, and has brought himself down to a 3 or 2 handicap. He has played in the Crosby and the big annual pro-am in Cincinnati, and he always carries his share of the load. Well, the winter the Nicklauses, the Hoags, and the Savics were together at Cabo San Lucas there was no golf, since there was no course handy. However, there was fishing to vie at and there were tennis courts, paddle-tennis courts, and a sand-on-cement croquet court, and we poured our energy and ego into those diversions. I had quite a streak there. I won at everything—I mean *everything*. Each morning I caught the first large marlin. In the afternoons I was the undefeated star of the tennis and paddle-tennis matches. At night, after dinner, we would play seven or eight games of croquet, and no one could touch me. I was a very poor winner, no question about it. I had no modesty, no reserve. I even took it upon myself to straighten Hoagy and Pandel out, whatever we were doing. They hated my arrogance but they put up with it until Friday morning, I think it was. Pandel, at long last, had hooked his first good-sized marlin, and as he was struggling to bring it in, I began telling him how he was doing everything wrong —how, if you're pumping a fish, what you want to do is to lean back and raise your rod, and then, as you drop your rod, you reel in as hard as you can to gain line. Pandel looked up panting and sweating. "La Boca Grande!" he exploded. "Old Big Mouth. Will you shut up for once and let me catch my own fish!" Everyone loved that. After that no one called me anything but La Boca Grande, and if I get out of line with this crowd even today, I can be sure the next sentence will be something on the order of, "La Boca, you're still as charming as ever."

As my education as a golfer continued, I came into increasingly

188

frequent contact with celebrities from the entertainment world, both on and off the course, and, like the rest of the fellows, gradually became more at ease in their company. Just when I was beginning to regard myself as a very smooth operator, I pulled one of the prize boners of my career at the Crosby. My birthday generally falls during the week of that tournament, and that particular year, as usual, a lot of people who were at Pebble thoughtfully remembered the date, January 21. One who did was John Swanson, from San Francisco. John telephoned my room in the Del Monte Lodge from the cocktail bar on the ground floor. Just as he was about to hang up, he told me to hold on, there was another fellow at the bar who wanted to say hello. This fellow came on very strong. He started to sing "Happy Birthday to You," taking his time, and went all the way through the song.

"To whom am I speaking, please?" I asked rather formally.

"Bing Crosby. Happy birthday, Jack."

I think I mumbled I was sorry but I hadn't recognized the voice. This is called, I believe, putting La Foota in La Boca.

XIII

Another Spring,
Another Masters

THE MASTERS IS NOT the most important golf tournament in the world. That distinction still belongs to the U.S. Open simply because it is the national championship of the world's leading golf nation. Among the four major championships, the Masters must be content to be ranked second, a notch above the British Open and the P.G.A. Yet what an achievement this is when you consider that where the British Open was started in 1860, our Open in 1895, and the P.G.A. in 1916, the Masters dates only from 1934 when it was begun as a modest invitational tournament, a spring get-to-gether at which Bob Jones, a co-founder and the president of the Augusta National Golf Club, acted as host to his old friends and rivals during a four-day event held over the course he co-designed with Alistair MacKenzie, the Scottish golf architect.

Looking backward, it is easy to see why the Masters grew to prominence so rapidly. It had all the necessary ingredients, and then some! Bob Jones' presence infused the tournament with flavor and spirit—the spirit of golf at its best. The course, which Jones annually improved in the early years, revamping certain features of certain holes to make them play better and stronger, established itself in no time as one of the most testing and interesting inland courses in the world, strategic golf at its finest. The beauty of the course, of the whole Augusta National plant, was overwhelming. The club occupied the site of one of the South's great nurseries, and the hillsides and banks beneath the tall, straight pines bloomed with azaleas, dogwood, red bud, camellias, and dozens of other flowers and flowering shrubs. You didn't have to be a golf fan to respond to the charms of the Augusta National, but if you happened to be, the Masters usually became your favorite tournament. It offered unrivaled spectator facilities, that's for sure: you could see much more of the play than you could at any other event. In fact, every phase of the Masters was clearly thought out and carefully executed, for from the outset the administration of the tournament was the province of a remarkable man, Clifford Roberts, a New York investment banker, whose chief purpose in life was (and is) to make the Masters the pre-eminent sports event in the world. As the perennial chairman of the Masters, Mr. Roberts works at this every week of the year.

In addition to all these pluses, the Masters has several other things going for it. Taking place as it does the first full week in April, it occupies a choice spot on the golf calendar: it heralds the coming of spring and another golf season. Moreover, as the only major championship held over the same course each year, it has become, like Wimbledon and the Kentucky Derby and the Rose Bowl, an institution as well as an event. When a golf fan attends the Open, by the time he gets to know his way around, it's time to check out of his hotel room and head home; it may be a decade before the Open is held at that particular club again. The Masters—it's like returning home, you get to know it so well from your yearly visits. Everybody is there.

Down in the press building (and occasionally out on the course), the golf writers from all over the country are gathered in force. On the winter tour, Lincoln Werden of *The New York Times* is the only man who makes most of the different stops, but all the fellows are at Augusta—Maury Fitzgerald from Washington; Joe Looney, Tom Fitzgerald, and Roger Barry from Boston; Joe Schwendeman and Fred Byrod from Philadelphia, Al Laney, Dana Mozley, Gene Roswell, and Des Sullivan from the New York metropolitan area; Waxo Green and John Bibb from Nashville; Wally Wallis from Oklahoma City; John Walter from Detroit; Jesse Outlaw and Furman Bisher from Atlanta; Jim MacDonald from Orlando; George Bugby and David Bloom from Memphis; Will Grimsley and Milt Richman from the wire services; Al Wright, Dan Jenkins, Dick Taylor, Dick Aultman, Ross Goodner, and Mark Mulvoy from the national magazines—and this doesn't begin to cover a tenth of the old familiar faces nor does it touch on the British press, golf's last aristocrats, or the innumerable fellows in radio and television.

The crowd that throngs the terrace between the clubhouse and the practice green comprises a veritable Who's Who in Golf—former champions and teen-age hopefuls, representatives of the golf equipment companies, players' wives and children, emissaries from most of the big tour tournaments, golfers and golf devotees from all over the globe, entrepreneurs like Mark McCormack and Fred Corcoran and Ed Carter, not to mention the members of the host club in their bright Augusta National green blazers, the officials of the U.S.G.A. crisply bedecked, the officials of the P.G.A. in their scarlet blazers, and, from time to time, Doug Sanders in his latest assault on the rainbow. This is golf's most complete annual gathering, no question about it. Everybody is "up" for spring and the first major championship.

I made my first visit to the Masters in 1959, qualifying for an invitation as a member of that year's Walker Cup team. I went down the week before the tournament with Bob Obetz, a good friend (later my best man at my wedding) and an Ohio State golfer. I didn't realize that I couldn't take a guest to the Masters with me, but an Augusta National member, Mr. Alec Osborne, kindly took Bob onto the course as his guest and we played some warm-up rounds together until Ward Wettlaufer, Deane Beman, and other players I knew began to arrive. Six young amateurs—Ward, Deane, Tommy Aaron, Dick Foote, Phil Rodgers, and myself—were put up in the Crow's Nest, a dormitory at the top of the clubhouse, just below the glassed-in cupola. Each morning we'd get up, climb the ladder in the center of the room that led to the cupola, and look out over the golf course. After checking the wind and the weather, we'd know whether we wanted to take a little more sack time or get out onto the course as soon as possible and play all those great holes.

It was marvelous at Augusta. I loved the way they let amateurs sign for everything. After four days, they clamped down on Phil Rodgers and me and wouldn't let us order two steaks apiece at dinner, but we were still allowed a double shrimp cocktail. I also loved the course. It has often been said—and one heard it continually when Arnold and I won six of the seven Masters between 1960 and 1966—that, with its extra-wide fairways and its almost complete absence of rough, the Augusta National favors the power golfer. To a degree, that's true. The big hitter has an advantage there, but, I hasten to add, only if he hits the ball in the right direction. When you look back through the list of Masters champions, you will come across the names of quite a few golfers who weren't exceptionally long: Henry Picard, Herman Keiser, Claude Harmon, Jimmy Demaret (a three-time winner), Jack Burke, Doug Ford, Art Wall, Gary Player, and Bob Goalby. While length helps a bit more perhaps than it does at some other courses, to win there takes sound all-round golf; you must really be in command of your irons to bring the ball in on the proper side of the flag, and you must be a very good putter to cope with the brisk contours and the subtle little rolls on the huge greens.

In my debut in the Masters I played pretty fair golf but my total of 150 for the first two rounds was a stroke too high to make the cut, although I was only nine shots behind the 36-hole leader, Arnold Palmer. The eventual winner, Art Wall, made the cut by only two shots. This was one of the reasons why the Masters revised its format so that any player within ten shots of the leader qualified for the last two rounds whether or not he stood among the low 44 scorers at the halfway mark.

My failure to get to play all four rounds was a keen disappointment. I had really played better than my score, hitting 31 of the 36 greens in regulation, but eight 3-putt greens finished me. I went right home after missing the cut. I didn't want to hang around if I wasn't playing. That's hard. It's sort of like attending a wedding where your girl friend is marrying some other guy.

In 1960 I stayed in the Crow's Nest a second time, but after that I did what many players do during the Masters—I went in with friends and rented a house for the tournament week. There are many nice homes available, for it has become a custom for the nongolf-minded local people to leave town during the tournament. For a number of years, Barbara and I rented the Myron Fogel residence, on Trafalgar Road, along with two couples from Columbus, Pandel and Janice Savic and Dr. Jack Lewis and his wife Diane. We lead rather quiet lives. If we want a change of pace, we drive over to Bellevue Avenue where my father and his friends rent the John Tobin home. The cast of characters in "Charlie's Gang" varies slightly from year to year, but, in addition to my dad and my uncle Frank, it usually consists of Asa Beavers, Bob Daniels, Bill Davis, Howard Hutchinson (whose son married my sister Marilyn), Al Johnson, and Wayne Brown—all of them Columbus businessmen. Jack Grout is also a regular, and some years Bill Foley, the wonderful photographer of the Columbus *Dispatch,* is also on hand.

"Charlie's Gang," ready for action at Augusta. (Uncle Frank stands behind my dad.) From the looks of things, it's early in the tournament.

When I think of "Charlie's Gang," the first thing that comes to mind is the size of their martinis—they're as big as a milkshake. When you enter the house, my father is usually standing in the middle of the living room replaying my round that day (saving at least three or four shots through headier management), and Uncle Frank is parading around the living room, a martini in one hand and a pitcherful of martinis in the other, seeing to it that nobody goes unnourished until the steaks or the chops finally appear. The men say otherwise, but I have an idea they all drink one martini less each year.

The fifth year I played at Augusta, in 1963, I broke through and won the first of my three Masters titles after finishing thirteenth in 1960, tying for seventh in 1961, and tying for fifteenth in 1962. I have described that 1963 Masters earlier and there is no need to reprise it. The following April, I tied for second with Dave Marr, but the tournament, as it always was those even-numbered years, was all Palmer. Never behind at any stage, Arnold won by six shots. All four days he played beautiful golf. My rounds—71, 73, 71, 67

—exceeded my expectations, in a way. That spring I was battling a tension problem. For some reason or other, my right wrist and forearm had become tight and rigid at address and during the swing. My hands had no life coming back, and at the top of the backswing I had no wrist-cock whatsoever. This frozen hand-action is what caused my bad shank on the twelfth.

During the tournaments that followed the Masters, this tension abated from time to time, but it still bothered me. It wasn't until late June that I discovered a cure for it one morning when I was on the practice range at Highland Park during the Cleveland Open. The high position of my right-hand grip on the club was what was tightening up my wrist and forearm, so I tried changing my grip, softening it by moving my right hand down a bit, more to the right. That fixed things up and I stayed with it, but I wasn't too happy with my revised grip. I felt I had a better grip when my right hand rode higher. However, as every tournament player knows, as you grow older and the elasticity goes out of your muscles, whether you like it or not, you must make certain compromises and adjustments in order to remain an effective golfer.

A few problems also popped up just previous to the Masters the next year, 1965. The fact of the matter, I suppose, is that a professional golfer is almost constantly beset by problems. If he's playing a circuit tournament, he can afford to let them slide, but he can't when a major championship is at stake. Most of us start getting ready for the Masters, for example, a good month before the tournament, and as we try to raise our games, we naturally get fussier and tend to become anxious when things aren't coming along the way we would like them to. This may explain in part, anyway, why so many years just previous to the Masters my game has caused me concern. In 1965 what troubled me was the way I was hooking my shots. I had begun hooking them at Jacksonville, and then when I went up to Augusta to begin my on-the-spot preparation the next week—the week before the Masters—I couldn't get rid of that hook. I decided to go down to see Jack Grout at La Gorce. Jack got me to move my hands up higher on the backswing and into a much better position at the top. Though I was still drawing the ball, I wasn't hooking it, and I was hitting it solidly. Besides, a draw isn't bad at Augusta. If you play the ball that way and you're on your game, you can certainly win there just as easily as a left-to-right player can.

195

However, when I returned to Augusta and played a practice round with Deane Beman, something new had gone wrong with my swing. I was spraying the ball all over the premises. Midway through the round, Deane thought he spotted my trouble. I always listen to Deane because he's a sound analyst of swings and he knows mine very well. "You're doing something I've never seen you do before," he told me. "Your feet are lined up correctly, but just before you start back you're closing your shoulders and your hips. You're blocked out when you come down, and that's what's causing your inconsistency." Deane had hit it right on the nose. When I corrected this closing of the shoulders and hips and took the club straight back from the ball, the other moves began to fall into place, I began to come more "under" the ball on my downswing, and I began to get a mild fade on my shots, which is what I like. I played a practice round with Ben Hogan the next day, Saturday, and played well. Greatly relieved, I flew home for a couple of days of relaxation broken only by an hour of practice each day. I got back to Augusta on Monday night, shot a 67 the next day and a 33 on a final nine-hole tune-up on Wednesday. My, I had been lucky! Not that I deserved much of the credit for it, but on the eve of the tournament, after all of these complications, my game was at its absolute peak.

My opening tee-shot on Thursday was the Jack Nicklaus Special, a snappy hook. I put my approach, an 8-iron, eight feet from the flag, but when I got down over the putt I was so nervous I could hardly concentrate. When I found myself half-backing away from that putt, I stopped and tried to goad myself into a positive mood: I had to bear down and get that ball into the cup—any jerko could miss it gracefully, I told myself. I managed to hole that putt, and this dispelled my nervousness then and there. As I recall, I made only one real error the rest of the way—a pulled iron off the twelfth. On that opening day, however, the Augusta National played as easy as I can ever remember. The 67 I shot was only one of ten scores under 70. Gary was in front with a 65, and Dan Sikes, Tony Lema, and Tommy Aaron also had had 67s. While I was happy at having gotten off on a good foot, I still felt like kicking myself. I hadn't taken full advantage of the perfect scoring conditions. One thing for sure—I hadn't worked hard enough on the greens.

On Friday the Augusta National was much more like its old self. The pins were tucked in hard positions, and a stiff breeze swept over the course. It took darn good golf to match par, 72. Only a handful of players broke 72 and only one man broke 70—Arnold with a 68. I had a 71 to share the lead at the halfway mark with Arnold and Gary at 138. Again I felt like kicking myself at the close of the round. Going to the eleventh I had been two under par for the day, but I had suffered a costly lapse on that hole and on the next two as well, dropping a stroke to par on each of them. On the eleventh I plain looked up on a chip from the rough behind the green; on the twelfth I fluffed another chip; on the thirteenth, eager to get rolling again, I tried to get home in two with a 3-wood from a sticky lie in the pine needles in the right rough and succeeded only in slicing the ball into the creek. I did finish strong, though, birdying both the fifteenth and sixteenth. If I could just stop being so sloppy, I felt I could win this Masters. I was splitting the fairways the way I had at Merion in 1960, and I was hitting the ball very long.

On Saturday, we again had practically ideal scoring conditions. There was scarcely any breeze. Friday's winds had dried out the fairways and made them fast, but the greens were still holding approach shots well and they were excellent for putting. (In the press tent after my round I declared rather grandly that "the greens are approaching proper tournament speed." I remember this because I was kidded so much about it—you know, a veteran of twenty-five leaning back and sounding so condescending when talking about one of the most carefully maintained courses in the world.) On this third round I finally did take advantage of the conditions. I was around in 64, tying the record low score for eighteen holes which Lloyd Mangrum had set twenty-five years before. It is a round that I am very proud of, and I would like to reconstruct it, if I may, hole by hole. One thing more. In enumerating the clubs I used on my approach shots, I am aware that I may forward the impression that the Augusta National is a short course. It is anything but. On this round I got a lot of flight on my tee-shots because the air was unusually light, and I got a lot of roll on them because, as I mentioned earlier, the fairways were hard and dry. Also, I happened to have one of the best driving days of my life.

Hole 1. Par 4. 400 yards. Driver and sand wedge. Two putts from 25 feet. 4.

Hole 2. Par 5. 555 yards. A terrible drive pushed into the pines 60 feet from the fairway. A lucky opening, a wide channel back to the fairway and also toward the green. A good lie, too. A 3-iron recovery 50 yards short of the bunker before the green. A wedge 25 feet past the hole. One putt. 4. (This fortunate birdie was undoubtedly the making of the round.)

Hole 3. Par 4. 355 yards. Driver and pitching wedge. Two putts from eight feet. 4.

Hole 4. Par 3. 220 yards. (We used the short tee this day, however.) A 4-iron hit fat which ran to within 10 feet of the flag, set front and left-center. One putt. 2. (Another big break.)

Hole 5. Par 4. 450 yards. Driver and 6-iron. Two putts from 20 feet. 4.

Hole 6. Par 3. 190 yards. 6-iron 20 feet from the pin. One putt. 2.

Hole 7. Par 4. 365 yards. Driver and pitching wedge two feet from the pin. One putt. 3.

Hole 8. Par 5. 530 yards. Driver and 3-iron 75 feet from the pin. Two putts. 4.

Hole 9. Par 4. 420 yards. Driver and pitching wedge. Two putts from 20 feet. 4.

(Out in 31. Five birdies, four pars.)

The 16th green, third round. A long one falls for a birdie 2.

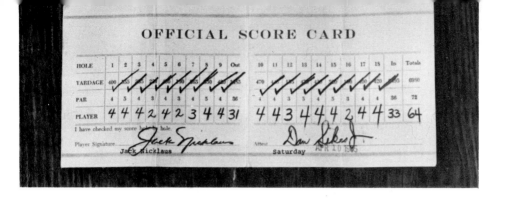

Hole 10.   Par 4. 470 yards (downhill). Driver and 8-iron. Two putts from 20 feet. 4.

Hole 11.   Par 4. 445 yards. Driver and 8-iron. Two putts from 50 feet. 4.

Hole 12.   Par 3. 155 yards. 8-iron four feet from the pin. Two putts. 3.

Hole 13.   Par 5. 475 yards. Driver and 5-iron 45 feet from the pin. Two putts. 4.

Hole 14.   Par 4. 420 yards. Driver pushed into the edge of the rough. 7-iron 25 feet from the pin. Two putts. 4.

Hole 15.   Par 5. 520 yards. Driver and 5-iron onto back fringe of green, 60 feet from the pin. Chip to two feet. One putt. 4.

Hole 16.   Par 3. 190 yards. 6-iron 14 feet from the pin. One putt. 2.

Hole 17.   Par 4. 400 yards. Driver and 8-iron onto front fringe 30 feet from the pin. Two putts. 4.

Hole 18.   Par 4. 420 yards. Driver and pitching wedge 25 feet from the pin. Two putts. 4.

(Back in 33. Three birdies, six pars.)

Score: Out 444 242 344 — 31
         In 443 444 244 — 33
                            ———
                            64

The round was made up of eight birdies and ten pars. I didn't have a 5 on the card. I missed two fairways off the tee but hit all the greens in regulation except the seventeenth where my approach landed on the green but spun back onto the apron. I took 30 putts.

This 64 gave me a five-shot lead over the closest man, Gary Player, and put me in a position to challenge Ben Hogan's record four-round total of 274, set in 1953. I would need a 71 to break it. I noted this, of course, but it occupied little of my attention then. My main concern was to go out and play a good strong fourth round, and win.

199

On the third round my playing partner had been Dan Sikes. Before entering professional golf, Dan was a lawyer, which may possibly explain why he doesn't feel right unless he's complaining about something. I like him very much. On the last round I had another most agreeable pairing—I drew Mason Rudolph. Mase is never dour, he's pleasant to chat with, and he's very courteous without calling attention to it—an ideal partner to have on a fourth round when you're leading a big tournament. Even when you're holding as comfortable a margin as five strokes, as I was, setting the pace on the last day of a tournament creates pressures and problems. The worst error you can make is to play too cautiously, too defensively, for pars can slip into bogeys only too easily; and then if someone else suddenly gets hot, you're in trouble. On that particular last round, I got off very fast, and that helped. I birdied the first, and after two pars, holed from 14 feet for a birdie 2 on the tough fourth. I missed my par on the fifth but then, playing good unfancy golf, made my pars on the next four holes to reach the turn in 35. It was another nice sunny day, perhaps a trifle breezier than Saturday but great golf weather. No one was making a rush at me, though. In fact, whenever I checked a scoreboard, I learned that my lead was widening if anything.

Two more pars and then I came to the twelfth, that unnerving 155-yarder over Rae's Creek. You can take any score there, as so many fourth-round leaders have learned. It had almost cost me the tournament in 1963. This day the pin was on the right side of the green, behind the bunker. I ignored it and played the percentage shot for the middle of the green. My 8-iron pulled up on the left side of the green about 25 feet from the pin. I hit my putt well, the ball had the line and struck the back of the cup and dropped. What a slew of putts I had made on the par 3s! All in all, I had picked up seven birdies on them, and they are as formidable a set of 3s as you'll find on any course. As a few people pointed out afterward, for all the distance I was getting off the tees, I may well have won the tournament on the short holes.

After that long putt went down on the twelfth, for the first time I felt fairly confident of victory; I was 16 under par now for the tournament and I think my lead was up to eight shots. For the first time, too, I really thought I had an excellent chance to break Hogan's record 274. Well, I wasn't going to think too much about that. If I broke the record I broke it, and if I didn't I didn't. My job was to win the Masters. I hadn't done that yet.

Over the last six holes, the only incidents were minor ones. On the fifteenth I ran into my first three-putt green of the entire tournament. I went too boldly for the 25-footer I had for an eagle, the ball twisted out of the cup, and I then missed the five-footer I'd left myself. On the seventeenth, where I wasn't really looking for a birdie, I made one. The pin was on the right side, toward the back, and I felt a 9-iron was the right stick. My caddie Willie thought it was only a wedge. I told him I wouldn't hit the 9 too hard. When my approach stopped a foot from the hole, I reached over and pulled the bill of Willie's cap down over his eyes—at that stage we were feeling pretty good about things. I parred the home hole for a 69 and a four-round total of 271, three strokes below the old mark, nine strokes in front of Gary and Arnold who tied for second.

What a wonderful day that was for me! The crowd was with me all the way, cheering and urging me on, and I hope I was able to express at least some of the gratitude I felt. To top everything off, at the presentation ceremony Bob Jones remarked that in his opinion my play in the 1965 Masters was perhaps the finest performance ever in a championship. "Jack," he added, "is playing an entirely different game—a game I'm not even familiar with." I must say that I'm not familiar with that type of golf myself. I have never since consistently hit my drives as far and as straight or my irons as accurately over 72 holes as I did in that Masters—and then there were all those long putts that fell for me. That week everything just happened to come together. Last but not least, when I needed to be lucky (like on the second hole on the third round), I *was* lucky.

In 1966 I successfully defended my Masters title and became the first player ever to help himself into the green jacket that is the emblem of victory. The next year, however, I played so poorly, on and around the greens in particular, that I didn't even make the cut and became the first player in recent history to suffer that fate as the defending champion in both the Open (1963) and the Masters (1967). Up you go, down you go—the game is like that.

While my victory in the 1966 Masters warrants no detailed examination, I would like to touch on a few aspects of it. Each tournament a golfer wins takes on an individual shape and coloration—

its own personality, you might say. I think of the 1966 Masters as a tournament I was extremely fortunate to win. To begin with, my golf was much spottier than the year before at Augusta. On top of that, I won out only after a playoff with Gay Brewer and Tommy Jacobs, and there might not have been a playoff had Gay holed the five-foot side-hill putt he had for his par on the 72nd green. It was a very strange tournament. Whenever a man played himself into the lead, he proceeded to lose it so quickly that after a while the standard comment around the clubhouse was that no one apparently wanted to win the 1966 Masters. It certainly didn't look as if I wanted to. I moved into the lead several times over the four rounds and couldn't hold it for the life of me. A opening 68 put me three shots ahead of the field, but on Friday, the day of the second round, I squandered them all, and more, by three-putting five greens, ending up with a swell 76. On Saturday I moved out in front again by playing the first eleven holes in three under par, and then I went and took a double bogey on the twelfth when I stuck my tee-shot in the bank behind the green. I settled down after that and going to the seventeenth I led by two. You guessed it. I succeeded in bogeying both the seventeenth and the eighteenth.

Some observers attributed the in-and-out character of my play to improper preparation, and I must agree with them. That winter I had taken things easier than I had in previous years. In February, Barbara and I made a trip to South Africa where we had a wonderful visit with the Players incidental to my playing a series of exhibition matches with Gary on his native heath. On my return I entered the Doral, the Florida Citrus, and the Jacksonville Opens—I finished thirteenth, second, and eighth—which I thought would give my game just the tune-up it would need for the Masters. Evidently it didn't. My practice rounds at Augusta were mediocre, and I was lucky that my private pro, Deane Beman, was once again on hand to diagnose my trouble: I was taking the club back at a correct tempo but I was rushing the downswing, and as often as not I was starting down before I had completed my backswing. Even when I had rectified this, I wasn't sharp enough to be able to bear down during the tournament and keep a lead once I had it. I did play a high number of very good shots, I thought, but I also played many more loose shots than I normally do.

The evening before the first round I suffered a deep personal loss. Bob Barton, a very close friend whom I admired so much, was killed along with his wife Linda and another couple from Columbus, Jim and Jeretta Long, also good friends of mine, in an airplane crash near Johnson City, Tennessee. They were on their way to the Masters, and Bob, an Air Force Reserve pilot with 4000 hours, was flying a Beach Travelair he had leased from a friend. Over the Great Smokies, very treacherous country, ice formed on the wings, and the plane crashed as Bob was trying to bring it down into an airport. Barbara broke the news to me just before we went to bed. She had learned about the crash from a local announcer with the N.B.C. affiliate in Augusta. I won't go into my feelings except to say that I didn't want to play in the tournament. Barbara thought that I should play, so I did.

I must say that after I had wasted so many chances in that 1966 Masters, I was proud of the way I managed to come back late on the fourth round when it looked as if I was definitely out of the tournament. With five holes to go, after I had failed to get the birdie on the par-5 thirteenth I had been counting on, I stood three strokes behind Brewer, who had taken over the lead on the ninth and had clung to it with an unbroken run of pars. Gay was playing two pairs ahead of me. Tommy Jacobs, a stroke behind Brewer, was playing just in front of me. I made up one of those three strokes on the fourteenth, a 420-yard par 4, where I hit my best shot of the tournament, a 3-iron six feet from the pin, to get my birdie 3. The reason why I needed so much club was that I had pulled my drive into the trees on the left and the ball had rebounded toward the tee. From that far back, getting into the pin was quite an assignment. The green on the fourteenth is made up of a large upper terrace—the pin was on the right—separated from a thin, lower strip in front by a real St. Andrews contour, an abrupt dip that breaks down toward the fairway like a cresting wave. I knew I couldn't hold a long iron on the green if I flew it all the way to the upper terrace—it isn't that deep—so I played the ball to land on the front apron and to climb up the face of the contour and onto the upper terrace, and it did.

I made up a second stroke on the long fifteenth with another good iron, a 2-iron which I had to hook around the pine tree on the left side of the fairway which stymied my direct route to the green. The third stroke—I got that one back when Brewer missed that curling five-footer and bogeyed the eighteenth. This opened

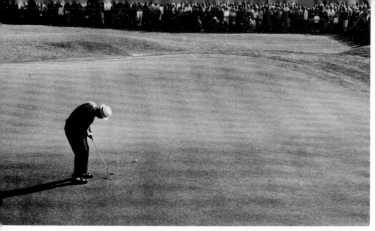

"The best putt I ever hit

the gate for Jacobs, too. Now he could tie Brewer by parring the eighteenth, which he did, thanks to a magnificent 3-wood second that he put 20 feet from the pin, centered on the lower level of that two-level green. The eighteenth is only 420 yards, but Jacobs needed a wood to get home since his tee-shot had caught the pines on the right and ricocheted laterally onto the fairway.

For a fleeting moment, Brewer's bogey placed me in a position to win the tournament outright, for seconds after that I put my 9-iron to the seventeenth just three feet past the hole. Man, the situation had changed fast! Now, if I could hole that little birdie putt, I'd be in the lead. I missed it. Did I ever! The ball was hardly on its way when it broke left. It didn't even touch the hole. A really bad putt. On the eighteenth I came awfully close to holing a birdie putt that was as difficult as the one on the seventeenth was easy. There my approach bounced up the green onto the upper level, about

that didn't go in the hole."

30 feet past the cup, which was cut at the bottom of the slope. When I was studying the line, trying to figure how many inches to the left the putt would break and how much I would have to allow for that, I noticed at the peak of the slope a small brown spot in the green, made by an old ball mark, that sat exactly on the line I had decided on. I couldn't have had a better guide-mark if I had placed a dime on the grass. I aimed for that brown spot and tried to tap the ball so that it would be dying as it reached it, barely moving when it caught the downslope. The ball rolled over the brown spot at just the right speed and came trickling down the grade. As it did, it swung two or three inches to the left and was heading dead for the cup. Eight inches away, it was in . . . and then it slid a quarter of an inch to the left and, instead of falling, ghosted over the rim of the cup. I think of it as the best putt I've ever hit that didn't go in the hole.

205

The 15th green: the crucial shot in the playoff of the 1966 Masters.

In the playoff Gay was not at his best but Tommy was. I don't believe I have ever seen him swing so rhythmically and meet the ball so solidly. The difference between my 70 and Tommy's 72 was that I holed three good-sized putts—a 20-footer downhill on the sixth, a 25-footer on the eleventh that put me in front by two, and a 14-footer on the fifteenth that I had to get to match Tommy's birdie and maintain my two-stroke lead. Some days you putt well and make nothing. Some days the ball rolls for you.

I look forward to being an annual starter in the Masters for many years to come. Indeed, I hope I'll be able to be on hand long after my best golf is behind me and when the teen-agers of that future generation, watching me paunchily puffing up the eighth fairway, will wonder what that old geezer's doing out on the same course with the current champions. Every golfer wants to remain a part of the game, and at Augusta, regardless of your vintage, you are in the midst of things, a member of the clan. I find it as hard to picture a year away from the Masters as a year away from my family at Christmas. No other occasion in golf compares with it, and I trust it never changes. I want to drive with my grandchildren down that breathtaking double lane of magnolias that leads to the clubhouse and show them everything—Ike's Cottage, and the Trophy Room with the portraits of Bob Jones and Cliff Roberts, and the Crow's Nest, and the par-3 course, and, out on the big course, the tenth with its towering pines, the Hogan and the Nelson Bridges, the great thirteenth, and perhaps even a few spots where their old man's old man hit one in the general direction of the flag.

Tommy Jacobs stands at the left, Willie Peterson performs at the right.

XIV

International Golf,
the British Open in Particular

A T ALL THE PRESTIGE TOURNAMENTS, and many of the lesser
events, one man in the galleries stands out like a sore
thumb. A tall, well-built, handsome, fidgety, blond young man in
his thirties, he has seemingly arrived at the golf course by mistake,
for he is always dressed in a light-gray flannel suit and is invariably
carrying an attaché case—the two symbols of that other world
where one walks on pavement and not on grass. He knows exactly
where he is, though; in fact, he probably knows as much about the
world of golf as any man living today. This tall young fellow with
the symmetrical good looks of a leading man in a B movie is
Mark McCormack, a lawyer from Cleveland, who presently acts
as the business manager for Arnold Palmer, Gary Player, and me,
his first clients, and also for Doug Sanders, Bob Charles, Bruce
Devlin, Mason Rudolph, Bobby Cole, the fine young South African star, and Tony Jacklin and Peter Townsend, the two best
young English prospects in years. Mark has now built a large
organization—Jay Lafave, his right-hand man, takes care of a good
part of my business—but Mark personally handles the most important contracts and the other major deals involving the members
of his stable. He is extremely able, to say the least. A low-handicap
golfer, he understands the game and is a competent judge of young
players. When he entered the world of professional golf in 1960
as Arnold's manager, he sensed far better than anyone had before
the public appeal and commercial potential that a top golfer possesses these days. A shrewd negotiator (he went to Yale Law
School after graduating from William & Mary), he has been able
to obtain excellent payment for his clients' services and to uncover
a hundred and one new sources of revenue for them.

Along the way, Mark has made a few bucks himself, which is as it should be. He surely stands as one of the outstanding success stories of this era, as well as one of its ranking "characters." For example, if you think Palmer or Player or Nicklaus has a large wardrobe, you should see McCormack's. It's so vast—at last inventory Mark owned something like 97 sports jackets—that to house it he had to build a clothes "closet" twenty feet by fifteen. When you walk into it, you think you're in Abercrombie & Fitch. So what does Mark do with all these clothes to choose from? He wears that light-gray flannel suit day in and day out. He's attached to it because he got it in Hong Kong for practically nothing.

At the time Mark entered the picture, professional golf was beginning to gain much more extensive popularity in America because of television, and, for a number of reasons, interest in the game was increasing at a rapid rate not only in America but all around the world. By the time I signed with Mark late in 1961, he had both learned the ropes of television and blossomed out as an international traveler, as much at home in Melbourne and Manila as in Cleveland. He was just beginning, though. Compare, for example, the first trip I made to Japan under Mark's aegis, in 1963, with the trip I made there four years later. The 1963 trip was underwritten by the Norfolk & Western Railroad, which was interested in selling more coal to Japanese steel companies, and I simply played "customer golf" with the Japanese executives. The 1967 trip started with my playing a television match with Chen Ching-po. Chen, a Formosan who has lived in Japan for quite some time, gave up his job as the pro at the Tokyo Golf Club a few years ago in order to accept an offer from the Japan Broadcasting Company to become the pro at the company's private club and to act as host on a television golf series—a most successful series, incidentally. Chen won our match by two shots. He had a 66 (with 25 putts) and I had a 68 (with 27 putts). His control off the tee was fabulous that day. He not only didn't miss a fairway, he was never more than three yards from the center of the fairway. I then joined Palmer and Player for a 54-hole Big Three match—18 holes at Kasumigaseki, 18 at Nagoya, and 18 at Osaka. Gary and I finished in a tie with totals of 211. We halved the first two holes of sudden death, and by then it was so dark there wasn't enough light for the cameras, so we called it a draw. The entire 54 holes were filmed for later showing on television. The Japanese television

209

crew, by the way, was terrific—much faster than ours generally are. We never had to wait. We just played along at our normal speed, and the crew, completely motorized, was always set up, ready and waiting for us. It was made up of 40 men, including 17 cameramen —the largest TV crew that had ever been assembled in Japan except for the wedding of the Crown Prince.

There is a great deal of fascination in international golf, but before proceeding further with this, I would like to discuss television and golf for a moment. As that 1967 trip to Japan brings out, in addition to carrying live telecasts of the top tournaments, the networks in many countries today present taped or filmed golf series. It occurs to me that if I simply set down, year by year, the different shows on which I have appeared, it would provide a serviceable index to the development of this side of golf.

In 1962, my first year as a professional, I participated in two television matches. On "Shell's Wonderful World of Golf," I had an exciting match with Sam Snead, at Pebble Beach, which I won with a birdie on the last hole, and on "Challenge Golf" I teamed with Phil Rodgers against Player and Palmer in a four-ball match, at the Los Angeles Country Club, which we lost 3 and 2. ("Challenge Golf" was the first television show with which Mark Mc-Cormack was connected. Gary and Arnold were the host stars and each week they took on a different pair of challengers.) . . . In 1963 I made a second appearance on "Challenge Golf." Mike Souchak and I met Arnold and Gary at Pauma Valley, and we went down 2 and 1. This, I believe, was my only appearance in a TV match that year. . . . In 1964 I joined Arnold and Gary for a series of eight "Big Three" matches, four of them filmed at the Firestone course in Akron and four at the brand-new Mauna Kea course on the island of Hawaii. They were shown the next winter. (I finished first in this series, with Arnold second.) . . . In 1965 we shot another "Big Three" series, only four matches this time, two at Firestone and two at Indian Wells, in Palm Desert. (Arnold finished first and I was second.) This series was shown in 1966. . . . In 1966 Mark branched out a bit. He arranged with the B.B.C. for a show called "The Big Three in Britain," and Jay Michaels, Mark's television specialist, directed the production—18 holes at Gleneagles, 18 at Carnoustie, and 18 at St. Andrews. Incredibly, Arnold, Gary, and I each ended up with the same total: 219. We later played off the triple tie at Dorado Beach, in Puerto Rico. (Arnold won.) We filmed "The Big Three in Britain" after the 1966 British Open. Before the championship I played a match at Wentworth, outside of London, against Peter Alliss, the English professional, for a series called "The U.S.A. Against The World," another McCormack-B.B.C. venture. The following year, also for that series, I played Roberto de Vicenzo at Birkdale. I beat Peter by one or two shots, as I remember it, and Roberto beat me by two. . . . Add to this the television matches in Japan in 1967 and we're up to date. Next year I think we should be ready for a sequel, maybe "Son of the Big Three."

The painfully slow crawl of a television match—some still take several days to complete if there isn't sufficient light for color—makes this form of golf much less enjoyable for me than tournament golf. I'm sure that one of the reasons why I've fared so well in the "World Series of Golf," the annual 36-hole match among the winners of the year's four major championships, is that the "World Series," while primarily a TV feature, is telecast live, and the foursome has to play along at a good golfing clip in order to complete the last six holes of each round, the usual televised segment, in the allotted time.

To get back to international golf. Growing up at Scioto as I did and learning about Bobby Jones when I was just a boy, it was natural for me to think of golf as at least a trans-Atlantic game; Jones' triumphs in the British Open and Amateur dramatized this. My trip to Scotland with the 1959 Walker Cup team widened my golf horizon, and so did the 1960 World Amateur Team Championship for the Eisenhower Trophy at Merion in which thirty-two countries were represented. The idea that golf was a universal game appealed enormously to me. When I turned professional and signed with Mark McCormack, I was allied with a man who had much this same point of view. Mark, of course, was interested in tapping the lucrative foreign markets for his stable of players, but I also believe that he should be given credit for certain uncommercial motives as well. The fact that golf is played wherever grass grows (and in some places where it doesn't) has always intrigued him and continues to. He has the gift of enthusiasm and can become almost as wound up watching some stranger play in the Honshu Amateur as watching his own horses in a major championship.

One of the first contracts with a foreign manufacturer which Mark negotiated for me was with the Slazenger company. I play their clubs and ball in the British Open. My contract with Slazengers has called for me to help promote sales by making periodic trips to Australia, a real hotbed of golf. I have visited that continent five times—in 1962, 1963, 1964, 1965, and 1968. Like most Americans, I am very fond of Australia. I haven't seen as much of the country as I'd like to—unfortunately, when you're playing in a tournament, you don't get to see much besides the course, your hotel, and maybe one or two private homes—but I've been most impressed by the Australians I've met. They're friendly and they're warm and they must be the most unaffected people in the world. They know their golf, too. If you split a fairway with a well-struck 1-iron, you get much more applause from the discriminating galleries than if you smash out a tremendous drive that's not quite on the right line. Be that as it may, on my first visit the best I could manage was a fifth in the Australian Open and a fifth in the Wills Masters. Thereafter I've played somewhat better. I was second in the Wills on my next try and I won the Australian Open in 1964 and 1968. Happily, my victories in the Australian Open came at the tail end of comparatively lean years, and they meant a good deal to me.

The 1964 Open was played over the Lakes Course, in Sydney, a first-class layout that had been the scene of the 1963 Wills. In that earlier tournament, I hit one of the best woods of my career. It came on the sixteenth, a par 4 on which the fairway swings out wide to the left from the tee. If you take that route, and you hardly have any other choice, the hole plays as a drive and a medium iron. The direct route to the green is over an expanse of water that fills the entire area between the tee and the green—325 yards of water. One day when I came to the sixteenth there was a gale at my back, so I decided to gamble and go for the green. I caught a 3-wood nice and flush, and the gale carried the ball over the water and onto the green, 25 feet from the flag. Someone measured the distance: 351 yards. (Small ball, of course.)

When I came to the sixteenth on the third round of the 1964 Australian Open, I was trailing Bruce Devlin by either two or three shots, I forget which. Anyhow, I was in a position where I had to gamble. The wind was slightly behind and coming across from the right—a good wind but no gale—but I figured I had nothing to lose and went for the green with my driver. I almost swung myself off my feet, but I made square contact with the ball, and then I stood back and watched it travel over the water. It was an awfully close thing. The ball just did clear the far bank. It landed on soft turf and finished short of the putting surface, on the fringe. That was one drive that didn't pay off: I missed the birdie. However, on the last round Devlin mis-hit his approach on the last hole, we ended up in a tie, and I eventually won in an eighteen-hole playoff.

You have to play top-notch golf to win a tournament in Australia. That home guard is formidable—Devlin, Thomson, Nagle, and Crampton to start with, plus a lot of young men like Bob Stanton, Gary Coxon, Ted Ball, Billy Dunk, and Len Woodward who can also play. On my next visit I hope to get in at least one round at Royal Melbourne, reputedly the best test in Australia, but the courses I have played have generally been of a high quality.

One of the most enjoyable golfing trips I've ever made was a visit to South Africa in the winter of 1966. Gary Player had been trying for a long while to persuade me to come over to his homeland, and he was pretty clever about it. While he talked about the golf courses at considerable length, knowing how much I love fishing he stressed first and foremost that South Africa was an incomparable sportsman's paradise. When I agreed to come over, the wheels started turning. A series of six Player-Nicklaus matches was set up, Gary to be sponsored by the Rembrandt Tobacco Corporation and I by the Riggio Tobacco Corporation, which puts out a cigarette called Lexington. The Lexington people kindly included Barbara in their invitation, so I asked my parents and Barbara's to join us and make it a real family expedition. We were there for seventeen days and had a superb time. We saw a good bit of the beautiful countryside and some of the astonishing wildlife, and I got in some fishing, which was as good as Gary had promised. (Gary is rather new to fishing but, as you would expect, he's very stylish with a rod —Joe Form himself.)

While we were in Johannesburg, Barbara and I stayed with the Players, and our folks stayed at a downtown hotel operated by Reg Taylor, a member of South Africa's 1960 Eisenhower Trophy team. Gary and Vivienne and their five children live in a lovely home in a residential district on the edge of Johannesburg. The house sits back a ways from the road, and you enter the grounds through a nice white gate. It is usual for well-to-do South Africans to have a good many servants—they come for the day and leave at night—and counting the nursemaids for the children, the Players have a staff of seven. They address Gary as "Master," which is customary in South Africa. Gary's house is called "Augusta" and his gorgeous timber farm in the rolling country 125 miles from Johannesburg is called "Bellerive" (after the course where he won the 1965 U.S. Open). I imagine it will be only a matter of time before he acquires more properties so that he can name one "Aronomink" (after the course where he won the 1962 P.G.A.) and another "Muirfield" (after the course where he won the first of his major championships, the 1959 British Open).

The format of the Player-Nicklaus matches called for six rounds at stroke play, the winner the man with the lower composite total at the completion of the Challenge Series, as the competition came to be called. The first match was on a Monday in Pretoria, at the Zwartkop Country Club, one of the country's best-known courses. Its rolling terrain reminded me of courses in northern California, but the trees bordering the fairways at Zwartkop—for the most part, pines and tall blue gums (something like our eucalyptus)—have more foliage. The course measures 6838 yards but it doesn't play too long, for that part of the Transvaal occupies a plateau some 6000 feet above sea level, and in the thin air the ball travels a great distance, particularly the small British ball which is standard in South Africa. If a player pounds out a 300-yard drive, no one runs for a tape measure. The grass on the greens at Zwartkop is roughly similar to Tifton 328, our improved strain of Bermuda grass. On a practice round the day before the match, I found I could read the grainy greens all right and I putted them reasonably well. This was a pleasant surprise. Golfers from other countries have always had a tough time with South African greens, for the heavy grain frequently influences the roll of the ball more than the contours do, and that's hard to get on to.

On that practice round I had the misfortune to break my driver, the one I'd been using since my fifth tournament as a professional. I have no idea how it happened. As I struck the ball on the eighth tee, the head split just behind the insert and along the neck. This was a Tommy Armour driver. The one I use now, a Jack Nicklaus club, is an almost exact copy: 13¼ ounces in weight, 42¾ inches in length, D-1 swing weight, Dynamic S shaft, leather grip 1/64 of an inch oversize, persimmon head finished a medium brown, slightly open face with nine degrees of loft, and a one-piece red fiber insert with six screws. I switched to a reserve driver that had the same specifications but a somewhat different feel. There are no such things as identical drivers.

During our match at Zwartkop we had another incident on the eighth. We were standing on the tee when a swarm of big yellow bees came out of nowhere and attacked us. I was the first to get stung—twice on the face and twice on the arm. The people in the gallery shouted to us, "Stand still, stand still." Gary stood still and got whopped four times in the face. Then the bees—there were hundreds of them—began stinging everyone. I just ran with the crowd. The next thing I knew, the swarm was gone and a nice calm lady was leading me down to a creek where she smeared mud over my face and arms, an old country remedy that relieved the pain of the stings. Rather than risk driving off the eighth, Gary and I decided to eliminate the hole, giving ourselves pars on it, and the match was resumed on the ninth tee almost as if nothing had happened. At that point I was one under par but two shots behind Gary. By the twelfth he had picked up two more shots on me, but on the last three holes I made up the whole deficit with two birdies and an eagle. We were both 69, three under par.

I didn't do nearly as well in our second match, which was held the next day at the Bloemfontain Golf Club in Bloemfontain in Orange Free State, south of the Transvaal and about 2000 feet above sea level. This was vastly different country—dry, flattish, sparsely wooded—and the course was not unlike an unwatered Texas course. The wind blew a lot and it was dusty out there. My troubles started early. On the second, a short par 4, I hooked my tee-shot into a water hazard and took a 7 to Gary's 3. Gary eventually brought in a one-under-par 70, a very good score on that 7027-yard course. I had a 75 which featured a few more hooked tee-shots and a couple of foozled short putts.

Next day, Port Elizabeth on the southern coast. This is a veddy, veddy English settlement, almost as English as some of the towns in New Zealand. The course we played, the Port Elizabeth Golf Club, was set in a strip of sand and pines; of the American courses I know, those around Virginia Beach and along the Carolina coast resemble it the most. Port Elizabeth calls itself "The Second Windiest City in the World." When you ask a Port Elizabethan, as who doesn't, what's the world's windiest city, he gives you a little twinkle

215

and says, "It blew away." Well, Port Elizabeth lived up to its billing. During our match it blew something like fifty or sixty miles an hour, and it rained hard. I don't think I've ever played golf on a windier day unless it was the first round of the 1964 British Open at St. Andrews. Under the conditions, Gary and I did extraordinarily well, I would say. Once again Gary seized the lead on the front nine, matching par with a 37 to my 40, but over the last four holes, when I was still trailing by three strokes, I rallied with three birdies and we each finished in 73, one under par.

After a day off, we went at it again in Durban, in Natal, north from Port Elizabeth on the Indian Ocean. It's a beautiful city, palmy and balmy, sort of a South African Miami Beach. We played the Durban Country Club, a seaside layout that struck me as the best course we visited during our series. The grass there is something like our St. Augustine grass but it is a much finer strain. On the fairways it was cut right down to the ground and it played well. For once I got off faster than Gary. I turned in 33 to lead him by five and I still held that margin coming to the last hole. In other words, after 71 holes, we were all tied in the Challenge Series. On the eighteenth, a par 4 of only 276 yards, I went over the green with a 3-wood and took a 6 to Gary's 4. Nicklaus 70, Player 73. Player in front by two after 72 holes.

We then flew back to the Transvaal, and the fifth match took place the next day at the Houghton Golf Club in Johannesburg, a 7114-yard layout, par 72, that was the venue of that year's South African Open. Up to this round my putting had been more than adequate, but now it started to disintegrate. I missed from three feet on the second and slowly went from bad to worse. I also hooked a couple of drives and smashed an approach into a tree for good measure. With a 68 to my 74, Gary, in effect, wrapped up the series. I couldn't quite see myself making up eight shots on a golfer of his class over eighteen holes.

The scene of our final match, fittingly, was the Royal Cape Golf Club, in Capetown, the oldest golf club in South Africa and, I believe, the oldest on the continent. It was founded in 1885, which would make it three years older than St. Andrews, the first permanent golf club established in the United States. Royal Cape's present layout is relatively short and on the flat side, but the fairways are tight and the greens heavily bunkered, and you have to play good golf shots. Gary did: he had a 69, one of those fine, crisp rounds of his when he hits one accurate shot after another. I was all over the place. Instead of whittling away Gary's lead, I dropped six more shots. Final totals: Player, 422; Nicklaus, 436. My pathetic golf in the last two matches had turned the Challenge Series, so closely contested most of the way, into a walkaway.

The Challenge Series had been the biggest thing of its kind in South Africa since 1947 when Sam Snead had opposed Bobby Locke in a similar series. (Locke was a decisive winner.) Gary is a national idol, and there had been a lot of pressure on him. He could hardly have acquitted himself better, as a golfer and as a host. I imagine he'll be trying to lure me over again one of these years. I stand ready to rechallenge him. He can name any six fishing grounds he desires, salt water or fresh water—it makes no difference to me.

Eight months later, in the autumn of 1966, Gary and I met in another head-to-head duel in the final of the (Piccadilly) World Match-Play Championship, at Wentworth, in England, and Gary defeated me 6 and 4. Mark McCormack was instrumental in organizing this competition, which was inaugurated in 1964 at Wentworth and which has since been held over that course annually. Eight of the world's top pros meet in an elimination tournament, all matches over 36 holes. It has already become an event of considerable stature because it gives us a chance to engage in that almost vanished form of golf, match play. I wish we had more opportunities to play it. It can be intensely dramatic, since a golfer directly confronts his opponent, and it can be very testing, since he must be able to answer a brilliant shot by his opponent instantly. I have, at this writing, played in the World Match-Play Championship twice, in 1964, when I was ousted in the first round by Bruce Devlin, and in 1966, when I lost in the final after defeating Dave Thomas, of Wales, and Billy Casper.

Unfortunately, the thing that stirred up the most attention in that final was not the match itself but an incident midway through the morning round which involved me and the referee, Colonel Tony Duncan. I disagreed with a ruling that Colonel Duncan made on the ninth hole, and when he subsequently asked if I would like a new referee, I said I would, and Gerald Micklem took over. I think what probably threw me off was not so much Colonel Duncan's ruling as his parade-ground manner, and after that I became

217

very stubborn myself. I don't think there is any point in pursuing the matter further, except to state that I feel I should have been able to handle the situation better—certainly the public relations phases of it.

The incident at Wentworth was doubly ironic: I have always loved playing in Britain, and earlier that year I had realized one of my greatest ambitions by winning the British Open. I had made only four previous attempts in that championship, and that isn't a large number, I appreciate, but I have never prized a victory more. To earn a rating among the world's finest golfers, a man must win the British Open, and I had begun to get it into my head that, for one reason or another, the British Open might always elude me.

I made my first bid for that championship in 1962. Bid is much too strong a word, for I was never in the running. That summer the Open was held at Troon, on the west coast of Scotland. Whereas Palmer adapted himself marvelously to the hard, baked-out links—his winning total of 276 is still the Open record—I couldn't do anything at all. I finished in a tie for thirty-second with rounds of 80, 72, 74, and 79, and I know that the spectators who watched me must have been wondering how I had ever managed to defeat Palmer a few weeks before in our playoff for the U.S. Open title. I had a handy excuse I could fall back on, privately. The set of clubs the Slazenger company provided for me had a balance and feel wholly different from my American clubs, and I didn't even begin to get used to them.

The next summer I didn't have the luxury of a built-in excuse: I brought over my MacGregor clubs. (Perhaps I should mention, since I have been this frank, that I found the clubs Slazengers made for me in 1964, and in later years, to be excellent.) In addition, the 1963 Open course, Lytham & St. Anne's, could not have been more to my tastes. There was a nice growth of turf on the fairways, and the greens were unusually receptive for British greens: unless you were playing a very long shot into them, you could fire your approach onto the green itself and the green would hold it. As you have no doubt perceived, I don't much care for courses that represent the extreme in British linksland conditions—courses where the fairways and greens are so hard and fast that on every approach shot you must land the ball many yards short of the green and hope that you have correctly estimated the amount of bound and run the ball will have. You can get all kinds of erratic kicks, and this, as I see it, puts too much of a premium on luck and not enough on ball control. An occasional pitch-and-run approach on a hole where the terrain is right for it—that's different, that's part of the vocabulary of golf.

At Lytham, as I described in an earlier chapter, I gradually overtook the early leaders, went in front on the 61st, and then, with only two holes to go, snatched defeat from the very jaws of victory by bogeying both the 71st and the 72nd. All the good golf I had played was tossed away. I finished a stroke behind Bob Charles and Phil Rodgers.

My collapse at Lytham bothered me more than a little. I wondered if I would ever be presented with a chance like that again in the British Open and concluded that I might not. My experience the following year in the championship seemed to support this pessimism. That was the year that Tony Lema won the British Open with his stirring performance at St. Andrews. I finished second. On the last day I broke the 36-hole record for the Old Course with rounds of 66 and 68, and when I reviewed the tournament as objectively as I could, it seemed to me that I had played well enough to win most British Opens. The only trouble was that Tony had played better.

The next summer, in 1965, the championship was at Birkdale, the scene of Arnold's first triumph in the Open four years before. There's nothing wrong with Birkdale—it has a lot to recommend it. However, from my first practice round on, I had the fixed idea it wasn't a good course for me. I don't handle hard-surfaced fairways as well as some golfers do, and Birkdale's were bone-hard. The layout, I also felt, favored a right-to-left player. Added to this, I was a little worried, as I always was in Britain, that I probably hit the ball too high to win in a country where the heavy winds off the sea are such an important factor. I ended up in a tie for twelfth, eleven shots behind Peter Thomson, who captured his fifth British Open by outplaying Lema down the stretch. It's stupid, to be sure, to approach a tournament with the attitude that the course isn't suited to you. You won't be at your best then. All you'll do is prove to yourself how right you were. All experienced golfers know this, but the fact remains that there are some courses you simply don't like, and sometimes you can't talk yourself out of it. Naturally, if

A spot of trouble at Birkdale, and a consoling pat from Gerald Micklem.

I had played prodigious golf at Birkdale, I would have grown to love the course—you know, discovered lots of subtle beauties I had somehow overlooked.

My attitude was much better the next year when I went over for the 1966 British Open. The championship was scheduled for Muirfield, which I knew and knew well from the 1959 Walker Cup match. Muirfield with its splendid turf, its moderate undulations, its honest "inland" character—that was my kind of course. When

I arrived there a week before the start of the championship, I was in for a shock. I hardly recognized the course. It didn't even look like a golf course; it looked more like a wide expanse of wheat whipping in the wind. Gerald Micklem, the captain of the 1959 British Walker Cup team who in 1966 was serving as the chairman of the R. & A. Championship Committee, explained to me what had happened. The Championship Committee had decided that Muirfield (6887 yards) didn't possess sufficient length or terror to provide a bonafide Open test. It would have to be made more severe. Taking a page from the U.S.G.A.'s book, Micklem & Co. had narrowed down the old swinging fairways by letting the grass along both sides grow up into rough. They had gone much farther, though, than the U.S.G.A. had ever gone. In the landing area for a long drive, 255 to 275 yards from the tee—British ball, remember— some fairways had been reduced so drastically they couldn't have been even 20 yards wide. From that point back toward the tee they broadened out to 25 or 40 yards. In other words, the long hitter who wanted to use his driver was welcome to, but he would have to hit the ball almost as straight as an arrow to keep it out of the rough. If he didn't feel up to that, well, he could drive with a fairway wood or an iron—he would have twice as much fairway to hit then. One walk around Muirfield convinced me that you had to be willing to sacrifice distance. You couldn't afford not to be on the fairway, because the rough was next to unplayable. It hadn't been cut at all. It stood a foot and a half high in many places, and the flowering stalks of grass beginning to go to seed did wave in the wind like wheat.

Instead of deciding to hate the new Muirfield, I made up my mind on that first walk round that I would just have to accommodate myself to it. I don't know what lay behind this stroke of intelligence, this sudden burst of maturity, but I think it must have been Muirfield itself. The memory of the 1959 Walker Cup match was still fresh in my mind. I had never stopped looking back to it, not only because that match had changed me from a good junior golfer into a good golfer, but also because that whole week at Muirfield—the preparation for the match as well as the match itself—had personified sport at its best, people at their best, the world at its best. Okay, so the course was set up different in 1966 than it had been in 1959. It was still Muirfield, and if anyone could handle it, I could. After all, I was an old Muirfield man.

221

It was a good idea to stay out of the rough at Muirfield.

On my first practice round, to feel out how the individual holes played, I used my driver off most of the tees. Each day after that, I narrowed down the number of holes on which I felt I could safely use a driver. By the eve of the championship, there was only one hole, the long fifth, where I planned to drive with my driver in any wind, and there were only a handful of other holes, all lengthy par 4s, where I planned to take my driver in certain kinds of wind. Everything considered, this amounted to the best preparation I had ever given a tournament in terms of learning a specific course. During the championship I stayed with my plan— I used my driver only seventeen times in all. Since I believe that this strategy won for me in the end as much as anything did, I would like to show you in chart form how my selection of clubs off the tee worked out.

HOLE	YARDAGE	PAR	TIMES USED DRIVER	OTHER CLUBS USED
1	429	4	0	1-iron to a 3-iron
2	363	4	0	1-iron
3	385	4	0	1-iron
4	187	3	(short hole)	
5	516	5	4	
6	473	4	3	3-wood once
7	187	3	(short hole)	
8	451	4	3	3-iron once
9	495	5	0	1-iron
10	475	4	0	3-wood
11	363	4	1	3-wood twice, 1-iron once
12	385	4	1	3-wood twice, 1-iron once
13	154	3	(short hole)	
14	462	4	3	3-wood once
15	407	4	2	3-wood twice
16	198	3	(short hole)	
17	528	5	0	3-wood once, 1-iron twice, 3-iron once
18	429	4	0	1-iron

Everything went smoothly for me the first two days. (Incidentally, this was the year the British Open relinquished the classic format of a double round on the third day and went to four days.) My opening round of 70, one under par, put me in a tie for the lead. The prevailing wind in that section of Scotland, just east of Edinburgh, is the west wind, but on the day of the first round it had switched around and was coming out of the east. This made for generally high scoring, for the course played altogether different than it had on the practice rounds. The second day the west wind was back, a mild west wind, and the scoring perked up. Peter Butler, of England, set a new course record with a 65, and Phil Rodgers had a 66. I had a 67 for 137 which put me into the lead after 36 holes, a stroke in front of Butler and three in front of Rodgers, Kel Nagle, and Harold Henning of South Africa. Doug Sanders was four shots off the pace, Arnold Palmer eight. Arnold and his wife Winnie, and Barbara and I were stopping at Graywalls, the wonderful inn right off the links where our Walker Cup team had stayed seven years before. Everything about Graywalls was as super as I had remembered it. I think it serves the best food of any inn or hotel in Britain. I was enjoying myself.

On Friday, the day of the third round, we had a stiff west wind and Muirfield played harder. I reached the turn in even par, however, to remain five under for the tournament, and this gave me a commanding lead. Butler, the nearest man, had fallen four strokes back, Rodgers seven. I started home with four pars, and then something happened. I missed my par on the fourteenth when I played a choppy chip from the back edge. I missed my par on the fifteenth when my approach rolled through the green and I again took three to get down. I was aware that the wind had dried out the greens and that they were playing much faster than they had, but all of a sudden, after having been so confident about my golf, I felt very, very jittery out there on the course. I missed my par on the short sixteenth when I took three putts from 40 feet. I almost missed my par on the seventeenth, a par 5 that was a possible birdie hole; I saved it with a seven-foot putt. Then I missed my par on the eighteenth when I pushed my second into the long bunker to the right of the green. That made it four bogeys on the last five holes, a 39 back for a 75. But that was only half of the story. While I had been floundering around, a number of the players had ripped the back nine apart. Rodgers, riding a great putting streak, had played it in 30! Palmer had played it in 32. The whole tournament had been turned around. Rodgers was now the leader after 54 holes with 210. I was two behind him, Sanders three, Palmer only four, and Thomas, the big strong Welshman, also four back after a 69.

Saturday. Wind from the west, blustery but subsiding. Five of us in contention. Rodgers and myself out last, Palmer and Sanders playing just in front of us, Thomas paired with Henning just in front of them. After the first hole, I was back in a tie for the lead: Phil bogeyed it and I holed from 25 feet for a birdie. I turned in 33 after two more birdies and six pars, and after getting my par on the tough tenth, I was comfortably out in front again—three strokes ahead of Thomas, four ahead of Rodgers and Sanders. Palmer was out of it. On the eleventh, a short 4, I was in a position to add another stroke to my lead after punching my approach seven feet from the flag. I jerked the putt, though, and it broke off a foot before the cup. I took pains with the 15-inch tap-in I had left for my par. I thought I hit it the way I wanted to, but the ball rimmed off the left corner of the cup and stayed out. That shouldn't have shaken me—I still had a two-shot margin on the closest contender —but it did.

I began to worry and I began to play jittery golf, exactly as I had on the second nine the day before. I got my par on the twelfth, a short 4, but only because I hooked my drive so badly it cleared the heavy rough and finished under the gallery ropes in rough the spectators had trodden down—I had a very playable lie. I didn't get my 3 on the short thirteenth, though. I was weak with my iron off the tee and way strong with my running, uphill chip. I couldn't pull myself together. I played the fourteenth poorly. There I pushed my tee-shot into an awkward spot in the bunker off to the right of the fairway and took a bogey 5. I'd lost three shots on four holes —my entire lead. Thomas, I learned, was in with a 69 for 283. Sanders, playing the eighteenth, was headed for 283 if he parred the home hole, which he did. I would have to par the last four holes to tie them. I wasn't at all sure I could.

On the fifteenth, 407 yards, I got my 4 but it was a wobbly one. A mediocre approach left me 40 feet short of the hole, and I had to putt over the humpy contour in the middle of the green called the Camel's Back. I managed to get down in two by holing from four feet.

The pin on the sixteenth, a 198-yard par 3, was at the back of a slippery green which slopes up from the front. The wind was behind me and I played a 7-iron. I had the ball on the pin but it was short, a good 30 feet short. And then I came through with the first good attacking stroke I'd played since the eleventh. I didn't hole that 30-footer but it was hit squarely, it was dead on line, and it couldn't have stopped more than an inch or two short of the cup. (I didn't want to go by the cup and leave myself a downhiller.)

Golf is not at all a logical game. There was no reason, really, why I should have lost my composure so completely after I had three-putted the eleventh from seven feet. There was no reason either why I should have suddenly regained it just as completely because I had made a firm putt and firm par on the sixteenth. That is what happened, however. I walked onto the seventeenth tee full of confidence, a different man. I was no longer thinking about how I might lose the championship, I was thinking about how I could win it. I thought I could. All I needed was a birdie and a par. The seventeenth—why, that was a very birdieable hole. The eighteenth —that was a tough 4 but I could make it.

A par 5 that measures 528 yards, the seventeenth is a rather unique hole. The tee-shot is semi-blind. The fairway slopes slightly up for 200 yards or so, and this cuts off your view of the landing area. After the fairway reaches the top of its rise, it twists to the left and continues on a relatively straight line to the green. About 100 yards from the green a high bunkered ridge thrusts itself into the fairway from the right, but a golfer doesn't have to concern himself with this ridge if he's hit a good drive—his second will carry it with plenty to spare. Beyond this ridge the fairway becomes very tight as it moves between a high mound of rough on the right and broken rough ground on the left, and it is nothing much more than a channel as it tumbles toward the left side of the flat circular green set in a hollow and banked by rough. From where you play your second after a good tee-shot, the left side of the green is visible, but most of the right side is hidden by that high mound of rough. An easy par, yes, but no giveaway birdie.

On Wednesday, when we had that east wind blowing against us on the seventeenth, I had used my 3-wood off the tee. On Thursday and Friday, with the west wind behind and right-to-left, I had used a 1-iron, aiming down the right side of the fairway and letting the wind take the ball in a little. No percentage attempting the shortcut over the corner: there was a series of bunkers along the left edge of the fairway but none on the right. On Saturday, as I stood on the seventeenth tee, it seemed to me that the wind was a bit stronger than it had been the two previous days. To be on the safe side I decided to play a 3-iron off the tee: there was always the danger, if you aimed down the right, that you might get the ball out past the corner and into the rough. The 3-iron proved to be almost too much club. My tee-shot finished in the fairway but only two yards short of the rough. I looked across the fairway at my yardage marker, the last bunker on the left, and consulted my yardage chart: since I was out equidistant with the front edge of that bunker, that meant I was 238 yards from the center of the green. Now to get the right club. With the big ball and no wind, 238 yards—that's easy: that's a 1-iron. Downwind with the small ball, 238 yards— that's more difficult to figure. I settled on a 5-iron. Not that I was able to go about things this scientifically, but I made my allowances more or less this way: one club less for the small ball; one and a half clubs less for the following wind; one club less for the run on the ball (it would have to be played to land on the fairway short of the green); and a half club less for the extra distance you get when you're charged up and the adrenaline is flowing. I could see the flag. It was in about the middle of the green, a little to the right. From where I stood, the flag was almost directly in line with the left edge of the big bunker in the face of the ridge jutting above the fairway. I took my line a shade to the left of the left edge of the bunker. I was going to try to play a straight shot but the kind of a shot which, if it slipped off, would slip off to the right.

My first reaction after I'd made contact with the ball with my 5-iron was that I had played as good a shot as I was capable of. I saw the ball fly over the ridge on the line I wanted and I saw it land on the fairway about 15 feet short of the green, and then—it seemed an awful long time later—a loud roar went up from the gallery packed around the green. The ball had gotten an ideal bounce onto the green, and as I saw for myself as I came hurrying up the fairway, it had finished about 16 feet from the flag, short and to the left. What a beautiful sight that was! By the time I walked onto the green, I felt comparatively calm. The important thing was not to go for the putt, just to get the ball as close as I could. I lagged it to within inches of the cup and holed the tap-in for my birdie. Now a par on the last hole would do it.

Muirfield's eighteenth is a 429-yard par 4, a straightaway hole from tee to green. It's a well-designed hole. To begin with, it demands an extremely accurate tee-shot. The fairway, a slim one, is bunkered on both sides, but you must particularly avoid the left side where three bunkers cut progressively deeper into the fairway. The green is bunkered front, left, and right, and you're playing a fairly long approach into it, so that's not an easy shot either. But the key to the hole is the tee-shot. In a west wind a left-to-right player like myself had a definite advantage, for that kind of wind blows across the eighteenth from the right and gives you a perfect bank to hit into. On my three earlier rounds I had taken a 1-iron off the tee. I went with the same club again, aiming down the middle and counting on the wind to cushion my fade. The ball ended up in the very center of the fairway, 208 yards from the heart of the green, according to my yardage chart. A 4-iron or a 3? I chose the 3. I didn't want to hit the shot hard, I just wanted to hang it in the wind, the way I had my tee-shot. Besides, the flag was set only 20 feet from the back edge of the green, and I wanted to be up. I'd be past all the trouble then. If my approach went over, there was nothing serious to worry about—just a little upslope and I could putt off of it. I hit that 3-iron well, my fourth good iron in a row. I cut it into the wind and it carried past the middle of the green and sat down softly about 25 feet to the right of the flag,

A big moment: two for it from 25 feet. This is the 429-yard 18th at Muir-field, last round of the 1966 British Open. Two putts will give me my par and a one-stroke victory. Phil Rodgers, my playing partner, watches as I study the line. I read the putt to break a shade to the left, and it worked out that way. I had just a tap-in left.

absolutely hole-high. I read the putt to break a foot and a half from right to left and reminded myself that the green was fast and that this was no time for hero stuff—just get that putt up close. I had the speed correct and the ball stopped seven or eight inches to the left of the cup. I lined up that little putt and carefully tapped it in. . . . I had won the British Open.

You sort of conk out at a moment like that. Five minutes later my head was clearer and I was telling myself, "I've won the British Open. That means I've won the four major championships. All I have to do now is make a good speech." At the presentation ceremony in front of the old stone clubhouse I felt relaxed and lighthearted as I sat back in my chair and listened to the joint runners-up, Dave Thomas and Doug Sanders, make graceful speeches. However, when the time came for me to get to my feet and receive the trophy, I got so choked up that tears came into my eyes and I couldn't talk. This had never happened to me before at a presentation. As I stood there, I began to understand why I was so overcome with emotion. Very simply, I hadn't been at all sure that I would ever be up there standing beside that trophy—a high-ball player like me who couldn't handle hard linksland fairways and who had always found a way to lose in the British Open and probably would continue to. "Excuse me," I said to the people gathered for the presentation. "Do you mind if I just enjoy this moment?" When I resumed speaking, it all came easily. I even remembered to thank the greenkeeper.

XV

Baltusrol

BARBARA AND I PRESENTLY make our home in Florida. We moved there in the winter of 1965, renting a house in Lost Tree Village, a lovely colony north of Palm Beach, while our own house was being built. It was ready for us the next year—a medium-sized Florida ranch-style structure, just large enough to take care of our three children. (Our third child and first daughter, Nancy Jean, whom we call Nan, had been born May 5, 1965.) It was I who instigated the move to Florida. Originally, my idea was that we would live there three months of the year and the rest of the time in Columbus, but it has turned out the other way round. Barbara likes Florida but I positively love it. For the weariness that overtakes you when you spend upward of thirty weeks a year on the road, it offers the perfect antidote. Professional golf, I know, must seem to the spectator like one long leisurely escape from the dull routine of day-to-day living, but it has its own pressures and exerts its own demands. Anyhow, the moment I leave the tournament world, I like to forget it totally, and in Florida I can do this better than any place I know.

Our home is situated on a quiet stretch of water just off the Inland Waterway called Little Lake Worth. I have two boats at my

"Uncle Gary" in a relaxed mood.

Fishing—not in Florida, as it happens.

disposal, a 16-foot Evinrude with a 100-horsepower Evinrude motor (which I keep at our dock), and a 37-foot Merritt powered by two Daytona 409 engines with 385-horsepower motors, capable of over 40 miles an hour (which I keep at Bill's Sailfish Marina up the road in Palm Beach Shores). When the urge strikes me—and it does almost daily—I either take out the smaller boat and do some "lake fishing," or take the larger one out into the Gulf Stream for some deep-sea fishing. No waters in the world can compare with those off the Florida coast for the variety of fish you can get— sailfish and dolphin, tarpon and marlin (over by the Bahamas), kingfish and bonito, shark and barracuda, snook and bluefish, mackerel and sea trout, to name just a few of them. My good friend Linc Werden, the gentleman from the *Times,* made his debut as a deep-sea fisherman on my boat. Linc landed an enormous barracuda, and when he had it mounted, his triumph was my triumph. That's the way you always feel when you take out friends who are newcomers to the sport.

I start my kids fishing as soon as they're old enough to stay in the boat—when they're two or three. Jackie, the oldest, has a real flair for fishing. When he was only three, he landed a 27-pound kingfish all by himself after a 25-minute struggle, and the winter

"Uncle Cary" in a relaxed mood.

of 1967, when he was six, he led the annual Silver Sailfish Derby of the Palm Beaches for two weeks by bringing in, on a 24-pound test line, a sail that measured 7 feet 9 inches and weighed 62 pounds. I think Jackie got more space in the sports pages that month than I did.

Lost Tree has a very good golf course (and the first fairway is literally in my back yard), but I rarely touch a club when I'm home. When the time comes round that I must rejoin the tour, I spend a few days on the practice tee, but that's about the extent of it. As my neighbor Cary Middlecoff likes to say with a little needle, "When the Golden Bear hibernates, he really hibernates." Cary agrees with me, though, that these almost complete vacations from golf seem to be the right diet for me and may even serve to lengthen my competitive career. I usually return to the tour feeling refreshed and eager to work hard on my game. Besides, these days when the tour offers so many big-money tournaments which you can't afford to pass up, and when the season runs full tilt from January through October, it is absolutely necessary to pace yourself.

Lost Tree is essentially a golfing colony. In addition to Cary, the second-slowest player in the history of the game, the residents include Don Moe, the star of the 1930 Walker Cup match, Mrs. Betty Probasco, the fine golfer from Tennessee, and a high number of low-handicap senior players. Scott and Betty Probasco have the house on our left, Cary and Edie Middlecoff the house on our right. We do quite a bit of informal partying with the Middlecoffs, who are perhaps our closest friends at Lost Tree. There was one party they had at their house last winter that I remember especially well. Barbara and I brought along an old friend, and among the people he met was Don Walker, a businessman from upstate New York who owns the house on the other side of the Middlecoffs'. "Tell me," our friend asked Don, "has living so close to Jack and Cary had any effect on your golf?" "Yes, indeed," Don replied emphatically, "yes, indeed. I used to play to a six handicap and now I play to a twelve. Not only that, it now takes me five and a half hours to complete a round."

While the last thing I want to do is to build myself up as a terrific father, I do love to spend my time with our three kids, and in Florida I can go fishing with them or take them water-skiing and swimming or just laze around with them in the sun. They're very

Jackie, our oldest, at age three.

different in personality. Jackie—he's seven now—is studious and somewhat quiet (except when he isn't). He's a pretty fair athlete, and, as I said, he's a darn good little fisherman. Stevie, who's five now, is a wild man who never listens to me or anybody, but he is loaded with charm and he really has exceptional athletic coordination. We're hoping we can get him into the first grade on an athletic scholarship. Nan is very bright and grown-up for her age, three—talkative, responsive, companionable. She shadows her mother from morning to night, and I sometimes get the idea she thinks she's running the house.

I believe I'm pretty good with the kids, but for some strange reason, I'm not the first time I see them. When Barbara went to the hospital in Columbus to have Jackie, I was out of town playing a match. I rushed home and out to the hospital. A nurse carried my new son out so that I could see him, and as I was walking forward, I sank to the floor and collapsed. Another nurse revived me with smelling salts. Terrific! When Stevie was born, I waited patiently at the hospital and then when he was brought out, I collapsed—another gutsy performance. Just before Nan was expected to arrive, Barbara told me I'd probably do the same thing again and accused me of never allowing her to have the spotlight for even a moment. I knew better. By this time I was much more relaxed about children. This time it would be a breeze.

To show you how untaut I was, a day or so before the baby was due, I played an exhibition for the American Cancer Society at Scioto with Bob Hope, James Garner, and Walker Inman, our club pro. After the exhibition, I took Bob, Jim, Walker, and two or three other fellows back to the house and told Barbara we wanted to play some snooker in the game room and to make some dinner for us. I don't know why I was so dense, but even after Barbara suggested that I grill some steaks for our guests, I still didn't realize how bad she was feeling or why. When we sat down for dinner, she excused herself and left the table after taking a sip from a Coke. We didn't miss her too much—the steaks were tasty, Hope was in great form, Garner was very funny. Forty-five minutes later Barbara reappeared. Her hair was all fixed and she was carrying sort of a weekend bag. "Let's go," she said to me. All my buddies cleared out in nothing flat. Then Barbara said, "You got out of taking me to the hospital once before. You're not getting out of it this time." It was eleven when we left. Nan was born ten minutes after twelve. They wheeled Barbara out so that I could see her, then they brought the baby out, and then I keeled over. Two interns and two nurses caught me. I was taken to the recovery room where I recovered consciousness fifteen minutes later. Barbara's doctor, Dr. William Copeland, insisted on following me home in his car to make certain I got there safely. I took that as an affront. When I asked him why he thought this was necessary, he really twisted the harpoon. "After all, Jack," he said, "you spent more time in the recovery room than your wife did."

The tournament that usually begins the new season for me is the Crosby. For many years it was the third event on the calendar, preceded by the L.A. Open and the San Diego Open. In 1967 there was a shifting-around of tournament dates: the San Diego Open led off, the Crosby followed it, and then we had the L.A. Open. I never expect to do too well in the Crosby, mainly because I come to it direct from Florida and six weeks of sun, surf, and snoozing. Some years, nevertheless, my golf has been much more creditable than I could have hoped for. Pebble Beach and Cypress Point make you want to play, they're such interesting and enjoyable layouts. Spyglass Hill—that's different; that makes you want to go fishing. In 1967, much to my surprise, I actually won the Crosby. Going into the last nine I was a couple of shots back of Casper and Palmer, but they both ran into trouble and I suddenly got very hot. I birdied 12, 13, 14, 16, and 17, and won by five shots.

It was a costly victory, in a way. The morning before the final round I woke up with a bad back and bad left side. Apparently I had strained some muscles the day before without knowing it. Many times before my back had bothered me, but it had never hurt this much: I could hardly get out of bed. When I did get up, I took a hot shower and then applied a heating pad to my back; then, after Barbara had massaged it, I decided to see if I could play. On the practice tee I couldn't get through the ball. The first hole was worse. My back was so painful that I broke into a cold sweat going down the fairway. I almost walked in, there and then. The only way I could get the ball out any distance at all was to play a right-to-left shot, hitting it hard with my right hand at the bottom of the swing. Fortunately, it was a nice warm day, and by the time I reached the turn the stiffness and pain had eased up appreciably. I had gone out in 37, making up for some sour holes with a couple of birdies.

Coming in, as I said, I started to play astonishingly well and brought it back in 31.

The next week, when we moved down the coast for the L.A. Open, my back felt good enough. I finished out of the money, however, tying for fifty-first place with George Archer, Dutch Harrison, Bobby Nichols, Bob McCallister, Babe Hiskey, and Steve Reid at 286, seventeen strokes behind Palmer's winning total. My trouble was that the right-to-left pattern I had fallen into the last day at Pebble had set in, and I found it hard to get out of it. I played better golf from tee to green the following week in the Bob Hope Classic, but I putted like a television star. Happily, my schedule called for me to return to Lost Tree Village then and not to pick up the tour again until early March when it swung into Florida. That suited me fine. I'd rest up the back, work a little on left-to-right, get my putting stroke straightened out, and be ready to go.

The first of the four Florida tournaments was the Doral Open. With seven holes to go, I led Doug Sanders by a shot, and while I finally ended up two shots behind Doug in a tie for fourth, all in all I hadn't played a bad tournament. (Incidentally, I've never won a tournament in Florida except for the 1966 P.G.A. Four-Ball Championship, which Arnold and I took.) My back hadn't bothered me at Doral, and my swing pattern was okay. One more tournament, I thought, and my game would be good and sharp.

I was mistaken. In the Florida Citrus Open, in Orlando, I finished in a tie for seventh with Bert Yancey and Bobby Nichols, four strokes behind the winner, Julius Boros, but I didn't like the kind of shots I was playing. I had slipped back into hitting them with that right-to-left draw action, and this disturbed me. I was trying to win a place on the 1967 Ryder Cup team, and to do this I would have to finish near the top in the next three tournaments on my list— the Jacksonville Open, the Pensacola Open, and the Masters. The Masters was the final event in which aspirants to the team could compile points. Having been admitted to a Class A membership in the P.G.A. only the previous June (and then largely because Leo Fraser, the vice-president, and Tommy Jacobs, the head of the Tournament Players Committee, had hacked an avenue for me through a wilderness of red tape) I had just nine months and not the full two years in which to collect Ryder Cup points. At Jacksonville, the best I could do was a tie for thirty-fourth. (Dan Sikes won.) I was no better at Pensacola, tying for thirty-third. (Gay

Brewer won there with a spectacular burst—rounds of 66, 64, and 61 before a final 71.) After those two weak tournaments, I would have to play a very strong Masters to have any chance at all for the team.

You know how when something starts going wrong a whole lot of other things seem to go wrong, too? Well, that had been happening to me. The Sunday evening after the last round at Jacksonville, I gave Gardner Dickinson a lift home in my plane. Gardner lives just a couple of miles away from me in North Palm Beach. I drove Gardner to his house and dropped in to say hello. His kids, I learned, had the mumps, so I got out of there fast—I'd never had them. The next morning I went to see Dr. John McRoberts, our children's doctor, and he suggested that, to be on the safe side, I take some mumps vaccine shots. He gave me the first shot then. That's a potent vaccine. It stiffened up my neck and the middle part of my back, and it didn't wear off much. I had trouble swinging freely at Pensacola. I got the second vaccine shot on my return from Pensacola and had the same severe reaction to it.

Nevertheless, in the middle of that week—the week before the Masters—I went up to Augusta as I had previously planned to, and after three or four days I had worked the stiffness out. My doctor had told me that the inoculations throw "instant uncoordination"

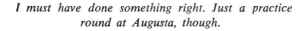

*I must have done something right. Just a practice
round at Augusta, though.*

into you for six weeks, but I honestly felt fine before the tournament and probably would never have thought of his statement again except that in the Masters I did play like a fellow with no natural coordination whatsoever. On the opening round, when I played a 72, I wasn't too bad, but on Friday, around the greens particularly, I looked like a 90-golfer who was having an off-day. I punched one simple chip at least 20 feet past the hole, and some of my short putts never came close to the cup. I was in with a 79 and out of the tournament: 151 was a stroke too many to make the cut. When I missed it, I missed the Ryder Cup team. Gay Brewer, continuing his fine all-around play, won at Augusta after a head-to-head battle on the last round with Bobby Nichols.

The week after the Masters, in the Tournament of Champions at Las Vegas, I thought I was pulling out of my slump. I actually had a chance to win the tournament, but on the last few holes, when I was bearing down as hard as I could, I just didn't have the shots. I finished fourth. This ineffectiveness under pressure worried me and magnified the lack of confidence that had been building up ever since Jacksonville. It was just as well that my schedule called for me to leave the tour for three weeks at that time to play a series of exhibitions and to go to Nicaragua to film a show on tarpon fishing for the "American Sportsman" television series. When I returned to the tour early in May at the Houston Champions International tournament, I was hitting the ball satisfactorily but my putting was still pathetic. At an exhibition I played at the Topeka Country Club, for instance, I took 21 putts on the first nine. Naturally, everywhere I went people were asking me, "Why are you playing so badly?" I didn't really know how to answer that. I had never been in such a long and severe slump in my life.

Things came to a crux of sorts at the Houston Champions tournament, an up-and-coming event held at the impressive club which Jimmy Demaret and Jackie Burke organized and operate. The course we play there is long, rolling, and very green for Texas, and I looked forward to getting at it. I had made up my mind about one thing: I was going to play everything left-to-right that week and every week even if I had to aim out-of-bounds on some holes to do so. My partners the first two rounds at Houston—a blind draw was used, which is customary—were Al Geiberger and my old Florida neighbor, Cary Middlecoff. I was moving along fairly well the first day until I cut my drive out-of-bounds on the fourteenth and then knocked my approach into the pond before the green. I took a big 8 there and ended up with a 77.

I was on the spot again. Unless I played a good solid second round, I wouldn't make the cut. I worked like the devil that second day. I don't think I holed a putt over six feet and I missed one of 16 inches, but I managed to bring in a 69. And then, just as I feared might happen, when our threesome walked off the eighteenth green Jack Tuthill was waiting for us. Jack, the P.G.A. Tournament Director, had warned us back on the eleventh that we were playing too slowly: we'd fallen a hole and a half behind the threesome in front of us. Unless we made up some ground, he told us, he would have to penalize us for slow play. After that warning, Cary and Al and I did our level best to speed up, but we hadn't succeeded in closing the gap, and, as Tuthill explained when we came off the eighteenth, he had no choice but to slap a two-stroke penalty on each of us. That turned my 69 into a 71.

For an hour or two, while I was sweating out the cut, I was really hot. I wasn't sore at Jack Tuthill. He's as fair as they come— the best man we've ever had in charge of the tour. He was right to assess the penalty. We'd broken a rule of golf by failing to hold our position on the course. What burned me, I guess, was that P.G.A. rules did not allow any adjustment of pairings. I've always felt that a certain flexibility is advisable. When you take a player who's as slow as Cary and stick him with a player who's as slow as me and add a player like Al Geiberger who's not exactly a speed merchant—well, you've got trouble, my friends. The funny thing was that after we had received that warning on the eleventh, the three of us had broken our necks trying to hurry and we had still lost ground. In any event, I made the cut, fortunately, went out with the dew-sweepers the next two mornings, had a 72 and a 71, and sprinted into a tie for thirty-eighth, my usual spot.

After Houston things began to look up. At New Orleans I was second to George Knudson, and at the Colonial a respectable eighth. However, at Memphis, my last tournament before the Open, I lost it again, tying for twentieth and playing pretty spotty stuff. My troubles started when I blew a run of four-foot and five-foot putts the first day. After you miss a few of those, you fall into that old vicious cycle: you try to stick your approaches so close to the pin you can't fail to make the putt; then, to give yourself the shortest possible approach to play, you try to hit your tee-shots harder and harder. Not very intelligent. You end up pressing every shot. When I headed for Baltusrol the following week—while most of the fellows were playing the Buick—to begin my preparation for the Open, I was in a rather confused frame of mind. I didn't know whether I'd played my way out of my slump or not. I knew one thing, though: Boy, I could use a good Open!

During the four years that had elapsed since Oakmont, I hadn't done much in the national championship. In 1963, at The Country Club, I failed to qualify for the last two rounds. In 1964, at Congressional, I was out of contention early in the third round and finished far back, tied for twenty-third. In 1965, at Bellerive, on the outskirts of St. Louis, I barely made the cut; it came at 150 and that's what I had: 78-72. After the first nine holes on the third round, I was definitely out of it and wound up in a tie for thirty-second.

From these performances no one could have guessed how diligently I worked each year to be ready for the championship— 1965 was typical. In late May when Gary Player came out to Columbus for a few days, I said to him, "The most important tournament in the world is the United States Open. Let's prepare for it right up to the hilt." I'd already gotten in two practice rounds at Bellerive, but an Open course needs detailed study, so I suggested to Gary that we fly out to St. Louis on Wednesday the week before the championship. We went at things systematically. We played nine holes at a time—occasionally less than nine—taking at least a half hour on each hole. We drove several balls off each tee, to different parts of the fairway, so that we could learn what was the most advantageous position from which to approach that particular green. We practiced from all the chipping positions around the green and familiarized ourselves with how each greenside bunker played. After we had done that for three days, I went home for the weekend. Gary stayed on and continued his practice.

When I got back to Bellerive on Monday, I could see that his game was tuned to a very fine pitch. When he's swinging well, Gary doesn't make that lashing-down move at the start of his downswing that causes him to lose his balance at the finish. Then he's hitting too hard for Gary Player. At Bellerive he was taking his hands back into a high position and starting them down smoothly. What is more, he wasn't trying to draw the ball; he was trying to hit it straight, which is the way Gary should play. He held that pitch throughout the tournament, putting together four beautifully consistent rounds: two 70s followed by two 71s. This tied him for first with Kel Nagle, and Gary took the playoff handily with another 71.

The odd thing about that 1965 Open was that Arnold and I, heavy favorites to win because Bellerive at 7191 yards was the longest course in Open history, were never in the running. No long hitter was. If a long hitter is sharp and a short hitter is sharp, the long hitter naturally has an advantage, but I think people are inclined to lay too much stress on power in analyzing the chances of the various players before a tournament. The men who are playing good golf that week—they're the men who'll be fighting it out. At Bellerive none of the first five finishers—Player, Nagle, Beard, Boros, and Geiberger—would be classed as a power golfer, but they are all steady, straight drivers and dependable putters, and those were the requisites for handling Bellerive with its tight, fast fairways and its colossal greens. It was nothing unusual to have an approach putt of a hundred feet. Interestingly enough, Deane Beman, the shortest hitter in the field, tied for tenth, despite the fact that he needed a wood to get home on a good many of the par 4s. It wasn't the first time Deane had showed his class on a big, stretched-out Open course. At Oakland Hills in 1961 he tied for eleventh, and the next year at Oakmont he tied for fourteenth. Golf is so illogical, though. The year the Open was at Congressional, where Deane knew every blade of grass, he didn't even make the cut.

I don't want my main point to get lost, however, and it is this: Gary won at Bellerive because he played the best golf, and the intensive preparation he had put in was a big factor in this. It doesn't automatically follow that if you practice hard for a tournament you'll get out there and sparkle. I certainly didn't at Bellerive, and Gary was the only man, I think, who had worked as seriously as I did to get to know the course. But I do believe that careful preparation at the scene of a championship is bound to improve a player's chances. That's the reason, anyway, why I have continued to check in at the Open, the British Open, and the Masters a week before the shooting starts.

I finally played a decent Open in 1966, at Olympic. With a round to go, I was only one shot behind Bill Casper who, you will remember, caught Arnold on that last round with a 68 and went on to defeat him in their playoff with a 69. Myself, I played a rather blah last round, a 74. While I finished third, I was seven full shots back. I hoped to do better than that at Baltusrol. It was about time I did! At twenty I'd finished two shots behind the winner, at twenty-one just three shots back, and at twenty-two I'd won the Open. Compare that was finishing seventeen shots back in both 1964 and 1965, seven back in 1966. It is all very good to rank among the top money-winners, as I had each year, but from the beginning of golf the true champions have had the stuff to be at their best in the national championships.

The fact that I had had such a dismal record in the winter and spring tournaments in 1967 hardened my resolve to play some real golf in the Open. I was no longer amused when I read those newspaper and magazine articles asking, "Whatever became of Jack Nicklaus?" The most eloquent answer I could make would be to win the Open. I wasn't sure I could do that, but I meant to give it everything I had.

Baltusrol is situated in the town of Springfield, New Jersey, about an hour's drive from New York City. One of our oldest clubs, it had been host to four previous Opens—in 1903, 1915, 1936, and 1954. After 1903, when Willie Anderson won the second of his four Opens there, Baltusrol had produced some rather offbeat champions: Jerome Travers, an amateur; Tony Manero, a real dark horse; and Ed Furgol, who had not been considered a serious contender. In 1967 we would be playing the Lower Course, the layout on which Furgol had won thirteen years before with a total of 284. The Lower Course, I gathered, had since been altered only in a minor way. Some of the bunkering had been revised and some of the greens resurfaced, but that was about it. The most bizarre thing about the course, as set up for the Open, was that you didn't get to play a par 5 until the seventeenth. At 623 yards, the seventeenth was the longest hole in Open history, unreachable in two since the green was elevated and bunkered. The eighteenth was also a par 5, 542 yards, to another plateaued green. Here a long hitter could get home with two big shots. My honest feeling, after my first warm-up rounds, was that any one of thirty golfers in the field could win at Baltusrol.

As at every Open course, the fairways had been narrowed down and accurate driving was the key to scoring, even though the rough was much less fierce than Open rough customarily is. (Three rainless weeks were responsible for this.) Putting was bound to be important—when is it not?—for the greens were filled with tricky little rolls and shimmers. At the same time, a golfer who was in top form could expect to have quite a few more cracks at birdies at Baltusrol than he usually gets in the Open, for the course was in amazing condition. The fairways (*poa annua* and bent cut very low) were marvelous, and the greens were firm and holding. Given good weather, I thought we might see some exceptionally low scoring, and I found that most of the other players I talked with shared this opinion. At 7015 yards, Baltusrol wasn't short and it had quite a few sticky holes, but you could see where, if someone got really hot, even Hogan's Open record of 276 might be beaten. Ben had set the record nineteen years before at Riviera.

Ben was one of the players who had to be taken into serious consideration in any evaluation of the Open field. He was fifty-four, granted, but two months before in the Masters he had reminded us all how masterful he still was by shooting a 66 in the third round— 36 out, 30 back. Palmer, of course, would be "up" for the championship, determined to show the golf world that his collapse at Olympic the year before was just one of those unaccountable things. Arn had been playing well all season. He had won at L.A. and at Tucson, and he had been the leading money-winner right along. In my opinion, he was driving the ball better than anyone on the tour. Who else could win at Baltusrol? Billy Casper, the defending champion, could, of course. Gary Player could. Julius Boros certainly could. At forty-seven, Julius was having his best season ever. He had won the Phoenix Open and the Florida Citrus Open and, the week before Baltusrol, the Buick Open. Don January would have to be watched. He was playing excellent golf and was always tough on a long course. There were two other names to add to your list of possible winners: Doug Sanders and Frank Beard. Never having won a major title and very conscious that he had to in order to increase his stature, Sanders now took the championships quite seriously. Beard had come to the front in the spring by winning the Tournament of Champions and the Houston Champions, nipping Palmer both times by holing a pressure putt on the 72nd green. On the tour we rated Frank among the best drivers and putters, a golfer with a sound style who would obviously continue to improve.

My personal long-shot choice was my old buddy, Deane Beman.

Following the Masters, Deane had finally turned professional at the advanced age of twenty-nine. He felt he would always be frustrated in a sense unless he gave himself a chance to see how good he really was. I played my practice rounds with Deane. I liked the way I was hitting my shots, but my putting, which had been plaguing me for five months, was still horrible.

After our round on Friday when Deane and I were tapering off on the practice green, I picked up his center-shafted Bull's Eye putter and tried it out. I had been using a center-shafted Ping putter with a much larger blade, hollowed at the back; a nicely balanced club, this putter is very popular with the touring pros. I had been effective with it the season before, and so I had persevered with it throughout 1967. There was no question, though, that I was stroking the ball much better with Deane's Bull's Eye, a straight-shafted model with a fairly light head.

The next morning when we were back at Baltusrol, Deane brought out four or five Bull's Eyes he had in the trunk of his car. "I can't give you mine," he explained. "I've made the mistake before of letting people try my putter and then they want it, but I need it myself." I liked Deane's other putters but, naturally, not as much as I liked *his* putter. Then a friend of his, Fred Mueller, who was out on the practice green with us, spoke up. He happened to have a Bull's Eye in his car which Deane had fixed up for him, and if I wanted to try it out, he would be glad to fetch it. It turned out to be an exact duplicate of Deane's putter except that Fred had painted the blade white to prevent sun glare. I loved the way it felt. Fred was kind enough to tell me I could have it if I wanted it. I practiced with it at home over the weekend and knew I did.

When I got back to Baltusrol, however, I didn't get the results on the greens I was hoping for. Tuesday night, when I was tapping those invariable three balls on the practice green, Gordon Jones walked over and we began talking about my stroke. Gordon is an old golfing friend from Alliance, Ohio, about ten years my senior, who had turned pro at an early age. He has played the tour from time to time, and he knows a lot about the game. My trouble, Gordon felt, was that I was quitting at the ball—not stroking through the ball. "Why don't you take a little shorter stroke and hit the ball harder?" he asked. As soon as he said this, big bells began to ring. That was how I putted as an amateur: I used a short backswing and then rapped the ball firmly, popping it at the hole. After I had thanked Gordon for his suggestion, I started to work on cutting down the length of my takeaway. The next day, Wednesday, I putted fabulously. It seemed that every time I drew the putter back I holed the putt. I was around in 62 even with a 5–5 finish. I couldn't remember when I last had a round like that.

The weather during the four days of the 1967 Open wasn't as blazing hot as it was in Dallas during the 1963 P.G.A., but the thermometer was well up into the 90s every day and the humidity was brutal. There was hardly a breath of a breeze. You'd look at the thick stands of oaks and maples and evergreens that framed the holes, and you couldn't detect the suspicion of a rustle. The greenkeeper—I think his name was Casey—stayed right on top of things. He had brought the course through a very rainy May and then through a drought in early June, and he brought it through the championship in wonderful shape. The fairways were easily the best I've ever played in this country. The ball was always sitting up for you, and if you weren't able to spin an iron under those conditions, the fault was with you, and you knew it.

On the opening day, Thursday, nine players broke 70, which is an awful lot for the Open. Marty Fleckman, a young amateur from Texas who had worked with Byron Nelson, had a 67. Palmer, Casper, Player, January, and Beman had 69s, as did Art Wall, Chi Chi Rodriguez, and Butch Baird. I had a 71, one over. From tee to green I thought I played pretty darn good, but my new putting stroke hadn't held up. I was worried about this. In a wearing tournament like the Open, you've got to drop an occasional putt to perk yourself up. There was a perfect example of this on the first round. Arnold was two over par playing the thirteenth, a drive-and-pitch 4. He pulled his drive into a hummock of rough there, and it looked as if he might lose another stroke, but he got his recovery onto the green and ran in a 45-footer. After that unlikely birdie, he made two more. That long putt had changed his entire round.

I got off on the wrong foot on the second round with a bogey on the first. I parred the next two holes, but then I missed the green on the short fourth. The most scenic hole on the course, the fourth, in general terms, is not unlike the famous sixteenth at Augusta; both measure about 190 yards and there is nothing between the tee and the green but water—at Baltusrol, a small pond. However, where the sixteenth at Augusta has a longish green with the trouble along the sides (water on the left and bunkers on the right), the green on the fourth at Baltusrol is wider than it is deep. What with the pond lapping against the stone wall that bulwarks the front edge and with four bunkers spotted at the back, your first consideration has to be length, not line. I played a 3-iron and it was the right club, but my timing was hurried. The ball started on the line I wanted—the left side of the green—but instead of fading back into the pin, it had draw on it. It bounced off the left edge of the green and ended up in the light rough behind the fringe. Nothing catastrophic about that. My ball was lying well and I was only 30 feet from the pin. I went to sleep on the chip. I hit it much too hard for that fast green, and it rolled 11 feet past the cup. A bogey 4 would put me two over par for the round, and, as no one had to remind me, with the way the scores were running I couldn't afford to be over 70 or I would be too far behind the leaders ever to catch up.

I worked hard on that putt and made it. It not only saved me a valuable stroke, it did for me what Arnold's putt on the thirteenth the day before had done for him: it lifted my whole game and changed my whole round. I birdied the fifth from 4 feet and the eighth from 12. A pushed drive cost me a bogey on the tenth, but I had momentum now and came back to birdie the twelfth from 15 feet and the sixteenth from 25 feet. On the eighteenth I got home in two and down in two from 40 feet for my fifth birdie: 67, the best scoring round I'd ever had in the Open. It put me only one shot behind the leader, Palmer (68-69–137), and a shot in front of Casper. Fleckman was a shot further back after a 73.

For the third and fourth rounds the U.S.G.A. follows a strict arithmetic progression in making the pairings. The man in first place plays with the man in second place, the man in third place with the man in fourth, and so on up the line. (When two or more people are tied with the same score, the man who posted that score first is considered to be the leader in that group.) This meant that Palmer and I were paired together on Saturday. We carried a huge gallery spearheaded by the most vocal detachment of "Arnie's Army" I'd ever encountered. We treated them to some dull, second-rate golf. When you're paired with Arnold there is always a tendency to play against Arnold. Maybe I did that unconsciously and maybe Arnold unconsciously was playing against me. Whatever the reason, the two of us were equally sloppy.

While we were frittering away a stroke here and a stroke there, Billy Casper wasn't idle. He overtook us and then passed us early in the afternoon, and with four holes to play he had built up a four-stroke lead. Nine times out of ten, when a golfer of Casper's ability and toughness gets that sort of a lead at that stage of a tournament, that's the tournament. This was the tenth time, the odd time. Billy bogeyed the fifteenth, sixteenth, and seventeenth to finish with a 71. Just about this time, Arnold and I finally woke up. Over the first sixteen holes we hadn't made a single birdie between us, but on the seventeenth I got down a 12-footer for a birdie 4—I misread the putt just right—and we both birdied the eighteenth. Nicklaus 72, Palmer 73. We had gotten out of the afternoon cheap.

Marty Fleckman had recaptured the lead with a 67 for 209, but Palmer and I were only one stroke behind him in a triple tie with Casper at 210. Beman, January, Gardner Dickinson, and Miller Barber were at 211. Hogan, Player, Sanders, Beard were out of it; so was Boros who was forced to withdraw because of illness in his family. In addition to Fleckman, the first amateur since Johnny Goodman in 1933 to lead the Open with a round to go, one other dark horse was in contention, a newcomer named Lee Trevino registered out of El Paso. I'd never heard of him, but he had shot rounds of 72, 70, and 71, and to do that in the Open you have to be a player.

Arnold and I were paired again on the fourth round. We went out just in front of Casper and Fleckman. Again an immense, boisterous gallery tramped along with us, a staunchly pro-Palmer gallery equipped with such luxury items (for the spectator-who-has-everything) as cloth signs inscribed "Right Here, Jack" to be held up behind a bunker or a water hazard. When you're accompanied by "Arnold's Army," you know it. You have to make up your mind to accept the Army as a fact of tournament life. When you're in certain moods, the presence of the Army can actually help you: it spurs you on to keep coming and not to let up. This assumes, of course, that you're playing very good golf, and on those days you probably wouldn't be distracted if you were followed by several rock-and-roll outfits, Everett Dirksen, a herd of buffaloes, and the Mafia Marching Band.

On this important round, from the third hole on, I happened to be playing just about as well as I know how. On the second I bunkered my approach and missed my par, but I got that stroke back with a birdie on the third: a good drive, an 8-iron to about 12 feet, and a putt that had just the right speed to topple in when it caught the high corner of the cup. That putt put me back into a tie with Palmer. It also gave me that lift, which I have spoken of before—the feeling that you're playing well, the assurance that you will be rewarded if you continue to, the expectation that the ball will drop for you if you putt it properly. I followed this birdie with another on the fourth where I hit a 3-iron four feet from the stick. This moved me a shot in front of Palmer. More than that, it put me into the lead in the tournament. Fleckman had dropped a stroke on the first after driving into the woods on the right, and another bad drive on the second had cost him a stroke there. (Later on, when he got his driving under control, his putting let him down.) Casper had also gotten off slowly, and, like Fleckman, he never did get into high gear. For all intents and purposes, very early in the fourth round the Open had narrowed down to a two-horse race.

More often than not, when you finally stick your nose in front after you've trailed throughout a tournament, it's difficult to keep playing as aggressively as you did when you were behind. I didn't have that problem at Baltusrol. Playing head-to-head with Palmer, the man I knew I had to beat, kept me charged up. My only thought was to widen my lead. Arnold is always dangerous. You can never lead him by too many shots. On the fifth I increased my margin to two strokes with a 15-foot birdie putt, but I lost that stroke on the very next hole, missing from 7 feet for my par. It was a ticklish putt, however, and my failure to hole it didn't disturb the confidence I had built up by sinking three good putts in a row. Curiously, after I had switched to the Bull's Eye and adopted a shorter stroke, my putting had followed a strange in-and-out sequence. On Wednesday (when I had that 62), it had been spectacular; on Thursday, only fair; on Friday, wonderful again; on Saturday, just fair again. If that pattern held up, I was due for another good day.

The next two holes, the seventh and eighth, may very well have decided the championship. The seventh, 470 yards long, plays as a par 5 for members of Baltusrol, but in the Open we played it as a 4. A dogleg to the right over flat terrain, it dips a little before the green, and the frontal bunkers hide the foot of the flagstick from view. The green is oval-shaped and falls away at the rear. Arnold and I both hit big drives, with Arnold away by a couple of yards. He had been playing sound, steady golf—six straight pars—and here on the seventh he came through with a really magnificent shot, a 1-iron that he smoked right at the flag and which finished just 12 feet past. Arnold hadn't holed a putt up to this pont, and this was a likely spot for him to begin. I took a 3-iron for my second and hit a high left-to-right approach about 22 feet past the flag and to the right of it—not a great shot like Arnold's but not a bad one. As Arnold walked onto the green he received a tremendous hand. I followed him onto the green and started to study the line of my putt. If I missed and Arnold holed, I was thinking, we'd be all even and Arnold would be psychologically primed to take off on one of those bursts of his. My putt looked like it had only a slight right-to-left break, but the texture of the grass in that area of the green seemed a little heavier than on most of the greens, and I wasn't too sure how hard to strike the ball or whether, in truth, I had read the speed of the green correctly. I hit a very firm putt and I had the ball dead on line, but I was afraid I'd hit it too hard. It kept running for the cup and dove right in. That turned everything around. It made Arnold's putt longer and tougher, of course, and on top of that, it shifted the psychological advantage to me: even if Arnold made his 12-footer, he would still be a stroke behind. He missed it by an inch. I went to the eighth unexpectedly leading by two.

The eighth is the shortest par 4 on Baltusrol's Lower Course, only 365 yards long. It is, nevertheless, a good strong hole, one of the best on the course. It is a tee-shot hole primarily. Over the fence on the left side is out-of-bounds, but the tee-shot must be played down the left or left-center of the fairway in order for the player to be in the correct position for the opening to the small, heavily bunkered green. If you let your tee-shot slide to the right of the fairway, your route to the green will be blocked by a tall, spreading tree whose branches extend well out over the narrowing fairway. I hit just the drive I wanted, down the left and long. Palmer's drive got away from him. Cut out to the right, it bounced into the rough, and ended up close to the trunk of a tree. He had no choice but to play out laterally onto the fairway and to try and recoup his 4 by dropping his pitch near the pin, tucked at the front of the green. He played it a fraction too much to the right, and the ball trickled off the fringe and into a shallow bunker. Palmer doesn't give you many openings like this and you have to seize them when they come. I'm not an especially good short-pitch player, but for once I produced a really nice shot, a sand wedge from about 85 yards out that hit four feet from the pin and stopped right there. Arnold got down in two for a 5, but I made the putt for my 3, and now I led by four strokes.

After that there was only one moment when my confidence in my ability to hold onto the lead wavered. Walking down the eleventh after three-putting the tenth, I had a flurry of self-doubt, but it passed relatively quickly. I pushed my lead to four strokes again with a birdie on the thirteenth where I put a pitching wedge about four feet from the pin. Another birdie on the fourteenth pushed it to five strokes. There I hit a 7-iron approach five feet from the pin. I had never before, in any tournament, played a succession of fine pitches like these. Pars on the fifteenth, sixteenth, and seventeenth for me, two pars and a birdie for Palmer. He had continued to play top-notch golf—the only real mistake he made had come on the eighth—but until the seventeenth Arnold hadn't been able to get down a birdie putt. . . . With one hole to go, I had four strokes in hand.

Down the stretch at Baltusrol. The expressions tell the story. Palmer has just missed a holeable birdie putt, and I move to my shorter one to see if I can drop it and widen my lead. I have never hit my pitches better.

The home hole at Baltusrol, as I mentioned earlier, is a 542-yard par 5 that can be reached with two big shots. However, you can go for a bundle on the eighteenth, a dogleg to the left with the break coming about 275 yards out from the elevated tee. On the drive you want to favor the right-hand side of the down-sloping fairway, for along the left there is water paralleling the fairway, clumpy rough, and a thick woods. (In the 1954 Open, Furgol drove into the woods on the last round and might not have gotten the 5 he needed to win had he not discovered an opening through the trees onto the eighteenth fairway of the Upper Course. He played out that way, put his third on, and got down in two putts.) On the other hand, if you aim your drive down the right and push it a little, there's trouble there, too—rough, bushes, trees. (Just such a tee-shot on the last hole in 1954 had cost Dick Mayer a 7 and possibly the championship.) I decided to play the safe, prudent tee-shot: a 1-iron. I didn't need to make 4. With a four-stroke margin, I just wanted to be sure I didn't make more than 6.

My 1-iron slid off a few yards to the right of the line I meant to take, but it was not hit far enough to reach the bushes and trees. It finished a couple of yards in the rough on a patch of bare ground close by a television cable drum. I was permitted a free drop to get clear of the obstruction, but with a tight lie on crusty ground I decided that the intelligent shot was to lay up short of the sizable water-hazard that crossed the fairway about 120 yards in front of me. I took an 8-iron, set myself up carefully to play a little three-quarter punch, looked up on the shot like a duffer, struck the ground a good two inches behind the ball, and advanced it barely 50 yards nearer the hole. Arnold, who had hit a perfect drive, then played his second—a fairway wood up and over the hillside bunker; it finished short and to the right of the plateau green. I took out my 1-iron. By my calculations I was some 230 yards from the green, all carry, and slightly against the wind. I didn't know if I could fly a 1-iron that distance, but that was the club I wanted to play. I have a great deal of confidence in it—much more than I have in my 3-wood—and I felt certain I could carry the ball far enough to at least clear the hillside bunker and that I could hit it straight enough to stay out of the bunkers to the left of the green. As a left-to-right player I was in luck here, for the ideal way to play the shot was to bring it in from the left: both the landing area before the green (which had been turned into light rough) and the green itself fall off to the right. I doubt if I have ever hit a better 1-iron. I know I've never hit a longer one. It carried the bunker, landed a few feet short of the green, hopped onto the green, and finished 22 feet from the cup. As I made the long walk up the hill, I knew I had that putt to beat Hogan's record, but this was irrelevant. I had the tournament won—that was the big thing, the only thing. I worked on the putt, of course, and I happened to make it, but records are just bonuses—the cherry on the sundae. Indeed, they're accidents most of the time. The importance of my total of 275 (71-67-72-65) was that it was the lowest score in the 1967 United States Open.

After what it had done for me in the Open, I stayed with the white-bladed Bull's Eye (which Fred Mueller had christened "White Fang"), and it had a lot to do with the good, solid, cheering golf I played the rest of the year. In the British Open, at Hoylake, I was the runner-up—and not unhappy to be, since the winner was Roberto de Vicenzo, a wonderful guy and a superb striker of the small ball, who had been trying for twenty years to win the British Open and had come tragically close a half-dozen times. Back home I tied for third in the P.G.A., the Canadian Open, and the American Golf Classic; I was second in the Thunderbird; and I won the Western (a tournament I valued winning), the Westchester Classic (the first $250,000 event), the World Series of Golf, and the Sahara. When December came around and my time was my own and I could laze in the sun and fish to my heart's content in Florida, the days were very sweet. No one was saying any longer, "Whatever became of Jack Nicklaus?"

Part Four

XVI

First Principles:
The Structure of the
Golf Swing

To instruct a golfer so that he really benefits is not an easy thing even when you are working together face to face on the practice tee. To do so through the printed word and illustrations and still get your points across is, of course, a hundred times harder. However, I believe that for all its difficulties this "remote" kind of instruction can be of considerable value to the average golfer-reader in helping him to understand what a sound swing consists of and in assisting him to improve his own. If I thought otherwise, I wouldn't attempt it.

It is my feeling that I will be able to get across my thoughts on golf and the golf swing more effectively—and that the reader, in turn, will best be able to digest them—if I present my points in "short takes," step by step. One other thing. While I trust that my philosophy of golf will be implicit as you read these instructional chapters, let me state it directly: The sensible way to approach golf is to make the game as simple as possible. It's hard enough as is without complicating it.

The golf swing, as I see it, is made up of a massing of many different coordinated components. If that seems like quite a mouthful, it is meant to be. A correct golf swing *is* an involved physical performance. To be a fairly good golfer, a man must coordinate a large number of the components of the swing. To be a truly first-class golfer, he must be able to coordinate all the components, and in order to do this he must have a great deal of natural ability.

What are the basic components of the golf swing? Well, to begin with, I would say that the most important one is the only non-moving part: the head. As such, it acts as the fulcrum of the swing.

A good head position.

If a golfer keeps his head still and steady, then if his club takes a reasonably good path through the ball, he will hit good golf shots. The best players invariably have very "quiet" heads. A chief reason why Arnold Palmer, for example, plays such fine golf is that his head remains in a perfect position throughout his swing. It *makes* his swing. The converse is equally true. If a golfer moves his head, it will throw his swing badly off.

On the backswing many moves must be coordinated, but in this segment of the swing what I try to do (along with maintaining a good head position) is to make the widest possible arc with the

256

club. The wider the arc you can make on your backswing without consciously cocking your wrists, the better. The role of the wrists here strikes me as critical, and I want to go over this point carefully. On the backswing you don't restrain your wrists from cocking, but you don't make a definite move to cock them. There's no need to. A wide arc with the arms on the backswing is the product of a full shoulder turn, and if you execute a full shoulder turn with your arms extended, you can't help your hands and wrists from cocking.

Some good players drop their wrists at the top of the backswing to gain what they think is an added cocking, the idea being that

The point in the downswing where the cocking starts to increase.

this will give them more hand power, added distance. They are mistaken. First, their hands and wrists were sufficiently cocked before. Second, when the golf swing is performed correctly, the hands naturally increase their cocking as they move into the downswing. Sam Snead, as I said earlier, stands out as a player whose arms and hands are in an ideal position at the top of the backswing, and I'm sure this is one of the main reasons why Sam has lasted so long. You see, if in your efforts to hit the ball a good distance you don't depend first and foremost on hands-play, then you have to rely on tempo and timing in your pursuit of distance—and the latter is a much superior approach to building a sound golf swing.

However, the average golfer is forced to use his hands because he doesn't move into a position on the backswing in which tempo and timing can be developed. To put it another way, he is forced to try and complete with his hands the cocking action that would have taken place automatically—and better—if he had executed a full shoulder turn with the arms fully extended.

You cannot make a full shoulder turn unless you make a full hip turn. If you inhibit your hips from turning, you'll inhibit your shoulders from turning. The amount of hip turn in a golfer's swing is governed by three things: the length of the club, the width of the stance, the position of the feet and legs. The first of these, the length of the club, takes care of itself. The second, the width of the stance, is quite simple. If a golfer widens his stance, it restricts his hip turn. If he takes a narrower stance, he can make a freer hip turn. Bob Jones, to cite one example, used a very narrow stance to facilitate the freest hip turn of any golfer of the 1920s. This set up his full, rhythmic swing and was the source of the power that made Jones, when he wanted distance, one of the longest wooden-club players of his time.

The third factor—how you stand, or, better yet, how you set yourself up at the ball—is more intricate. Stance has a decisive effect on the backswing, for it ordains your alignment on your target, and faulty alignment will cause you to make a bad move with your body or your arms or hands on the backswing. Since the whole swing is interrelated, one bad move leads to another bad move and another and another. Indeed, I would say that proper alignment along with a proper head position are the two most important parts of the golf swing.

When you set your feet in place before the ball, your hips must be in correct alignment and your shoulders must be in correct alignment, for the route your hips and shoulders take when they turn determines the path your club will take. A great many errors in golf stem from the player's failure to align his hips and shoulders on the target; his clubhead follows the path they have set up, but it isn't the path to the target. Just as many errors result when this same player, aware that his shots have been off-line, doesn't correct his alignment on his subsequent shots but attempts instead to cure his problem by steering the ball toward his target with his arms and hands. He can't possibly hit a good golf shot then, not when he's moving simultaneously in two different directions—one with his shoulders and hips, the other with his hands and arms.

I think I can best get across what correct alignment is all about by describing how a sound golfer—say, Billy Casper—approaches it. Billy, who has the ability to simplify golf, lines up a little to the left of his target, since he usually allows for a slight fade. Then Billy forgets about his target, entirely. He concentrates solely on executing his fine repeating swing *in terms of the stance he has taken.* He knows that if he makes a good swing, the ball will go where he means it to go.

If you don't execute the backswing properly, you can't execute the downswing properly. Since the downswing is an almost wholly reflexive action, let's take another look at the backswing, the controllable part of the swing.

Let's start with the hands. Contrary to the opinions of many golfers and golf scholars, I don't believe that a great deal of power is generated by the hands themselves. The hands, to my mind, function as a connection between my clubhead and my arms—a flexible link which, in effect, extends my arms another 43 inches, the length of my driver. I feel I play my best golf when my left arm is perfectly straight, when that arm, the back of my left hand, and the shaft of the club form one unbroken line. *I think of my right arm as a brace for my left arm.*

When a golfer has placed his hands on the club and settled into his stance, his next concern is starting his backswing. It's difficult to start it cold. It has to have some ignition. There are two ways you can achieve this. First, you can initiate the backswing with what is called a forward press—a slight move toward the target with the legs or the hips that, you might say, untracks a golfer from his stock-still position before the ball. (Gary Player, for instance, makes his forward press by pushing his right hip forward, and then, having gotten himself moving, slides into his backswing.) Second, you can initiate the backswing with a stationary press, the method I use. I call it a stationary press since the legs and the hips don't move, remaining just where they are at address. What takes place is this: Standing with your hips and legs and everything else relaxed, you firm up your hands, pressing them together on the shaft once or twice. This tiny move pulls your arms closer together, but that is almost irrelevant. The true purpose of the press is that it is an affirming. It puts feel not only in your hands but also in your feet and legs and hips—it seems to alert the muscles you'll be using on your backswing. By readying them for the moves they make at the start of the swing, it helps the golfer to make these moves more easily and more fluently. I prefer the stationary press to the forward press. A forward press is bound to vary more, and so, it follows, will your takeaway. The big thing is not the degree of the press you make but its uniformity.

The next stage of the swing is a terribly forced, ridiculously slow movement of the club away from the ball. This is where a good press helps you enormously: it enables you to move everything together—hands, arms, shoulders, hips, legs, feet. Over the first 10 or 12 inches of the backswing, in addition to moving everything in "one piece," you should move them as slowly as you can. You should be thinking in terms of maintaining this tempo throughout the entire swing. You can't, of course. Because you're swinging a long-shafted club with a relatively heavy head, the rate of speed of your swing is bound to pick up. However, there's no such thing as being "ridiculously slow" with the hands and arms, which is why I purposely use that phrase. By attempting to be ridiculously slow, you at least insure that your tempo will be unhurried and satisfactorily slow.

The harder I want to hit the ball, the slower I start my takeaway. I want it to be just fast enough to avoid being jerky. Though I'm conscious in a corner of my mind that I'm trying to hit the ball

Try for a ridiculously slow movement of the club away from the ball.

as far as possible, I know that I don't have to move my arms and hands fast to gain maximum distance. It is clubhead speed in the hitting zone that will give me distance, and that's a wholly different thing from the speed with which the arms and hands make their movements going back and coming down. Clubhead speed, as we all have been told, depends largely on leverage and centrifugal force, but let me say at this point that I don't believe it is much help to get involved with the influence that the laws of physics have on the golf swing. I translate leverage into the width of the golfer's arc—the wider it is, the greater potential force he is able to build up. I translate centrifugal force—the force that impels an object away from a center of rotation—as the power generated, chiefly by the legs and hips, in the actual hitting zone. The faster the correct movements are made, the greater the power generated.

At the start of the backswing, the club is taken back on a straight line away from the target. It then swings inside that line, directed by the turning movement of the hips and shoulders. The return path to the ball on the downswing is just about the same, except that the clubhead will be moving at a sharper angle on the downward path. Do not work for an inside-out arc or an outside-in arc coming down. You will only foul up the cohesion of your swing.

The downswing, as I stated earlier, is for the most part a reflexive action. It takes place so quickly that even the most accomplished golfers are lucky if they can think of doing just one thing during that phase of the swing—and do it. Though nearly every top-rung golfer arrives at approximately the same position when he enters the actual hitting zone, each one has his own individual method for getting there. One will start his downswing with a pulling-down motion of the left arm. Another will start it by pushing off the right foot. Another will lead with the hips, the left hip in charge. Another will throw his right shoulder under. There are countless variations. Each golfer uses the move that works best for him. Sometimes it came to him naturally, other times he mastered it by hard work. Either way, it is a move that has become second nature to him and which he can execute almost without thinking about it. My own method of starting the downswing combines raising the left shoulder and pushing the right hip down and under. This allows me, as I hit through the ball, to extend my right arm full length toward my target—somewhat similar to the way the right arm swings all

The golf swing is a massing of many different components. Coordinating them correctly is no simple thing—one bad move leads to many. I find it useful to make a stationary press with my hands (note photograph 1) before starting my backswing. It helps me to ready the components in advance, whether I'm playing a full tee-shot or, as in this sequence, just a wedge pitch.

the way through when you bowl or when you pitch a softball.

As your weight starts to reach your left side on the downswing, your left side should become progressively firmer until you have passed impact. (We'll go into that further in the next chapter.) The main point I want to make, though, is that once you've begun your move into the ball, almost everything you do is the result of what you've done earlier in the swing. *You've played as good a swing as you set up.* All you can consciously do is to finish the swing right, making sure that you stay on your left side until the swing is completed and that your head remains fixed and steady. You will seldom finish with your hands nice and high and with your head in a good position unless you've made a good swing.

One further word about the head. After you've hit through the ball, your head will swivel toward the left, but it shouldn't tip or bob or turn or raise up. It is the neck, really, that stays fixed, since the head does swivel slightly, but I think a golfer will profit if he thinks of the head remaining in just about the same position it was at address.

I am reminded at this point to bring up the fact that a golfer can execute a good swing only if he is on balance. The two keys to balance in Jack Grout's judgment were (and are) keeping the head still as you swing your hands to the highest possible point on the backswing and the finish, and, secondly, keeping your weight in balance in the area between your two feet—that is, not permit-

A correct finish: right shoulder lower than left; hands high; head not raised.

ting it to tip too far to the right going back or too far forward coming down. I consider these two keys to balance so invaluable that when I start my young sons off in golf, I will see to it that no other part of the swing has a higher priority.

What I have done, I trust, in this chapter is to give you an idea of the basic structure of the golf swing, introducing the fundamental movements and their interrelationship. The more of the movements you execute right, the better swings you'll make and the better shots you'll hit.

Your local golf professional is the man who can teach you to make the fundamental moves the way they should be made and, later on, check on how well you are continuing to make those moves. Most club pros are competent at handling not only beginners but golfers who have played quite a bit but who haven't had the opportunity to study the game, not to mention those experienced golfers who have an excellent understanding of the game but who have taken themselves as far as they can go and need instruction to improve further. Even the best shotmakers, as you may or may not know, have to have their swings checked continually. I know I need to be looked over at regular intervals, because when I'm playing a run of tournaments I'll usually fall into some bad habit or other. It's hard not to. There are countless things you have to remember to do, and when you're engaged in a competition you can only think of a limited number of them. I play my best, I find, when I try not to think of more than two things during a swing—maybe some move on the backswing and some move on the downswing. However, what often happens is that while you're concentrating on executing, say, move F, you forget to execute move C or G as well as you should, and you won't know this until someone who is professionally familiar with your swing points it out.

Speaking of what one consciously thinks about during the golf swing, it may be helpful if I tell you what were my thought processes during the summer of 1967 when I enjoyed an extended stretch of good, solid golf. I'd carefully set up to the left of the target—ten yards to the left off the tee—and open my clubhead a shade since I was playing for a left-to-right flight. On my backswing I gave primary consideration to preventing my head from moving. It had been. It needed attention. The one thing I thought of on the downswing was keeping my head well behind the ball and keeping it steady. It had been moving and this had upset my balance and made my path through the ball inconsistent. Some days when my head seemed good and still, I then worked on making sure that I didn't let my hands roll over until I was actually completing my follow-through. On those particular days, I would suppose, I hit a higher percentage than usual of accurate golf shots . . . but I probably threw it away on the greens.

XVII

Power: The Four Sources

COMPARED TO MOST GOLFERS, I hit the ball quite long. It's a tremendous asset, power, as long as you control it. A big drive on a par 4 allows you to use a much shorter iron on your second shot; the shorter the iron, the closer to the flagstick you should be able to put the ball. A big drive on a par 5 occasionally allows you to get home in two when the green is out of the range of the only moderately long hitter. Power intrigues all golfers, and since I am associated with it, just about three out of every four questions I'm asked have to do with "How do you get your distance?" While I am flattered by this, at the same time I feel a little like those solid all-round golfers who also happen to be excellent putters and who, publicity being what it is, tend to become known only for their putting—the implication finally being that all they can do is putt, and if it weren't for the monsters they hole on the greens they'd be selling used cars. I think I have a pretty good golf swing, power aside, so I relish it when some free soul at a tournament asks me to elaborate on how I achieve such exquisite timing with my medium irons or to reveal what lies behind my stunning mastery of the feathered wedge. But, in a way, I'm not kidding. The majority of golfers are so bewitched by power that they never get it into their heads that no one can hit the ball long and straight as a regular thing unless he is a sound technician. The secret of power is having a good golf swing.

Now that I have made it clear, I trust, that building a correct golf swing comes first and that long yardage is strictly a by-product, I would say that there are four chief sources of power: (1) a club of the proper weight and balance; (2) a long, wide arc; (3) speed of movement from the right side to the left at the start of the downswing; (4) the speed with which the left hip, having stopped its forward move, spins to the rear in the hitting zone. Let's look into these factors one at a time.

1. Swinging a club that is correctly weighted and balanced deserves more attention than most golfers give it. If I tell you about my own experiences in arriving at the driver I use today, I believe it will bring out the various considerations one should bear in mind. My present driver is 42¾ inches long, it has a square face with nine degrees of loft, it weighs 14 ounces, it has a Dynamic S shaft, and it has a swing-weight of D-1. How did I arrive at these specifications? The answer, of course, is through trial and error.

The first change I made from the stock drivers I used as a youngster came about when I decided to investigate the problem of swing-weight. Swing-weight is a concept of achieving overall balance in a club. In a simplified way, it is the ratio of the weight of the club-head to the weight of the grip, with the aim being to keep the feel of each club in a set the same regardless of the length of the shaft. Most pros use clubs with a medium swing-weight, between D-1 and D-3. As an amateur, I used a D-5 or D-6 driver. I found, though, that very often when I had to play 36 holes a day—which is not unusual in amateur golf—I couldn't swing that heavy a club for seven hours or more and swing it well. Through experimentation I learned that if I went down to a D-1, I could move that amount of weight all day without losing my effectiveness. Fine. However, I discovered that when I reduced my swing-weight to D-1, I had come down to a 13-ounce driver. This presented a complication: early in the day I would swing that light a club too fast. To offset this, I gradually increased the weight of my club to 14 ounces. Then I had a driver that was perfectly balanced for me— or at least I thought so. In any event, I've stayed with this distribution of weight.

Now the shaft. Generally speaking, the golf manufacturers put out shafts with four standard degrees of flexibility. The designations for these different types of shaft vary somewhat with the manufacturer, but as a rule it goes like this: an A shaft is a whippy shaft (which gives a player added distance but is hard to control); an R shaft is a regular shaft, neither stiff nor whippy; an S shaft is a stiff shaft; and an X shaft is extra stiff. When you are using a relatively light swing-weight, such as D-1, the shaft doesn't flex as much as it will with a heavier swing-weight. With a D-1 swing-weight, a

Dynamic S shaft reacts about the same way an X shaft would if I used a D-5 or D-6. After a brief, woeful period in 1962 in which I experimented with an X shaft, I stayed with the Dynamic S until 1968 when I moved to a slightly softer shaft, the TTW.

Next, I discovered that, for some silly reason, a 43-inch driver, which is standard length, played a touch too soft, too whippy for me. To stiffen the shaft just that touch, I had a quarter of an inch taken off the end of the shaft that enters the clubhead; hence my driver's present length of 42¾ inches. With this slightly shorter shaft, I naturally lose a little distance. However, distance isn't my problem. Accuracy is my problem. The shorter club makes sense for me, because it's easier to control and this increases my accuracy.

I should interject here that I have been discussing only one club, my driver—*the* power club. Forgetting about the putter, the rest of my clubs, with one exception, have Dynamic S shafts of standard length and they swing D-2. The exception is my sand wedge, in which I have an X shaft which I took from a discarded driver. Regard this as an idiosyncrasy of mine: I think a wedge with minimum flex improves my sense of clubhead feel. You, too, through trial and error, will hit upon the weight, swing-weight, and shaft length specifications that are best for you, but I would guess that, unless you are ultra-serious about your golf, you won't need to be half as finicky as I've been about my driver. To repeat, I could certainly hit the ball farther if I used a club with a heavier swing-weight and a longer shaft, but distance is not the name of the game. The name of the game is consistency.

2. In the era of the wooden shaft and for some time after the steel shaft came in, most golf pros taught their pupils to keep the right elbow in close—so close that if they tucked a handkerchief in the armpit, it would remain there snugly throughout the backswing. The weakness of the type of swing which this old-style teaching bred was the narrowness of the arc, and this necessarily produced hands-players—men who bunted the ball down the fairway. Even the best hands-players don't last many years. That style of play demands the ultimate in timing, and no golfer can manage this under pressure once he loses the fantastic coordination of youth.

At the same time, in the old days—the days of Old Tom Morris and the subsequent decades—power golf was not a very big part

269

This sequence shows how my right elbow moves away from the body on the backswing and tucks in and returns to the orthodox position on the downswing. A real "flying elbow" points to the sky at the top of the backswing.

of golf. The champions were not the men who were colossal hitters. They were the men who were straight and sure. It is Harry Vardon who is remembered, not Ted Ray.

Golf is different today. This is the era of the power golfer. You see more and more of the young players employing the modern power swing. The arc is very wide going back. The hands are very high. While the right elbow doesn't exactly "fly," it isn't tucked in as tightly as it once was. I probably exaggerate the elbow-away-from-the-body move more than any other player, but the difference is only a matter of degree. All the young power players have the elbow out a bit, since it permits a wider arc, and, as we noted earlier, the increased leverage a wide arc creates is a much more trustworthy means of gaining clubhead velocity than speeding up your hands, no matter how strong they are.

3. On the backswing, weight and tension are stored up on the inside of my right foot, the inside of my flexed right knee, and the inside of my right thigh. When I'm in this position, I feel sort of like a sprinter crouched and eager at the start of a 100-yard dash. My body feels all wound up, coiled with energy, ready to spring for-

On a full tee-shot it is very important that the head, the fulcrum of the swing, be still and steady. At impact and during the hit-through, it remains in its original position: behind the ball.

273

The driver, from the rear. Two big points to emphasize. On the backswing, work to start the club back on a straight line from the ball. (Note photo-

274

graphs 2 and 3.) Work also for the fullest possible shoulder turn. It will enable you to achieve full extension through the ball. (Note photograph 12.)

A good full shoulder turn helps store up the tension.

ward. I begin my downswing by pushing off the right foot with the
right knee, and my right thigh drives me forward. As my right side
moves forward, my left side moves with it.

I will not embroider on this simple description except to underline once again that *how well a golfer moves on the downswing
depends directly on how well he has moved going back.*

4. The first push forward on the downswing is succeeded by a
whiplash motion that results when your left leg firms up and your
left hip moves out of the way as you enter the hitting zone. Let me
describe this slowly. On that first push forward, your hips move
forward—laterally. Your shoulders have begun to move, coordinated with the hips. At this point in the swing, your arms are just
beginning to start down from the top—they haven't moved much
at all compared with your hips and shoulders. You're moving the
upper part of your body—the hips and shoulders—faster than the
arms can move. Accordingly, at this stage of the downswing your
arms need an added acceleration, "more throttle," in order to catch
up. What happens is this. As your hands are about to enter the
hitting zone, your hips stop moving forward and start to turn, to
spin, to the rear. *The speed of your body is slowed down by the
turning of the hips, and this produces a slinging action in which
your arms, your hands, and your clubhead are released with such
speed that they do catch up with your body as you hit through the
ball.* The faster you can move your hips forward and then whip
them out of the way, the faster will be your slinging action—an
action that continues well past impact, with the arms reaching full
extension only after the ball has been struck.

The controlling factor for me on this vital phase of the downswing is my left side. Let me be more specific. After I have made
the initial push forward off my right foot, right knee, and right

thigh, my hips move laterally and my weight shifts to my left side. When I feel that the bulk of my weight has been transferred to my left side—actually it hasn't been, but it feels that way for every golfer—*then I want my left hip to brake its forward motion. I do this by firming my left leg with a conscious movement—firming the left knee.* The left leg becomes almost straight but it retains its flexibility. This act of firming the left leg forces the left hip to rotate to the rear—what is commonly called "clearing the left side." I have very strong legs and thighs, and so I am able to turn the left hip out of the way very, very fast. This is the principal reason, I think, why I am able to generate a great deal of clubhead speed and to hit the ball longer than most golfers.

Different golfers emphasise different things to gain their distance. Arnold Palmer, as you can tell by watching him, stresses the shoulders and the arms. On the other hand, Gary Player, since he's a comparatively small man, has to integrate the action of his shoulders, arms, and legs with the virtuoso athlete's ability to move himself into an ideal releasing position. I concentrate on the legs and hips. I don't think of the hands at all. Their action is entirely instinctive.

Incidentally, I have rather small hands and small pudgy fingers, which surprises most people since they associate big hitting with big hands. My fingers aren't especially strong either. When Barbara has trouble removing the top of, say, a mayonnaise jar and passes it to me, I usually can't twist it off. Back it goes to Barbara and I look on with amazement, and discomfort, as she applies a little more elbow grease and—flick!—the top slides off.

A key source of power: The left leg firms just before impact and the left hip rotates to the rear. These photos, by the way, were taken in 1959.

XVIII

Accuracy, the Product of a Good Swing

ONE OF THE MOST DISCOURAGING features of golf is that there are no shortcuts to learning how to play the game acceptably well. This is true, really, of all sports: to excel at them one must master the fundamentals, and that takes application and patience. Far more than any other sport, though, golf has a strange quality of illusion about it. For example, when a sports fan sees a linebacker ride off a block and move in for a driving tackle, or when he watches a shortstop hustle deep into the hole for a hard-hit ground ball and drill the ball to first ahead of the runner, he knows it isn't done with mirrors. However, when he watches a golfer fire an approach right to the flag, it all looks so deceptively effortless that he persists in believing that if some inside tip on technique (which the pros know but won't let out) were revealed to him, he would be knocking down the flags, too.

The explanation, I would think, lies in the unique nature of golf. As the only major game in which a man hits a stationary ball from a stationary position, it requires neither brawn nor speed of foot nor athletic agility nor endurance. Anyone can play it. Besides, at least once every round, the average golfer will hit a first-class shot that would do credit to a Littler or a Boros. He knows, consequently, that it's in his power to hit a fine golf shot. If he only knew what he did on that shot so that he could repeat it, he would tear up the course. No other sport intoxicates a man with such dreams of glory. He realizes that if he stood at the plate for an hour during batting practice he could never hit one pitch out of a major-league park; he knows he could barely get his racket on Rod Laver's serve if he stayed out on the court all day; he knows that never in a

278

thousand tries could he fake Jerry West out of position and drive around him into the basket; and so on. But golf is different. Today the secret, tomorrow the British Open Championship.

Accuracy, the foundation of good golf, is the product of a correct golf swing. The golfer who can execute most of the fundamentals sets up a desirable swing pattern. The better the golfer's swing pattern, the more accurate he will be. It is all as simple and unmysterious—and as dull—as that.

What are the principal errors that break down a golfer's swing? I'd say there are four: (1) a bad grip; (2) bad alignment; (3) a bad head position during the swing; and (4) bad, jumpy rhythm that causes bad timing. This applies whether a golfer shoots in the 70s or the 90s.

All right, you say, there are a number of successful pros who don't have picture-book swings and who obviously don't execute every fundamental perfectly—men like Bob Rosburg, Deane Beman, Billy Maxwell, and Jim Ferrier, to name four who come to mind quickly. What are the fundamentals which these men execute that make them far better players than many golfers who appear to have better swings? The answer, I think, must be somewhat oblique. Whatever their idiosyncrasies, these unorthodox stars all arrive in the correct hitting position when they enter the hitting zone: a sufficient amount of weight has moved to the left side; the head is behind the ball; the left arm and hand and the shaft are in a relatively straight line; and the club is moving squarely on the path to the target. I think that all these talented nonstylists would agree that they might possibly have become even better players had they developed more orthodox swing patterns, but in the area where it really counts, they are exceedingly sound—much sounder than they appear to be.

Unless you are one of these gifted nonconformists—and there aren't many of them—the only way that you can reach a correct hitting position and complete a correct swing is to learn to perform the fundamentals. That isn't easy. I know of only one way in which you can simplify golf for yourself, and that is by being as natural as possible in setting yourself up for the golf swing.

First. Don't get all pretzeled up affixing your grip. When you stand normally, it's natural for your arms to hang with the palms of your hands facing in. Don't change that. Just bring your hands together as you form your grip.

279

The hands naturally hang with the palms facing in. Just bring them together.

Second. When you take your stance, your feet should be a comfortable distance apart—the same distance apart as when you're standing around doing nothing in particular. If you set your feet too far apart or too close together, you'll destroy your natural equilibrium, and you won't be able to swing with ease and balance. Your weight should be evenly distributed between the balls and the heels of your feet. Your weight should not tip forward even though you have a golf club in your hands and are extending it toward the ball.

Third. As regards your posture before the ball, don't overwork at it. Don't shove your hips out toward the ball. Don't drop your right shoulder way down. Your right shoulder has to be a little lower than your left only because your right hand grips the club lower down the shaft than your left hand. Don't force your head into an artificial position. Your head is set squarely in the middle of your shoulders—leave it there. Don't tense up your arms, or any part of your body. Stand at the ball just as if you were standing on the corner watching all the girls go by. Tony Lema looked great at the ball. There was no trace of strain. Sam Snead and Jack Burke look wonderful. They make assuming the position of address seem as instinctive as opening a door or picking up a phone.

While it is true that the golf swing must be learned and that the

280

muscles must memorize their functions, I think it is misleading to say (as many do) that there is nothing natural about golf. Once a golfer understands the moves he should make, how well he performs them depends on his coordination. The more natural his position at the ball, the better his chances of utilizing his natural coordination during his swing and producing a correct, smooth stroke.

It is hardest to control the golf ball when you try to hit it straight at your target. To say this a little differently, the golfer who takes dead aim on the pin and tries to hit the ball so that it will travel toward it on an absolutely direct line is attempting the most difficult shot in golf. It's almost a sure thing that he'll hook or slice the ball. The intelligent golfer appreciates this. Therefore, he thinks of accuracy not in terms of a slim pin type of target but in terms of an area target—the whole fairway, the whole green.

Let me illustrate. Say I'm playing a 5-iron shot to a green 80 feet wide, with the pin positioned in the center of the green. If I aim at the pin, that leaves me only 40 feet of green on either side if I hook or slice the shot. As a left-to-right player, I give myself a much greater margin for error if I aim 20 feet to the left of the pin and try to work the ball in. I can make a 40-foot error and still keep the ball within 20 feet of the hole. The same in reverse would apply for the right-to-left player, of course.

Assuming that a golfer has learned how to fade or draw the ball —whichever has become the most dependable method for him— ten percent of the time he will make a mistake and his fade or draw won't come off, but the percentages are with him. Furthermore, golfers make much freer and better swings when they're playing for an area; they know they have ample margin for error and they go about their shots in a relaxed manner. It is significant, I think, that the two most consistently accurate shotmakers the game has known, Harry Vardon and Ben Hogan, didn't try to bisect the fairway or split the pin, but being left-to-right players, they aimed to the left of their target and let the ball fall in.

Speaking for myself, when I'm playing left-to-right really well, off the tee I allow for the ball to swing half the width of the fairway. I aim for the left edge of the fairway, so that if my fade doesn't come off, I'll still be in the fairway and not in the rough. With a 3-iron, I'll aim about 20 to 30 feet to the left of the flag; with a 5-iron, 15 or 20 feet to the left; with an 8-iron, about 10 feet; with

Alignment for left-to-right drive: I aim for the left side of the fairway.

a wedge, just a shade to the left. It's harder, of course, to fade or draw a short iron, intentionally or unintentionally, than a long iron or a wood.

Since a hooked ball will generally have a low, hard, buzzing flight and will roll a good ways, hitting the ball from right to left gives a golfer more distance than hitting it from left to right. I like to play left-to-right because distance is not what I'm after—I'm long enough. Control is my main concern, and left-to-right gives you more control. Left-to-right spin is gentler than draw or hook spin, and, as a result, the degree of swerve or break in the flight of your ball is less extreme. A faded ball usually flies higher, too, and this contributes to the fact that the ball will land more softly and sit down more quicky and safely.

Because of these reasons, a fair proportion of golfers have always been left-to-right devotees, and down through the years a number of different methods for fading the ball have been advanced. I don't care for most of them. They're too complicated for me, and I would think the same must be true for the average golfer.

To start with, most of the old how-to-fade methods prescribe an exaggeratedly open stance. That can throw you into too many bad habits. When I want to fade the ball, I take my regular stance, aligning myself squarely on my primary target—say, the left side of the fairway if my ultimate target is the center of the fairway.

Then, there are methods for fading the ball that are based on a grip adjustment—turning the left hand farther to the left, into the so-called "weak position." Few golfers feel natural with this kind of grip, and what frequently happens is that they lose the correct path of their swing without knowing it. I advocate maintaining your regular grip. The only modification I make when I'm trying to fade the ball is to open the clubface slightly. If I want to increase the fade, I open the face a shade wider. In this connection, you must remember that the more you open the clubface, the more loft you put on the clubface and, it follows, the shorter you'll hit the ball. As a rule a left-to-right player will need to take one more club than he would ordinarily to reach his target—a 4-iron instead of a 5.

The most injurious method for fading the ball, as I see it, is the one that calls for the golfer to try to swing, consciously, from the outside in. This can really ruin a swing. It isn't necessary to swing outside-in in order to fade the ball if you aim to the left of your target and open the face of the club. Once you've aligned

The basic modification for left-to-right play: open the clubface slightly.

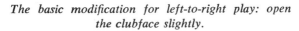

yourself on your primary target, as I said earlier, you should try to swing squarely through the ball—just as you do when you're not playing a fade. It's hard enough to develop one reliable, repeatable swing, let alone two or three. Ben Hogan, who plays a fade better than any other golfer I've seen, stays away from all the gingerbread. Ben just aims down the left side, opens his clubface a shade, and lets it rip.

When I'm playing from left to right, during the swing itself I try to stress two things: on the downswing I make sure that I move very fast to my left side, and when I hit through the ball, I try to get the feeling that I'm delaying my right hand from rolling over my left as long as possible. Left-to-right takes plenty of practice. I would be less than honest, too, if I did not say that it also requires some natural ability. However, I believe that a golfer who can break 90 usually possesses sufficient coordination and timing to handle the controlled fade.

The most common pitfall for a left-to-right golfer, whatever his skill, is a tendency to work himself more and more open. He hits wider and wider fades, and ends up by slicing the ball—cutting across it—instead of hitting squarely through the ball with a slightly open clubface. To make certain I'm not unconsciously slipping into a slice action, when I'm warming up on the practice tee I make it a habit, periodically, to hit two fades and then a draw. If the draw comes off, then I'm reasonably sure that my clubhead is moving on the correct path through the ball, that I'm still playing a proper fade and not a slice. Right-to-left players have to watch out for a corresponding pitfall—a tendency to become more and more closed and flatter and flatter until they're swinging way out to the right of their target and playing a looping, roundhouse hook instead of an elegant, cultivated draw.

To sum things up, if you are a golfer who has learned an inside-out swing and who now hits the ball from right to left, you should stay with it—a golfer should always stay with what has become natural. However, if you are a young player, you should know that the inside-out, right-to-left swing, though still taught universally as the standard method, is not the only way to play golf. Moreover, you should know that, at the top echelon, left-to-right has been an accepted method of play for many years now, mainly because it bolsters a man's consistency and strengthens his accuracy. Surely it stands to reason that the game of golf can be played better if at address a man faces his target or a trifle to the left of it, as a left-to-right golfer does, rather than having to look over his shoulder and pull the ball around to his target, as the right-to-left golfer does. Since the left-to-right golfer is on the path to his target so much longer, surely it is much easier for him to hold his groove than it is for the right-to-left golfer. Surely the right-to-left golfer suffers more when he loses his groove, for he invariably ends up "coming over the ball" with his shoulders and arms, and that's a much more destructive error than the left-to-right golfer succumbs to. At least he's still coming under the ball. His mistakes are bound to be more moderate. He can still stop an approach somewhere on the green. And surely if you're right-handed and play right-to-left, under tension you're more likely to overaccentuate the hitting action of the right hand, which can be disastrous. All in all, I'm convinced that when the pressure is on, the left-to-right golfer has a marked advantage.

The best golfers can move the ball both ways. On a championship course, they have to be able to. There are always some shots that must be brought in from the left and some that must be brought in from the right. Take the Augusta National, for example. (I choose the Augusta National, for today golf fans seem to know it better than any other course, a consequence of its being the only course over which a major championship is held annually.) As I see it, there are two holes at Augusta on which a right-to-left tee-shot is just about a requirement—the ninth and the thirteenth. On three other holes, the fifth, tenth, and fourteenth, a right-to-left tee-shot is certainly preferable. While there is only one hole, the eighteenth, on which a left-to-right tee-shot is called for, two other holes, the first and third—and perhaps one more, the seventh—play more easily if you play a left-to-right tee-shot.

Over the course of four rounds on a championship layout, apart from how you choose to play your drives, you're invariably confronted with a fair percentage of approach shots on which you must bring the ball into the green with a definite draw or a fade. In the 1966 Masters, for instance, when I was chasing Gay Brewer and Tommy Jacobs down the stretch on the last day, to keep my chances alive I had to birdie the fifteenth, the last of the par 5s, 520 yards long with a small pond separating the fairway from the green. I put my tee-shot just where I didn't want to—behind the two

For most golfers the long irons are the hardest clubs to control. The lack
of clubface loft (plus the length of the shaft) intimidates them. While the
1-iron, 2-iron, and 3-iron require almost as full a swing as the woods, I
believe it is very helpful when playing these clubs to try to swing them with
the same tempo and ease with which you swing a 7-iron.

287

pines that stand in the left-center of the fairway. I had just enough room to shoot to the left of the first pine, if I wanted to, and to try to fade the ball into the green, but I didn't like that shot; the left side of the fifteenth green is hard and fast, and you never know how a long approach will behave on it. Instead, I elected to play to the right of the first pine and try to hook the ball in. I took a 2-iron, and since I had to aim far to the right of the green to get around the tree, I concentrated on hitting the ball as high as I could and with as much controllable hook as I could. I really hit a darn good shot. The draw took beautifully. The ball came hooking into the green almost at a right angle, and finished 15 feet to the right of the pin. It makes you feel like a golfer when you can maneuver the ball.

Let me close this chapter with a tip that I think will be of value to all golfers—those who play left-to-right, those who play right-to-left, and those who play right-to-right or left-to-left, as I have done on too many occasions. You will never see a good golfer plant his left foot first when he steps up to the ball. You block yourself out if you do, and then you're forced to peer over your left shoulder when you try to get aligned. Place your right foot in position first. This way you'll be facing your target and you'll be able to set yourself up much better as you move your left foot into position and complete your stance. . . . Oh, yes. When you're standing at the ball and squinting down the fairway and wondering if you'll be able to avoid the rough, the bunkers, and the trees, keep in mind that accuracy is the product of a good swing. The narrower the fairway, the better you must swing in order to hit it.

XIX

Technique: The Grip, the Stance, the Swing, the Finish

EVERY SO OFTEN when my father meets me after following me on a tournament round, he'll say something on the order of, "Jack, I thought you played very well today. At the same time, I didn't think your swing was slow and smooth enough. I love to watch you when it doesn't look like there's any effort at all to hitting the ball—the way you looked in the Masters."

I'll usually reply with something on the order of, "I'd like to be swinging that way myself, Dad. I just can't do it all the time."

My dad knows golf very well, and he has understood ever since he was a young boy trying to emulate Bobby Jones that good tempo can't be superimposed on a bad swing. On those days when he calls to my attention that I am not swinging as smoothly and easily as I sometimes manage to, I can only deduce that he must think that I have more ability than I have—that if I put my mind to it, I could swing lyrically every day. Of course I can't or I would. But up to a point my dad is right. If a golfer tries to swing with a nice even tempo, a lot of times the faulty movements that were jamming up his swing will disappear. I know that when my swing is quick and jerky, most of the time the seat of the trouble is that I'm moving my hands too fast. As a result, I'll jab my right elbow out of position going back, instead of allowing the elbow to fold into a correct position. Or I'll be in such a hurry that I won't let the clubhead swing itself all the way to the top on the backswing—I'll push it there. When you rush things, you force yourself into bad moves.

289

*Two bad moves. Left, club in too tight, no extension. Probable result: a draw
or hook. Right, "crossing the line" at the top. Probable result: spray.*

Sometimes, as I remarked, you can correct the errors in your
swing by correcting the tempo, but other times when you're making
certain kinds of bad moves, you can't swing slowly or smoothly no
matter how hard you try. You have to correct the bad moves first.
Tempo—the overall rate of speed of your swing—is function, not
ornament. So is rhythm—the flow that knits together the various
moves that make up the swing. So, too, is timing, the result of
tempo and rhythm.

I mention these points because in this chapter, having previously
discussed the golf swing in general terms, we'll be studying the
technique of the swing more closely. On one hand, tempo, rhythm,
and timing serve to make a sound and refined technique possible,
and, on the other hand, they are created by technique—the detailed
procedure for executing the swing properly. That's rather intricate
stuff and we'll leave it right here. The last thing I want to do is to
make golf or the golf swing any more elaborate than is necessary.

In that connection, let me say that I am a one-swing man. I
believe that a golfer should use the same swing for all the conventional or normal shots. There's no sense in talking about how
to play the driver, how to play the 1-iron, or how to play the

5-iron, as if they required separate techniques. The different clubs merely modify the arc of the swing. Myself, with the driver I hit the ball the instant before the upswing begins, and I hit the ball with all the other clubs the instant before I reach the bottom of the downswing—just before the club enters the turf and goes through the turf as it moves from the downswing into the upswing. In line with my philosophy that one should always try to make golf as simple and consistent as possible, I might add that unless I'm playing a shot from a fairway bunker or a shot from high grass around the green or some other shot on which precise contact is absolutely essential, I never aim for a point on the ball—just for the ball. Also, I never try to actually hit the ball, as if the hit were a distinct action in itself. I try to swing through the ball.

The first thing I'd like to go into in a little more detail is the grip. Let's begin with the left hand.

When you hit a golf ball, the left hand, being the forward hand, is going to receive all the blow, all of the shock. It follows that you want to hit the ball with the most solid part of that hand. That's the reason why golfers long ago developed the four-knuckle left-hand grip; it enabled them to use the butt of the hand to absorb the shock of impact. The difficulty here, as I see it, is that you're forced to get your left hand into a very unnatural position in order to strike the ball with the butt. I feel that the back of my hand is nearly as strong as the butt and that it's a far more natural part to hit with —and to hit with consistently. That is why I place the club crosswise in the palm: it facilitates hitting the ball with the back of my left hand, directly behind the palm.

A supporting reason why I place the club crosswise in my left hand is that I have very small hands. The crosswise angle permits me to wedge the club in my palm, and the more a golfer's grip is in the palm of his left hand, the better he can take advantage of the solidness of the back of his hand. Even with my relatively small hands I use a club-grip that is a little larger than the average club-grip to keep my fingers from digging into the heel of my hand. I want to feel the palm, not the fingers. The bigger a golfer's hands, the more his left-hand grip will be in his fingers unless he offsets this (as many professionals do) by building up the size of his club-grip.

The right hand is another story. Although I don't necessarily

291

emphasize the right hand when I hit through the ball, it is the acceleration of the right hand that finally brings the clubhead back to a square position when your hands are racing to catch up with your body in the hitting zone. As I try to stress when I give a clinic, a man uses his right hand in golf much the same way he uses it in throwing a baseball. If a golfer placed the club in his right palm, it would take a huge effort for him to get the clubhead back to square. Similarly, if a ballplayer placed the baseball in his palm, throwing the ball across the diamond would be a job and a half. However, if a golfer puts the club in the fingers of his right hand or if the ballplayer puts the baseball in his fingers, it takes far less effort to achieve the same objectives. That is why, probably since the beginning of golf, golfers have held the club more in the fingers than in the palm of the right hand.

In my opinion, the method by which the two hands are joined together on the club doesn't make too much difference. The three more or less standard grips—the Vardon or overlapping grip, the interlocking grip, and the baseball or four-finger grip—don't change the position of the hands on the club. They are just different methods of linking the hands.

I use the interlocking grip—the little finger of my right hand is locked between the index finger and the big finger of my left. I use the interlocking grip for three reasons: I started with it. I have small hands. I feel it keeps them compactly together. With the Vardon grip, my hands feel like two units rather than like one.

The Vardon or overlapping grip, the most popular grip by far, has the advantage of putting four fingers of the left hand on the club—the little finger of the right hand laps over and rides behind the index finger of the left. The baseball grip goes one better: it puts four fingers and the thumb of both hands on the club. Its weakness is that it spreads the hands out. The farther apart your hands are, the more inclined they are to work against each other and the more this reduces your chances of developing maximum clubhead speed. (For example, when you slide your hands six inches or so apart on a baseball bat in order to bunt, you have wonderful control of the bat but no power.) As a matter of fact, I honestly believe that the interlocking grip is a better grip than the Vardon. I think it provides better linkage. But then, I suppose that's only natural since I'm an interlocker. Sewsunker Sewgolum, the South

A good view of my interlocking grip. (On the first tee at Merion in 1959.)

African who is the finest cross-handed player in the world, undoubtedly is convinced that the cross-handed grip is the only grip.

In discussing stance earlier, I made the observation that unless you stand comfortably before the ball, you set up limitations as to how well you can hit your shots. Your stance must be narrow enough so that you can move with ease, and it must be wide enough so that your weight does not sway to the right of your right foot going back or to the left of your left foot coming down.

The angle at which you place your feet has a significant influence on both comfort and function. The right foot—the foot you place first at address—should be positioned either square (straight, that is) or pointed slightly out, depending on your build. A thin man can set up with a very straight right foot because he's apt to be supple and needs something firm and stabilizing to keep him from turning his hips too far around to the right on the backswing. (Ben Hogan, who has a very supple physique, employs a straight right foot to help him limit the extent of his hip turn going back.) Con-

293

On all shots except the woods and long irons, I make it a point throughout the swing not to raise my left heel from the ground. As this sequence depicts—I'm hitting a 5-iron—the left ankle and heel roll in to the right on the backswing, then roll back to the left on the downswing, but the stabilizing heel remains securely on the ground.

295

versely, a bigger, heavier man, who needs to increase the freedom of his turn, will benefit if he opens his right foot by pointing it a shade to the right, maybe five or ten degrees.

The position of the left foot should be much the same for all golfers—pointed out toward the hole at about a thirty-degree angle. There's a simple reason for this: if a golfer were to set up with a straight, or square, left foot, he would find that when he came into the ball and tried to clear his left side out of the way, this would restrict him from doing so. He wants to be restricted on the backswing, yes, to prevent an overturn, but he certainly doesn't want to be on the hit and the follow-through. There he wants to move as fast as he can and as far through the ball as he can.

Ball position is, of course, an integral part of the stance. Trying to simplify the game as much as I can, I play every standard shot with the ball in the same position in reference to my feet. *On all these shots the ball is positioned in line with my left heel.* There is only one point on the downswing at which the clubhead is absolutely square to the line of flight, and if you cut down the number of variables at address, your clubhead has a much greater chance of regularly reaching that point of squareness right at the ball. By positioning the ball in line with your left heel for all normal shots, you have only two variables: (1) the distance you stand away from the ball with both feet to accommodate the different lengths of the shafts of your clubs; (2) the amount you narrow your stance by moving your right foot in toward the left when you play the shorter-shafted clubs. The big thing is that the relationship of your left foot to the ball remains constant. Under the old system of ball position-

My ball position on all standard shots:
in line with the left heel.

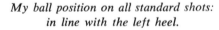

ing, it didn't. That system called for the ball to be moved back progressively nearer to the right foot as a golfer played the shorter-shafted, more lofted clubs. When the ball is moved back in this manner, the clubface is inclined to be opened at impact—it hasn't yet reached the square position. To compensate for this, a golfer has to open his stance a bit, and then he's aiming left. This introduces altogether too many variables: How far back do you play the ball? How much do you open your stance to equalize the open clubface? It stands to reason that this system has to produce a much more erratic, much less precise striking of the ball. When you keep changing the low point of your downward arc, you keep changing your swing.

I think of the high-speed, stop-action camera as a two-edged sword. It is most instructive for a golfer to be able to study photographs that can show him how the components of his swing are functioning at the various stages of a particular shot. It allows him to spot, and to take steps to correct, an error he has been making that has been throwing off his backswing, his downswing, or both. Today, however, what with so many stop-action photos paraded before them, many diligent club golfers make the mistake of trying to push themselves into some definite position during the course of the swing—say, just as they enter the hitting zone—in an attempt to copy the position of some successful golfer which the camera has caught. This is a bad idea. You shouldn't think of the swing as being made up of many segments, each of them consciously controlled. The successful golfer knows better. The position in which you see him frozen is a consequence of his earlier movements, and he reaches it only by performing those movements correctly. He doesn't confuse cause and effect, but the average golfer does.

To say this same thing another way, you can't govern the swing segment-by-segment when you're playing a golf shot. You can't exercise muscular control over where you want the clubhead to be halfway through your backswing, where you want your hands to be at the top of the backswing, where you want your right hip and shoulder to be at impact, and so on ad infinitum. *The whole golf swing happens in less than two seconds.* That's much too fast for point-to-point control. You should, nevertheless, know what happens in a good golf swing. Then you have a much better chance of making the correct moves, not to mention a much better chance of

297

A full 4-iron, front view. On all standard shots with all clubs except the driver, the clubface contacts the ball the instant before it reaches the bottom of the downswing. The clubface then enters the turf and cuts through the turf as it moves from the downswing into the upswing.

knowing where the fault may lie when you're not playing well. With this in mind, let me tell you what happens in my golf swing. Some of this will necessarily be a recap of information we talked about earlier; some of it will be new.

My swing is initiated by a stationary press. My hands are set a little forward, to the left, of the ball. I then move the club away from the ball, with my hands, arms, shoulders, and hips all working together. This starts the transfer of my weight to the inside of my right foot, and as this takes place, my left ankle rolls in toward the right. (Only when I'm playing a wood or a long iron does my left heel leave the ground at any time.) At this early moment in the swing, the first twelve inches or so, my clubhead is moving on a very straight path away from the ball. As the turning of my shoulders and hips continues, the club will follow a somewhat inward path because the shoulders and the hips do. When the clubhead is about belt-high, my wrists will begin to cock, automatically, due to the weight of the moving clubhead. This action continues until the backswing is completed, which arrives when your hips and shoulders have made their maximum turn.

A few additional comments on the backswing. The amount of shoulder turn is governed by the amount of hip turn, and this is governed by the positioning of the feet, the right foot in particular. At the top of the backswing, both the right and left wrists are under the shaft; my right elbow, away from the body, points down; the back of my left hand and my left forearm form a relatively straight line; the club points at the target. At the top of my backswing, my chin is canted a bit to the right, for at the start of the backswing it swivels in that direction. The axis of my neck, however, remains in a fixed position in relation to the ball. This swiveling of the chin is a peculiarity of mine. I do it because it permits my shoulders to turn more freely. It serves no other purpose.

As I mentioned earlier, my downswing is initiated by a push forward from the inside of my right foot, a push that moves my hips laterally toward the target and also raises my left shoulder slightly. At this moment in the downswing, my clubhead hasn't started down —it's still in the position it was when I reached the top of the backswing. This may seem confusing and I had better explain it. When I make that push forward off my right foot, my hands are still occupied with changing the direction of the club—ending the backswing and beginning the downswing. As my hips continue to move forward, the shoulders follow them, as do the arms, the hands, and finally the club. When I feel that my weight has been transferred to my left side and I begin to enter the hitting area, I firm up my left side, my hips finish their lateral move, and my left hip spins around to the rear. The stopping of that swift lateral action sets up a reaction—a sudden releasing of all the energy stored up on my backswing and downswing. My right knee kicks in toward my left. My right hip drives down and under, as does my right shoulder. My left shoulder comes up higher. This combination of movements during the release triggers the hit, the hit-through, and the follow-through. It is all one continuous action, like the breaking of a wave.

At the finish of my swing, 95 percent of my weight is planted on my left foot, if only for an instant. (I swing so hard with my driver that the force of my follow-through creates a reaction—I rock back onto my right foot.) When I finish, my body is virtually facing my target, my hands are high, and my right shoulder and hip are lower than my left shoulder and hip, indicating that I continued to stay "under the ball" long after impact. While my neck remains in the same position as at address, my head swivels to the left during the course of the follow-through. It doesn't jump up way above my shoulders or anything as drastic as that, however. Indeed, I like to feel that my head is still down low when I pick up the flight of the ball and that, as I follow the ball, my eyes sort of hug the ground as they peer up. In a word, I try to stay down a long time.

While I think I have a clear idea of what happens during my swing—I should after all these years of practice and study—let me emphasize that the only things a golfer can actually control are the preparations for the swing and the start of the backswing. That is why both are supremely critical. Maybe, if I'm concentrating well and swinging well, I can also focus my attention on the proper execution of one move on my backswing or downswing, but that's all. Beyond this, it's strictly a matter of feel. While you are swinging you can sense if everything is proceeding as it should or if something is going wrong or has gone wrong. Instinctively you try to compensate for the error you think you're making. There's not too much you can do about it—it all takes place so fast and the elements of the swing are so tightly interrelated. (I suppose a musician who senses he's going wrong during a solo passage is in a similar position. Instinct alone can help him.) Anyhow, when you have made a poor swing, or a succession of poor swings, try to isolate

301

the point at which you felt your swing went sour, and then try to remedy this by working extra hard on your ensuing shots to execute correctly the fundamental on which that particular phase of the swing is built. Sometimes your diagnosis will be awry, but at other times you'll find that you can straighten yourself out.

This is perhaps the logical spot to voice my thoughts on that old controversial topic, the flat swing versus the upright swing, and on one other aspect of technique: how hard should you swing at the ball?

A golfer's build determines the plane of his swing. The shorter he is, the flatter his plane will be, since the ball will be proportionately farther away from him. The taller he is, the better his chances of approximating what is theoretically the perfect arc for the golf swing: the arc of a pendulum on which the clubhead would always be square to the line of flight. Byron Nelson is usually recognized as the man who pioneered the modern upright swing. Some of the present players who belong to the upright school are Billy Casper, Allan Geiberger, Terry Dill, and young Bob Dickson. I am a decidedly upright swinger. The more upright a golfer can swing the club without artificially forcing it, the simpler it is for him to keep the club on the right line. One of these days a very tall player with excellent coordination will come along who will hit the ball straighter than anyone before him. It is just one of those inexplicable things that a towering, talented golfer-athlete hasn't appeared up to now. Down through the years medium-sized men have generally been the game's finest exponents, but there's no real reason why a very tall man should not be just as well coordinated for golf.

How hard should you swing at the ball? For myself, the only club I hit full force is the driver. With all the others, I try to swing well within myself. If I am, say, 160 yards from a green and another fellow about the same distance out elects to play an 8-iron, I'll still stay with a 6-iron. I'm not interested in how far I can press a club; I'm interested in playing the club that will get the job done best. However, after I get to the driver, there ain't no more. If I need every yard of distance I can muster, I've got to go after it with that club. I will only go all-out for distance, however, when I believe it won't hurt to sacrifice a degree of accuracy. I might do this, for illustration, on the long fifteenth at Augusta where the fairway in the driving area is a good 75 yards wide. When I shoot the works for distance, I concentrate on taking the club back slower than usual to give myself the time to complete the fullest backswing I can make. The wider my arc, the farther I should be able to hit the ball. Then, on the downswing I try to move my hips as fast as I can.

To repeat, except for certain situations where I have ample margin for error on the tee-shot, I never hit the ball with everything I have. It's too risky—you can lose your balance and your timing so easily if you try to hit the ball too hard. As a matter of fact, I would class myself as an only moderately long iron-player. Here, in any event, is how I chart my range with the various clubs under normal playing conditions:

> sand wedge: up to 80 yards
> pitching wedge: 80 to 105 yards
> 9-iron: 105 to 135 yards
> 8-iron: 130 to 145 yards
> 7-iron: 140 to 155 yards
> 6-iron: 155 to 170 yards
> 5-iron: 170 to 185 yards
> 4-iron: 185 to 200 yards
> 3-iron: 195 to 210 yards
> 2-iron: 205 to 220 yards
> 1-iron: 215 to 235 yards
> 3-wood: 235 yards and up
> driver: 250 yards and up

XX

Putting and the
Short Game

T HE HALLMARK OF A FIRST-CLASS GOLFER is the ability to play
a respectable round on those days when he is decidedly off his
game. Intelligent course management helps a great deal on those
rounds—knowing where you can afford to gamble off the tee,
planning your approaches so that you will be on the advantageous
side of the green if you should miss it, having the hard sense when
an error has gotten you into a serious predicament not to try to bail
yourself out with a wonder shot and to accept the probable loss of
one stroke instead of inviting the possible loss of two or three. On
those hard-work rounds, of course, a golfer's best friend is a dependable short game.

You can talk all you want about the lift a man gets from a big,
booming tee-shot, but I honestly believe that nothing raises a golfer's
spirits as much as telescoping three shots into two with a deft little
pitch next to the pin or saving a stroke on the green by holing from
two-putt range. After all, good golf is two things: playing fine shots
and scoring well. Even on those days when a man is hitting the ball
like a dream, he has to be neat and effective around the greens and
on them or the quality of his tee-to-green play won't be reflected in
his score. I would go as far as to say that on at least half of my best
scoring rounds my golf wasn't especially brilliant. I split few fairways and I put few irons close to the flag and I made a number of
outright errors, but I managed to cancel out those errors by pitching
and chipping adroitly, and I nailed down my figures by sinking a
half-dozen or so putts I normally wouldn't get. While there is no
real substitute for a sound swing and steady on-the-green-in-regu-
lation shotmaking—in the long run the percentages are against the

304

scrambler—in order to defeat your opponent in match play or out-score a field of opponents in medal play you must get the ball into the hole in fewer strokes than your competition, so there's no sense priding yourself after a defeat on the fact that you hit the ball straighter and farther than the winner or consoling yourself with the reflection that the only clubs he played well were the wedge and the putter. They're darn important clubs to be able to play well, the wedge and the putter, every bit as much a part of golf as the driver and the 5-iron. You had better learn how to handle them yourself.

Most tournament golfers think of the "scoring area" as beginning about 125 yards from the green: from there on in, if you play a very good shot, you can either save a stroke or pick up a stroke. I agree with this and only wish that I could get nearer the hole on many more of the short pitches I get to play. Some of my friends like to kid me by claiming that I'm the only golfer in the world who is more accurate with the 1-iron than with the 9-iron, but they're not entirely wrong. My short game can stand plenty of im-provement. Be that as it may, when I'm playing a shot with the 9-iron, I use the same swing I do on all the longer shots. This also applies to the pitching wedge, which I play from 80 to 105 yards out. From a fine lie you can spin the ball back with the pitching wedge, but if your lie is not too good you must expect to get a little run on the ball, just as you do with the other pitching clubs, the 9, the 8, and the 7.

From 80 yards in, I use the sand wedge for conventional pitches and I also use it for those difficult little pitches of under 55 yards—half-wedge shots. I have two ways of playing the half-wedge, a low, backspin shot and a high, soft shot. These and the other finesse shots in the green area require a somewhat different technique than the full shots, so we'll take them up one at a time.

I play the low, spin half-wedge when the pin is so positioned that there is sufficient room for the ball to take one big bounce before it settles down. The trajectory of this shot is too low for the ball to stop instantly. On a short pitch like this, since I can't strike the ball as forcefully as I can on a full shot, I have to find another way of putting good, active backspin on it. What I do is to move my hands a bit more forward at address and play the ball an inch farther back, to the right, than I customarily do; I also use a

305

The backspin half-wedge. This shot is very serviceable from 80 yards in when you're pitching to a pin that's not positioned too tightly. At address the hands are set forward and the ball is played an inch farther back in the stance. The arc on both the backswing and downswing is steep. The ball will fly low but the backspin on it will stop it quickly after one big bounce.

The best "percentage" pitch shot is the high, feathered half-wedge. The key points are these: the ball is positioned an inch farther forward than usual; the club is taken back a shade outside the line, and coming down you cut slightly across the ball; and at the very start of the downswing you start to release the clubhead so it can slide under the ball and waft the ball into a high soft-falling flight.

slightly more open stance to compensate for moving the ball back. I set up with my weight predominantly on my left side, and I keep it there. These adjustments give me a steeper arc going back and coming down into the ball. This enables me to make purer contact with the ball, and the purer the contact—the less grass between your clubface and the ball—the stronger the backspin. (As is no doubt obvious, this shot can be played only from a good lie.) Because of the steepness of my swing on this half-wedge, I open the clubface slightly to compensate for the hooded position it would otherwise be in. Indeed, I generally try to put a little cut on this shot, cutting across the ball just a shade from the outside in. As I say, the ball flies in a low trajectory and usually takes one big hop before the backspin starts to take, but there are many situations that accommodate this kind of shot, and I use it a lot.

When I have to throw the ball over a trap and stop it quickly, I play a different kind of half-wedge—a high, soft shot. On this type of pitch you're trying to produce some backspin but you're depending at least as much on the floating flight of the ball and the close-to-vertical angle at which it falls to reduce the amount of roll to a minimum. You use a square stance and at address your hands are in their normal position, but you play the ball an inch farther forward than usual. You open the face of your club a trifle, and you take the club back a little outside your regular path on the backswing and cut across the ball from the outside in. However, the main thing you do differently on this shot is this: as you begin the downswing, you immediately start to release the clubhead so that you can slide it under the ball and loft the ball high in the air. When you execute this properly, you get a very gentle shot, a feather shot. This kind of half-wedge comes in extremely useful, for you can play it from almost any fairway lie.

I play three different types of wedge chips, all of them with the sand wedge. Two are simply abbreviated versions of the two half-wedges, a low chip with spin and a soft lob chip. The third is hit with a square face and a conventional swing. On this last shot, the ball carries only moderate backspin and doesn't check too quickly, so I employ it just in those situations where there is a lot of green between my ball and the hole and where, as I look the shot over, I get the feeling that the contours will cradle the rolling ball best if I drop it onto the green with a wedge.

310

Whatever style of wedge chip you're playing, you must remember never to let the right hand cross over the left. This will give you a very "hot ball," one that jumps forward fast when it lands and keeps rolling. Work for a grooved rhythm and you'll acquire the knack of getting almost the same action on shot after shot—which is what touch is. (Deane Beman, Gary Player, and Jerry Barber have wonderful touch, and they're able to "invent" all sorts of little wedge shots to get them out of sticky situations.) The more I play golf, the more I use the sand wedge. I think I must use that club on about 90 percent of my chips now—again because it limits the variables.

A standard chip is more or less an extension of a putt.

I chip with the other irons, the 9 through the 5, when I'm a fair distance from the pin on a large, flattish green and feel that I can probably get the ball up closest if I play for lots of run on it. I address the ball much as I do when I'm putting. I play the ball off my left heel, but I take such a narrow stance that the ball is in about the middle of it. I hit down on the ball a fraction, for it should be contacted crisply. Essentially, this kind of chip is an extension of an approach putt—I'm using a lofted putter that just happens to be a 6- or 7-iron.

On these chips I use my right hand more than I do on a full shot. Just how much right hand I use depends on the feeling I get as I set up before the ball, and this varies from day to day. Some days I increase my right-hand action, other days I lessen it, and occasionally I try to equalize the role of both hands. Maybe this fluctuation explains why I'm not a better chipper than I am. Bobby Nichols and Art Wall are two fellows who are outstanding in this department. Bill Casper is another. When Casper chips from the fringe, the ball runs for the hole like a putt.

One always keeps learning more and more about golf, which is as it should be. I have always thought of myself as a fairly decent bunker player but not the artist that a number of today's golfers are. Until a couple of years ago, bunkers with very soft sand gave me a great deal of trouble. I'd dig down too deep in the sand. Though I seldom missed the shot so badly that I left the ball in the bunker, I seldom put it tight to the pin. During the 1967 season, thanks to Jack Grout's help, I revised my whole approach to bunker play and became, I believe, much more effective in dealing not only with soft sand but with all kinds of sand. There are, naturally, a half dozen and more varieties of bunker shots in a professional's repertoire, but I think the best service I can render the average golfer and the ad-

Before I learned to play bunkers. Wide-open stance, wide-open blade, swing not upright or abrupt enough. I could play only a small variety of shots.

312

vanced golfer is not to go into all the special shots but to describe my new approach to bunker play in general. It's not too involved, and the beauty of it is that you can apply it to the full variety of sand shots.

I went to see Jack Grout about my indifferent bunker play on the Friday of the 1967 Florida Citrus Open, flying from Orlando to Miami after completing my round that day. I explained to Jack that on short bunker shots I hadn't been able to get the ball up in the air quickly and stop it quickly. I knew I'd been hitting too deep, but I hadn't been able to correct it. We went out onto the course at La Gorce, and Jack had me hit a few shots from a greenside bunker. I used the method I had followed for years, the method that I had, in fact, learned as a boy at Grout's knee: stance—same as for conventional shots; clubface—open, wide open; ball position—opposite the left toe (so that I'd contact the sand at virtually the same spot where I'd contact the ball on regular shots played off my left heel); backswing—upright.

Grout then suggested I make a few minor adjustments, all of them tied in with the new basic approach he advanced: the principal thing to consider on any and every bunker shot was the amount of sand I wanted to take. If I wanted to hit a shallow explosion, the key was to move my hands farther back—actually behind the club-head. If I wanted to hit a less shallow explosion, the farther forward I moved my hands, the deeper into the sand I'd hit. As simple as that. If I needed to put extra spin on the ball, then the ticket was to move my hands forward, position the ball a bit farther back in my stance, and hit down sharply behind the ball. This, by the way, is how Gary Player plays all his bunker shots.

Grout also suggested a change in the way I swung at the ball on these shots. At the start of my downswing, he counseled, I should try to release the club, with my right hand in control. I always did this when I feathered a little pitch with the wedge. Why I didn't do the same thing when I played from sand, I just don't know. It gives you a skimming action instead of a chopping action, and you get a softer shot that behaves much better.

My bunker game responded immediately to Jack Grout's treatment, and a few weeks later one further change suggested itself to me. Why should a sand shot, I asked myself, be different from any other shot in regard to the importance of playing it with a firm left side? When I played from sand, I'd been letting my left side flow

313

314

5 6

To my way of thinking, how far you hit behind the ball is not the critical thing in playing an explosion shot from a bunker. That distance can vary from an inch to three inches, depending on how the ball lies and where the pin is set. What is far more important is the amount of sand you take—the depth at which your wedge passes through the sand.

12 13 14

In recent years my bunker play has become less erratic because of two modifications in technique. First, starting down I try to release the club with the right hand in control—as I do when feathering a wedge. (Note photographs 6 and 7.) Second, I work to keep my left side firm in the hitting area—as I do on all other shots. (Note photographs 8 through 12.)

5   6

8   9

3   14   15

forward in the hitting area. That certainly could have been a contributing reason for my inconsistency. Directly, I began working for a much firmer left side on my bunker recoveries rather than letting my knees and hips sag forward ahead of the ball. It helped immensely.

Because of these three modifications, there was a noticeable improvement in my bunker play in 1967. It didn't matter whether I was dealing with honest-to-goodness sand or with silica sand. Silica, a by-product of the glass industry, is no favorite of mine. It's so squishy, it never packs, and since it doesn't give your club anything to bounce off of, it drags the club down deep and snuffs your shot out. However, as I say, I began to look like a different man even when dealing with synthetic sand.

A lot has been made of how far behind the ball you should hit on bunker shots. I don't think it's all that critical. Depending on your lie, it can vary from half an inch to three inches. What *is* critical, as I trust I have brought out, is the depth at which your club passes through the sand. A long bunker shot is, of course, the toughest to play. Your club must enter the sand close to the ball and take a relatively shallow route through the sand. If it strikes the sand close to the ball and then plows in deep, you have no chance. By the way, don't worry about how you finish any bunker shot. Concentrate only on playing the shot assertively. The right hand, the dominant hand from the top of the backswing on, will swing through and finish according to the type of recovery you're playing. Just remember that, the same as in chipping, the right hand never turns over.

As goes without saying, no part of golf is more important than putting. Not all of the great champions have been extraordinary putters, but they have been very good putters. An incomplete golfer cannot be a champion.

To putt effectively, as I see it, a golfer must first be comfortable over the ball. After that, putting is largely a matter of carrying through certain hard-and-fast fundamentals.

Comfort comes with the stance. If you feel best with a wide stance, take a wide stance; if you feel best with a closed stance, take a closed stance; and so on. I don't think the kind of stance a golfer takes means a darn. *The only thing that means anything, when all is said and done, is the alignment of your eyes and hands in conjunction with the blade of the putter and the line to the hole.*

My natural method: eyes over the line but sighting down line to the cup.

There are two equally correct methods of alignment. In the first—Method A, we'll call it—the golfer's eyes are directly over the line to the hole and his left eye is directly over the ball. In Method B both eyes again are directly over the line to the hole but they are set behind the ball, allowing the golfer to take in both the ball and the hole. You should use whichever method makes it easier for you to see the line. It's a personal thing. Palmer, Beman, and Casper like to have their left eye over the ball. Jackie Burke, another prodigious putter, likes to get his head more behind the ball.

Not that I belong in the same class with these fellows, but I used Method B as an amateur and today, after a fling with Method A, I have gone back to Method B. Either way, if you don't have your eyes over the line, you'll throw everything off. I remember a classic example only too well. On the 71st green of the 1966 Masters, the lead was mine for the taking—all I had to do was to get down a three-foot putt with a slight break. I not only missed it, on the left, but the ball didn't even touch the cup. Later that afternoon I happened to see the video tape replay of that putt on the television broadcast. The camera was positioned so that it looked right down the line from the back of the green, catching me in profile from the rear. The reason I had blown that putt leaped right off the screen at me. My head was bent too far over the ball, so that my eyes were well past it. They weren't over the line to the cup—my nose and mouth were. My putter was aligned with my eyes, which meant it was misaligned. I thought I had the blade squared with the right-hand corner of the cup. Not at all. It was aimed to the left of the cup. No wonder I hit the ball there! That night, the eve of my playoff with Tommy Jacobs and Gay Brewer, I spent an hour on the practice green working just on alignment. In the playoff, after that session, I putted very well. The three long putts I holed made the difference, unquestionably, in my duel with Tommy.

Most of the top professionals use the reverse overlap grip for putting. I use it because it gives me the greatest control of the putter. Putting is basically a right-hand stroke, and the reverse overlap puts four fingers of the right hand on the putter. Also, I find it a very comfortable grip, no doubt because I've used it ever since I started to play golf. Once again, though, I don't think that good putting depends to any considerable extent on the kind of grip you employ. It is, much as stance is, a matter of what feels comfortable and works for you. There are a hundred and one tiny variations in putting grips, and trial and error is the only way that each individual can arrive at the one he feels is right for him.

As regards the position of the hands in putting, there's only one point I would emphasize: your hands should be far enough forward so that the shaft is either perpendicular—at a right angle to the line of your putt—or leaning ahead. If you putt with the shaft perpendicular, you are then in a position to take the putter back low along the ground and still keep the blade square to the hole all the way. If you putt with your hands ahead of the ball, you have to pick the club up slightly going back in order to keep the blade square, and

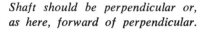

Shaft should be perpendicular or, as here, forward of perpendicular.

coming forward you catch the ball more on the downstroke. To compensate for this, you should use a more lofted putter. Some golfers fall into the habit of setting up with their hands behind the ball when they putt. This is not a sound idea. Very often on the backswing the blade, blocked for a straight takeaway, will strike the ground, and this will divert it either inside or outside the line. (On the full golf swing your hands should be ahead for the same reason.) A good number of club golfers also try to hit the ball on the upstroke. Not that it really matters, but you see very few first-class putters who putt that way. The best putters either hit the ball at the base of the downstroke (as Casper does) or they keep the blade level throughout the stroke (as Palmer does).

Another aspect of putting that is purely a matter of individual preference is the type of stroke you choose to use—all arms, all wrists, or a combination of arms and wrists. I'm an arm-and-wrist putter, and like many people who subscribe to that style, I take the putter back with the blade square and bring it forward with the blade square—square to square, as we call it. Some wonderful wrist putters, Palmer and Casper among them, use a close-to-open stroke, closing the blade just a bit going back and opening it coming through. A number of equally outstanding putters, such as Player and Locke, use an open-to-close stroke. I never did get to watch Bobby Locke when he was at his peak, but they tell me he literally hooked his putts into the cup.

Though many fine putters do, I don't try to contact any particular part of the ball. I don't try to hit the ball with a definite rap either. I try to putt through the ball, the same as I try to hit through the ball on regular shots. If there is any one thing I concentrate on, it's contacting the ball with the solidest part of the putter, the sweet spot, just as I do with all the other clubs. In the interests of consistency, I do one other thing when I putt that conforms with my procedure on the other shots: I start the stroke with a stationary press, a very mild press just with the fingers. It firms up my grip.

In summing up these thoughts and suggestions, let me repeat that the first essential in putting is to be comfortable, and the second is to be correctly aligned with the eyes and hands. After that, it's up to each golfer to decide for himself if he wants to putt from a closed stance, adopt a reverse overlap grip, hold the shaft angled forward, use the wrists only, cultivate an open-to-close stroke—or to assemble some other amalgamation that suits him. You can be sure of one thing, however. Whenever you're playing with a fellow who has one of those days when putts are falling for him all over the greens, you always get to wondering if his method, whatever it is, isn't the only way to putt. I can provide you with a classic illustration. The other day, after I had played nine holes with my wife Barbara and had watched her roll one sizable putt after another right into the center of the cup, I was even ready to change over to her method. It features an awkward stance, faulty alignment, a spread grip with the right thumb off the shaft, a fast backswing followed by a jerky forward stroke on which her head bobs up as the blade bounces off the turf before the ball, and finally an irritating Bolt-like strut as the ball plinks into the cup and she walks forward to retrieve it.

XXI

Some Aids to Better Golf

THERE IS REALLY NO LIMIT to how deeply one can probe into the theory and technique of golf. A man could write a book just on how to drive or how to play the wedge. The variety of shots is almost infinite, and as you go into increasing detail about them, finer and finer points keep presenting themselves, endlessly. You have to draw the line somewhere or else you put yourself in somewhat the same position as Thor, in that tale from Norse mythology, when he set out to empty a goblet of water and, for all his monumental efforts, failed to do so, though, as he was later informed, he had drained several oceans in the process. What I propose to do, accordingly, is to round out this section on instruction by discussing, in separate takes, several unrelated facets of golf that I haven't touched on yet and which I think are important to understand. Some of them have to do with the intellectual side of the game, some with more or less general problems, and a few are simply expanded tips. All of them, however, should be of value, I believe, in assisting you to become a more knowledgeable golfer—and a better one.

Practice

On the tour there's a not uncommon type of golfer who, up to a point, is sort of a mystery man. Al Soran, as we'll call him, has never met with much success, though he has conspicuous natural ability and practices as hard as anyone. What's holding Al back? Well, one thing that frequently does is the way he practices. On the practice tee he goes through the same unthinking ritual every day. He doesn't know what he's working on or why. He's out there because he's heard that practice is supposed to make you better. It does, but only to a negligible degree unless you know what you're doing, and Al Soran hasn't a clue. He's just banging balls out.

On the practice tee the smart, truly conscientious golfer is always working toward some definite goal. For some of our very best golfers—Gary Player is an excellent example—reaching that goal is, as a rule, a long, laborious affair. They have a general idea of what they're after, but it takes many, many sessions to achieve the specific result they have in mind. A number of the top players are just the opposite. Billy Casper, for example, practices very little, but when he does go out and practice, he knows exactly what he means to do, and it doesn't take him long to do it. Like so much of golf, practice patterns are a personal thing. I fall into a middle category about halfway between Player and Casper: it takes me a while to master some correction, but from the outset I have a clear idea of what I'm pursuing. I'd say Arnold Palmer is pretty much the same as I am in this respect. What we're really after when we practice is a sense of feel—the feel that enables you to time and control your swing so that you can produce the type of shot you're trying to play.

Sometimes when I'm on the practice tee I'll be meeting the ball squarely and flying it a long way with a nice little draw on it—in other words, hitting what would seem to be fine golf shots. Some of the fellows on the tour, watching me on these days, must wonder why I still stay out there hitting balls instead of wrapping things up contentedly. The explanation is that I'm not hitting the ball the way I want to. What I want is not a nice little draw but a nice little fade, and it might take me an hour to hit thirty or forty shots that behave that way. I'm out there trying to get the feeling that I'm working *under* the ball—the kind of action that gives you a fade and not a draw. A slight draw on the practice tee may look okay, but I don't want to go out on the course with the germ of a hook, not when I know that I'm a better left-to-right player.

Some days when I'm practicing before starting a tournament round, I'll look as though I'm hitting the ball very badly. One shot will veer to the left, the next will veer to the right, the next couple may fly straight but very low. Then I may follow this seemingly patternless sequence with three shots that move left-to-right and two or three that move from right to left. I really have more control of the ball than it might appear. What I'm attempting to do is to find out how much feel I have that morning. Can I play a slowly rising draw? Can I play a soft fade that doesn't tail off until the very end of its flight? Can I hit a low, boring, straight shot? And so on.

There are many days when, after I have moved to the first tee to start my tournament round, my opening drive bears no resemblance to any drive I hit on the practice tee. Some mornings my drive off the first will have much more authority than any of my practice drives. (I can imagine some of my fans giving me too much credit and saying, "Man, does he ever know how to pace himself! Took himself to the perfect point of preparation!") Other mornings, when I've gone through what has struck me as an impressive warm-up, my opening drive will be a terrible duck hook. I've done that more than once in the Masters. Why is there such a disparity, both good and bad, between what I do on the practice tee and what I do only a short time later when the round begins? I wish I knew. That deep-down awareness all golfers have that things can suddenly go much better or much worse than logically they should—this is what makes golf such a wonderful and confusing game.

On the practice green, whether it be before a round when I'm in the throes of a bad putting streak or right after a round when I've been just awful on the greens, I never try to take my stroke apart. My stroke doesn't vary that much. What I practice is timing and feel. I'm after two things: I want the ball to feel right when I strike it, and I want to develop an instinctive sense of the speed of the greens on that particular course so that I have a feel for distance. During a round I pay a good deal of attention to touch, on all putts. If I have an 8-footer, for example, on my practice stroke I don't simply swing the putter through—I try to simulate the feel of an 8-foot putt. A 15-footer or a 45-footer, same thing: I try to tailor the practice stroke to the putt coming up. I've been doing this so long I honestly can't remember when I started it, but I recommend it unreservedly to all golfers.

Placing the Drive

Distance lends enchantment off the tee, but, as I have mentioned several times, raw power by itself amounts to a very small part of the game of golf. Particularly if he is a power hitter, a golfer must always keep in mind the position he wants to play his second shot from. On many holes, in order to gain the most advantageous opening to the green or to provide himself with a level lie for his approach on a fairway that begins to tumble farther out, he should sacrifice yardage, gladly. As I also stated earlier, one reason why my victory in the 1966 British Open was so gratifying was that I won it

4

5

6

10

11

12

16

In this sequence—I am playing a 3-wood—I have correctly executed (on this particular shot) one very important move in the swing: I have hit *under* and *through* the ball, not *over* and *around* it. Also, my clubhead has moved squarely into the ball and squarely through it on the proper path.

on a course that really didn't suit a power game. On most courses I know, there are a number of holes on which a long-hitting club golfer would stand to profit if he left his driver in his bag and played for position with an iron or a 3-wood or 4-wood.

The Long Irons

The long irons are the nemesis of the average golfer. I'm convinced that the underlying reason for this is that he keeps hearing how hard they are to handle. They're not that difficult, truly.

When my long-iron play is not up to standard, I will often resort to an old, reliable exercise during my practice sessions. I'll hit out a batch of 7-irons to get my rhythm going. Then I'll grab a 2-iron or a 3 and, imagining that I still have a 7-iron in my hands, I'll try to duplicate the rhythm of a 7-iron shot. It isn't necessary, by the way, to hit a 2-iron any harder than a 7. The club is designed to get the distance for you. That's why it has less loft and a longer shaft.

I realize when I say those words—less loft and a longer shaft—that they constitute the precise reasons why the long irons frighten the average golfers. They don't think they can get the ball up with that straighter face, and this leads them into making the most common error golfers make with these clubs: they hit the ball down as hard as they can, hoping this will somehow do the job. Three out of four times they'll hit the shot "fat"—strike the turf before the ball. I would like to suggest to the average golfer that he try to hit the 2-iron and the 3 cleanly, without taking any divot. He's usually so hostile to the 1-iron he won't even carry it, but if he does, the same thing applies. Concentrate on making sharp, square contact with the ball. Don't worry about power. Think about producing your very best swing.

Let me pass on one small tip that may be useful. When I'm playing a 2-iron or a 3-iron on a par 3 where carry is of the utmost importance, I'll tee the ball very high—almost a half-inch off the ground. This way I have a much better chance of meeting the ball in the center of the clubface, where the power is packed.

The All-Purpose Rough Shot

The chief concern of most golfers when they're playing from the rough is to be sure to get out of it. Consequently, whenever they face a shot when the ball is lying in high or coarse grass, they feel they must go down and dig it out with an extra emphatic action. In their preoccupation with getting down under the ball, they tend to forget that they're bound to get some grass between the clubface and the ball. The result is a "flier," a shot which, as we mentioned earlier, carries overspin and not backspin and which flies one or two clubs farther than an ordinary shot with that particular club. When a flier lands on a green, it bounds on like a jackrabbit and frequently ends up in a rear bunker or in worse trouble over the green.

In order to avoid hitting a flier when I'm approaching a green from the rough, I play a different kind of shot than I would if my ball was on the fairway. I move the ball an inch or two back to the right, open the clubface, aim to the left of my target, and, as I bring my club down at a steep angle, I work to contact the ball as cleanly as possible, just at the start of the upswing. If my execution is correct, these modifications will give me a soft-flying recovery with a little cut on it, and the ball will usually plunk itself down on the green with a minimum of get-up-and-go. This type of shot doesn't require a professional's skill. Moreover, it can be played with all the clubs from the 4-iron through the wedges, and in most kinds of rough. It's a very useful kind of shot to play, too, when you're not trying to hit and hold a green but trying merely to advance the ball dextrously down the fairway on a long hole.

As a general rule, the rough does strange things to golfers. They stop thinking. Even experienced club players try to pull off circus shots they would never dream of hitting from a fairway lie. Conversely, I have played with few club golfers who seem to understand the value of what I think of as the "mature recovery." (When I first had enough brains to play it, I felt I had suddenly grown up as a tactician.) Very simply, if you're in the rough, say, a 5-iron away from a green that is fairly open in front but has lots of trouble over it, forget about the 5-iron and take a 7-iron or an 8. If the ball comes out of the rough faster than you had counted on, which frequently happens, and keeps on running and running, you're in no trouble. Occasionally it will run all the way to the green. Fine. If it comes out of the rough with less steam on it, as it normally will, and ends up well short of the green, you're in good shape, too. You have a relatively routine little pitch or pitch-and-run left, the kind of shot that you can often stick in one-putt range. On the other hand, if you attempt the Metro-Goldwyn-Mayer 5-

329

An 8-iron shot. I recommend using the same swing on all shots. The different clubs—having shafts of different lengths—merely modify the arc of the swing. One good swing is hard enough to learn.

iron, the immature recovery, you can end up much worse off than you started.

Flight

On a full shot, the ideal flight is one on which the ball rises gradually until it peaks, and then, having spent all its forward thrust, drops as softly as a snowflake. Golf clubs are designed to give you this kind of flight if you strike the ball correctly. There are four factors which in combination get the ball in the air for you: the loft of the clubhead, the grooves in the face of the club, the weight of the clubhead, and the flex of the shaft. To approximate ideal flight, however, you must have certain weather and turf conditions. It follows that young golfers who are lucky enough to grow up in areas where the turf is excellent and there isn't much wind will generally develop a good flight on their shots. This goes a long way toward explaining why California and east Texas produce so many top-notch golfers. It works the other way, too. Few golfers from west Texas, for example, where the turf is poor and the wind blows free, acquire the ability to flight their shots properly. One of the principal reasons, I would say, why British golfers haven't been successful on the American tour stems from the fact that, while they play on excellent turf at home, they must regularly contend with blustering winds that knock a player off-balance unless he has adopted a restricted pivot and an extremely compact hitting action. (In this connection, there's no doubt in my mind that the larger American ball helps a man to develop into a much better striker.)

When golfers grow up in difficult climates and play under difficult conditions, it is natural for them to accept as a good shot a so-so shot that happens to work out. For illustration, say a young golfer comes from a region where the ground is very hard. He soon learns that a low, hooking tee-shot will give him much more roll than a tee-shot that peaks and then drops gently, so he gravitates toward a draw action and uses it on all his shots. Say he hits an approach with a long iron that has a dipping flight but which bounces onto the green and ends up in the same position a well-struck, well-flighted iron would have. He's likely not to be as critical as he should be of this shot. Generally, he comes to think too much in terms of his score and not enough in terms of how he made his score. He settles, without realizing it, for a lower standard of play and a rougher technique than golfers who are fortunate enough to live in areas where conditions are better and where a promising young player quickly learns that he is expected to hit the ball to his target with a superior type of flight that he can repeat on shot after shot. The habits of youth are hard to break. Some golfers of undeniable talent never unlearn all their early bad habits. In tournament play under average weather conditions they cannot keep pace with the better strikers, the better flighters. In a word, then, a serious young golfer, whatever his local playing conditions, must understand what good flight is and work continually to achieve it. How your ball gets to the green is just as important as the fact that it gets there.

Playing in the Wind

It takes a very capable golfer to control the ball on a windy day. Continuous adjustments are necessary. Let me describe some of the elementary considerations.

Downwind. When the wind is behind you, it becomes more difficult, of course, to stop a ball on a green. Though I flight the ball rather high as a rule, downwind I try to hit it even higher. My aim is to achieve, in effect, the same type of shot I'd be able to hit on a windless day when you can play an approach to peak out and drop almost vertically. With this in mind, I take one club less than the distance calls for—an 8, say, instead of a 7—and I hit it hard. I want to get it up high, so I concentrate on staying behind the ball and on working under it.

Against the wind. Here you want a boring flight, the kind on

Into the wind—weight forward, extension low. You don't have to dig deep.

which the ball never seems to peak out but keeps driving forward. The only way you can accomplish this is by hitting shots that don't carry backspin; if they do, they'll climb into a head wind. Since it's impossible to hit a golf shot that doesn't have any spin, the thing to do is to play the ball for sidespin—preferably for hook spin, which bores through the air much better than fade spin. To do this, I drop the ball back a little in my stance and I close the face of my club a shade. However, I use a hook-spin shot only when conditions make it absolutely necessary, for my natural style is left-to-right and I believe in cutting down the variables. However, a fine natural draw player, like Frank Beard, would have no reservations at all about this.

Cross winds. A cross wind that's blowing partially against you amounts, really, to a head wind. You must treat it that way, along with making the obvious allowance in the line you take in order to offset the force of the cross wind. A cross wind that's blowing with you to some degree is another thing. Old-time golfers as a rule used to play *into* this kind of a wind: if it was coming off the left, they would draw the ball into it and "hold the ball up" in the wind. Same thing if the wind was coming across from the right: they'd fade the ball into the wind. This is a useful, sensible way to control the ball, but there are some situations in which you stand to gain more on the tee-shot if you ride *with* the wind. For example, on those days at St. Andrews when you have a following wind that's sweeping over the fairways on the second nine from the left, there are certain holes on which you should try to use the wind to pick up yardage on your drive. The famous Road Hole, the seventeenth, provides a convenient example. This is a long par 4 of about 460 yards on which the fairway angles to the right about 225 yards from the tee. On a calm day the most desirable route off the tee is directly over the new hotel that has replaced the old sheds in the elbow of the dogleg. That's out-of-bounds, however, and the out-of-bounds line continues all the way to the green along the right. As you can realize, this makes cutting the corner a little dangerous in a following wind that's coming from left to right. If you play to draw the ball into the wind and the draw doesn't come off, you can be blown out-of-bounds; in addition, there's always the likelihood that you will overaccentuate your draw action, to be on the safe side, and hook the ball across the fairway and into the rough on the left. The golfer who can play the ball both ways—fade it as

334

well as draw it—is much better off in this kind of wind if he aims a few yards to the left of his calm-weather line over the corner and plays for a fade that will catch the wind as it swings with the fairway. The wind will push the ball many yards farther, and this can be important: instead of having to play a longish iron to the ticklish green on his second, he has a much shorter, safer, more controllable shot. While the Road Hole offers an exceptionally dramatic illustration of the value of riding with the wind, you will see Casper and Palmer and other accomplished drivers utilizing a cross wind in this fashion, either with a fade or a draw, whenever the direction of the wind and the shape of a hole encourage it.

Keeping Your Swing Sound

How do slumps begin? They begin from neglect, and neglect finally leads to a loss of confidence.

You can practice a lot but still be neglectful—neglectful of the fundamentals. During the long stretch of poor golf I suffered through in the winter and spring of 1967, I tried to rouse my game by attempting to bring off increasingly complicated shots. What I should have done was to back up, return to the fundamentals, and get one thing at a time under control.

It's not easy to keep a golf swing tuned up and functioning correctly. This is one of the reasons why I play two or three tournaments and then take a week off from the tour—and take it off completely. After a few tournaments, you see, I will have developed quite a few bad habits, and I want to get them out of my system. When I start practicing again after that week's layoff, I go right back to fundamentals and build from there. I do the same thing at the start of every season when I haven't touched a club for a month or six weeks. I start with the grip, the stance, the turn— the ABCs. When my swing is in fairly good working order, I go down and see Jack Grout and have him check me over to see how well I'm performing the fundamentals.

When you do fall into a protracted slump, life becomes involved, to say the least. There is never any shortage of people who want to help you. They are all sincerely well-intentioned, none more so than your fellow professionals. Every professional, though, is inclined to see your troubles in terms of his troubles, and to see his solutions as your solutions. The pro who thinks that the rotation of the hips is the basis of correct action invariably discovers that your hips are off—you're turning them too little or too much, too soon or too late, too fast or too slow. The pro who has always had a problem staying behind the ball nearly always diagnoses this as your problem. And so on—a new prescription from each specialist. This is why you must have an unconfused understanding of your swing. Ultimately, you must straighten yourself out. Even if you're lucky enough to have a dependable teacher you've known for years to go back to, he can help you only so much and no more.

If your slump continues—well, lots of luck. You'll need it. You'll be overwhelmed with unsolicited advice from every quarter. Very often today, if a man can't be a great golfer, it's his ambition to be a great teacher—old Doctor Golf himself. These fellows, some of whom can actually break 80, pop up in every town. The ones I especially have to avoid are my hometown friends. If I had a bruise on my swing, they'd treat it as a heart attack. I gather from my colleagues on the tour that it's the same all over. It probably always was, for human nature doesn't change. I'll bet that every time Harry Vardon hit a shot off-line, which wasn't very often, he was flooded with suggestions by dozens of admirers, each of whom wanted to be "the man who straightened Vardon out."

When I'm not playing well during the course of a tournament, I continually try to locate the source of my trouble and do something about it. But I experiment only within reasonable limits. I confine myself to minor adjustments, and I know pretty well how these will affect my shots. I never make radical changes. The ball might go anywhere then. Let me tell you of one happy occasion when I managed to hit on a successful minor adjustment. During the 1967 World Series of Golf, at the Firestone Country Club in Akron, I wasn't hitting my shots at all the way I wanted to. My scores for the two nine-hole stretches on Saturday's round and the first nine on Sunday's concluding round were three 37s, two over par for each nine, but I wasn't playing nearly as well as those figures might indicate. I kept experimenting and examining my swing for whatever ailed it. Meanwhile, I forced myself to make slower, smoother swings so that, at least, I wouldn't accentuate my errors. At length, on the ninth tee on Sunday, I discovered what was throwing me off: I was taking the club back too much inside. To rectify this, on my next shot and all subsequent shots I picked out a spot six inches behind the ball and made sure my clubhead passed over it at the start of my backswing. This helped my swing and my shotmaking, and my scoring as well. I had a 33 on the back nine and nipped Gay Brewer by a stroke. Emphasizing a straighter take-away wasn't a complete cure, naturally, but as a temporary expedient it did the job.

Course Management

Course management, I'd say, is the part of golf most overlooked by the average player. He has little or no conception how much thinking should go into a round or how beneficial good planning can be.

To begin with, he would be wise to walk off the yardages on his home course, selecting a bunker or a prominent tree or some other permanent feature in his normal drive zone on each hole, then measuring the distance from that marker to the center of the green. Then he should carry out the second part of the operation: he should go to the practice tee and determine accurately how far he ordinarily hits the ball with each club. It is surprising how many strokes can be saved simply through correct club selection.

Herb Shriner, the night-club comedian from Indiana, used to lead off a funny monologue about a hometown friend called Doc by explaining that his friend wasn't really a doctor but he'd got the nickname because he acted so much like a doctor—"For example, he loved to double-park." I am reminded of this because, as we all know, many club golfers who have watched the pros on television try to behave just like the pros—and they do superficially. They wear puffy-sleeved sweaters and shoes with flaps, they talk the lingo of the circuit, and they take forever to putt out on the greens. Unfortunately, their observations seldom go deeper and they miss the very points that might make their golf more professional. For example, take the fairly competent club golfer—the man with about a 10 handicap. Does he ever play an iron off the tee on certain holes to gain the best position for his approach? He should. Does he ever deliberately aim his tee-shot for the rough on one side of the fairway when there is major trouble on the other side to be avoided at all costs? He should. Does he make it a practice when he's snarled in the rough to play what we've called the "mature recovery"? Does he think out each approach so that, if he should mis-hit it, he'll wind up on the most advantageous side of the green? Does he think out his chips so that he'll leave himself with the most holeable putt? Does he gear himself up when he has an opening so that he can cash in on it? He should do all these things, of course. There's nothing hard about them. All they take is an understanding of golf and where the percentages lie, for everyone. I would say that one of the most satisfying statements a golfer can make after a round would be this: "I played just fair but I managed my game very well."

Acquiring a Better Temperament

As a general thing one runs into three main types of temperament in golfers: there are the fellows who never learn to control their emotions; the fellows who have no emotional problems; and the fellows who have temper and fire but who have learned how to use this to their advantage rather than disadvantage. To reach the top in golf, as in everything else, you have to have lots of drive. I've

At Oakmont in '62 I was, as the saying goes, too young to know how hard putting is. Putting takes discipline, and discipline comes from temperament.

never met a champion who didn't. Some of them may look pacific and others may express their worries perpetually, but the resolution and the spark are there in both cases. Outward demeanor is just a matter of the golfer's personality. Who would have ever thought a person with Bobby Jones' remarkable composure would be burning up so much fuel inside that during one Open he lost sixteen pounds?

Most golfers can develop self-control, if they really want to. No young athlete ever had a more terrible temper than Jones. When he was nineteen, he tore up his scorecard in disgust during the 1921 British Open, and the shame he felt afterward gnawed so deeply into him that from that day on he proceeded to set a standard of conduct and sportsmanship that was matchless. In a much lesser way, I went through the same thing myself. My second year in golf, when I was eleven, I played with older kids who threw their clubs whenever they hit a bad shot. I thought this was the thing to do and began doing it myself. One day when I was playing with my father at Scioto, I hit an 8-iron to the fifteenth and missed the green completely. I whirled and hurled that 8-iron just as far as I could. I was standing there fuming when I heard my father speak in a tone he seldom used. He was outraged. "Young man," he said, "that will be the last club you throw. If I ever hear of you throwing a club again—well, that will be the last round of golf you'll ever play." There was no misunderstanding him. He meant every word he said. That injunction faced me in the right direction, immediately. It wasn't long before I began to take pride in harnessing my temper, not indulging it. I cannot begin to tell you how much good it did me. It was incalculable.

Most of the successful professional golfers, as goes without saying, have acquired fine, stable temperaments. They keep themselves well under control and they have a winning attitude. The very best have the capacity to keep working on a poor round and often they end up with a respectable score through sheer doggedness. They also have the ability not to get frightened of their scores when things are going great, which is just as hard. Beneath his sheath of outward calmness, though, a seasoned tournament player frequently experiences all sorts of qualms and tribulations, the same tortures that afflict the average player when he learns on the seventeenth tee that he can win the Saturday tournament if he finishes with two 5s

—and then finds that his knees are knocking and his hands are shaking. I know I have these spells of anxiety.

Baltusrol and the 1967 Open come quickly to mind. A number of my friends have told me that they have never seen me in such a commanding mood as on the last day of that championship. No, sir. After I bogeyed the tenth, as I can remember only too vividly, I suddenly had a bad attack of nervousness. As I walked down the eleventh fairway, I tried to calm myself. "Here you are, starting to get afraid of winning the Open," I said to myself. "You're leading by three strokes with eight holes to go. You've obviously played well or you wouldn't be in this position. You're still playing well. You're doing something you enjoy, so enjoy it. Play each shot as well as you can, and when you hit a really fine shot, savor it." This was one time when a little talk with myself helped me to renew my poise and my confidence, and down the stretch I played good aggressive golf. Some days it is easier than it is on others to settle yourself down or to rise to the occasion. In addition, no matter who you are, it always takes a little luck, too, to be able to come onto your game at the right time or to be able to stabilize it in a crisis.

The basic point I'm trying to make, however, is that the average golfer can develop a better temperament. Instead of burning up with frustration on your bad days or becoming a bundle of nerves at the prospect of victory on your good ones, I would say to you, "Think of the wonderful challenge that golf provides and try to meet that challenge." That's where the real kick lies—not in being a lion in the locker room and a lamb on the links. Don't try to be foolishly heroic, to play way over your head. Keep your feet on the ground. Just try to do yourself justice. Accept the challenge and enjoy the challenge.

Part Five

XXII

Some Thoughts on
Golf Architecture

GOLF IS THE ONLY GAME that is not played on a specially pre-pared court or field but on natural terrain, and this is un-doubtedly the reason for its incomparable fascination. Moreover, since there are no strict measurements that a golf course must abide by, each course is free to develop its own form, its own flavor, its own personality. Say the word *Pinehurst* to a golfer and it conjures up in his mind's eye the No. 2 course—eighteen green holes weaving their way through a forest of longleaf pines, holes with tumbling fairways and with splendidly sited greens that challenge the golfer sometimes with adroit bunkering and other times simply through the canny contouring of the putting surface and the green area in general. Say the word *Carnoustie* and a totally different prospect presents itself—the gray coast of eastern Scotland, a chilly wind off the North Sea sweeping over eighteen linksland holes on which there is scarcely a tree, eighteen holes that look undramatic and banal until you tackle them and learn that it is no easy matter to keep the ball in play, let alone control your approaches to the fast, slanting, unbanked greens. Whether it be Pinehurst or Carnoustie, Kasumigaseki or Persimmon Ridge (that brand-new layout that has no persimmon trees, no ridge, and nothing much else), when you think of a course you automatically assess it. Your assessment takes in a hundred and one facets, from the type of fairway grass to the color of the flags, but eventually it comes down to the char-acter and the beauty of the holes, individually and collectively.

For me, golf beauty means two things: the natural suitableness of the land for golf, and the skillfulness with which its topographical features were utilized to create holes that arrest you and intrigue

343

you and never become stale no matter how many times you play them. There are a lot of beautiful golf courses spread throughout the world—meadowland courses and parkland courses, seaside courses and mountain courses, courses of penal design (which frankly punish each wayward shot) and courses of strategic design (which encourage initiative and reward a player in proportion to the difficulty of the shot he chooses to play and successfully executes), courses on which water hazards abound and are the chief threat, courses on which the wind amounts to the principal hazard, courses on which each hole is separately shut in by woods, courses that play well only when the fairways are fast and the greens slick, courses on which control of the tee-shot is the key, courses where the second shot is more important than the first, courses on which power is an invaluable asset and those on which it is a treacherous ally, courses that throw one tough hole after another at you with positively no letup, courses that start somewhat leniently and then demand increasingly heady shotmaking, courses that force you to play defensively and courses that incite you and make you want to gamble—an endless variety, each requiring the golfer, if he is to cope with it effectively, to make certain modifications in his thinking, in his method of "taking the ball," and in the type of shots he plays. It is not to be wondered at that when a golfer, up against a fine course on a fine morning, happens to be in top form and brings in a low score, there are few pleasures in life as gratifying.

All first-class golf courses and all outstanding golf holes have one thing in common to the golfer's eye: they look absolutely natural, as if the terrain had always been that way, waiting to be discovered for golf. That is seldom if ever the case, to be sure. Even in Britain and Ireland where some seaside stretches need only minor alteration to emerge as eighteen holes of good golf, some work must always be done. This is where the golf architect comes in. As he visualizes and stakes out his holes, his job is to make the best possible use of the natural features of the terrain, then to use his modern earth-moving equipment with taste and imagination in shaping the supporting features that his holes need. Regardless of the type of land he is given to work with and the amount of "artificial" construction he may feel impelled to undertake, if he is a truly competent architect every hole, every feature of every hole, will have a natural look to it. The stream in the tee-shot landing area will cut across the fairway at the proper point; the key bunker in the green area will be set at just the right angle to the entrance; the size and shape of the green will suit the approach shot perfectly.

It has been said that every golfer is a golf architect at heart. I agree with this statement but I'm not terribly impressed with it. I don't see how it could be otherwise, considering the nature of the game of golf. While I'm not an especially artistic or creative person, even when I was a boy making my first visits to new courses something inside of me responded instinctively whenever I came upon a hole that appeared to have exceptional golf quality and played as nicely as it looked it might. Just as one never gets tired of studying the golf swing and trying to separate the true fundamentals from the jerry-rigging, one never becomes bored thinking about golf holes and trying to arrive at the exact reasons why certain holes have both charm and shot value while others have nothing except yardage. Golf architecture interests me so much, in fact, that I hope to become increasingly involved in it in the years ahead. With this in mind, some time ago I joined a young architect's firm as a consultant, and the experience has proved to be so stimulating that it has confirmed my long-range intentions to spend more and more time in that field as I cut down on the amount of competitive golf I play.

Golf architecture in a vast subject, almost as big as all outdoors. Accordingly, in discussing it here, I'm not going to attempt to do much more than present some of the observations and ideas that have formed in my mind over the last dozen years while playing hundreds of different courses around the globe. Many of my remarks will be critical, because one of the things that has struck me hardest is the mediocrity of the majority of the courses that have been designed in comparatively recent years. Many of my remarks will be appreciative, for, more often than not, I have truly been impressed by the celebrated courses and holes. I think you build up your opinions about equally from the good courses and bad courses you play. In any event, here are some of mine.

First Thoughts

Golf architects too often accept an inferior piece of property just to get the job. The result, almost inevitably, is an inferior course.

Gently rolling land is best for golf. That's why most desert courses are boring—the fairways have no contours. They don't have to be that way. You can bulldoze flat land into undulating land, and bulldozing isn't that expensive considering the results.

The terrain itself should create or suggest most of the hazards. I don't favor inserting too many bunkers. The Augusta National, I believe, has only 32 or so bunkers. This makes it pleasantly playable for the members. For the Masters, merely by moving the tee-markers back and changing the pin positions so that the bunkers come sharply into play, the Augusta National becomes a wholly different course—a test for experts.

Speaking of the Augusta National, it is, among other things, a triumph of routing. The first nine runs counterclockwise, the second clockwise. No two holes look alike or play alike. No two consecutive holes run in the same direction. As a matter of fact, you don't meet with two par 4s back to back until you come to the ninth and tenth.

Fairways must swing. This then makes it imperative for a golfer to "work the ball." I hate to play a hole where you stand up and hit two straight shots to the green. On the other hand, I admire holes where on the tee-shot the golfer faces a definite feature he must carry or avoid—water or a mound or a tongue of rough or a depression or trees—in order to gain the preferred position for his second shot.

Each green should have a variety of rolls and breaks so that the members, however familiar they may be with the greens, cannot play a putt from memory but must re-read the putt each time. This keeps a golf course fresh.

Holes in General

I prefer a course that begins softly. In my judgment, a par 4 makes the best starting hole. I don't like to tackle a par 5 until I'm fully warmed up.

Whether a hole be a par 3, 4, or 5, you should have to play one great shot to make a birdie. For illustration, take two of my favorite holes, the thirteenth at the Augusta National, a short 5, and the third at Pebble Beach, a short 4. On the thirteenth—475 yards, dogleg left, a creek before the green and curving along the right side—you can set yourself up for a birdie by playing (1) a great tee-shot around the corner that enables you to get home easily in two; (2) after an only fair drive, a great second over the creek and onto the green; or (3) if you have laid up short of the creek

There's no better finishing hole in golf than the 18th at Pebble Beach.

with your second, a great wedge pitch that puts you in one-putt range. On the third at Pebble—355 yards, dogleg left, a tiny green bunkered front-right and side-left—you can put yourself in position for a birdie by playing (1) a great controlled right-to-left drive around the corner to a point near the green from which you should be able to get down in two; or (2) after an only adequate tee-shot, a great little flip pitch which has perfect touch and sits down next to the stick.

Par-3 holes, I think, were meant to be played with an iron. There should be no demand for a wood on them. The new courses that make a big deal of short holes that measure over 230 yards have succumbed to a confused set of values. The fact that players make high scores on a hole doesn't necessarily mean that it's a good hole. The ideal combination of par 3s on a course would, I believe, give you one hole that calls for a long iron (a 2 or a 3), two holes that call for a medium iron (a 4, 5, or 6), and one hole that calls for a short iron (a 7 or an 8).

There is a definite shortage of top-class par 5s today. In some cases the distance the modern player hits the ball has taken the bite out of holes that were formerly fearsome, but it would be wrong to deduce from this that length alone can make a good par 5. I personally like Bob Jones' concept (which the Augusta National dramatizes) of building par 5s that are intrinsically par 4½s, the green within reach in two if the golfer puts a pair of long, accurate shots together. I have no objection at all to par 5s that are beyond the big-hitter's two-shot range, but these holes can be dull and

A beautiful and exacting par 3: the 16th at the Augusta National.

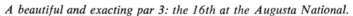

Merion's 11th—the approach to the green. A great drive-and-pitch hole.

dreary if the drive and the second shot are just a matter of slugging away and eating up as much yardage as possible. On a lengthy par 5, the second shot should present the golfer with some problem to surmount—say, placing the ball on the high side of a two-level fairway in order to open the entrance to the green, or carrying some hazard (sand or water) in order to gain some other distinct advantage in playing the third shot.

In regard to par-4 holes, the wider the variety, the better off a course is. There should be some 4s—in the U.S. Open we meet plenty of them—that are both long and stringent; to get home, you must follow a well-placed drive with a precise long iron, or, in the case of a short hitter, a fairway wood. In recent years, however, there has been a tendency to build courses where all the par 4s are well over 400 yards, and this seems a real mistake to me. There should be one or two (and maybe more) drive-and-pitch 4s, not merely to create a change of pace but to present the golfer with a crack at a birdie now and then. A good example of this type of short par 4 would be the eighth at Baltusrol, which is only 365 yards long. If you position your tee-shot on the proper side of the fairway, you have a shot at a bird; if you put it on the wrong side, you have your work cut out to make a par. The 378-yard eleventh at Merion, the famous Baffling Brook hole—the brook cuts in front of the green and then hugs the right side—is another excellent example of how much golf a drive-and-pitch hole can pack. In the old days the terrain in the green area on this type of hole was usually quite severe, the idea being that the golfer, called on to play only a short iron on his approach, should be penalized more drastically if he missed the green than if he were playing a longer iron. In any event, few architects today build sharp slopes on their short par 4s, and they give as their reason the difficulty and the high cost of maintenance. This is incorrect. Sharp slopes are not hard to maintain—they did it for years—and the cost need not be high.

A sensible way to require the long-hitting modern golfer to play good golf shots (and not just long ones) is to provide for a fair percentage of dogleg par 4s and semi-dogleg par 4s among your eighteen holes. To place your tee-shot on the fairway and in good position on a dogleg takes judgment and execution. The long hitter is forced to be as accurate as the medium-distance hitter or the short hitter, and this is as it should be.

I don't believe that a long par 4 should necessarily have a large green and a short par 4 a small green. The size of the green on any hole should depend primarily on the nature of the terrain it occupies. The fourth at Pebble Beach, for instance, has an extremely small green and it should, not because the hole measures only 325 yards, but because the terrain in the green area is rather humdrum. The architects had to create a certain amount of hazardousness to offset this, and they achieved it by devising a small green with "quick" contours and by cutting their bunkers right to the edge of the putting surface.

Some of the holes I find most engaging are "sleepers"—holes that are neglected when enthusiasts discuss a particular layout but that have a subtlety that an observant golfer learns to respect. The short twelfth at Lytham & St. Anne's is just such a hole. Only about 170 yards long, a flattish little stretch with an unspectacular green set off by shallow bunkers, it looks like nothing. It really plays, though. You see, the bunker at the left-front of the green commands your attention, so you play away from it and in doing so, you wind up on the tougher side on the green—and frequently off the green. There's nothing wrong with a hole like this which deliberately misleads you. It's up to you to stay awake.

350

Tee to Green

As I have stated earlier, I do not think much of holes where yardage is stressed out of proportion and where the golfer merely puts the ball into play on the tee-shot, hitting it as far as he can in the bargain. The tee-shot should be more than just a reflex action. On the other hand, as an advocate of strategic as opposed to penal architecture, I don't think the tee-shot should set the golfer too hard a problem, such as overly harsh fairway bunkering creates. A fairway bunker, as I see it, should catch a bad shot but not a shot that is only a few yards off-line. Most of the courses we play on the tour are faulty in just the reverse way: they give you too much room on the drive. Not only are the fairways extra-wide but the fairway bunkers present no danger since they can be carried. Furthermore, the rough is so sparse and mild that a scatter driver is hardly worse off for missing the fairway.

The courses on which the U.S. Open is played come fairly close to my ideas on how championship courses should be set up. I very much approve of the Open's insistence on narrow fairways, as long as they're not too fast. The heavy rough that invariably borders the fairways on an Open course makes sense to me: after an erratic drive, you shouldn't expect to be playing from as congenial a lie as if you had hit the fairway. The main trouble with rough as a hazard, of course, is that it is too capricious. Sometimes it penalizes you too severely for your error, at other times not at all.

Naturally, there are a few measures the U.S.G.A. regularly follows in the Open that I'm not so keen about. I don't see the point of those occasional strips of rough between the fairway and the green—fairway grass that has been permitted to grow into rough. I've never been enthusiastic about the now traditional procedure of bringing the rough in close to the green, providing only a yard or so of clipped fringe between the actual putting surface and the rough. As a result, the Open almost completely eliminates chipping and substitutes chopping. I would also like to see the U.S.G.A. be somewhat less rigid in preparing individual holes. Off the tee, I believe, a golfer should have the opportunity to take a chance occasionally—not just the long hitter but the average Open contestant. Ideally, a well-designed hole should offer an alternate route to the green, and while this is sometimes impossible, it should at least allow more options than most Open holes do. Too often they can be played just one way and one way only. This tends to muffle initiative and it makes golf too much a game of repetitive accuracy —too close to bowling. Accuracy is the first essential of good golf, to be sure, but at its best and most exciting the game should also make provision for maneuver, finesse, and outright gambling.

Since the advent of the bulldozer, unconscientious architects—and they are not at all rare—have made it a practice to flatten out green areas and then to add a few bunkers in an almost automatic fashion. This is a surefire prescription for a nothing-ball golf course. A green area can't have any life unless it is built on interesting land and unless the bunkering is tied in with the flow of the land. Mounds and roll-offs and hollows in the green area work out extremely well; they give the average golfer a shot he plays better than the explosion from sand, and they give the expert much more to think about than a bunker shot does. Personally, I am not as partial to mounding in the green area as some people are—the lie you end up with depends too much on luck. I prefer decisive roll-offs at the edge of the putting surface, for then, if you miss the green with your approach, you must play a delicate chip or pitch to get the ball near the cup—a true golf shot.

In this connection, I am reminded of the first hole on Pinehurst No. 2. Some 415 yards long, it has a medium-sized green guarded by only one bunker, situated to the left of the green and extending three-quarters of the way back. Most golfers, understandably, play away from this bunker, and in doing so many of them end up in the pronounced hollow to the right of the green. Then they face a much more difficult shot than the one they would have had from the bunker, for the hollow is filled with undulations, and it takes an exquisite touch chip to run the ball up the bank at just the right speed and have it roll dead near the cup. I have seen many seasoned players hit this chip too soft to get it up onto the green and as many others hit it too hard to stay on the green. If Donald Ross, the architect of Pinehurst, had put in a second bunker to the right of the green—and most architects would have—it would have made the hole blunter, easier, and much more prosaic.

Greens

The hardest thing to do in constructing a golf hole is to build a green into a hillside and make it look as if it was always there. Whenever you can, of course, you must use the natural terrain and

352

not disguise it by carting in soil and erecting a "mail-order" green on top of it. Britain's courses are made by their bold use of the terrain, although at first glance it doesn't hit you that way.

The vogue for the super-large green is subsiding, and this is a good thing. On paper, the advantage of a super-large green is that it offers you four or more separate pin areas that can make the hole stiffer or easier, as required. The one course I know where it works out that way is the Augusta National, and it works there because the course as a whole has a monumental scale and because the individual holes have been designed with care and knowledge. All in all, the only circumstance in which I think that the super-large green is justified is on a course that handles a great amount of traffic. Then, certain sections of the greens can be rested while others are being used.

Although there is nothing wrong with having a few plateau greens on a course, I think we have possibly been going in for them disproportionately. I may be wrong about this; I may be looking at it too much through the eyes of a touring professional. Most of my colleagues, as you probably know, are so set against elevated greens that they speak of shots on which only a part of the flagstick is visible as "blind shots." Perhaps this attitude is bred by the fact that a touring pro usually gets to play only one or two practice rounds before a tournament, and not knowing the layout as well as he would like to, he naturally prefers to be able to see every yard of the greens. Be that as it may, I believe that an able architect should create a good many downhill shots to his greens—or at least build a fair percentage of his greens so that they give the impression that they are sitting below you. When a player can see all of a green, you can raise your demands on him. Take the second and third holes at Pine Valley, both of them beauties in their separate ways. The second is a 350-yard 4 to a green perched at the top of a steep ridge strewn with sand and rough. From the fairway below you can see only the front rim of the green, so the pin positions should always be rather moderate. The third, a 175-yard 3, is played from a raised tee to an island green (surrounded by sand) that is well below the tee. Here, with all the green visible and readable, much more extreme pin positions are entirely acceptable.

Random Thoughts

You can't create a golf course on a piece of paper. The holes never turn out the way the "paper architect" imagines they will. After a hole is built, the architect must go back to it, see how it actually plays, and then modify the hole to bring out its golf charm and its shot values.

In the practice area, the prevailing wind, ideally, should come from the right and be slightly against the golfer. Since they ordinarily occupy whatever ground is left over after the holes have been laid out, most practice areas are not all that they should be. Some of the best, in my judgment, are those at Doral, Firestone, and the Champions in Houston.

The quality of practice greens has improved noticeably in recent years. Today there are quite a number where the grass and the undulations are much the same as they are on the greens out on the course—which is the idea behind having a practice green. Since a practice green can be one of the handsomest features of a golf club—it is at Oakmont, for example, where it flows right into the ninth green—considerable attention should be paid to it. The pleasure it gives the older members is justification enough.

In laying out a course, the architect should see to it that the golfer doesn't begin or end his round shooting into the sun. The ninth hole, as goes without saying, should be routed back to the clubhouse, as many of them are. A series of strong, assertive finishing holes is a tremendous plus for any course. The excellence of the home-stretch holes at Pebble Beach, Carnoustie, Merion, Muirfield, Hoylake, and Baltusrol contributes a great deal to the stature of those courses.

Televised golf tournaments have earned large and devoted audiences, but television golf will come into its own only when the full eighteen holes of the big championships are shown. That day, I would guess, isn't so far off, for the advances in mobile television equipment have been remarkable. In constructing a new course that is intended for championship play, the best approach—and I hope to be a part of just such a project—would be to anticipate the needs of television from the outset. This would mean installing the cables and wires under the ground when the fairways are being built and the drainage system put in, as well as providing for suitable ridges and knolls that would give the cameras the choicest positions possible without disturbing the natural aspect of the course or impeding the circulation of the gallery. If the job is done properly, the cameras should be able to catch all the shots a player hits in the course of a round and, what is more, follow the ball on each shot. Watching the flight of the ball is at the heart of golf's appeal, and until the day when the viewer is able to do this, television golf will continue to be only an abbreviation of the game that doesn't begin to capture its true texture and spirit.

XXIII

The Golf Scene Today

N O ONE EVER DREAMED that golf in America and throughout the world would grow as it has during the past twenty years, particularly in the past ten. Each year the tournaments have become better attended, the purses higher. Half the weekends of the year a professional tournament is televised. The top pros have become celebrities, recognized wherever they go, swarmed over like movie stars. Golf has become a national game: even the people who don't play it now understand a little about it—enough so that they realize that Oakmont, Oakland Hills, and Oak Hill are golf courses and not fashionable finishing schools for girls. Like pro football, golf is now deep in the country's blood. And again like pro football, the fears in some quarters that the game was being overexposed and would suffer as a consequence have so far proved to be unfounded. It is difficult to guess where it will all end, but most people feel that the country's absorption in golf will continue to increase as long as the national economy continues to thrive.

Speaking for the men who have been involved in the game, I believe we appreciate how lucky we have been and are. Whenever pro golfers gather and talk seriously, there is one expression you are bound to hear: we must keep the standards of the game very high, or else we will kill the goose that laid the golden eggs. So far, despite some individual and collective mistakes, things have gone fairly well, but I hasten to add that this has happened not because of what we have done for golf but simply because of the nature of the game. Golf is something! If anyone tried to invent a game with the beauty, the competitive kick, the technical subtleties, and the endless fascination of golf, he wouldn't even come close. The least we can do is to see that golf remains the great game it is by approaching the problems that come along with all the wisdom we can muster.

These remarks, as is probably apparent, are made by a professional golfer addressing himself primarily to the world of professional golf. I think about that microcosm a good deal—all of us have had to in 1968—and I have reached certain conclusions about what must be done to keep it healthy and strong. Let me go into them briefly.

To start with, I think we have arrived at that point where we must have two tournament circuits—a major league and a minor league, if you wish. Today there is such a large number of young men who want to make a career of professional golf that the tour, as we know it, simply doesn't offer room enough for all of them. In the average winter tournament 500 players are trying for the 144 places in the starting field. Each year a few of the new young pros prove that they have the stuff to meet the fast pace on the tour, but they are the exceptions. The vast majority of the young men need a stepping-stone between college competition and the tour, and at the present time there is no such place where they can develop their skills. In baseball, few kids can come straight off their college team and pitch to Willie Mays, but after gaining experience in the minors, a number of them will be ready.

My suggestion is that we ask the sponsors who want to hold a tournament featuring the Palmers and the Caspers and the Januarys and the rest of the "name stars" to put on a second tournament for the young developing players that same week at a course in the same general area. For example, the New Orleans Open might well be scheduled the same week as the Jackson Open in Jackson, Mississippi. The golfers who haven't qualified to play New Orleans would play Jackson and have a crack at a modest purse which the sponsors of the New Orleans tournament would put up. A hopeful young golfer must play lots of competitive golf, and it doesn't hurt if in the process he can make enough money to support himself and not fall into the bad habit (as too many youngsters have) of thinking that the world owes them a backer. We should begin organizing this second circuit as soon as possible. The population explosion on the tour isn't around the corner, it's here already. To say it another way, if fifteen or twenty years from now my kids want to play tournament golf, I want them to have the same chance I had.

It is also time, I believe, for the formation of an international players' association. Its main purpose would be to work with the various national professional associations and reach an accord on tournament dates throughout the world so that there would be no conflicts, such as there was in 1968 when a new tournament, the $200,000 Greater Milwaukee Open, was scheduled the same week as the British Open. After all that the British have done for golf, the minimum we can do is to give their championship our active support. We should encourage our best players to participate in it. In 1968 I was half-planning to skip the British Open—I'd gone over for it six straight years—but when I learned that a big new tour tournament had been arranged for that same week, that made up my mind for me: I decided I'd play in the British Open.

Today we are very, very close to attaining that age-old ideal, a universal set of rules for golf. The U.S. Golf Association and its counterpart, the R. & A., meet every four years to discuss rules and regulations, and at their meeting in Sandwich in 1967 they came to a full agreement on just about every point. Those of us who play the pro circuit would like to comply to the letter with these rules. Presently there is only one U.S.G.A. rule that we don't follow, the one that calls for continuous putting. We have tried it, and it doesn't seem to work out under tour conditions. For example, decreeing that the ball can be lifted and cleaned only once on each green would be unfair to the early starters who must cope with dew-covered greens. We aren't being different just for the sake of being different, and we would welcome the opportunity to talk over this matter with the U.S.G.A. and see if we can hit upon something agreeable to both parties.

Besides being very much for the idea of a single set of rules for all golfers, the pros also are in favor of the movement toward one universal golf ball. A significant step in this direction was taken in 1968 when the British P.G.A. decreed that the entrants in their tournaments would have to play the large-size American ball that year and the next two years. I hope that this trial period will prove to be extremely successful. There's no doubt in my mind that our large ball is the better ball, and I believe it can be played effectively even in stormy British weather.

The time is long overdue for us to make our national professional championship, the P.G.A. Championship, what it should be. Today it stands a poor fourth among the four major championships, hardly worthy of comparison with our Open, the Masters, and the British Open. It should be the proud showcase of American professional golf—as conscious of tradition as the British Open, administered as crisply as our Open, staged as handsomely as the Masters. First and foremost, it must be held on courses of undisputed championship quality. It hasn't been. In my time we have played it at Aronomink (near Philadelphia), the Dallas Athletic Club Country Club, the Columbus (Ohio) Country Club, Laurel Valley (near Pittsburgh), the Firestone Country Club, Columbine (in Denver), and Pecan Valley (in San Antonio). The members of most of these clubs went all out to make the championship a great event—my, there are a lot of nice, hard-working people in golf!—but there was just so much they could do. None of the courses was without merit, and some were very good, but we should not be satisfied with anything less than the finest courses, such as Oakmont, the Los Angeles Country Club, Merion, Seminole, Baltusrol, Olympic, Pinehurst No. 2, and Medinah, to list just a few. I am sure we can get these courses if we really want to. (The selection of the National Cash Register Course in Dayton, Ohio, for the 1969 championship is certainly a step in the right direction.) For another thing, I think we've been holding the championship at the wrong time. Most years it has come so close on the heels of the British Open that it doesn't give the players who have made the trip to Britain time to get reacclimated. The logical time to hold the championship is in late August or early September, at the conclusion of the important summer tournaments. Then it would serve as a natural climax to the season. One thing more. We should go all out to set new standards of television reportage at the championship. For example, the flight of the ball on drives and approaches should be covered by the cameras. Golf is not just a putting contest, though it is made to seem so in most telecasts today when the action is switched from this green to that green with confusing rapidity.

When you read this, several of the criticisms and suggestions I have noted may have been acted upon, for I am writing this at a time when the administration of professional golf in this country is in the throes of important changes. The golfers who regularly play on the tour have voted to leave the Professional Golfers Association and to establish our own organization—the American Professional Golfers—to conduct the tour tournaments and to handle all contingent matters in the future. As is fairly common knowledge, we, the touring professionals, have been far from happy with the way the tour has been operated—to say the very least. For many years the Tournament Committee, which ran the tour, was set up so that the representatives of the touring players were outnumbered four to three by the members of the P.G.A. Executive Committee who sat on the Tournament Committee. In 1967, after numerous attempts by the players to rectify this, we were able to gain a modification in the composition of that committee: it would, henceforth, be made up of four player representatives and four members of the P.G.A. Executive Committee; in the event of a four–four deadlock, the matter under consideration would be turned over to an advisory panel of men close to golf, and its decision would be final. Although this was an improvement, it did not cure the basic ills rooted in the conflicting philosophies of the P.G.A. and the tournament players. You see, we think of the tour as an enterprise quite separate from the P.G.A. That organization is composed predominantly of golf professionals, club pros, as distinct from professional golfers, tournament players. In round figures, there are at the present time some 5800 club pros in the United States and about 300 year-round tournament players. Just as we wouldn't presume to tell the P.G.A. how to run its affairs, we think we should have the authority to run ours.

Although the P.G.A. had very little to do with founding the tournament tour and developing it, the tournament players would have been happy to have remained within the framework of the P.G.A. if we were recognized as a separate section and were granted administrative autonomy. These things we needed, for (1) we feel that the P.G.A. does not understand the problems of modern tournament golf, and (2) the many attempts to adjust our differences all resulted in failure. That is why the break finally came in mid-August of 1968. It produced a fresh series of misunderstandings, a succession of countermoves by the P.G.A., a flurry of personal attacks, and a number of proposals by individuals and groups (such as the International Golf Sponsors Association) aimed at healing the breach. At the moment none of these proposals has been acceptable to both parties. I don't know how it will all come out, although I have been, as it happens, closely involved in the situation, first, as one of the four player representatives on the Tournament Committee and then, after the split, as vice-president of the American Professional Golfers. I do not believe that this is the time or the place to discuss point by point the changes that we, the players, think must be instituted, but I would sum up my position this way:

There is no question at all in my mind that the tour can best prosper and develop as it should only if the men who really understand its problems have the power to direct and govern it.

My golf year starts in January when I go out to California for the Crosby. I always like to play in that event, partly because of my admiration for Pebble Beach and Cypress Point, partly because I am very fond of Bing and enjoy the people who gather for the clambake, and partly because I've had a good long rest by that time and need to get back to golf. After the Crosby I usually play one or two other West Coast tournaments. I return to Florida then and wait until the tour hits that state before rejoining it. From that point on, my entire schedule revolves around the four major championships. I regard the tour tournaments I play in March as the start of my preparation for the Masters, which is held the first full week in April. Similarly, I approach the tournaments I play late in the spring as the start of my preparation for the Open, which is held in mid-June. Next comes the British Open, during the first or second week in July. I like to get to the site of that championship a full week before the bell rings, for adjusting to the small ball and the different playing conditions takes a while. Then, the P.G.A. Championship. After that, even if you're tired and overgolfed, you simply can't afford to pass up the late summer tournaments because of the tremendous prize money that's at stake. Appropriately, they are held on much better courses than we generally get to play. Autumn has its own pace. Some years I've entered the Pacific Coast tournaments that close out the schedule, but most years autumn means traveling abroad for the World Match-Play Championship or the Australian Open or the World Cup (if I've been selected). Autumn is also the time when most television golf shows are filmed for winter showing, and this can mean more foreign travel. By late November, when I finally get home, I've been playing competitive golf for six months without a break, and I can't wait to get away from the game. I sleep late, I get reacquainted with my family, I put away my spikes and get out my sneakers, and I do a little fishing. A few days before Christmas, Barb and I and the kids go up to Columbus to spend the holiday with the rest of the tribe. Then, gradually, I have to rouse myself to get ready for the Crosby and another tournament season.

Most years, between tournaments, I sandwich in about fifteen exhibitions, regular meetings with manufacturers whose products I am

At home in Columbus with a couple of tigers, Jackie (swinging) and Stevie.

connected with, and some consultant work in the golf architectural projects that Pete Dye is engaged in. (I chose to work with Pete, I might add, because he tries to make it a rule never to be involved in more than three courses simultaneously. He believes that the architect must be present during the building of a course and personally direct his crew in shaping the greens, the hazards, and the rest. This is the way I feel that you must go about constructing a golf course.) All this adds up to a full schedule, and to make things as easy as possible for myself, in 1967 I turned in my Aero Commander and leased a Lear (Model 24) twin-engine jet which has a cruising speed of 550 miles an hour and a range of 1500 miles. Stan Pierce, my old pilot, flies the Lear now, and despite Stan's startling lack of tact in assessing my golf, I'd be lost without him. I also have another pilot, Rex French, supplied by Gates Aviation, from whom I lease the plane.

Except for the Masters, our Open, and the British Open, where I like to get to the course early, I follow a more or less set procedure at tournaments. When the event is being held on a course I know, I ordinarily arrive in time to play in the pro-am on Wednesday, the day before the tournament starts. This serves as a practice round for me; it gives me a chance to learn how the course is playing and also how I'm playing. On my trips I carry along a portable card file of the tournament courses—a separate card for every course. On each card I have noted, hole by hole, the distance to the green from various points on the fairway, and on my practice round I check these distances and other pertinent data. If the course is a new one for me, then I'll arrive on the Tuesday so that I can play that day and chart the eighteen holes. Oh, yes—when there's a tournament in Las Vegas, I also try to check in on Tuesday, so that I can get in a day of bass fishing at Lake Mead.

All of us on the tour learn to adopt rather fixed daily schedules during a tournament. For myself, I like to arrive at the course an hour and a quarter or an hour and a half before I'm due to tee off. That means I'll get up about three hours before my starting time— if I have an early starting time, that is. (If I have a fairly late one, then things can be looser.) I eat a good-sized breakfast: juice or melon, eggs with bacon, toast, and a glass of milk. I can't drink coffee or tea in concentrated form, because it keys me up too much. Iced tea, which is diluted, suits me fine, and I probably drink more iced tea and Coke than any other beverages.

As a rule I spend about a half hour warming up on the practice tee. I follow an almost unvarying system here. I begin by hitting seven or eight shots with the pitching wedge. Then I hit about the same number of shots with the 8-iron. I move on to the 5-iron, the 2-iron, and the driver, in that order, hitting about four or five shots with each of them. If I'm not satisfied with the way I'm driving the ball, I'll work longer with that club. Sometimes the layout we're playing will call for a 3-wood off some tees or some fairways, and in these cases I'll also bang out a few 3-woods. After my tune-up on the practice tee is finished, I go to the practice green and spend about ten minutes there, concentrating mainly on getting my timing right and on trying to pick up the speed of the greens. I make it a point to be on the first tee at least five minutes before I'm due off. When I was thirteen and was playing in my first U.S.G.A. Juniors, at Southern Hills, Stanley Ziobrowski and I were scheduled to be the first pair off. I sauntered over to the first tee thirty seconds before our starting time and was informed by the starter, Colonel Lee S. Reid, that he had just called my name for the third time. He told me that I should have been present on the tee after the first call and that he would be watching to see that I was in the future. His friendly but serious lecture evidently sank in, for I have never since been late in getting to the first tee.

During the hour and more you spend at the course before beginning your round, there are quite a few interruptions, naturally, as you go about your preparations. Golf fans love to talk with the players, and if my warm-up has gone well, I enjoy chatting with them. Knowing I'm a Ohioan, a lot of people give me buckeye nuts for good luck. (The buckeye is the state tree of Ohio, and the nut, a shiny brown, is very pretty.) Then, too, there's always a little conversation with my colleagues on the practice tee and the practice green. I get a kick out of hearing Dan Sikes air his latest gripes. I enjoy bantering with Phil Rodgers—he loves to be irreverent— and just plain talking with Deane Beman and Tony Jacklin. Dave Ragan and I are good friends, so I'll look for him. I'll also look for Gay Brewer. He's got an exceptionally good sense of humor, and you can always count on him for a couple of laughs. Jackie Cupit and Bobby Nichols can be very amusing, too, and, of course, there's always Chi Chi. I'll watch him slap out a couple of long, hard-hit drives, and he'll turn around and say, with a straight face, "Jack, I don't know how thee ball can take eet!" If Arnold or Gary is around, we always visit with each other. We've spent a lot of time together over the years, and we've grown to have a great deal in common.

When I'm marking time on the first tee I check my golf bag to make sure I've got everything I want. I want fourteen clubs and no more. I want some tees and a dozen of those zingy MacGregor DX Tourney balls that go so far for you. I carry an umbrella and, in the large compartment of my bag, a rain jacket and rain trousers and a rain hat. Also in the large compartment: a sweater, a turtleneck dickey for cold weather, a towel, spare golf gloves, a package of Band-Aids, the U.S.G.A. rulebook, the rules sheet for that week's tournament, and a metal ball-ring. (If a ball can slip through the ring, I know it's not regulation size.) On trips to tournaments I customarily bring along an extra driver and an extra putter. I keep them in my locker, but one good reason for counting my clubs before a round is to double-check that the extras haven't gotten into my bag by mistake.

During all the rounds I play in the big championships, and in many other tournaments, two excellent writers from the Columbus papers walk every hole with me. One is Paul Hornung, the sports editor and columnist of the *Dispatch,* the afternoon paper, and the other is Kaye Kessler, the star sportswriter of the *Citizen-Journal,* the morning paper. Although Paul is not a golfer—Big Ten football is his specialty—he knows golf very well. He is an extremely kind and understanding man who I feel has a genuine interest in me, and I count him among my closest friends. The same applies to Kaye Kessler. Kaye, who is a darn good golfer, is a first-rate analyst. He not only perceives with accuracy how well or how poorly I may be playing that day, but also has a pretty shrewd idea of the reasons why. It does me a lot of good to have these two pleasant gentlemen at my side. At a number of events they are joined by Bill Foley, a photographer on the *Dispatch.* There's never been a nicer guy than Bill. He has known me ever since I was a kid. As a matter of fact, I think Bill was at Scioto the first day I started golf: he was out to take a group picture of Jack Grout's Friday morning class. Before he became a photographer, Bill was a golf professional, and when he makes an observation, I pay attention. Not many fellows in sports are as lucky as I am when it comes to the quality of the hometown fellows who cover them.

During a round in a regular tour tournament, I may talk a bit more to my playing partners than I do in a major championship, but, at the same time, I try to bear down all through the round. That's the only way I know how to play golf. Besides, each year the number of competent golfers on the tour increases. Some of the younger ones still suffer from inconsistency—one week they play up a storm, the next they slide off—but this means that every week a fair proportion of them will be in contention. Consequently, unless you stick to business, you may not even make the 36-hole cut. That's a distinct possibility these days, for everyone. In a tour event, I try to make intelligent use of the advantage my length gives me, just as I do in the championships, but good driving and not long driving is what a low-scoring round is built on. Then, too, I'm not in a class by myself when it comes to big hitting. Today there is quite a group of powerful young men on the tour who can stay with me and some days hit it past me. In my opinion, Tom Weiskopf, who came so fast last year, is the best swinger and the best striker in this group. Tom can play both ways, left-to-right and right-to-left. Paul Bondeson and Ray Floyd can also hit the ball a mile. They can also both fade and draw it. The player with the most golf knowledge in this group is Terry Dill. He should be; he learned about the golf swing from Harvey Penick, one of the game's great teachers. Terry hits exceptionally long irons. This is true as well of Rod Funseth, who, as everyone knows, can also move those woods. Pete Brown is another powerhouse. I don't think anyone pulverizes a 3-wood the way he does. Funseth and Brown play the ball from right to left. And then there's Marty Fleckman—a really fine striker—and Bob Lunn, who plays so well under pressure. If I have a suggestion to make to the young sluggers coming up through the ranks—I'm not referring to the men named above—I would tell them to devote more time to their irons. As a general rule, they haven't developed their iron game to the same degree as they have their woods, and this delays their achieving consistency.

It is a common practice now for a golfer who has played a low round or a round that has kept him among the tournament leaders to be escorted to the press tent, when he comes off the eighteenth, for a mass interview over the P.A. system. There must be an awful lot of ham in me, because I love to go down to the press tent for these sessions. In fact, I'm supposed to have exclaimed after finishing a so-so round in the 1965 P.G.A. Championship, "Boy, I'm glad I got that last birdie! For a minute I was afraid I wouldn't

Pressure in the press tent: "Let me see, I think I hit a 7-iron there."

make the tent!" There are two reasons for the pleasure I find in these mass interviews: first, they help me to unwind from the tension that accumulates during a tournament round; second, I simply enjoy talking golf with a lively, interested audience, and the press fellows are that. In Britain they have adopted this mass-interview practice now, and, let me tell you, it puts you on your mettle when you have to answer some delicately phrased question like, "I wonder if you would care to explain—and I daresay you might find this trivial—why it was that, when the wind began to puff up so mischievously on the tenth, you hesitated such a frightfully long time before hitting your recovery stroke from that patch of bracken?" In a spot like that you just can't answer, "Jeez, was that bracken?" or even, "Well, I didn't know if I had enough club." You've got to talk the language, old boy. "My delay was caused," you hear yourself saying, "by my uncertainty as to whether or not a 5-iron, which was my initial choice, would suffice under the altered circumstances." Barbara made her first visit to a British press tent one afternoon at Muirfield when I had a really terrific day at the microphone. When I went up to her afterward to see what she had thought of my performance, she was wearing an expression that is best translated as "Well, I never!"

After a round is over and you've finished talking with the press and taping interviews with the radio and TV fellows, you're free to return to the practice tee and get in some hard work. It's a rare day when I don't practice after a round, because it's a rare day when something or other hasn't gone wrong during my round. Late in the afternoon you can count on having a fair amount of company on the practice tee. The atmosphere is both chatty and experimental. You try out new moves in your swing, you try out new clubs, you watch what the other fellows are working on. You may make some comment to one of your friends about his swing, if he asks you, and you may hit a couple of shots with somebody else's clubs, or vice versa. One afternoon in 1967, for illustration, Gay Brewer picked up the extra driver I was carrying—the one I'd used in the 1966 Masters—and began banging out some shots with it. Gay was having trouble off the tee at that time, and he really liked the way he was meeting the ball with that driver of mine. I didn't have any need for it just then, so I told Gay he could have it. In a couple of weeks, if I hadn't known that Gay's new driver was my old one, I wouldn't have recognized it. He'd added some weight to the head, put a couple of plugs in the end of the shaft to lengthen it, and had stuck a new rubber grip on it. He used it for a while and then passed it on to Chi Chi. What Chi Chi did to it I have no idea—I lost track of it then. As you can gather, it's a good rule to hold onto any club you might want to use later yourself. You give a guy a club that looks like Brigitte Bardot and, by the time he's finished making his changes, it looks like something out of a horror movie.

During a tournament I take it pretty easy in the evenings. After dinner I'll watch a few TV shows and get to bed by eleven or eleven-thirty. Occasionally I play some bridge in the evening. Harold Henning, I'd say, is probably the most advanced bridge player among the pros. I play with him now and then, but most of the time I play with Deane Beman or with Arnold. Palmer's bridge is basically like his golf: he goes for everything. Sometimes he'll play a hand very well and make what had seemed like a foolhardy bid, and other times he'll go down for a ton. One night during the second World Series of Golf, I think it was, Arnold and Charles Goren, the world-famous bridge authority, played a couple

368

of rubbers against me and Forrest Evashevski, now the athletic director at Iowa. I was quite relaxed during this session because I'd just gotten through an ordeal: Howard Schenken, a leading tournament bridge player, and I had just played Evvy and another Goren teacher—with Goren himself leaning over my shoulder. I learned then how an 18-handicap golfer must feel when he tees off in a pro-am: I was scared to death to make a bid or pull a card. Anyhow, when Evvy and I later played as partners against Goren and Palmer, I felt under much less pressure. There were two hands I remember. In the first we set Arn, who had bid with his usual abandon, six something or other. In the second, we set him one. In that hand, as I remember it, I made a brilliant discard on the next-to-last trick which enabled me to take the important last trick with a nine of spades to Arnold's eight. When Goren wrote up that hand in his column in *Sports Illustrated*, it came out a little different. As he described it, Arnold successfully made his bid by playing the hand like a master. Knowing I had to be holding the eight of spades, *he* made the great discard and *he* won the crucial last trick with a nine of spades. Arnold thought the article was a lot better than I did.

Like everyone who travels the tour, I have my favorite tournaments and my favorite cities. Most of the time, the explanation is that I have good friends at those stops. One reason why I enjoy playing the Memphis Open, for example, is that I stay with Curtis Person, Jr., and his wife Peggy Joyce that week. On the West Coast I make sure I see Buck Laird, a fraternity brother from O.S.U., and his wife Vonda. In Chicago I arrange to spend at least one evening with Fred and Sally Blesi; I went to high school with Sally and to college with Fred, a very good golfer. In Cleveland I look up Barbara's brother Ray and his wife Marilyn. I always have a wonderful time in New Orleans. My close friends there are Gavic and Susie Schoen, Jack and Louise Weiss, and Gene and Dessa Rutter. The Rutters always have a great crayfish spread. Not that I am trying to set myself up as sort of a spiked-shoe Duncan Hines, but I'd say that New Orleans is the best town for eating—a strikingly unoriginal statement, I appreciate. I love the oysters, crab, and shrimp, and, for my taste, the food at Manale's is the best I've ever come across. By the way, as far as hotels go, for me the Century Plaza in L.A. is in a class for itself. Another place I always look forward to visiting is Las Vegas, and Barbara does, too. If she misses the Tournament of Champions, she comes out for the Sahara—usually with our Florida friends, Jack and Grace Leggett.

Then there are two tournament stops in Texas I always enjoy, the Colonial in Fort Worth and the Champions in Houston. No one works harder to give their tournament distinction than the members of Colonial, and, to be sure, Ben Hogan's identification with Colonial gives that event a special aura. The Champions is held at the Champions Golf Club, which was started about ten years ago, on a very modest scale, by two Houston boys, Jimmy Demaret and Jackie Burke. They have developed the club magnificently. Today they have two 18-hole courses—the Cypress Creek Course (which we play) and the Jack Rabbit—that are routed through a handsome forest of hickory, pecan, oak, and pine. The club's real estate operation has flourished, and many lovely homes now border the fairways. The club has also developed a colony of some forty-odd brick cottages which individual members own. (Don Cherry bought the first.) Jimmy and Jackie have had exceedingly capable assistance along the way—for instance, from Howard Daugherty, who is the club manager and quite a bit more—but they deserve a great deal of credit for the financial astuteness and the excellent taste they have demonstrated in guiding their baby from a wobbly little club too far out of town into one of the most attractive golf communities in the country. It is difficult to know if other pros have the special abilities and the local position to achieve what Jimmy and Jackie have, but the Champions shows what can be done.

Speaking of tournaments I enjoy, I must not overlook the British Open. The flavor of the British Open varies with the particular course you're playing, as it does in our Open. At the same time, wherever the British Open is held, be it St. Andrews or Hoylake, Muirfield or Lytham, Carnoustie or Birkdale, its basic atmosphere remains intact. Golfers come to play in it from most of the European countries and from the far corners of the world. Golf fans from all over (such as Gary's good friends from Johannesburg, George and Brenda Blumberg) annually plan months in advance to be on hand. Accordingly, the British Open stands as the golfing equivalent of that other great international assembly, Wimbledon. When you are a foreign golfer and have played in the Open over a period of years, the galleries, though less vocal than ours, definitely let you know how glad they are to see you and how much they appreciate your coming over for the event. They respect their

370

championship deeply, and they are extremely warm and hospitable toward old campaigners, like Roberto de Vicenzo, who return year after year because they, too, respect the championship. That is the reason why Roberto's victory at Hoylake in 1967 was such a tremendously popular one.

Because Britain is relatively small in size as countries go, the British golf world is much more closely knit than ours. Year after year you meet the same people at the Open—the same R. & A. officials, the same clubhouse and hotel "characters," the same gentlemen of the press—and pleasant relationships grow into friendships. For example, I now feel completely at home with the British golf writers, almost as if they all came from Ohio. They're a very interesting and enjoyable group: Leonard Crawley (with his ginger moustache and his well-worn Walker Cup blazer), Henry Longhurst (who also handles the television commentary with great skill), Pat Ward-Thomas of the *Guardian* (a most entertaining man who writes beautifully), Peter Ryde of the *Times* (who has filled Bernard Darwin's shoes just about as well as anyone could), Bob Ferrier (a very congenial fellow and a very knowledgeable writer), Ron Heager of the *Express* (surely one of the most courteous journalists in the world), and many, many others—Mark Wilson, Peter Dobereiner, Willie Allison, Fred Tupper, Frank Moran, John Stobbs, Norman Mair, Jack Wood, Paul Mac Weeney, Donald Steele, Tom Scott, John Farrow, Raymond Jacobs, Ben Wright, Tom Reedy, Percy Huggins, John Ingham, Ken Bowden, Maurice Hart, Michael McDonnell, Charles Scatchard, and John Ballantine. George Simms handles the press setup for the R. & A. Without exception, they give one the impression that they honestly love their work.

As I remarked earlier, from a commercial standpoint this is the golden age for a professional golfer. No other athletes have the opportunity to do as well as we do, especially when you take into account the subsidiary gravy that comes our way. Since I have gone into the other aspects of the current golf scene in some detail, I think you might find it interesting if I touched briefly on my present business affiliations. First, I play MacGregor clubs and balls. I have been under contract to MacGregor since turning professional. Indeed, I used MacGregor equipment as an amateur. The three men I have worked most closely with are Leon Nelson, Bob Rickey, and Bob Lysaught, and they are wonderful associates. In

371

foreign tournaments, as I have mentioned, I play Slazenger clubs and balls. Under a deal that Mark McCormack arranged, golf balls bearing my name are merchandized at Firestone outlets—three balls for $1.33. This has been a most successful venture. As regards golf shoes, I endorse a line made by the Plymouth Shoe Company. The ones I wear are kangaroo leather and Corfam, with anodized gold spikes. (If you want to pivot properly, you've got to have anodized gold spikes.) In the clothes department, my principal affiliation is with Hart, Schaffner, and Marx, who sell Jack Nicklaus slacks and sports jackets. I also have tie-ins with Hathaway-Peerless shirts and sweaters, Robert Lewis rain jackets, Spatz young men's and boys' jackets, Stern, Merritt ties, Host pajamas and robes, Kramer Brothers hosiery, and Hat Corporation headgear. (In Japan a company called Asahi-Kasei put out men's wear that bears my name—something like Nickirasu.) In a different realm of operation, I do a series of golfing tips and occasional articles for *Sports Illustrated*. We began our relationship back in 1962, and it has been an enormously happy and satisfying one for me. The Hall Syndicate handles an illustrated instruction feature I prepare which appears in over a hundred newspapers around the world. I have two fine new contracts with Eastern Airlines and Pontiac. I play some customer golf for the United States Banknote Corporation, I have a promotional arrangement with the Mauna Kea golf resort, I reach for a Coca-Cola when I'm thirsty, and—let me see—I think that's about it. I am not in the laundry business, but I do endorse lawn mowers through Murray-Ohio.

As goes without saying, when you're a young athlete and things are going your way, you must bear in mind that these good times will not last forever. Like most of my colleagues, I spend considerable time studying the investments I've made or may be making. I want to continue to play competitive golf as long as I can play first-class golf and as long as I enjoy playing tournaments, but the day will come, inevitably, when I'll be on the sidelines, and it will be most important then to have set things up so that my boys will have sound businesses they can step into, if that is what they want to do.

In this connection, I was thinking the other day that my son Stevie, the five-year-old, will probably be able to use a strong helping hand. To give you an idea of what I mean, last winter, when our daughter Nan was christened, the minister gave Jackie, the seven-year-old, the bowl of water to hold and gave Stevie the napkin—the better to keep them quiet and attentive during the cere- mony. When it was over, Barbara said to Stevie, "I bet you enjoyed helping out, didn't you?"

"No," Stevie answered. "I only got to hold the rag. Jackie got to hold the trophy." Then he turned to Barbara's folks. "That man doesn't know how to use a trophy," he continued, pointing to the minister. "He put water in it. My daddy never puts water in his trophies."

XXIV

Adding It Up

QUITE EARLY IN THIS BOOK, when I was discussing the great
pleasure I got in playing the last two rounds of the 1960
U.S. Open with Ben Hogan, I mentioned that during that tournament I had a wonderful feeling whenever I set up to play a shot:
my right knee seemed right under me, so to speak, and I could pivot
very easily on the backswing and move into a strong hitting position
on the downswing with equal ease. I also mentioned that countless
times afterward I tried to recapture that particular feeling before
the ball and was never able to. In a later chapter, when I was recalling the second World Amateur Team Championship (for the
Eisenhower Trophy), which we played at Merion in 1960, I remarked that my hands felt absolutely marvelous on the club that
week: my left wrist formed an almost straight line with the back
of my left hand. Having the sense that I was perfectly aligned on my
target, I stopped thinking about how I was executing my swing
and devoted all my attention to playing each shot as well as I could.
No wonder I had such a fine tournament! Naturally, I tried to establish that same ideal coupling of the left wrist and hand on many
subsequent occasions, hoping to rediscover the sense of correctness,
comfort, and confidence I had at Merion, but I never managed to.
I bring up these two incidents—it would be no trouble to add a
dozen more—because they serve to point up the recurring problem
I've had holding onto a position, a move, or just a feeling which
worked wonders for me and which I wanted to make a permanent
part of my game.

There are, thank goodness, some phases of golf technique that
a man can master (change to *almost master*) through hours and
hours of repeating a certain action. However, looking back, I would
guess that one of the principal themes of this book would be how
elusive golf is even for those of us who have made the game our

profession. I remember, for example, reading how Henry Cotton, after a putting session in which he had holed everything in sight, tacked some brown paper around the grip of his putter and had a friend trace with a pencil the exact position of his hands. The idea behind this, of course, was that Cotton was hoping that if he placed his fingers in precisely the same position the next time he went out, he might perhaps be able to summon up again the same astonishingly effective stroke and touch. The following day he tried it out. With the brown paper still tacked around the grip of the putter, he carefully positioned each finger where the guide lines indicated. And what happened? It didn't feel the same at all. The stroke he had wanted to re-create had entirely vanished.

When I was an amateur, I had the notion that if I did turn professional I would play a great deal better. I used to think that my erratic stretches resulted from having other commitments that kept me away from competitive golf for months at a time. I thought that if I turned professional and was able to play or practice every day, I would never lose my groove—I would be able to check things out so regularly then that I would detect any faulty move before it had time to catch hold and become a habit. Well, part of my education has been learning what a starry-eyed vision that was. I've found it just about impossible to avoid picking up bad habits, and it's no easy matter to break them once they set in. I think most pros would subscribe to this.

Sometimes you have an excuse for losing your groove. I think I did when I lost my left-to-right action in 1963. Because of the bursitis I had in my left hip, I couldn't move that hip out of the way as fast as you must to play left-to-right. In fact, right-to-left was the only way I could play for a while without hurting myself. In 1967, when I once more fell into a bad right-to-left pattern, I couldn't be too critical of myself again, for I had been forced to adopt that style of play after straining my back in the Crosby. Okay. But physical miseries had nothing to do with that bad putting grip and stroke that Jack Burke had to straighten out for me in 1962; or with that fatal hook off the 72nd tee at Lytham in the 1963 British Open (just one of the many unexplained hooks I hit on the concluding holes in a number of tournaments when I hadn't hooked a single shot up to that point); or with the tension trouble in my right arm and shoulder that affected my swing in the winter and spring of 1964 (which I cured, at length, by altering my right-hand grip);

375

or the spell of hooking I fell into in 1965 (which Jack Grout got me out of by getting me to raise my hands higher on the backswing —I had thought they were high all along); or that unconscious closing of my hips and shoulders the second before I moved into my backswing (which Deane, that invaluable doctor, caught just before the 1965 Masters); or that awful addiction to playing too slowly which grew worse and worse until, in 1966, I couldn't speed up no matter how hard I tried; or the several occasions when, all of a sudden, I would find my confidence quivering when I hadn't done anything that should have shook me that much (for example, my jitters at Muirfield in the 1966 British Open); or losing not only my putting touch but my whole conception of putting so completely in 1967 that 37 putts a round were about par for me. These are just a few of the problems I have encountered, and mentioned earlier, but there have been many, many others.

Golf, I have been forced to conclude, is a game of constant adjustment. Sure, at the back of your mind you continue to seek perfection, and, now and then, the law of averages will be on your side and you will produce an almost uninterrupted sequence of practically perfect swings and practically perfect shots. However, the wise golfer learns to accept his limitations. This doesn't mean that you should just sit back and play the role of the happy little philosopher after you've blown a tournament by pull-hooking into unmapped territory a couple of drives you meant to fade. Quite the reverse. You must stay in there and keep working. On each round you must work as hard as you can. It's like the story someone told me about Bach. Each Sunday he had to have a new oratorio ready for the church where he was the organist, so each morning he got up and went to work on that week's composition. Some days the best he could produce wasn't anything special, but other days it was some of the greatest music ever written. You must approach golf in a similar way. If you keep working at it on every round, some days, sooner or later, you will play some genuinely first-class golf, and occasionally you will even surpass your own talent.

Since I have been stressing how hard it is to avoid falling into bad moves, I think it might be helpful to bring out that a golfer can play very respectable golf without possessing the inhuman regularity of a machine. To say it another way, there are certain components of the swing that can be performed somewhat differently each time without this substantially affecting the quality of your shotmaking. An interesting illustration that comes to mind concerns Harry Vardon. Around the turn of the century when Vardon was in his heyday, he was so much straighter off the tee than any other golfer of that era that a group of golf scholars decided that some tests should be made with Vardon from which they might be able to deduce, in a semi-scientific fashion, the secrets of his accuracy. One of the experiments they set up was for Vardon to hit a series of drives from a dirt tee: on each drive, they charted the position of Vardon's feet in relation to the ball, and then, after he had driven, they erased his footprints so that there would be nothing to guide him when he stepped onto the tee again and addressed the next ball. Vardon hit about two dozen drives and split the fairway with every one of them. And what did the scholars find when they studied the charts they'd made? They found out that Vardon's stance had varied slightly each time. On one drive his left foot was angled a shade more open; on another, the distance between his heels was wider; on another, the right toe was nearer the ball than usual; and so on. Their conclusion, necessarily, was that the variations in Vardon's stance didn't seem to have any effect on how he hit the ball.

In general terms, the same thing is true of *some* other aspects of the golf swing: you can vary your execution of certain moves and continue to play well, providing you are blessed with the athlete's instinctive coordination of hand and eye—and providing that the basic components of your swing remain sound. Those basic components, of course, are what the best golf minds have arrived at as the true fundamentals. While a golfer now and then can get away with a shot, or even with a series of shots, on which some fundamental is faulty, he won't be able to get away with it for long. This is why nearly all top-flight golfers, when they fall into a really bad swing pattern, retreat to the practice tee, return to the fundamentals, and start to reconstruct their swing from the ground up.

One of the difficulties every golfer faces is the impossibility of knowing when some mannerism or habit of his that usually has no real bearing on his swing—such as Vardon's minute changes in his stance—will, for some reason or another, start to affect the correct execution of the fundamentals. Since a golfer can't see himself in action and check what he's doing, he must depend a great deal on feel. This is not a simple matter. I know my swing feels different

377

from week to week. At each tournament some segment of my swing is sticking out more that week than it generally does. Consequently, I find myself fastening on some little gimmick that will help me either to feel right or to swing right for the duration of that tournament. It might be raising my right shoulder a little higher at address (because that helps me to feel more relaxed and facilitates a freer turn), or it might be slowing down the push off my right foot at the start of the downswing (because that seems to help my balance in the hitting area). The next week it will be something else. When I mention to friends that I am forced to rely on this succession of gimmicks, I can sense that a number of them are let down to learn this. They would much rather hear that a professional golfer has everything securely under control, that each year he gains an increased mastery of his technique. All I can say is that I wish this were so.

One of the reasons why I may have been led to underline the will-o'-the-wisp nature of the game of golf is that I am writing this final chapter at the conclusion of a somewhat disappointing year in which I was reminded of it all too often. Things did not go exactly as I hoped they would in 1968. At the start of the season I set myself two goals: (1) to improve my driving; (2) to win one of the major championships. However, a number of problems I hadn't anticipated popped up, and due to one thing or another, my golf was an in-and-out proposition and I didn't win a tournament during the first seven months. In August I finally began to put it all together, as the saying goes, and played four strong tournaments in a row, winning the first two, the Western and the American Golf Classic. (In the autumn I won my second Australian Open.) Since those summer tournaments are rich ones, my share of the purses enabled me to exceed $100,000 in official prize-money for the sixth straight year and to move close to the top of the list of the leading money-winners. Because of this late rush, I know that many people thought that 1968 was a very good year for me. I don't think it was, despite the fact that I prospered financially. Making money is important, but it isn't all there is to golf.

When I set out to improve my driving at the start of the year, what I had in mind was to gain more control of the left-to-right method, my regular method. The previous season I had made life hard for myself by missing too many fairways. Reluctantly, I had had to agree with both friends and critics who pointed out that they

How to break a 5-iron. This happened in the 1968 Australian P.G.A.

were most aware of the advantages my power gave me not when they watched me drive but when they watched me dig a recovery out of thick rough. I can't tell you how many hours I spent working on the moves that would give me a safe, gentle fade I could depend on, but, in any event, I never did get it. In competition, as a general rule, I would play a series of drives in which the ball moved from left to right the way I wanted it to, but for reasons I was never able to put my finger on, a good part of the time, instead of getting a fade, I'd get a big, wide push—a right-to-right shot, you might call it. Worst of all, every so often I'd snap the ball far to the left in a low, diving hook. Jack Grout, the one man who could have helped me, was unavailable at this time, for he was seriously ill and eventually had to be operated on. (In midsummer, when he had recovered completely, we got together at the P.G.A. Championship and talked things over then. That was the best part of the tournament for me.)

For all this, I finally did succeed in improving my driving. This came about late in the Spring when I switched to a new driver with a slightly softer shaft. Theoretically, a soft shaft is wrong for a golfer like myself who swings hard at the ball. In actuality, it worked out because it forced me to keep my swing slow so that I wouldn't overpower the shaft. In a short while, I was timing the shaft very well and driving very well. While I couldn't get my old left-to-right flight back—the ball had a tendency to fall in a little from left to right, but that was all—I discovered that I could hit the ball straight with the new club. I changed my style: I began to aim down the middle consistently. In the U.S. Open and the British Open, I couldn't have asked for better driving. (At the British, by the way, I learned from Byron Nelson that he had used the same shaft as my new one—a TTW.)

I stayed with the straight drive the rest of the year, and that's where I am at the moment—playing the ball for the middle of the fairway and, in truth, driving fairly effectively. I am still convinced, nevertheless, that the percentages are on the side of the golfer, be he a fader or drawer, who can aim down one side of the fairway and so have almost the full width of the fairway at his disposal. And feeling this way, I have not altered the remarks I made in the instruction section on the virtues of the left-to-right method.

The goal I failed to achieve in 1968 was that annual goal of mine: to win a major championship. I don't know why it is, but I never fare well in this direction in Olympic or election years.

In 1964, I was shut out in the big ones, and in 1960 I made a poor defense of my U.S. Amateur title. I won't review in close-up detail my unsuccessful bids in the four major championships in 1968, but I would like to tell you something about them. An athlete seldom learns anything in victory, but there is a lot to be learned in defeat.

In retrospect, I believe I lost whatever chance I had of winning the Masters by the sloppiness of my play on five and a half holes—the last five and a half holes on the third round. My first two rounds, a 69 and a 71, had placed me in an excellent position, just a shot behind the leaders, Gary Player and Don January. As you may recall, I'd failed to make the cut in the Masters the year before, so on the first two days making certain I would be around for the last two days was always at the back of my mind. I was primarily concerned with avoiding doing anything stupid. After I had made the cut, however, I meant to attack the course as I normally do. Midway through the third round, after dropping two shots to par, I got it going. I birdied the eighth and ninth, and, following two pars, birdied the twelfth. Throughout the first three days of this Masters, a dozen or so players were all jammed together, fighting for the lead—and tossing it away whenever they got it—but my recollection is that after my birdie on the twelfth had put me five under par for the tournament, only January was in front of me.

On the long thirteenth I reached the green in two to be in position for another birdie, and then came that dazzling stretch of five and a half holes. I three-putted the thirteenth—bye, bye birdie. I pulled my drive off the next tee into a tree and ended up with a bogey 5. On the long fifteenth, a very possible birdie hole, instead of getting a stroke back, I dropped another one. My drive, a short one pushed into the edge of the rough, left me with a rather sticky lie, but I decided, anyhow, to try and carry the pond before the green with my second, a 3-wood. I made a stiff swing and didn't catch all of the ball, and you know the rest: splash! After pars on the next two holes, I bogeyed the eighteenth when I put my tee-shot into the fairway bunker on the left. I had choked down on a 3-wood off the tee and was certain I couldn't reach the bunker, but I guess I wasn't thinking too clearly by that time. On the last day, once the horse was out of the barn, then I was Mr. Concentration, Dr. Precision, and Professor Fight all rolled into one. Ordinarily, since I had started the day only four strokes off the pace, my closing 67 might have done something for me. On this particular Sunday at

Augusta, it was all but irrelevant. This was the day when Roberto de Vicenzo and Bob Goalby waged their great duel, matching each other birdie for birdie (and eagle for eagle) throughout the long afternoon as they converted the Masters into a two-man show. . . . I finished in a tie for fifth, four strokes off Goalby's winning total of 277.

The Open was played at Oak Hill, in Rochester, a rolling, wooded Donald Ross course over which Middlecoff had scored his second victory in the championship in 1956. I finished second, four strokes behind Lee Trevino. Lee played some golf! He put together a 69, a 68, a 69, and another 69 to become the first man in the history of the Open to break 70 on all four rounds, and his total of 275 tied the record I'd set the year before at Baltusrol. Lee's a very talented player, somewhat on the order of Billy Casper in that he keeps the ball beautifully in play off the tee and is fabulous around the greens—a remarkable wedge player and a sure, confident putter.

I left Oak Hill much more downcast than I usually am after an unsuccessful bid in a major event. I was disgusted with myself for throwing away some of the best sustained tee-to-green golf of my life by putting like a timid old lady. Now, I think we are all sick and tired of listening to golfers who blame their failures on their putting. The first implication is that they played their usual marvelous golf up to the greens—the part of golf that tells you who the *real* players are. The second implication is that they would have won in a walk if they had gotten any breaks with their putts—you know, putting is more luck than skill. Let me be slightly different, anyway. Bad luck had nothing to do with my bad putting. I have rarely played truer greens than those at Oak Hill. The simple fact of the matter was that I had been shaky with the putter all year, and the harder I tried to rectify this at Oak Hill, the more pathetic were the results.

As I say, I could have kicked myself, for every tournament golfer lives in the hope that when a big one comes along he will be someplace near the top of his game, and at Oak Hill I was at the very top. On all four rounds I drove extremely well. According to the tabulations of the I.B.M. machine, I hit more greens in regulation than any other player—61 out of 72. I not only hit the greens, I put my approaches much closer to the pins than I had ever done before in the Open or, for that matter, in any championship.

My play on the opening nine proved to be only too accurate an index of my pattern throughout the four days. Five times on the first eight holes my approaches set up very makeable birdie putts—three of them from about 15 feet, two of them from 7 feet. I made none of them. No golfer can afford not to cash in on such opportunities— he won't get them very often. To top things off, I took three putts on the ninth. On the scorecard I had played only average golf, one over par.

For all my continuing ineptness on the greens, at the start of the final round I still had an outside shot at it. I stood at 212 (72-70-70), seven shots behind the leader, Bert Yancey, and six behind Trevino. They were paired together, playing directly behind Charley Coody and me. To get back into a contending position, I would have to mount a big rush and mount it early. On the third, a 208-yard par 3, I hit a 3-iron 25 feet from the stick and actually holed the putt—the first one of any length I'd made in four days. This charged me up, as did the news that both Yancey and Trevino had bogeyed the first. On the fourth, a par 5 of 571 yards, two good woods put me off the front edge; I chipped to four feet and holed for another birdie. Yancey, meanwhile, had bogeyed the third, which meant that I had already picked up four shots on him and three shots on Trevino and now trailed both of them by only three. That was as close as I ever got. Over the next four holes I wasted three fine birdie chances, missing once from 12 feet and twice from 10. Trevino, who was playing with great resolution now and matching par on hole after hole, then made a wonderful counter-rush, and after he had birdied the eleventh and twelfth, he was as good as home. I finished with a 67 despite missing nine putts for birdies of 12 feet or less. The moral of this story is obvious: no golfer can expect to win a championship unless his putting is of championship quality.

There were quite a few similarities between my golf in our Open and in the British Open, which was held at Carnoustie, a long, tough, primitive-looking links which had been scrupulously prepared for the big event and which played very well indeed. To begin with, I again finished second—more accurately, in a tie for second. This time I was two shots behind the winner, Gary Player. (I was nothing if not consistent. Between the two championships I had finished second to Bob Charles in the Canadian Open.) For another thing, my putting at Carnoustie remained well below the

Gary and I, bundled up, begin the final round of the 1968 British Open.

standard of the rest of my game. (I had one encouraging putting round, the second, when I holed six 5-footers; the catch was that all but one of these were saves for pars after overly bold approach putts.) And third, when I was chasing Gary down the stretch, I couldn't produce that extra something you must produce to win golf tournaments.

On the final day Gary and I were paired together, just ahead of the last twosome, Bob Charles and Billy Casper. Casper had taken the lead on the second round with a 68, four under par, and still led after a third round of 74—a stroke ahead of Charles, two ahead of Player, and four ahead of me. It was an overcast and windy day—as what day isn't at Carnoustie—and when Casper slid over par on the second, the fourth, and the fifth, the championship was wide open again. Word travels slowly in a British Open, and although Gary and I were just ahead of Casper, preparing to drive on the long sixth, we had no up-to-date information on the troubles that had befallen him. Anyhow, on the sixth, I hooked my tee-shot over the fence and out-of-bounds, and took a 6. Gary birdied the hole. This vaulted him into the lead, and he held onto it the rest of the way. He made a fairly high number of errors en route, but he holed some big putts and he had the stuff to come up with the big shot at the critical moment.

The last five holes at Carnoustie comprise one of the best and most demanding finishes in golf. When we came to them, Gary led me by two strokes. I had just picked up a stroke on him on the thirteenth, and I had the feeling that with some luck I might pick up the other two, and possibly more. On the fourteenth I drove badly, very close to a stand of trees in the right rough. A par 5, the fourteenth is only 485 yards long, but it is no pushover birdie when the wind is against you, as it was that afternoon. It is called the Spectacles hole because of the two oval bunkers cut close together in the face of a quick rise in the fairway about 60 yards or so from the green. I got a terrific break on that drive. I was just far enough away from the trees to be able to take a full swing, and managed to slash a 3-wood over the Spectacles. It finished in the light rough to the left of the green, about hole-high. This put a lot of pressure on Gary. He was down the middle after a fine drive, but he needed a wood to get home. He took a 4-wood, a club he plays very well, and hit the shot with an exceptionally smooth action. When the ball passed out of sight on the far side of Spectacles, it was heading dead for the flag. It would be on, all right. The only question was how close it would be. An excited cheer went up from the gallery clustered around the green: it had to be stiff. It was —about four feet past the pin. I made my birdie but Gary made his eagle, so with four holes to go, his margin was back to three shots again.

On the fifteenth, a mean par 4 that is 460 yards long, Gary was in trouble off the tee and his recovery wasn't particularly good, but he fought me off by getting down in two from a hundred yards out. However, on the sixteenth I did cut a shot off his lead. Usually I took a 1-iron on this 243-yard 3, hoping to hit the front part of the long, slippery, snugly bunkered green. With the wind directly against us and the pin in the extreme back left-hand corner, I went with the driver. I hit one of the best shots of my life—the ball almost struck the pin as it came down. It finished 20 feet past. Gary was bunkered off the front of the green on his tee-shot, maybe 30 yards short of the flag. For a moment it looked like he was going to salvage another fantastic par, for he put his bunker shot 12 feet from the hole. However, after I missed my bid for my deuce, he missed his putt for his par.

Two strokes down, two holes left. The seventeenth is a 458-yard par 4. The main hazard is the Barry Burn, a ditch about 20 feet wide that twists twice across the fairway, the second time about 270 yards from the tee. I had to go for everything now. I hit my tee-shot just as hard as I could, and helped by the wind, behind us on this hole, my ball carried the far coil of the burn and ran to within 100 yards of the green. Gary played his tee-shot short of the burn, the correct tactical move in his position. His approach, a long iron, stopped a few inches off the front edge of the green, 70 undulating feet from the cup. Now, if I could pop my pitch next to the pin, there was a chance I might be able to get back not only one stroke but possibly two; even a stalwart putter like Gary wouldn't find it easy to get down in two from 70 feet if my ball was up there in birdie range. I took a pitching wedge and played the ball to land 30 feet short of the pin on the hard-surfaced green and to run the rest of the way. The shot didn't come off. The ball pitched where I wanted it to but it sat down after bobbling forward only four or five feet. I'd hit it with too much spin. I was still fretting about this miscalculation when Gary rolled that long, long putt of his to the edge of the cup—an amazing stroke under the circumstances. My try for the birdie grazed the cup. Two 4's.

One more chance—the eighteenth, a 525-yard par 5, into the wind; out-of-bounds all along the left; two coils of the Barry Burn to contend with—the first some 235 yards out from the tee, the second smack in front of the green. I went all out on my drive, necessarily, and swatted a big one down the middle. Gary, coolly playing the percentages, aimed away from the burn, down the seventeenth fairway—the long route but the safe one. His plan was to fly his second across the strip of rough between the seventeenth and eighteenth, dropping the ball on the eighteenth fairway 60 yards, say, short of the burn before the green. A par 5 was all he needed. Here he made a mistake. He came off his second shot, badly. The ball, half-hit, failed to carry the rough and fell in the high grass, just beyond a bunker, a good 140 yards from the pin. I still had a chance to catch him. It would take a super shot—that for sure. From 240 yards out, playing into the wind, I would have to put my ball not only on the green but close enough to give me a putt for an eagle. That would change the picture. The club for me was the 1-iron. I have confidence in my ability to maneuver the ball with that club. I'd have to here. I didn't think I could get

Walking to the 18th at Carnoustie. Still two shots to make up on Gary.

the ball all the way to the pin—it was at the back of the green—
if I played a straight shot. What I'd do, I decided, was to take aim
on the bunker to the right of the green and draw the ball. That
would give it the additional run it would need to get up to the pin.
I didn't bring it off. The draw didn't take. I must have hurried the
shot a fraction. In any case, the ball flew straight for the bunker
and carried into it. Thirty seconds later the championship was over:
Gary came through with a champion's shot. Playing an 8-iron,
he made clean contact with the ball and it came rising out of the
tall grass in a perfect parabola—you knew it was going to be good
the instant you saw it start. It landed near the center of the long
green and rolled to within 25 feet of the flag. He had won his
second British Open.

The next week I was in San Antonio, at the Pecan Valley Club,
for the fourth and last of the major championships, the P.G.A. I
was all concentrated out. I began with a 71 but after a 79 on the
second round, I missed the cut by a stroke.

There was a good deal to think about when I went home after
my quick exit from the P.G.A. Some nine months had elapsed since

387

my last victory in a tournament—the Sahara Open the previous autumn. This was the longest drought I'd ever experienced. As I saw it, there had been six tournaments in 1968 in which I'd had a reasonable shot at a win or a tie: the Crosby, the Florida Citrus, the Houston Champions, the U.S. Open, the Canadian Open, and the British Open. What were the reasons why I hadn't won any of them? A good many came to mind. Wildness off the tee early in the year—that had been injurious. In the Florida Citrus, Dan Sikes had gone into the lead on the last round when I hooked my drive off the 68th into a water hazard. At Houston, I had found the woods with a pull on the 68th, then with a push on the 69th. (At Carnoustie, the drive I hooked out-of-bounds on the 60th hole hadn't cost me the championship—I had a lot of holes left in which to do something about it—but it hadn't exactly helped.)

Weak-kneed putting—that had been another major reason, for sure. In the Crosby, the first tournament of the year, had I holed the three-footer I had for a birdie on the 71st, I would have needed only a birdie 4 on the last hole to gain a tie—a fair possibility. That glaring miss on the 71st green seemed to have set the pattern for the whole year.

But many other shortcomings had been apparent in my game and, as I thought about them, I began to perceive more clearly not only why I had failed in the tournaments I had a crack at winning but also why there had been so many other tournaments in which I hadn't scored well enough even to become a secondary factor. My management had been poor on a large number of occasions, much less sound than it had been in my younger days. A high percentage of my gambles hadn't been sensible. No wonder I had run into so many big holes for the first time in my life—those 7s and 8s that crush your chances. I hadn't been very bright either when it came to making the adjustments that a smarter golfer would have made during the course of a round or a tournament when something patently wasn't working. At Oak Hill, for instance, instead of persevering with a putting method in which I had less and less confidence, I should have tried to devise some modification.

There was one other thing that I was careful to bear in mind during these stock-taking sessions. It is all very well and good—indeed, it is essential—for an athlete to have a high opinion of his ability, but whenever someone plays better than you do, it is a mark of maturity and wisdom to acknowledge it. In the final analysis, I had been outplayed very often—by Sikes in the Florida Citrus, by all the other contenders at Houston, by Trevino in the Open, by Charles in the Canadian, and by Player at Carnoustie, to name just the obvious occasions. No different from me, they could have pointed out mistakes they had made which they needn't have. Golf *is* a game of mistakes. But they had also summoned the winning shots, and that takes something. Winning always does, in every sport.

I also began to realize at this time that, while many people still referred to me as "young Jack Nicklaus," I wasn't so young any more, certainly not in terms of golf. I was twenty-eight, the same age Bob Jones had been when he retired from tournament play in 1930 following his Grand Slam. It was a full twelve years since my first significant achievement, winning the Ohio State Open. I was already in my seventh season as a professional. It was about time I grew up a bit.

In late July, the week after the P.G.A. Championship, I made a decision I probably should have made months before. I decided to change putters. "White Fang" was sent into temporary retirement, and I went back to the Bristol blade I had used my first four years as a pro. I also decided to change my putting style. I had been standing fairly erect, with my left eye a fraction of an inch behind the ball. On the practice green this had worked for me but out on the course it hadn't. I went back to my old method—both eyes well behind the ball, sighting down the line. It wasn't as pretty a style— much more bunched up, much crouchier—but looks were my last concern. I had frittered away too many months thinking too much about the stroke I was making with the putter. It was about time I thought about getting the ball in the hole.

As luck would have it, when I returned to the tour after a week of rest and practice, I won the first tournament I played, the Western Open at Olympia Fields, and I won it chiefly because I had two rounds of adequate putting and two rounds of splendid putting. The following week I won the American Golf Classic, at Firestone, after a terrific battle with Lee Elder in a protracted sudden-death playoff. That week my putting was not as efficient, but on the crucial holes it rescued me. On the 72nd green, I holed the eight-footer I had to make to get into a three-way playoff with Lee and Frank Beard. On the first extra hole, the 625-yard six- teen—we were on TV and had to return to the holes on which the

389

cameras were set up—Frank went out with a par 5; Lee sank a 25-footer there for his 4; and I got down a 16-footer from the fringe for my 4. On the seventeenth, 365 yards, I looked like a gone goose. After a great iron, Lee lay two just six feet from the cup, and I lay three 30 feet away after dumping my approach into the front bunker and playing a mediocre sand shot. I made that putt, and when Lee missed his short one, I was still alive. On the eighteenth, a 465-yard 4, two pars. Back to the sixteenth again. Two 5s this time. Lee got his by exploding four feet from the pin after being bunkered on his third—a magnificent shot in that situation. On to the seventeenth. This time I played a much better approach, a 9-iron that stopped about nine or ten feet from the hole. I hit a good firm putt and it dropped, and that was it. I learned the next day that practically the whole television audience had stayed with the playoff to its conclusion and that golf fans everywhere were still buzzing about it. I could understand that. To hang in there, Lee and I had each played a succession of darn good golf shots, and it isn't often, really, that you find two men getting hot at the same time in a head-to-head confrontation. I think we almost brought back match play.

Apart from the marked improvement in my putting, was there anything else I had going for me in the Western and in the American Classic that helped to explain my generally solid play and my firmness in the pinch? I think there was—the best kind of determination, the kind that manifests itself in the clearness of your thinking. It enabled me to avoid two closely intertwined tactical errors I had been making: not bearing down hard enough from the start and, consequently, leaving myself more to do at the end than I was up to.

Clear thinking isn't a very dramatic quality, but the player himself definitely feels its presence. It makes a big difference even when you're just practicing. You get more work done. I remember vividly my final practice session at home before I left for Olympia Fields and the Western. I went out about six-thirty in the evening, perhaps the nicest time of the day for golf. At that hour I had the practice tee at Lost Tree to myself. It was all very quiet and still, and in the shadows the turf on the practice fairway looked rich and green. I began to practice, as usual, by hitting out half a dozen wedges, then moved on to the 8-iron, the 5-iron, and the 2-iron, in that order. Everything went along well until I hit three

2-irons in a row that drifted way to the right. I made a slight change at the top of my backswing: my swing had felt too upright, my hands too close to the back of my head. This seemed to straighten things out. I went on to the driver.

As usual, I first tried to see if I could hit a few drives with a good left-to-right flight. The first two were satisfactory, but the third was a low burning hook. So was the fourth. The fifth was a wide push. The sixth was another hook. Enough of that. I then set up to play the ball straight, aligning my feet, my hips, and my shoulders on a small palm tree at the far end of the practice fairway. The next batch of drives I hit were relatively on target—on the average golf hole they would have finished on the fairway—but there was something wrong with my timing. I was having to strain in the hitting area to get to the ball. I kept checking my alignment on the next batch of drives to make sure I was set up correctly—apparently I was—but I was still having trouble getting to the ball and releasing properly as I hit through it. Then it occurred to me to check the position of the ball in relation to my stance. Well, no wonder I was late! I'd been playing the ball at least a half-inch forward (to the left) of my left heel. I moved it back so that it was opposite the heel. Night and day! After that, I found I could move easily into the ball. There was no longer any need to make a special effort with my hands to catch up. The full release I wanted came automatically.

I banged out about twenty more drives, practiced a few long bunker shots and a few short ones, spent five minutes on the practice green rehearsing the old putting method I'd gone back to, and then I called it a day. I was delighted with the way the session had gone. The fact that I had slipped into playing the driver with the ball incorrectly positioned had disconcerted me a little—one always thinks that he has checked the fundamentals—but I was pleased that I had been clearheaded enough to have caught the error and saved myself a ton of confusion.

I went home and ate a big dinner.

This past season, as I said, was my seventh as a professional. My freshman season seemed much farther away than seven years, though, so many new faces had joined the tournament circuit since 1962 and so many of the older players had either drifted away or ceased to be really prominent. Not everything had changed. Arnold was still the number-one attraction, Billy Casper was still winning

Autumn, 1968. With the Australian Open trophy.

tournaments left and right, and Julius Boros seemed to be playing better than ever as he closed in on fifty. But a lot *had* changed. It strikes me that an exceedingly effective means of presenting this would be simply to list the tournament winners and the runners-up for those two years, 1962 and 1968.

392

— 1962 —

TOURNAMENT	WINNER	RUNNER-UP
Los Angeles	Phil Rodgers	Bob Goalby, Fred Hawkins
San Diego	Tommy Jacobs	Johnny Pott
Crosby	Doug Ford	Joe Campbell
Lucky International	Gene Littler	George Knudson
Palm Springs	Arnold Palmer	Gene Littler, Jay Hebert
Phoenix	Arnold Palmer	Don Fairfield, Bob McCallister, Billy Casper, Jack Nicklaus
Tucson	Phil Rodgers	Jim Ferrier
New Orleans	Bo Wininger	Bob Rosburg
Baton Rouge	Joe Campbell	Bob Rosburg
Pensacola	Doug Sanders	Don Fairfield
St. Petersburg	Bobby Nichols	Frank Boynton
Doral	Billy Casper	Paul Bondeson
Azalea	Dave Marr	Jerry Steelsmith
Masters	Arnold Palmer	Gary Player, Dow Finsterwald
Greensboro	Billy Casper	Mike Souchak
Houston	Bobby Nichols	Dan Sikes, Jack Nicklaus
Texas	Arnold Palmer	Doug Sanders, Mason Rudolph
Tournament of Champions	Arnold Palmer	Billy Casper
Waco Turner	Johnny Pott	Mason Rudolph
Colonial	Arnold Palmer	Johnny Pott
Hot Springs	Al Johnston	Bill Collins
500 Festival	Billy Casper	George Bayer, Jerry Steelsmith
Memphis	Lionel Hebert	Gene Littler, Gary Player
Thunderbird	Gene Littler	Jack Nicklaus
U.S. Open	Jack Nicklaus	Arnold Palmer
Eastern	Doug Ford	Bob Goalby
Western	Jackie Cupit	Billy Casper
Buick	Bill Collins	Dave Ragan
Motor City	Bruce Crampton	Dave Hill
P.G.A.	Gary Player	Bob Goalby
Canadian	Ted Kroll	Charley Sifford
Insurance City	Bob Goalby	Art Wall
American Classic	Arnold Palmer	Mason Rudolph
St. Paul	Doug Sanders	Dave Hill
Oklahoma City	Doug Sanders	Johnny Pott
Dallas	Billy Maxwell	Johnny Pott
Denver	Bob Goalby	Jack Fleck, Billy Maxwell, Bob Duden, Bill Johnston, George Bayer, Art Wall

393

TOURNAMENT	WINNER	RUNNER-UP
Seattle	Jack Nicklaus	Tony Lema
Portland	Jack Nicklaus	George Bayer
Sahara	Tony Lema	Don January
Bakersfield	Billy Casper	Tony Lema
Ontario	Al Geiberger	Tommy Jacobs, Chick Rotar, John Ruedi, Bob Goalby, Gardner Dickinson
Orange Country	Tony Lema	Bob Rosburg
Beaumont	Dave Ragan	Don Massengale, Lionel Hebert, Dow Finsterwald
Cajun	John Barnum	Gay Brewer

— 1968 —

TOURNAMENT	WINNER	RUNNER-UP
Crosby	Johnny Pott	Billy Casper, Bruce Devlin
Kaiser International	Kermit Zarley	Dave Marr
Los Angeles	Billy Casper	Arnold Palmer
Bob Hope	Arnold Palmer	Deane Beman
Andy Williams	Tom Weiskopf	Al Geiberger
Phoenix	George Knudson	Julius Boros, Jack Montgomery, Sam Carmichael
Tucson	George Knudson	Frank Beard, Frank Boynton
Doral	Gardner Dickinson	Tom Weiskopf
Florida Citrus	Dan Sikes	Tom Weiskopf
Pensacola	George Archer	Tony Jacklin, Dave Marr
Jacksonville	Tony Jacklin	Gardner Dickinson, Don January, Doug Sanders, Chi Chi Rodriguez, De Witt Weaver
Greensboro	Billy Casper	George Archer, Bobby Nichols, Gene Littler
Masters	Bob Goalby	Roberto de Vicenzo
Tournament of Champions	Don January	Julius Boros
Azalea	Steve Reid	Gary Player
Byron Nelson Classic	Miller Barber	Kermit Zarley
Houston Champions	Roberto de Vicenzo	Lee Trevino
New Orleans	George Archer	Bert Yancey
Colonial	Billy Casper	Gene Littler
Memphis	Bob Lunn	Lee Trevino
Atlanta	Bob Lunn	Monty Kaser

394

TOURNAMENT	WINNER	RUNNER-UP
500 Festival	Billy Casper	Frank Beard, Mike Hill
U.S. Open	Lee Trevino	Jack Nicklaus
Canadian	Bob Charles	Jack Nicklaus
Cleveland	Dave Stockton	Bob Dickson
Buick	Tom Weiskopf	Mike Hill
Milwaukee	Dave Stockton	Sam Snead
P.G.A.	Julius Boros	Bob Charles, Arnold Palmer
Minnesota	Dan Sikes	Ken Still
Western	Jack Nicklaus	Miller Barber
American Classic	Jack Nicklaus	Lee Elder, Frank Beard
Westchester	Julius Boros	Bob Murphy, Dan Sikes, Jack Nicklaus
Philadelphia	Bob Murphy	Labron Harris
Thunderbird	Bob Murphy	Bruce Crampton, Bob Lunn
Greater Hartford	Billy Casper	Bruce Crampton
Kemper	Arnold Palmer	Bruce Crampton, Art Wall
P.G.A. Team	Bobby Nichols, George Archer	Monty Kaser, Rives McBee
Sahara	Chi Chi Rodriguez	Dale Douglass
Haig National	Bob Dickson	Chi Chi Rodriguez
Lucky International	Billy Casper	Ray Floyd, Don Massengale
Hawaiian	Lee Trevino	George Archer
Cajun	Ron Cerrudo	Charley Sifford, Bobby Mitchell

A few short comments suggested by these lists seem in order. First, six players scored victories in both seasons: Casper, Palmer, Nichols, Pott, Goalby, and myself. I think Bob Goalby deserves special credit. After his big year in 1962, Bob, a self-taught golfer, went through four seasons in which nothing went right for him. However, he didn't quit the tour in disgust, as most men would have. He stuck with it and he fought his way back. It took a lot of guts.

Among the older players who did well in 1968, we'll begin with Dickinson. I know Gardner very well. We've been on the Tournament Committee together, and since we're neighbors in the North Palm Beach area, we get together from time to time with our families and go on beach picnics. I have long held the opinion that Gardner is a much better golfer than he thinks he is. He's a very straight driver and deceptively long. He's a dependable middle-iron player and perhaps the best 8-iron and 9-iron player on the tour today. He doesn't hole as many putts as some of the other boys do, but he never leaves himself a hard second putt. He has been an enormously hard-working and devoted chairman of our players' committee. . . . Miller Barber has a decidedly individual golf swing, but he understands it well, and that's the big thing. He draws the club far inside going back, and then sort of cups the rest of his backswing. However, that strange move permits him to make a good full turn, and he comes down into and through the ball impressively—always on the same path. . . . Don January has improved his technique every year. I especially like the way he sets the club before the ball and his position at the top of the backswing. A right-to-left player, he has a long, smooth arc. Very good temperament. . . . There haven't been too many tall men who've gone to the top in golf, but Al Geiberger stands out as a solid shotmaker and a really sound swinger. I've known Al since we were junior golfers together in 1954, and his game has remained fundamentally the same over the years. Like Littler, he has a nice pacific nature and goes about his business without blowing any trumpets to attract attention. . . . George Knudson—an individual if there ever was one —is, to my mind, one of the finest swingers and strikers in the game. No one is any better at repeating his swing, the forte of his idol, Ben Hogan. (George used to rush out after finishing his own round and watch Ben play.) Most of us think that George could build up an even stronger game if he would work a little harder. . . . This last comment would also apply to Frank Beard, another first-class golfer —straight, neat around the greens, confident. Frank Beard knows how Frank Beard should play, and when he's right, he's very hard to beat. . . . I don't believe that Dan Sikes gets a tenth of the credit he deserves for his great skill off the tee. We've played together often, and he always drives beautifully, long and straight, but when we were paired at Rio Pinar in the Florida Citrus last year, he outdid himself: I have never seen anyone drive as superlatively well as he did on that last round. Fine putter.

Now, some of the newer and younger standouts. Tom Weiskopf has as much natural talent as any golfer I've ever known. When he gets his emotions more surely under control, he'll become one of the best players of all time. Tom is that exception to the rule: an extraordinary golfer with an only ordinary grip. His hands don't fit together well on the club because the big finger on his right hand is arthritic, and this makes it necessary for him to sort of squeeze

396

his fingers together. Beautiful tempo on his full shots, and quite a fantastic putter. . . . Bert Yancey is another fellow who strikes me as being a better golfer than he thinks he is. I would like his swing better if he extended more fully when he hits through the ball. I may be this critical because I admire his backswing so much. It is simplicity itself—a perfect turn. Bert practices his putting an hour every day, and he does a lot for himself on the greens. . . . In contrast with Yancey, Dave Stockton has overflowing confidence in himself. This is one of the reasons he plays tight golf courses so successfully, and it also helps to explain why he is one of the best and boldest putters among the tournament regulars. . . . However, if I were asked to name the top putter in golf today, I would pick George Archer. No one putts the five-footers and six-footers with a surer, cleaner stroke. He is excellent from all distances and on all types of greens because he is so square at the ball and putts with such a consistent tempo day in and day out. . . . When I played my first round with Bob Lunn in the Andy Williams tournament, I don't believe I had ever heard of him. I thought he was probably a club pro from the area. I was surprised at what a big, strong player he was. Bob is also a much more polished golfer than he appears to be at first look. We'll be hearing a lot more from him. . . . Kermit Zarley should be a big winner, too. He has one of the soundest swings among the younger players. . . . When Tony Jacklin took the Jacksonville Open, he became the first British pro ever to win a tour tournament in which all the players of reputation were competing. The surprising thing about Tony is his temperament—he's more American than most Americans, buoyant and high-keyed. When he's playing well, he's got a funny story to tell you off every tee. He's a darn good all-around golfer, but I believe he would benefit from slowing down his swing and refining his hitting action. . . . The young foreign player with the rosiest future is Bobby Cole from South Africa. His hitting action is remarkably similar to Gary's, but he has a much wider arc, being a bigger fellow, and he can be very, very long. . . . Young Bob Murphy is one of the most accurate drivers in captivity. He's got a real sense of shot-making, he can putt, and he can compete. The same would apply to young Bob Dickson. . . . These kids—and a number I haven't mentioned—are coming very fast these days. We used to think they were scared of winning the big-prize-money tournaments. Well, we know better now.

If you're a golfer and you're on your game, life is a bowl of cherries. During your lean periods, though, try as you may to go along placidly, you never stop brooding about your poor play and grasping at possible panaceas. But the point I want to make is that in both good times and bad a golfer inhabits a wonderful world. He gets to meet a wide variety of stimulating people. He gets to spend time with celebrities—who have earned their celebrity— men like Hope and Crosby and Como who not only have prodigious talent but prodigious size as persons. He gets to go to fascinating places with perfect companions. In 1968, for example, just before the Andy Williams tournament, Barbara and I went down to Mexico and visited with Mauricio Urdenata, whom I had gotten to know back in 1960 and 1961 when we played against each other in the Americas Cup match. On our holiday, Mauricio taught me how to water-ski with one ski. I may make Cypress Gardens yet. All in all, if a man can't enjoy the world that golf makes available to him, he can't enjoy any world.

Even in 1968, when my golf was a tormenting thing for long stretches, life was still very sweet: I had the company of so many likable and interesting people in an atmosphere that was always vital, youthful, and pleasant. Something amusing was forever popping up. For example, I remember the second day of the Phoenix Open when Barbara forgot to bring her contestant's wife's badge out to the course with her. Instead of making herself known at the gate, she bought a ticket. I don't know who started the crack, but it soon got around that since I had shot a 77 on the first round, Barbara had decided that no one would have known who I was if she had tried to identify herself at the gate. My second round wasn't so hot either and I missed the cut, and that prompted the remark that considering the kind of golf I'd played, Barbara *should* have been required to pay her way in. That was an expensive week for me.

And then there was that blustery afternoon in July at Carnoustie when Gary and I were walking toward the 70th green, fighting it out for the British Open—a taut situation even for two fellows who know each other as well as Gary and I do. That's a gargantuan par 3, the 16th, and I had just hit one of the great shots of my life: a full driver, into the wind, about 20 feet past the pin. As I'm walking I'm thinking, "Now, if I can hole this putt for a 2 and Gary takes a 4, I'll be only one shot behind him." And at this moment my old buddy, the South African charmer, pipes up plaintively, "Jack, what are you trying to do to me?" That absolutely floored me. "Do to *you?*" I said. "I'm trying to beat you. Look what *you* did to *me* on the last hole—you hit that blind wedge ten feet from the pin and sank that putt! And the hole before—all you did was knock that wood stiff to the pin for an eagle! What am *I* trying to do to *you?*" At that point we both began laughing, in the midst of all the tension that a British Open thrusts on you. It must have flabbergasted the gallery.

The longer I play competitive golf, the longer I think I'll want to play it. That's a sort of scrambled statement, but I'm sure you understand what I mean to say. I certainly hope to be a regular tournament player for at least another ten years, all things being equal. I do notice some changes in my attitude, however. For instance, it is a little harder now to get myself "up" for the average tour tournament; my drive seems to center more and more on the major championships. As I grow older, too, I find that it takes me longer to solve certain problems connected with my swing. In fact, it seems to me that in subtle ways the structure of your golf swing changes without your realizing it or being able to do much about it. But I mean to try to be a much better golfer. I hope I'm not yet at my peak. How I fare in the years ahead, I realize, rests on my own shoulders. It will depend on how hard I work, how well I am able to sustain my keenness and my desire. They ebb and flow a bit more now than they used to, but on my good weeks, I'm happy to say, I don't feel much different than I did when I was a boy chewing up the practice range at Scioto and setting out to emulate Bobby Jones.

PICTURE CREDITS

INDEX

[Page numbers in italics refer to illustrations.]

411

Royal Melbourne, 213
Royal St. George's (Sandwich, Eng-
land), 83, 92
Royal St. George's Challenge Vase,
92
Royer, Hugh, 65
Rubber City Open, 1958: 81
Rudolph, Mason, 129, 200, 208, 393
Ruedi, John, 394
Ruffin, Bobby, 64
Rule, Jack, 66
Runyan, Paul, 30
Rutter, Dessa (Mrs. Gene), 369
Rutter, Gene, 369
Ryde, Peter, 371
Ryder Cup match, 87
1931: 14, 44
1957: 87
1967: 236, 238
See also Scioto

Sahara Open, 252, 370
1962: 394
1967: 388
1968: 395
St. Andrews (Scotland), 86, 163, 175,
210, 216, 334, 370
Old Course, 83, 106, 176, 219
See also "Big Three matches";
British Open (1964); World
Amateur Team Championship
(1957)
St. Andrews (near Chicago, Illinois),
95
St. Louis Country Club, 103, 109
See also U.S. Amateur Champion-
ship (1960)
Saint-Nôm-la Bretèche (near Paris),
34
St. Paul
1962: 393
St. Petersburg Open
1962: 133, 393
1963: 156
Sanders, Doug, 31, 45, 105, 115, 182,
192, 208, 236, 243, 247, 393,
394
at the 1966 British Open, 223, 224,
225, 229
San Diego Open
1962: 131, 393
1967: 335
See also Stardust Country Club
Sands Point club, *178*
Sarazen, Gene, 29, 31, 52, 152
Sarnoff, General David, 41
Savic, Janice (Mrs. Pandel), 187, 193
Savic, Pandel, 187-88, 193
Scatchard, Charles, 371
Schenken, Howard, 369
Schoen, Gavic, 369
Schoen, Susie (Mrs. Gavic), 369
Schoener, Helen *See* Nicklaus, Helen
Schweizer, Hans, 109
Schwendeman, Joe, 191

Scioto Country Club (Columbus,
Ohio), 13, 14, 15, 16, 20, 44,
50, 51, 53, 56, 57, 60, 65, 68,
69, 104, *108,* 109, *123,* 124,
148, 150, 187, 211, 234, 339,
365, 399
See also U.S. Open (1926)
Scott, Tom, 371
Seattle Golf Club, 117
See also Walker Cup Match (1961)
Seattle World's Fair Open
1962: 148, 394
Seminole, 359
Sewell, Douglas, 86, 88, 89, 91, 116
Sewgolum, Sewsunker, 292
Shepperson, Alec, 87, 88, 89, 91, 117
Siegfried, Larry, 64
Sifford, Charley, 82, 395
Sikes, Dan, 31, 129, 136, 192, 200,
236, 364, 388, 389, 393, 394,
395, 396
Sikes, Dick, 31
Silva, Duarte Espiritu Santo, 109
Simms, George, 371
Slazenger company, 149, 212, 218, 372
Smith, Dave, 97, 119
Smith, Dick, 90, 91
Smith, Steve, 78
Snead, Sam, 14, 15, 30, 66, 67, 140,
157, 158, 159, 161, 183, 210,
217, 257, 280, 395
Snyder, Larry, 56
Souchak, Mike, 22, 23, 24, 115, 129,
156, 210, 393
Southern Amateur. 68
Southern Hills (Tulsa, Oklahoma),
64, 80, 364
See also U.S.G.A. Junior Cham-
pionship (1953)
Southern Ohio P.G.A., 122
Southern Open, 68
Southport & Ainsdale (north of Liver-
pool, England), 137
Spatz company, 372
Spalding Top-Flite golf clubs, 56
Sports Illustrated magazine, 369, 372
Spring Lake Invitational
1947: 53
Spyglass Hill, 235
Stanton, Bob, 213
Stardust Country Club (San Diego,
California), 131, 134
See also San Diego Open
Steele, Donald, 371
Steelsmith, Jerry, 393
Stern. Merritt company, 372
Still, Ken, 395
Stobbs, John, 371
Stockton, Dave, 395. 397
Stranahan, Frank, 30. 66, 113
Sugimoto. Hidevo, 34
Sullivan, Des, 191
Sunnehanna Invitational (for ama-
teurs)
1956: 66
Swanson, John, 189